Main Street Oklahoma

Main Street Oklahoma

STORIES OF TWENTIETH-CENTURY AMERICA

Edited by

LINDA W. REESE

and

PATRICIA LOUGHLIN

UNIVERSITY OF OKLAHOMA PRESS : NORMAN

Library of Congress Cataloging-in-Publication Data

Main Street Oklahoma : stories of twentieth-century America / edited by Linda W. Reese and
Patricia Loughlin.
  pages cm
Includes index.
ISBN 978-0-8061-4401-6 (pbk. : alk. paper) 1. Oklahoma—History—20th century. I. Reese,
Linda Williams, 1946– II. Loughlin, Patricia, 1971–
F700.M35 2013
976.6'053—dc23

2013009236

To the memory of Louise Welsh

for her abiding love of Oklahoma history

Contents

List of Illustrations   ix

Acknowledgments   xi

Introduction   3

CHAPTER 1.   "For Our Own Safety and Welfare": What the
             Civil War Meant in Indian Territory
             Bradley R. Clampitt   9

CHAPTER 2.   The Mock Wedding of Indian and Oklahoma Territories
             Malia K. Bennett   29

CHAPTER 3.   "The Land We Belong To Is Grand!" Environment and
             History in Twentieth-Century Oklahoma
             Sterling D. Evans   46

CHAPTER 4.   Oil and Natural Gas: Putting Oklahoma on the Map
             Dan T. Boyd   76

CHAPTER 5.   Petroleum, Planning, and Tribal Property: Oil Field
             Development on the Osage Reservation, 1896–1950
             Houston Mount   92

CHAPTER 6.   Butchers against Businessmen: The 1921 Packinghouse Strike
             and the Open Shop Movement in Oklahoma City
             Nigel A. Sellars   110

CHAPTER 7.   "Spirited Away": Race, Gender, and Murder in Oklahoma
             in the 1920s
             Christienne M. McPherson   134

CHAPTER 8. Native American Art in Oklahoma: An Interpretation
Alvin O. Turner   154

CHAPTER 9. Let Us Help You Help Yourselves: New Deal Economic
Recovery Programs and the Five Tribes in Rural Oklahoma
James Hochtritt   175

CHAPTER 10. The War on Poverty in Little Dixie, 1965–1974
Jennifer J. Collins   201

CHAPTER 11. Conservative Oklahoma Women United: The Crusade to
Defeat the ERA
Jana Vogt Catignani   221

CHAPTER 12. On the Illinois: The Making of Modern Music and Culture in
the Oklahoma Ozark Foothills
J. Justin Castro   239

List of Contributors   257

Index   261

Illustrations

Figures

1.1. Rose Cottage, home of Cherokee principal chief John Ross   19

2.1. The original Miss Indian Territory, Mrs. Leo Bennett   30

2.2. Oklahoma "Tom Thumb" wedding performed at a bridal shower   35

2.3. Mr. Oklahoma Territory and Miss Indian Territory, 2007 Statehood Day reenactment   35

2.4. "Reverse Wedding" reenactment, 2007 Statehood Day   40

3.1. Coal mining with a water drill, c. 1915   61

3.2. Oil wells on the Oklahoma Capitol grounds, c. 1940s   63

3.3. Picher lead and zinc mines   66

4.1. Early-day "gusher" oil well, Yale, Oklahoma   79

4.2. Oklahoma oil and gas production, 1902–2007   81

4.3. Oklahoma well completion history, 1904–2007   83

5.1. Bartlesville Oil Field, 1905   99

5.2. Osage Tribal Council   105

6.1. Entrance to Packingtown, Oklahoma City, 1914   115

6.2. "Two Packing Workers Dead in Early Fire"   115

6.3. Oklahoma City mayor John C. Walton   118

7.1. 1921 lynching near Mannford, Oklahoma   137

7.2. Ku Klux Klan gathering in Oklahoma, 1923   143

8.1. Oscar Jacobson with the Kiowa Five   159

8.2. Artists Woody Crumbo and Charles Banks Wilson   163

9.1. Members of Civilian Conservation Corps–Indian Division building flood control structure   178

9.2. Cherokee Nannie Hogner leading a basket-making class 180

9.3. Bull Hollow Camp orchestra, CCC–Indian Division 189

10.1. Representative Carl Albert and Job Corps director Wayne Keenan
at the dedication of the Arbuckle Job Corps Conservation Center 206

10.2. Jess Swearingen and children in garden funded by Emergency
Food and Medical Service 214

11.1. STOP ERA handbill, Oklahoma, 1978 222

11.2. "Ads Termed 'Misleading,'" *Daily Oklahoman*, March 2, 1977 227

12.1. Fiddler Randy Crouch, 2007 249

Maps

1.1. Civil War battle sites map 14

3.1. Oklahoma ecoregions 49

4.1. Oklahoma oil and gas production 77

Acknowledgments

The editors wish to express their appreciation to each of the twelve scholars who contributed exceptional essays to this collection. From the beginning they were as enthusiastic about this endeavor as we were. They often graciously put aside their own work schedules to meet the demands of our timeline. We are especially grateful to Carolyn Hanneman at the Carl Albert Archives and Jacqueline Slater in the Western History Collections at the University of Oklahoma for their help in choosing photographs. The Oklahoma History Center remains one of the finest research facilities in any state, and we continually appreciate the guidance of their staff. Our administrations and colleagues at East Central University and the University of Central Oklahoma served as a nurturing environment for our scholarship. We are enriched by their support. The late Kirk Bjornsgaard first encouraged the idea of this book, and Jay Dew at the University of Oklahoma Press has given us invaluable advice and support. We also want to remember our mentors from graduate school days, David Baird, Arrell M. Gibson, and William W. Savage, Jr. They planted a love of Oklahoma history in our hearts and showed us the tools to use in our work. Finally, we thank our families who love us the most and know how to keep us humble.

Main Street Oklahoma

Introduction

The little town of Holdenville, Indian Territory, announced Oklahoma Statehood Day on November 16, 1907, in a spectacular way. The men of the community raced up and down the main street on horseback whooping, waving their hats in the air, and firing off their rifles in celebration. Most of the Native peoples of Holdenville were not so delighted with the news. They had fought for the retention of their lands until the final proclamation. Life in Oklahoma towns during the early twentieth century was like that. Everything happened on Main Street: the parades and the hangings, the church services and the saloon fights, politicking and elections, dry goods sales and horse races. After Sinclair Lewis published his classic novel *Main Street* in 1920, small-town American life frequently took on negative connotations. Existence for Lewis's main character was stifling. The intellectual climate was unrefined, conservative politics reigned, businessmen were petty, and revivalist religion captured the emotions of the people. Some Oklahomans today would grudgingly agree with these criticisms, but most would loudly denounce many of Lewis's characterizations. In the mass media parlance of the twenty-first century, "Main Street" has a different meaning. As opposed to Wall Street, Main Street is the domain of common sense, economic realities, and popular American values. All Oklahomans would prefer to emphasize the accomplishments of a people who survived dust storms, oil busts, bank failures, and homegrown terrorist attacks to arrive in the twenty-first century proud of their resilience and positive about their opportunities for the future.

Oklahoma was barely a teenager in 1920, and now the state has passed its hundredth birthday. It is fitting that historians now move beyond a long-standing fascination with territorial Oklahoma toward engaging and analyzing the major themes that reflect Oklahoma in statehood. This collection of essays incorporates a cross section of Oklahoma events in order to provide a snapshot of place, time, and culture. The chapters suggest significant social conversations among Oklahomans that may have taken place in the grocery store, at church, in the halls of power, and on the street corner. The topics reflect the singularity of the Oklahoma experience as well as Oklahomans' connection to the broader American experience. Each of the authors examines a major issue that directly affected the everyday lives of people and communities in Oklahoma, sometimes positively, sometimes negatively. In many ways, Oklahoma exists as a near perfect representation of the American nation. It is multiracial and multicultural. There are big cities and tiny hamlets. Fortune 500 companies and "mom and pop" businesses compete in the marketplace. Prosperity and cultural achievement exist alongside poverty and ignorance. The best of community spirit and action can be seen on Main Street as well as the worst examples of prejudice and violence. Life in Oklahoma is like that.

This book begins with a new interpretation of the origins of the statehood movement. Most works introduce this topic with the well-known "Boomer" intrusions into Indian Territory in the 1880s. It might seem strange that this collection starts with a chapter on the Civil War, more than forty years before statehood. It was the decisions that the Native peoples confronted during the Civil War, however, and the punitive aftermath of the war, that created the environment for Indian dispossession and statehood. The final rush toward incorporation of the Indian lands into a territory and eventually into a state, and the rapid development of Indian Territory by non-Indian intruders, resulted directly from the circumstances of the Civil War. When factions of the Five Indian Nations and some of the Plains tribes chose to fight for the Confederate States of America and against the United States, they doomed themselves to some form of retribution. The Reconstruction Treaties in 1866 with the Five Nations meted out that punishment. Bradley Clampitt skillfully presents the trajectory of decisions the Native peoples and their leaders made during the Civil War. Unlike many historians, Clampitt defines the experience in terms of a "quest for sovereignty" and protection of the homeland rather than an identification with either government or a position on the continuation of slavery. He reminds the reader that simple labels fail to reveal the reality of historical actors and events, especially ones as momentous as those of the Civil War.

Malia K. Bennett adds another dimension to consideration of Oklahoma history. She sketches the journey of mock wedding ceremonies from Irish folklore to the United States and finally to Oklahoma. The Statehood Day wedding ceremony in Guthrie, Oklahoma, of Miss Indian Territory and Mr. Oklahoma Territory on November 16, 1907, became over time an iconic staple of the unification of the Twin Territories and their peoples into one state. Characterization, costuming, and the script preserved in photographs, popular culture, artistic medium, and historical record varied in time and place, and reflected the ambiguous understanding of this union among white, black, and Native American residents. The 2007 centennial protest wedding illustrated the continued negotiation of the historical past. Bennett discusses the implications of race, gender, identity, and historical re-creation of this event over the one hundred years of its reenactment.

The next three chapters address the significance of the environmental history of the state, a topic fundamental to the lives of every Oklahoman. While it is simplistic to assert that environment determines destiny, the contours of Oklahoma's geography and its abundant natural resources shaped both the wealth of its people and the darkest trials of their lives in the twentieth century. Sterling Evans chooses lyrics from the state song, "Oklahoma!," created by Rodgers and Hammerstein and adopted in 1953, as a framework to depict the relationship of Oklahomans to their land. His is a realistic appraisal of the development of the state's natural endowment that has made it a prosperous and significant contributor to the national union. Evans draws clear connection between the people and the environment from earliest habitation through the twentieth century, and reflects on the benefits, costs, and dangers of their history together.

Dan T. Boyd and Houston Mount each examine the development of the oil industry in Oklahoma, but from different perspectives. After more than one hundred years of oil and gas extraction, Oklahoma ranks sixth in the nation in oil and third in natural gas production. Boyd, at the Oklahoma Geological Survey, traces the first recognition of oil deposits on Oklahoma lands by way of contaminated water wells, through the three major oil booms, to the emergence of natural gas as the primary energy source in the state. He believes that both of these fossil fuels represent a "secure bridge" to sustainable sources of energy for Oklahoma's future.

Houston Mount uses the Osage Nation oil development as a case study that presages the successful modern business enterprises of Oklahoma's Indian nations. The early extraction of oil in the United States from any location was fraught with legal complications regarding subsurface ownership rights. Allotment of Oklahoma Indian lands in the midst of oil discoveries exacerbated those issues. Unlike other tribal groups in Oklahoma, when the Osage government accepted allotment, they retained tribal ownership of mineral rights. They initially suffered from the same complications of overproduction, waste, and insufficient infrastructure as other oil-producing areas. In 1949, however, tribal leadership initiated a conservation project that resolved many of these problems and led to greater production and recovery levels. Unified ownership made the success of this project possible. Mount maintains that the Osage example refuted the Dawes Act theory that private ownership is always superior to tribal ownership.

World War I disrupted U.S. social, economic, and political traditions. For Oklahoma too it unsettled the social fabric of the state. In times of insecurity and economic stress, capitalism, race, and patriotism frequently become subjects of tangled and volatile conflict. This nexus of issues provides the focus of the next two chapters. In the first, Nigel A. Sellars analyzes labor relations in Oklahoma City in the aftermath of the war. The 1921 strike by the Amalgamated Meat Cutters Union began in response to pressure from the major companies to impose an "open shop" and thereby break the power of the fledgling city unions. In describing the evolution of the strike, Sellars presents the positions of the big companies, leading Oklahoma City businessmen, state politicians, and union leaders. This collision of interests led to charges of disloyalty, a lynching, violence in the streets, and the defeat of unionized labor. Christienne M. McPherson's chapter tackles a topic that many Oklahomans find embarrassing and most want to deny: the extent of racial prejudice and injustice in the early decades of the twentieth century. Publication of the 2001 report of the Commission to Study the Tulsa Race Riot of 1921 helped to reveal the fault lines of race relations in Oklahoma. McPherson outlines the aspirations of African American migrants for freedom and prosperity in the Twin Territories and their disappointment at the institution of legal and social Jim Crow laws following statehood. Using the 1922 case of the conviction for murder of a thirteen-year-old African American orphan named Elias Ridge, she discusses the Tulsa Race Riot of 1921 and the post-riot racially charged atmosphere in the state. McPherson draws a connection between Oklahoma and race relations nationwide. In spite of conflicting evidence and determined legal efforts by the black community, justice was dubious in the prosecution of Ridge's case and in the failure of the appeals process.

Oklahoma arts are the focus of the book's next chapter, by Alvin O. Turner. The state has often failed to receive just recognition and appreciation for its early encouragement of Native American art but here Turner bridges the gap between art history and state history to develop the framework behind the Native American art known as the Bacone or Oklahoma style of painting. Examples of Native American artistic expression date back to prehistory, but it was not until the collaboration and nurture of Oscar Jacobson and the Kiowa Five at the University of Oklahoma in the 1920s that the state began to emerge as a leader. In 1935 Acee Blue Eagle (Alex McIntosh), an OU graduate, created the art program at Bacone College that defined the model for subsequent Native art education. The economic hardships of the Great Depression, conflicting definitions of cultural expression, and the expansion of competing art venues and programs led to the decline of the state's supremacy, but for a time

Oklahoma provided the unique environment for the cultivation of some of the earliest great Native American artists.

Native Americans—and the Great Depression—are also the focus of the next chapter, by James Hochtritt. Nearly every Oklahoma family passes down to younger generations stories about their Great Depression experiences, and this includes families of Cherokee, Choctaw, Chickasaw, Seminole, and Muscogee people, who had already endured many hardships over the course of their long history in the region. Hochtritt challenges the historical record of the 1930s in evaluating both the plight of Five Nations people and the impact of federal New Deal programs designed to improve their circumstances. Hochtritt maintains that in contrast with non-Indians, members of the Five Nations utilized traditional cultural values and practices to maintain group survival. They pragmatically either adapted or abandoned federal intervention efforts based on their own ability to integrate the programs into their communal culture. Hochtritt assesses the value of some of the government projects but also illustrates the reasons for failure of other well-intentioned actions.

Jennifer J. Collins examines another period of severe economic distress in Oklahoma and federal programs that were intended to alleviate poverty. The Third Congressional District of Oklahoma, known as Little Dixie, experienced the worst conditions in the state between 1965 and 1974 with more than half of the resident families below the poverty line. President Lyndon Johnson's "War on Poverty" legislation signed in 1964 had as its original intention a progressive model of local participation and community action. Collins notes that most of the evaluation of the War on Poverty measures has focused on urban locations. Her study of this rural area reveals a mixed success. While the programs failed to construct their original model, they succeeded in bringing demonstrable improvement to the lives of local citizens. Education, nutrition, health, and housing all made positive gains from the impact of federal intervention.

One of the most controversial national political issues of the last half of the twentieth century was the proposed Equal Rights Amendment, which ultimately failed passage. In her essay on the proposed ERA, Jana Vogt Catignani illustrates the power of women in organizing resistance to this measure in Oklahoma. Initially the amendment seemed likely to pass in the state, but organized groups of conservative women united to insure its defeat. Rallying behind decades-old attitudes of female moral superiority, Protestant religious teachings, fear of communism, and antipathy for the sexual revolution of the 1960s, they became vocal and politicized as never before on this issue. Vogt suggests that the successful activism surrounding the defeat of the ERA may have been a factor that hastened the political realignment of the state to its current makeup.

In recent years, Oklahoma has become renowned for the musical talent it has produced. For the concluding chapter of this anthology, J. Justin Castro provides a tour of the state's musical landscape. Castro believes that music and song provide a tool for investigating the cultural history and composition of Oklahoma. Beginning with the forced removal of the Cherokee people and their slaves—and their migration to Oklahoma, the Illinois River area of Oklahoma cultivated a mixture of musical forms. He cites Indian customs, African American traditions, Southern white society, and New England missionary presence as shaping forces in the early music of the state. Jazz and western swing were later incorporated, and modern media helped these adapt and interact with earlier styles. Today "Red Dirt music" illustrates the blending of the sounds, rhythms, and histories that have developed in the twentieth century of Oklahoma.

This collection of essays marks a starting point for further research on the first hundred years of Oklahoma statehood. Just as the days of the Twin Territories were filled with remarkable people and events, so too have been the decades following statehood. The great Oklahoma historian Angie Debo once wrote that all of the forces of American history can be seen in the development of this state. No single volume can capture the multiple histories of Oklahoma, but we have chosen stories about the people who walked the main streets of the state's communities. Their concerns, triumphs, and tragedies contributed greatly to the texture of our common heritage. Enjoy.

Linda W. Reese
Patricia Loughlin

CHAPTER 1

"For Our Own Safety and Welfare"

WHAT THE CIVIL WAR MEANT IN
INDIAN TERRITORY

Bradley R. Clampitt

From 1861 to 1865 the American Civil War raged after decades of sectional animosity between North and South, and the fratricidal bloodbath lives on in the imaginations of countless Americans. The endless public fascination with the Civil War has prompted one prominent historian to describe it as "the war that never goes away."[1] One need not be a native of a former Confederate state to fall spellbound to the tragic "war for Southern independence," and one need not hail from a Northern state to appreciate the Union's heroic effort to preserve the nation and eventually dismantle the abomination of chattel slavery. But clearly the distinctiveness of one's home state—"where we come from," as some would have it—influences individual perceptions, and many Americans understandably seek to comprehend the role of their state in their country's most transformative event.

The Civil War began forty-six years before Oklahoma statehood, but its ravages transcended political distinctions such as statehood. The residents of what was then known as Indian Territory experienced its horrors vividly. When Oklahomans and students of history consider the region's role in the Civil War, do they think first of individuals who remained loyal to the United States, or do those who struggled for Southern independence first come to mind? Perhaps the answer should be "neither." Oklahoma history presents a unique interpretive framework, a war within a war: the American Indian population waging their own war for independence, and indeed survival, within what began as someone else's conflict. That quest for sovereignty most accurately frames the story of the Civil War in Indian Territory. The story of the Indians' Civil War also serves as a reminder that history is rarely about "good guys" and "bad guys" and that people tend to defy simple categorization.

Relative to the war's primary theaters of operations and the economic and political centers of the Union and the Confederacy, Indian Territory must be considered remote and sparsely populated. Approximately seventy thousand individuals resided primarily in the territory's eastern half on lands claimed by the nations known as the Five Tribes—Chickasaws, Cherokees, Choctaws, Creeks (Muscogees), and Seminoles—who had been forcibly relocated from the southeastern United States decades earlier, while settlers and members of Plains tribes occupied the western portions of the territory. Confederate officials in particular hoped that the territory might provide resources that they could ship to more important locations east of the Mississippi River, but claims that the two belligerents desperately sought to control an Indian Territory rich in resources exaggerates reality. What Indian Territory offered paled in comparison to the resources found in other contested border grounds such as Kentucky. Two other factors—geography and the question of the Indian population's allegiance—contributed far more to the territory's significance. Its location made Indian Territory potentially important and placed its residents in a precarious situation. Union-controlled Kansas bordered the territory to the north, while the Confederate states of Texas and Arkansas loomed to the south and east respectively. To the northeast, Missouri included residents with divided loyalties. A Confederate-controlled Indian Territory might serve as a military buffer zone to protect the more important Texas and could potentially provide a base of operations for Confederate invasions of Kansas or even the rich gold fields of Colorado. Conversely, Union officials viewed the territory as a buffer to protect those regions and as a potential highway of invasion to Texas. Its location between the belligerents increased the likelihood of competition for control of Indian Territory and virtually guaranteed the involvement of the region's Indian population in the conflict.[2]

Neither side could realistically assume that the Indian nations sympathized with its cause. Union officials could hardly be surprised if Indian leaders exhibited no great affection for the U.S. Army. Confederate officials recognized that southeastern states bore great responsibility for the removal of the Five Tribes to Indian Territory and that Texas had forcibly removed other Indians to the territory in more recent years, and that resentment certainly lingered.

Still, because Union and Confederate officials displayed interest in Indian Territory, Indian leaders needed to be concerned about the looming war.

Neutrality appeared virtually impossible and was perhaps ill-advised anyway because war threatened to envelop the Indians' homelands. Perhaps the Indians' best course of action was to enter the war on their own terms—and that is what they did. The vast majority of residents of Indian Territory chose a side, but they did so for myriad reasons unique to their own experience, not necessarily out of affection for the Union or the Confederacy. Old grievances (intertribal and intra-tribal) made a united front unlikely, and each nation acted individually, with most tribal leaders motivated by what they considered the best course of action for their people.

Most of the territory's Indians supported the Confederacy, some chose the Union, a relative few changed allegiance during the war and others attempted to remain neutral. Numerous concerns factored into the tribes' decisions. Existing treaties with the United States, dependence on the U.S. government for a degree of financial support, and reliance upon its military for physical security motivated some remaining loyal to the Union, while resentment, genuine belief in the propriety of slavery, and/or a stronger cultural connection with the South motivated others to support the Confederacy. Members of the Chickasaw, Choctaw, Cherokee, and Creek Nations collectively owned approximately seventy-seven hundred slaves. An 1860 speech by Republican William H. Seward, who would become Abraham Lincoln's secretary of state, also alarmed many Indian leaders. Seward pointed to American expansion into western lands as the key to suppressing the intense sectional conflict and called for yet another relocation of Indians to clear the way for white settlement. Therefore, while a Republican victory in the presidential election of 1860 likely promised an end to the expansion of slavery into the western territories, it promised absolutely nothing to the inhabitants of Indian Territory. For all of these reasons, the Civil War would explode into more than simply a "white man's war."[3]

The Choctaws and Chickasaws doubtless displayed more affection for the Confederacy than other tribes would demonstrate for either side during the war.[4] Before either the North or South took official action to secure alliances in Indian Territory, and months before the war began, the Five Tribes planned a meeting to determine their roles in the looming conflict. That meeting occurred February 17, 1861, though neither the Chickasaws nor the Choctaws attended. Although there remains no official explanation for their absence, Chickasaw and Choctaw leaders likely anticipated and rejected the cautious response of the other groups, who at the urging of the Cherokee delegation

resolved "simply to do nothing, to keep quiet and to comply with our treaties."
Ten days earlier, the General Council of the Choctaw Nation had approved a
resolution that plainly expressed their sentiments. In the event of the permanent division of the United States, Choctaw loyalty would rest with the new
Confederate States of America. The Choctaw council's resolution concluded,
"We shall be left to follow the natural affections, education, institutions, and
interests of our people, which indissolubly bind us in every way to the destiny
of our neighbors and brethren of the Southern States." Two months before
the famous shots at Fort Sumter, South Carolina, started the Civil War there
could be no doubt where the Choctaws stood. According to the council, an
alliance with the Confederacy best served tribal interests because longstand-
ing cultural connections with Southern states linked the tribe's future to that
of the would-be Southern nation and because such an alliance conformed to
the sentiments of the Choctaw people. The Chickasaws followed suit May 25.

Meanwhile, during February and March 1861, the provisional Congress
of the Confederacy took initial steps toward securing official alliances with
the nations of Indian Territory by enacting legislation that created a Bureau
of Indian Affairs and appointed a commissioner of Indian Affairs. Also in
February, the Texas secession convention appointed representatives to visit
the Five Tribes in hopes of enticing their hosts to support the Confederacy.
The Texas commissioners found considerable support for the Confederate
cause among the Five Tribes, although they found the least sympathy among
the Cherokees. The Texans' report claimed that the tribes feared "Northern
aggression," and that as soon as the Indians were in a "defensible position"
they would declare their allegiance to the Confederacy and raise thousands of
good fighting men. According to the Texans, one Indian leader declared that
"Lincoln may haul his big guns over our prairies in the daytime, but we will
swoop down upon him at night from our mountains and forests, dealing death
and destruction to his army." Regardless of whether any Indian leader actually
made such a boast, only the official Confederate representatives could form
alliances with the nations of Indian Territory, and dramatic events would soon
hasten those arrangements.[5]

The famous events at Fort Sumter in April 1861 and Lincoln's subsequent
call for volunteers to suppress the rebellion forced the hand of the eight slave
states that had not seceded immediately after the presidential election of 1860,
as seven had. Four states—Missouri, Kentucky, Maryland, and Delaware—
remained loyal to the Union, while the other four—Virginia, North Carolina,
Tennessee, and Alabama—seceded and joined the Confederacy. Meanwhile,
activities in and near Indian Territory in April 1861 more immediately affected

the course of the war there. As fighting loomed, federal soldiers occupied three forts in the territory and one just across the Arkansas border: Fort Smith. The latter served as a supply depot to the three others, which helped to protect the Five Tribes from Plains tribes. Fort Washita stood in the southeastern portion of the Chickasaw Nation, about sixty miles southeast of Fort Arbuckle. Farther west, Fort Cobb was located in present-day Caddo County, approximately forty miles north of present-day Lawton. Fort Cobb supplied the nearby Wichita Agency, which served a number of small bands that had been removed from Texas, including Wichitas, Caddos, Anadarkos, Penateka Comanches, and others, and protected them against bands of Comanches, Kiowas, and Kickapoos.[6]

After a sequence of orders that initially called for the concentration of federal forces at Fort Washita, Union officers ultimately ordered the evacuation of the military posts in the territory, leaving the Five Tribes without the military protection guaranteed them by federal treaties. From the Union perspective, this action did not represent a calculated decision to abandon the Indians. Union officials ordered the evacuation of military posts elsewhere in areas threatened by Confederates and considered the soldiers' presence in the East more important. Moreover, the subsequent Confederate occupation of the territory and Confederate ascendancy in Arkansas rendered federal control of the posts tenuous anyway.[7]

Not surprisingly, however, some Indians considered the federal evacuation tantamount to abandonment. The evacuation certainly cleared the way for Confederate diplomats who sought to form official alliances with the Five Tribes and other groups within the territory. Considering conditions in Indian Territory in 1861, the cultural connections between many members of the Five Tribes and the Southern states, and the perception that the federal government had abandoned them, it is hardly surprising that most members of the Five Tribes now cast their lot with the Confederacy. One historian has argued that federal ineptitude with regard to Indian policy in general significantly enhanced the Confederates' chances for success in securing the services of Indian allies.[8] An even simpler point should not be overlooked—in the minds of many Indians the Confederacy presented them with at least the opportunity to fight for the lands supposedly reserved for them.

To secure the Indian alliances, Confederate officials wisely appointed Arkansas resident Albert Pike, well known to many members of the Five Tribes and Plains tribes. Pike spoke several languages, fancied himself a poet, and possessed considerable experience working among Indian peoples. The Confederate envoy met with Cherokee leader John Ross on June 2, but the

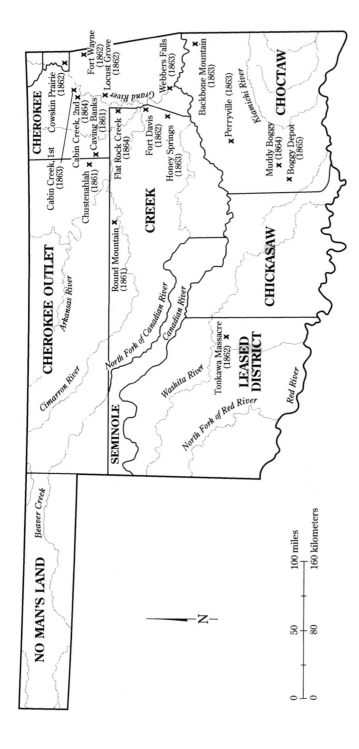

Map 1.1. Civil War battle sites, 1861–65. Map from W. David Baird and Danney Goble, *The Story of Oklahoma*, rev. 2nd ed. (Norman: University of Oklahoma Press, 2013), p. 160. Reprinted by permission of the publisher. All rights reserved.

14

chief stood firm in his commitment to his nation's neutrality, first announced on February 22. Ross sought to maintain relations with both governments, pointed to his nation's extant treaty obligations with the United States and the financial considerations involved, and hoped not to alienate the majority of his nation who supported the continued relationship with the United States. Ross also worried that he might lose his position as principal chief to his rival, Stand Watie, who represented a growing pro-Confederate minority within the Cherokee Nation. Finally, the chief understood that concluding a formal alliance with the Confederacy would equate to a declaration of war by his nation against the United States. For the time being, Ross declined Pike's proposed alliance.[9]

Pike next traveled to the Creek Nation, where he met also with Choctaw and Chickasaw leaders. Among the Creeks, Pike found divisions that dated back to the days of removal. The pro-Confederate faction included "mixed-bloods" who had formally endorsed removal, while the group who insisted upon continued loyalty to the United States arrayed themselves behind the aged leader Opothleyahola, a "full-blood" who had been an ardent opponent of removal. On July 10, Pike concluded a treaty with the pro-Confederate faction, led by the McIntosh brothers, Chilly and Daniel, and Principal Chief Motey Kennard. This would not be the last the Confederates would hear of Opothleyahola, however. The passionate divisions among the Creeks and Opothleyahola's determination to resist a Confederate alliance would ultimately lead to the first Indian bloodshed in the territory during the Civil War.[10]

Just two days after he arranged the compact with the Creeks, Pike easily concluded an official joint treaty with the Choctaws and Chickasaws. The diplomat then journeyed to the Seminole Nation, where, despite resistance from traditionalist leaders who wished to remain uninvolved in what they considered someone else's war, Pike concluded a treaty on August 1. Having formed official alliances with the Creeks, Choctaws, Chickasaws, and Seminoles, Pike headed west to the Wichita Agency with plans to treat with the various groups who resided there and, if possible, the Comanches, Kickapoos, and Kiowas who frequently tormented them.[11]

On August 6, Pike reached the Wichita Agency with a large escort that included other Confederate representatives, Seminole principal chief John Jumper, Creek principal chief Motey Kennard, and some sixty Creek and Seminole horsemen. To Pike's delight, upon his arrival he found representatives from the agency groups, but also envoys from the Kickapoos and certain bands of Comanches (Naconis, Taneiwes, Yaparihcas, and Cochoticheas). Kickapoo leaders, already suspicious of the entire spectacle, withdrew from the council without reaching an agreement with the Confederates, while the Kiowas simply declined to attend. For several days Pike stated the Confederate case, reminded Indian leaders of Union designs on the tribes' hunting grounds, and lavished gifts upon the Indian representatives. Eventually, on August 12, Pike secured agreements with the agency tribes and the Comanche bands that placed all parties under the authority and protection of the Confederacy and obligated the Plains tribes to cease all hostilities with their old enemies the Texans, now their brethren under the Confederate banner. The accords promised the reserve Indians the right to remain in the region known as the Leased District and obligated the Confederate government to supply the signatory groups with rations and agricultural tools and supplies.[12]

What happened at the Wichita Agency in the summer of 1861 illustrates perfectly that the residents of Indian Territory acted in the best interest of their respective peoples. Deeming themselves abandoned by the American military and meeting in a council that included their former federal Indian agent and the representatives from Indian nations who had already signed treaties with the Confederacy, the reserve tribes' decision likely proved uncomplicated. In fact, as a historian of the Caddos and Wichitas has explained, the reserve tribes had little choice but to sign with the Confederates, who now controlled Indian Territory in the absence of the Indians' former federal "protectors." In the end the residents of the Wichita Agency and those Comanches who signed the treaties clearly did so, quite understandably, out of concern for their own well-being rather than as a display of affection for the new Confederacy.[13]

In the meantime, back in the Cherokee Nation, John Ross had carefully reconsidered his nation's neutrality. A number of factors weighed on his mind, not the least of which was the increasing isolation of the Cherokees. The other large Indian nations had signed agreements with the Confederacy, and Ross knew that Pike would likely find further success in western Indian Territory. In the bigger picture, Ross perceived that the Confederacy appeared to be winning the war. The Confederates had scored a well-publicized victory at the Battle of Bull Run in Virginia on July 21. Closer to home and more important to Ross, the Confederates had temporarily seized control of the war in the trans-Mississippi theater with their August 10 victory at the Battle of Wilson's Creek in Missouri. That triumph temporarily secured Confederate control of northern Arkansas and southern Missouri and for the moment dashed any hopes Ross might have entertained of reconnecting his nation with the Union. Obviously Pike knew all of this as well, and the wily diplomat wrote to the chief to remind him of the growing Confederate sentiment among the Cherokees and to urge him again to ally with the Confederacy.[14]

Historians have long agreed that Cherokee unity lay at the heart of Ross's decisions throughout his life, though maintaining his leadership of the nation also proved a powerful motive for the chief. If Ross held out and refused to ally with the Confederacy, Pike would simply formulate a treaty with Stand Watie's mixed-blood faction. Pike had signed agreements with the mixed-blood factions of the Creeks and Seminoles, and Ross knew all too well the divide-and-conquer approach employed by American leaders during the days of removal. A shift to Confederate allegiance thus made sense for Ross at that moment and such a move proved consistent with his long-term goals. He had always sought to protect the independence of the Cherokee Nation and preserve the material well-being of its citizens. Now clearly without federal support and increasingly isolated, Ross sought to avoid the probable rupture of his nation and Watie's prospective rise to power.[15]

Similar to the decisions made by the various groups discussed thus far, Ross and Watie each acted in what they considered the best interest of their people and themselves. Ross desperately sought to maintain control of the Cherokee Nation not out of a selfish desire for power but because he considered himself the nation's best leader and because he distrusted his rival. Watie genuinely supported slavery and worked to stamp out abolitionist activity within the Cherokee Nation. He made no secret of his attachment to the Southern states and their shared culture. In fact, throughout the summer of 1861, Watie proved increasingly popular among those Cherokees with Southern sympathies and among the Confederates themselves. In July he received a commission as a colonel in the Confederate military and authorization to raise a small force to assist in the protection of Indian Territory. Ross knew all of this and thought that a Confederate treaty with the Watie faction would prove disastrous for the Cherokee Nation.[16]

For all of those reasons, Ross believed that the time had come to join the rebellion against the United States. The chief called a conference of the Cherokees in Tahlequah on August 21, 1861. There Ross addressed a crowd of what he described as "about four thousand Males" that included mixed-bloods almost certain to favor the Confederate alliance and full-bloods who would prove far more difficult to persuade. In his address Ross twice predicted Confederate victory, proclaimed the interests of the Cherokee people inseparable from those of the pro-Confederate Indians and Arkansas, and insisted that the Cherokees could not stand alone. He defended his previous call for neutrality as proper under the conditions at the time but insisted that circumstances had changed. In an obvious but effective attempt to inflame the emotions of his audience, Ross employed fiery language. "The great object with me has been to have the Cherokee People harmonious and united. . . . Union is strength, dissension is weakness, misery ruin! In time of peace together! in time of war, if war must come, fight together. As Brothers live; as Brothers die!"[17]

The Cherokees ultimately approved their chief's proposed alliance with the Confederacy and voted to raise a regiment, under Ross loyalist John Drew, and offer its services to their new allies. Pike soon returned to the Cherokee Nation, where he concluded a treaty with the Cherokees at Tahlequah on October 7, only days after securing the pledges of allegiance from the Senecas, Shawnees, Quapaws, and Osages at Park Hill. Ross, now officially using his considerable influence in support of the Confederate cause, had written to the leaders of each group in an effort to persuade them to accept Pike's offer.[18]

Ross wrote other letters during that tumultuous time. The Cherokee leader also wrote to Opothleyahola, the head of the full-blood pro-Union Creeks, or "loyal Creeks" as they preferred to describe themselves. Ross wrote to his fellow chief in an attempt to convince the Creek leader to join the other Indian nations and cast his lot with the Confederacy. Although Opothleyahola was apparently stunned by Ross's plea, in hindsight the Cherokee leader's action was predictable. Ross had previously written to Opothleyahola in order to urge him to avoid a Confederate alliance. He had also attempted to prevent the western tribes from signing Confederate treaties, only later to encourage the small tribes that lived within the Cherokee Nation to do the opposite.[19]

All of this demonstrates again that Indian leaders frequently acted without regard to deep sentiments toward either Civil War belligerent. When Ross had considered neutrality the best option, he had urged other leaders to follow the same course in the interest of Indian unity and self-preservation. Now, when he urged Opothleyahola to ally with the Confederacy, he did so with the same motives. Ross proclaimed that it would be "a great disgrace and a shame upon the Indian character" for Indians to find themselves opponents in the conflict and pleaded with Opothleyahola to agree to a meeting that might "strengthen the Bonds of Brother Hood between the several Nations of Red People!" Despite Ross's dramatic language, however, Opothleyahola no longer trusted his former ally from the days when both men challenged their peoples' relocation from the Southeast.[20]

What followed brought tragedy, bloodshed, and civil war to Indian Territory, initially in the form of Indians versus Indians. Several thousand loyal Creeks, accompanied by like-minded Seminoles and Cherokees who had also rejected their nations' Confederate treaties, gathered near Opothleyhola's

Figure 1.1. Rose Cottage (1860), home of Cherokee principal chief John Ross, burned during the Civil War by Confederate Cherokee officer Stand Watie. Courtesy of the Western History Collections, University of Oklahoma Libraries (Morris, 36).

home, fearful of the pro-Confederate factions of their respective nations. Isolated fighting had already occurred between the Creek factions, and an undetermined number of individuals from various tribes had already fled to Kansas in hopes of finding shelter with the U.S. military. Now the unionist individuals who remained in the territory looked to Opothleyahola for guidance and protection. Confederate military officials had been dispatched to meet with Opothleyahola in an attempt to mediate the disputes between the Creek factions but the aged chief declined to meet with them. Confederate leaders, meanwhile, grew increasingly concerned about Opothleyahola's communications with federal officials in Kansas and the threat of the old chief's influence upon Confederate Indians, especially the Cherokees. Although Opothleyahola's band of refugees presented no immediate military threat, that does not mean that Confederate leaders had no reason for concern. The wise old man's potential influence among the Cherokees, never the most ardent of Rebels, could have undermined Confederate control of Indian Territory. Thus, rather than mediate an intra-tribal dispute among the Creeks, Confederate officer Douglas Cooper proclaimed his intention to apprehend Opothleyahola or drive him and his followers out of Indian Territory.[21]

While the Confederates formulated a strategy, Opothleyahola and several thousand of his followers began a trek toward safety—heading to the Kansas border with livestock, wagons, and whatever personal possessions they could carry. The Confederates soon pursued the fleeing families, initially with a force composed of Creeks, Seminoles, Chickasaws, Choctaws, and part of the white Ninth Texas Cavalry. The pursuit ultimately led to three small battles: the Battle of Round Mountain (November 19), the Battle of Chustotalasah (December 9); and the Battle of Chustenahlah (December 26). In the first two engagements, Opothleyahola's warriors and followers skillfully eluded their attackers. At the Battle of Chustenahlah, however, the Confederates finally got the better of the unionist Indians and scattered Opothleyahola's followers with tragic results.[22]

After the first engagement, Opothleyahola had indicated his willingness to negotiate, whereupon Cooper sent members of Drew's Cherokee regiment to meet with the chief. While the Confederates waited, however, almost all of Drew's Cherokees deserted. Sources offer conflicting explanations for the deserters' motives, but clearly many felt sympathy for the refugees and at least some simply proved unwilling to attack fellow Indians, many of whom were friends, neighbors, and even relatives. The mass desertion should have surprised no one. Drew's Cherokee regiment comprised mostly full-blood Cherokees who had enlisted in Confederate military service primarily to protect the interests of their nation and because of their loyalty to Ross. As one historian has written, the Cherokee soldiers "knew an intertribal fight when they saw one and wanted no part of it."[23]

That fact points to the larger issue here and reinforces the relevance of the Opothleyahola campaign to a discussion of the problematic quest for Indian sovereignty during the Civil War. Indian soldiers who enlisted to protect their nation predictably questioned the need to attack a band of refugees that included thousands of women and children. Confederate leaders evinced legitimate concern with regard to Opothleyahola's ability to undermine Indian support for the Confederacy, but the Indian soldiers' different perspective highlights the weak link between the Confederate quest for Southern independence and the Indians' search for their own national autonomy. Many participants clearly recognized even during the war's first year that the Confederate-Indian alliance rested upon a shaky foundation of similar goals and that the strategies for how to accomplish those war aims would not always coincide.

The brutal aftermath of the Battle of Chustenahlah demonstrates the conflicted loyalties and tortured emotions the war's Indian participants faced. The battle turned into a rout of tragic proportions as men, women, and children scrambled for their lives across the cold countryside in a desperate effort to make their way to Union-held Kansas. During ensuing days, Confederate forces, primarily Confederate Indians, captured stragglers and frequently killed those who resisted. Those loyal Indians who escaped their vengeful enemies continued their trek to Kansas in small groups through a severe winter storm, though an untold number died along the way. Thus the first meaningful military action of the war in Indian Territory had featured Indians on both sides and culminated in fratricidal conflict with tragic results. As 1861 closed, some Indian leaders must have wondered whether they had chosen the proper path to secure their autonomy.[24]

A few months later, Union forces scored a significant victory in Arkansas at the Battle of Pea Ridge, March 6–8, 1862, against Confederate forces that included Indian soldiers. That Union victory removed the threat of an organized Confederate military presence in Missouri and northern Arkansas and forced a chaotic Confederate retreat. Most of the soldiers from Indian Territory under General Pike retreated to the Choctaw Nation in the southern portion of the territory, while a smaller number remained farther north under Stand Watie in the Cherokee Nation, an alignment that helped open the door for a Union invasion of the territory. That summer 1862 campaign, sometimes referred to as the Indian Expedition, included two Union Indian regiments recruited from Opothleyahola's followers and resulted in the first Union capture of the Cherokee Nation.[25]

More important regarding Indian sovereignty, federal soldiers who invaded Indian Territory in 1862 "captured" John Ross. Never a true Confederate, Ross had always hoped for an opportunity to repudiate his nation's treaty with the Confederacy and reconnect with the United States because he believed that an alliance with the Union promised better long-term benefits for his people. The Confederacy's inability to meet treaty obligations and provide for the residents of Indian Territory doubtless further motivated Ross, who had already written to Confederate president Jefferson Davis regarding the deplorable conditions in the territory. So Ross allowed himself to be captured, thus maintaining the image that he had kept his word with regard to the Confederate treaty. In reality his capture allowed him to travel to Washington to plead with federal officials on behalf of the Cherokees. Soon thereafter those Cherokees loyal to Ross confirmed their support for their leader and renounced the Confederate treaty, while those who remained committed to the Confederacy reaffirmed their allegiance and elected Watie their chief. The Cherokee schism was official.[26]

Ross's unenthusiastic support for the Confederacy was perhaps the worst-kept secret in the territory. Individuals on both sides grasped the situation and even expected Ross to shift to the Union side when availed of the opportunity. One Union colonel who took part in the invasion wrote, "John Ross is undoubtedly with us, and will come out openly when we reach there." Confederates suspected Ross too, as evidenced by the diary and letters of Texas cavalry officer James C. Bates. The Texan more than once expressed his suspicion of the chief, even after hearing Ross deliver pro-Confederate speeches to audiences of Cherokees and Choctaws. Bates wrote to his brother-in-law, "Ross is regarded here by every Southern man with distrust. You need not be surprised to hear that we have trouble with him yet."[27]

Regardless of real or perceived loyalties, the war raged on inside the borders of present-day Oklahoma, though both governments largely ignored the region and its inhabitants after the Union secured control of the Mississippi River in 1863. Indians and whites on both sides and black Union soldiers fought occasional small battles and skirmishes, while Stand Watie gained a degree of recognition for his exploits in guerrilla warfare. Civilians suffered intensely at the hands of forces on both sides and because neither government adequately provided for Indians.[28] None of the military activity in the territory significantly affected the outcome of the war and neither the military campaigns nor the civilian suffering proved especially urgent to officials in Richmond or Washington. Thus when the war ended in 1865, it proved a mixed blessing to the residents of Indian Territory. Peace and stability eventually returned, but the war's end also meant surrender negotiations and yet another round of treaties with the federal government.

As the war's closing scenes played out, Confederate-allied Indians, Plains Indians, and Confederate officials held an important conference May 25–27 at Camp Napoleon, near the Washita River and present-day Verden, Oklahoma. The meeting proved to be one of the largest-ever intertribal gatherings in Indian Territory, with estimates that ranged from five thousand to twenty thousand attendees. Confederate officials sought peaceful relations with all Indian groups and vowed that the Confederate Trans-Mississippi Army would surrender separately from the Confederate Indians because the latter had entered the conflict as "independent" entities, because they demanded separate surrenders, and because the Confederate officer in command of Indian Territory insisted that to surrender the Indians with his own forces would endanger his life. Confederate Indians also turned their attention to their postwar fate. Before the meeting, Choctaw principal chief Peter P. Pitchlynn revealed those concerns and expressed the Confederate Indians' position when he insisted upon separate surrenders for Indian forces, "that we may be enabled to take steps for our own safety and welfare."[29]

Thus events at Camp Napoleon, perhaps more than any other event, illustrate the Indians' ongoing search for sovereignty and their attempts to protect their interests during what began as someone else's war. The delegates pledged peace between the Plains tribes and the Confederate-allied Indians. Indeed, the authors of the remarkable document known as the Camp Napoleon Compact chose for their motto "An Indian shall not spill an Indian's blood" and promised, "The tomahawk shall be forever buried. The scalping knife shall be forever broken." The compact features dramatic and emblematic language that lamented the decline of the Indian populations and placed some of the blame squarely on Indian shoulders, thus the pledge to avoid intertribal conflicts. Delegates called for a united front among all Indians in an attempt to protect themselves against their common enemies.[30]

During the next several weeks, all Confederate Indian forces surrendered. If Indian leaders still pondered their postwar fate, U.S. emissaries cleared up those uncertainties at a meeting with representatives of the Five Tribes and other groups at Fort Smith in September. Because the Indians had made war against the United States, proclaimed the American envoys, they forfeited all rights and expectations from previous treaties. Tribes would be expected to make peace with each other and with the United States, abolish slavery, surrender portions of their lands for the relocation of other tribes into Indian Territory, and submit to a policy that united all Indian groups in the territory under one government. Federal officials made no distinction between tribes who had supported the Confederacy and those who had not. Indian delegates understandably rejected the terms and refused to conclude an official settlement at Fort Smith, though all eventually negotiated Reconstruction treaties with the federal government. Those Reconstruction treaties essentially made official the American demands announced at Fort Smith and enumerated exactly how much land each Indian nation would cede.[31]

In the end, the Indians' determined but problematic pursuit of sovereignty best illustrates the distinctive character of the Civil War in Indian Territory. Although the territory was similar geographically to bordering states such as Missouri and Kentucky, the residents of those states were U.S. citizens who shared their national and cultural identities with other U.S. citizens in the North or the South or both. While some Indians exhibited genuine loyalties to either the Union or the Confederacy, they were not U.S. citizens, and the protection of their own people understandably motivated them more than any other factor. They found themselves fighting to protect a precarious position as semi-independent nations with the unusual dual status of communities distinct from the U.S. citizenry yet legally wards of the federal government.

Unfortunately for the Indian groups, the Civil War presented a threat to their sovereignty more than an opportunity to secure it. A Union victory delivered only a step backward from true independence, while a Confederate victory at the very least would have further divided Indian peoples and prolonged slavery within the Indian nations. Ultimately that paradox demonstrates yet another in the long list of tragedies associated with the Civil War. The Indian nations almost certainly stood to gain nothing from their participation, yet neutrality proved unrealistic for groups of quasi-independent peoples caught between two powerful belligerents. Still, the Indian participants for the most part were not innocent bystanders. They played an active role in their theater of the war, and for that the Union victors punished them severely during Reconstruction. The disastrous dimension of Reconstruction in Indian Territory was not that the Confederate-allied Indians were punished. They had fought an armed rebellion against the United States, and for that they expected and received punishment. The great transgression was that the federal government treated all Indians in the same manner and punished even those who chose not to support the Confederacy. Moreover, in the long-term the United States government penalized the Confederate-allied Indians more harshly than they punished the residents of the eleven former Confederate states.

The same U.S. government that waged a heroic war effort to preserve the nation and destroy slavery perpetrated the moral crimes of the Indian Reconstruction treaties. Some of the same Indian groups who fought courageously to protect the interests of their peoples switched sides when it proved convenient, Indians on both sides owned slaves, and certain Indian participants willfully endeavored to preserve chattel slavery. The story of the Civil War in Indian Territory is one of shades of gray rather than black and white heroes and villains.

Notes

1. James M. McPherson, "The War That Never Goes Away," in McPherson, *Drawn with the Sword: Reflections on the American Civil War* (New York: Oxford University Press, 1996), 55–65.

2. Douglas Hale, "Rehearsal for Civil War: The Texas Cavalry in the Indian Territory, 1861," *Chronicles of Oklahoma* 68 (Fall 1990), 233–34; Robert L. Kerby, *Kirby Smith's Confederacy: The Trans-Mississippi South, 1863–1865* (New York: Columbia University Press, 1972), 4; Lary C. Rampp and Donald L. Rampp, *The Civil War in the Indian Territory* (Austin, Tex.: Presidial Press, 1975), 1; Clarissa W. Confer, *The Cherokee Nation in the Civil War* (Norman: University of Oklahoma Press, 2007), 4–7. The term "Five Tribes" has generally replaced the

traditional term "Five Civilized Tribes" in scholarly usage in large part because of the elusive definition of "civilization" and because of judgments of other cultures implicit in the term. "Five Civilized Tribes," the term formerly used by whites and the tribes themselves, referred to the parallels between Five Tribes cultures and mainstream American cultures. The tribes also used the term in part to distinguish between themselves and Plains tribes, whom they considered more "wild" or "savage." See David La Vere, *Contrary Neighbors: Southern Plains and Removed Indians in Indian Territory* (Norman: University of Oklahoma Press, 2000), 21–22.

3. Laurence M. Hauptman, *Between Two Fires: American Indians in the Civil War* (New York: The Free Press, 1995), ix–xii, 1–13; John C. Waugh, *Sam Bell Maxey and the Confederate Indians* (Abilene, Tex.: McWhiney Foundation Press, 1998), 29–30; *The Works of William H. Seward*, ed. George E. Baker, vol. 4 (Boston: Houghton, Mifflin, 1884), 346–67; Rampp and Rampp, *Civil War in the Indian Territory*, 3.

4. Dean Trickett, "The Civil War in Indian Territory, 1861," *Chronicles of Oklahoma* 17 (September 1939), 316–18; "Resolutions . . . of the General Council of the Choctaw Nation, February 7, 1861," in *The War of the Rebellion: A Compilation of the Official Records of the Union and Confederate Armies*, 128 vols. (Washington: Government Printing Office, 1880–1901), ser. 1, vol. 1, 682 (hereafter cited as *Official Records*); "Resolutions of the Senate and House of Representatives of the Chickasaw Legislature," in *Official Records*, ser. 1, vol. 3, 585–87.

5. "Edward Clark to Jefferson Davis, May 15, 1861," in *Official Records*, ser. 4, vol. 1, 322–25; Kinneth McNeil, "Confederate Treaties with the Tribes of Indian Territory," *Chronicles of Oklahoma* 42 (Winter 1964), 408–409.

6. "E. D. Townsend to Secretary of War, March 27, 1861," in *Official Records*, ser. 1, vol. 1, 659–60; F. Todd Smith, *The Caddos, the Wichitas, and the United States, 1846–1901* (College Station: Texas A&M University Press, 1996), 78–84; A. M. Gibson, "Confederates on the Plains: The Pike Mission to Wichita Agency," *Great Plains Journal* 4 (Fall 1964), 8. Fort Gibson, in the Cherokee Nation, had been abandoned in 1857 but would witness extensive wartime activity.

7. See various orders, reports, and correspondence in *Official Records*, ser. 1, vol. 1, 648–53, 656–57, 659–67; see also Trickett, "Civil War in Indian Territory, 1861," 318–22.

8. Hauptman, *Between Two Fires*, 25–26; Confer, *Cherokee Nation in the Civil War*, 45–46.

9. Alvin M. Josephy, Jr., *The Civil War in the American West* (New York: Alfred A. Knopf, 1991), 323–27; McNeil, "Confederate Treaties," 411–12; Gary E. Moulton, *John Ross, Cherokee Chief* (Athens: University of Georgia Press, 1978), 166–69.

10. Josephy, *Civil War in the American West*, 327; McNeil, "Confederate Treaties," 412–13. For the Confederate treaty with the Creek Nation and related documents, see *Official Records*, ser. 4, vol. 1, 426–43.

11. Josephy, *Civil War in the American West*, 327–28. For the Confederate treaty with the Choctaw and Chickasaw Nations and related documents, see *Official Records*, ser. 4, vol. 1,

445–66. For the Confederate treaty with the Seminole Nation and related documents, see *Official Records*, ser. 4, vol. 1, 513–27; Gibson, "Confederates on the Plains," 8–9.

12. Gibson, "Confederates on the Plains," 8–16; Smith, *Caddos, the Wichitas, and the United States*, 83–85. For the two treaties signed at the Wichita Agency and related documents, see *Official Records*, ser. 4, vol. 1, 542–54.

13. Smith, *Caddos, the Wichitas, and the United States*, 83–85; Gibson, "Confederates on the Plains," 8–16; McNeil, "Confederate Treaties," 413. The Confederate and Indian obligations under the new treaties essentially duplicated those stipulated in the Indians' previous treaties with the United States.

14. Josephy, *Civil War in the American West*, 328–29; McNeil, "Confederate Treaties," 414–15; Jay Monaghan, *Civil War on the Western Border, 1864–1865* (Lincoln: University of Nebraska Press, 1955), 216–17; Kenny A. Franks, *Stand Watie and the Agony of the Cherokee Nation* (Memphis: Memphis State University Press, 1979), 118. For excerpts of Pike's letter to Ross, see Ross to Joseph Vann, September 10, 1861, in *The Papers of Chief John Ross*, ed. Gary E. Moulton, vol. 2 (Norman: University of Oklahoma Press, 1985), 484–85.

15. Moulton, *John Ross*, 163–73; Confer, *Cherokee Nation in the Civil War*, 47–58.

16. Franks, *Stand Watie*, 114–19; Moulton, *John Ross*, 163–73.

17. "John Ross to the Chiefs and Headmen of the Creek Nation, August 24, 1861," in *The Papers of Chief John Ross*, vol. 2, p. 482; "Address to the Cherokees," in ibid., 479–81; Monaghan, *Civil War on the Western Border*, 216–18; Josephy, *Civil War in the American West*, 328–29.

18. "Ross to Chiefs of the Osage Nation, September 19, 1861," in *The Papers of Chief John Ross*, vol. 2, pp. 485–86; "Ross to the Chiefs of the Shawnees, Senecas, and Quapaws, September 10, 1861," in ibid., 486–87; Josephy, *Civil War in the American West*, 328–29; McNeil, "Confederate Treaties," 414–15; Monaghan, *Civil War on the Western Border*, 216–18. For the Confederate treaty with the Cherokees and related documents, see *Official Records*, ser. 4, vol. 1, 669–87. For the Confederate treaty with the Senecas and Shawnees, see *Official Records*, ser. 4, vol. 1, 647–58. For the Confederate treaty with the Osages and related documents, see *Official Records*, ser. 4. vol. 1, 636–46. For the Confederate treaty with the Quapaws and related documents, see *Official Records*, ser. 4, vol. 1, 659–66.

19. "Ross to Opothleyahola and Other Chiefs and Headmen of the Creek Nation, September 19, 1861," in *The Papers of Chief John Ross*, vol. 2, 487–88; "Ross to Opothleyahola et al., October 8, 1861," in ibid., 491–92; ibid., 173; Confer, *Cherokee Nation in the Civil War*, 59.

20. "Ross to Opothleyahola, October 11, 1861," in *The Papers of Chief John Ross*, vol. 2, 495–96.

21. "Report of Col. Douglas Cooper," in *Official Records*, ser. 1, vol. 8, 5–14; Rampp and Rampp, *Civil War in the Indian Territory*, 6–7; Josephy, *Civil War in the American West*, 330; Whit Edwards, ed., *The Prairie Was on Fire: Eyewitness Accounts of the Civil War in Indian Territory* (Oklahoma City: Oklahoma Historical Society, 2001), 3; Confer, *Cherokee Nation in the Civil War*, 58–62; *A Texas Cavalry Officer's Civil War: The Diary and Letters of James C. Bates*, ed. Richard Lowe (Baton Rouge: Louisiana State University Press, 1999), 35–40.

22. "Report of Col. Douglas Cooper," in *Official Records*, ser. 1, vol. 8, 5–14; "Reports of Captains M. J. Brinson and R. A. Young on the Battle of Round Mountain," in ibid., 14-15; Edwards, *Prairie Was on Fire*, 3–4; Rampp and Rampp, *Civil War in the Indian Territory*, 7; Josephy, *Civil War in the American West*, 330–31.

23. *A Texas Cavalry Officer's Civil War*, 37–38; "Report of Col. Douglas Cooper," *Official Records*, ser. 1, vol. 8, 5–14; Confer, *Cherokee Nation in the Civil War*, 62–64.

24. Rampp and Rampp, *Civil War in the Indian Territory*, 8; *A Texas Cavalry Officer's Civil War*, 60–62; Josephy, *Civil War in the American West*, 332–33.

25. Arrell Morgan Gibson, "Native Americans and the Civil War," *American Indian Quarterly* 9 (Fall 1985), 389–90; Rampp and Rampp, *Civil War in the Indian Territory*, 8–16; Kerby, *Kirby Smith's Confederacy*, 30–32; Franks, *Stand Watie*, 124–26; Confer, *Cherokee Nation in the Civil War*, 75–76; Josephy, *Civil War in the American West*, 354.

26. Moulton, *John Ross*, 173–78; Rampp and Rampp, *Civil War in the Indian Territory*, 13–20; Franks, *Stand Watie*, 129–31; Confer, *Cherokee Nation in the Civil War*, 78–79.

27. *A Texas Cavalry Officer's Civil War*, 42, 52–53; Moulton, *John Ross*, 174.

28. Steven E. Woodworth and Kenneth J. Winkle, eds., *Atlas of the Civil War* (New York: Oxford University Press, 2004), 310; Gibson, "Native Americans and the Civil War," 390–93; Rampp and Rampp, *Civil War in Indian Territory*, 11–146.

29. Brad R. Clampitt, "'An Indian Shall Not Spill an Indian's Blood': The Confederate-Indian Conference at Camp Napoleon, 1865," *Chronicles of Oklahoma* 83 (Spring 2005), 34–53; "J. J. Reynolds to James Harlan, June 28, 1865," in *Official Records*, ser. 1, vol. 48, pt. 2, 1018; "Camp Napoleon Compact, May 26, 1865," in ibid., 1102–1103; "Edmund Kirby Smith to Albert Pike, April 8, 1865," in ibid., 1266–69; "C. S. West to W. D. Reagan," in ibid., 1279–80; "Kirby Smith to D. H. Cooper," in ibid., 1270; "Cooper to James W. Throckmorton, May 16, 1865," in ibid., 1307; "Cooper to W. P. Adair, May 16, 1865," in ibid., 1307–1308; "Cooper to Throckmorton, May 22, 1865," in ibid., 1317; "James C. Veatch to J. Schuyler Crosby, July 20, 1865," in ibid., 1095–97; "Interview with Charles Stewart Lewis, March 11, 1938," in Grant Foreman, ed., *Indian-Pioneer History*, 112 vols., unpublished manuscript in Research Division, Oklahoma Historical Society, Oklahoma City, vol. 109, 157; "Testimony of James Webb Throckmorton," *Congressional Record*, 49th Cong., 1st sess., March 9, 1886, serial 2236, pt. 3, 17; Maurice Boyd, *Kiowa Voices: Myths, Legends, and Folktales* (Fort Worth: Texas Christian University Press, 1981), 163; "Council Minutes, May 13, 16, 20, 1865," Peter P. Pitchlynn Papers, Gilcrease Institute, Tulsa, Oklahoma; "William P. Adair to Stand Watie, May 13, 1865," in *Cherokee Cavaliers: Forty Years of Cherokee History as Told in the Correspondence of the Ridge-Watie-Boudinot Family*, ed. Edward E. Dale and Gaston Litton (Norman: University of Oklahoma Press, 1939), 224–25; "Pitchlynn to Smith, May 17, 1865," Peter P. Pitchlynn Papers, Western History Collections, University of Oklahoma, Norman.

30. Clampitt, "Camp Napoleon," 43–47; "Camp Napoleon Compact and Camp Napoleon Minutes, May 25–27, 1865," Pitchlynn Papers, Gilcrease Institute; "Reynolds to Harlan, June 28, 1865," in *Official Records*, ser. 1, vol. 48, pt. 2, 1018; "Cooper to S. S. Anderson, May 15,

1865," in ibid., 1306; "Camp Napoleon Compact, May 26, 1865," in ibid., 1102–1103; United States Commissioner of Indian Affairs, *Annual Reports*, 39th Congress, 1st sess., 1865, H. Ex. Doc., vol. 2, pt. 1, serial 1248, 202.

31. Gibson, "Native Americans and the Civil War," 405; M. Thomas Bailey, *Reconstruction in Indian Territory: A Story of Avarice, Discrimination, and Opportunism* (Port Washington, N.Y.: Kennikat Press, 1972). Several Plains tribes, including Comanches, Kiowas, Cheyennes, Arapahos, and Kiowa-Apaches, played a relatively minor role in the war. At a meeting in Kansas in October 1865, U.S. officials assigned those tribes to various reservations in Indian Territory, Kansas, and the Texas Panhandle.

CHAPTER 2

The Mock Wedding of Indian and Oklahoma Territories

Malia K. Bennett

T he Wedding Consummated": so read a front-page headline in the *Oklahoma State Capital* on November 17, 1907. The newspaper was published in Guthrie, the first state capital and main location of the November 16 ceremonies marking Oklahoma's admission to the United States. There the presidential proclamation declaring Oklahoma's statehood was read, the elected officials of the new state's executive branch were sworn in, and a mock wedding symbolizing the joining of the Twin Territories was performed.[1]

A woman from the city of Muskogee, Mrs. Leo Bennett, played the part of Miss Indian Territory, according to historian Muriel Wright. Mrs. Bennett was reported to be part Cherokee, but certainly did not dress in buckskin as Miss Indian Territory was portrayed in the Fred Olds statue in Guthrie, Oklahoma, dedicated years later. In reality, Mrs. Bennett wore "the latest fashion of the time," described as a long lavender dress of satin, complete with "a large picture hat and gloves" (fig. 2.1). C. G. Jones of Oklahoma City, a successful businessman and community leader, portrayed Mr. Oklahoma Territory. In her article based on an interview with William A. Durant, who "gave the bride away" in 1907, Wright describes Jones as tall and fair-haired, and his attire was said to include striped pants and a black coat "suitable for such an occasion." No known photographs of Jones in his wedding attire exist.[2]

Historians would later misrepresent the mock wedding as being performed by actors dressed in nineteenth-century costume—as in the Fred Olds

Figure 2.1. The original Miss Indian Territory, Mrs. Leo Bennett, in Statehood Day gown. Courtesy of the Research Division of the Oklahoma Historical Society.

statue, in which Oklahoma is represented by a man in a settler's garb—rather than that described by Wright. David Baird and Danney Goble, for example, in their 1994 book *The Story of Oklahoma*, write, "A man dressed as a cowboy 'married' a woman made up like an Indian. . . . Miss Indian Territory was barely Indian at all."[3]

This description contradicts fact. In addition to Wright's article, a story in the *Daily Oklahoman* from November 16, 1930, recounts the story of the mock wedding with an artist's rendering of the couple, dressed in Edwardian clothing. Furthermore, as a mixed-blood member of the Cherokee Nation, Mrs. Leo Bennett was considered one of the Cherokee elite, who were upper-class and well educated. As to whether her appearance was "barely Indian at all," a November 17, 1957, article in the *Daily Oklahoman* offers a different view: "Her selection as the woman to represent Miss Indian Territory was a natural. A tall dark-haired beauty, she was part Cherokee Indian, part Irish and all woman. Enthusiastic newspapermen described her as one of the loveliest women of Indian blood of the day."[4] Baird and Goble declare that the bride didn't look Indian, but by 1907 many Cherokee women wore contemporary non-Native clothing as part of their cultural assimilation. Further, mixed-blood people then may even have looked like their European ancestors more than their Indian ones.

Why the confusion? Why have reenactments of the mock wedding used the stereotypical imagery reflected in the Olds statue? Have they been influenced by decades of mass media images, well-worn portrayals of Indians in movie and television Westerns? The Olds statue was dedicated in the 1970s and may have influenced Baird and Goble. The curators at the Oklahoma Territorial Museum maintain that the statue was Olds's artistic interpretation of the event. We can only speculate as to why Olds chose to dress his figures as he did.

Wedding reenactments held in Guthrie after 1907 did not include the cowboy and Indian costumes, but performances elsewhere did. An April 10, 1938, photo and cutline, "Uncle Sam Marries Them," from the *Daily Oklahoman*, shows such an interpretation. Students from the Capitol Hill neighborhood of Oklahoma City are seen in costume for a mock wedding of the territories, part of an upcoming pageant to celebrate the fiftieth anniversary of the 1889 land run. The photo shows Miss Indian Territory wearing a fringed buckskin dress with a headband and feather. Mr. Oklahoma Territory is dressed as a cowboy, complete with hat and boots. In this reenactment, a student dressed as Uncle Sam is officiating the mock wedding. Clearly, this is a far different representation than in the ceremony performed in Guthrie in 1907, closer to the interpretations of Olds, as well as Baird and Goble.[5]

A performance in Duncan in June 2007 included actors dressed in attire similar to those in the 1938 Capitol Hill celebration. Organizers explained that they knew that the original mock wedding had been done in Edwardian clothing, but their local community theater had no such clothing. They did, however, have costumes on hand similar to the clothing depicted in the Olds statue. It was simply a matter of convenience and economy.[6]

Although the full script of the 1907 mock wedding ceremony was printed in some of the newspapers that covered the admission day events, the accompanying articles shed no light on who wrote the ceremony or who came up with the idea of using matrimony to represent the merging of the Twin Territories into a single state. It can be assumed that organizers were simply adopting a popular form of entertainment in a way that helped dramatize the union.

An explanation may come from a surprising source. Materials archived by the Folklore of Ireland Society in the 1930s contain accounts of games played at Irish wakes in the 1800s that included mock weddings. A 1938 article on Irish wake games by Henry Morris quotes an earlier article on this topic: "Lady Wilde, in her *Ancient Legends, Charms and Superstitions of Ireland* (1887, Vol. 1: 228), tells about 'wake orgies' of which she remarks: 'From ancient times the wakes or funeral games in Ireland were held with many strange observances, carried down by tradition from the pagan era. Some of the rites, however, were so revolting and monstrous that the priesthood used all their influence to put them down. The old funereal customs, in consequence, have now been discontinued almost entirely among the people and the traditional usages are unknown to the new generation.'"[7]

While the playing of games, including mock weddings, at wakes may seem puzzling to Americans today, Patricia Lysaght with the National Folklore Collection of Ireland explains that "this was one of a range of Rabelaisian-type 'games' performed at wakes and has been interpreted by some scholars as a strong and sometimes explicit expression of the continuation of life in the midst of death."[8]

Although the occasions when mock weddings were performed in North America did not include wakes, it is logical to assume that immigrants would have brought such games and plays with them, giving these dramas a new home and new traditions. We know that mock weddings were performed throughout the United States and Canada in the nineteenth and twentieth centuries, and are still performed today in some parts of North America. Michael Taft, director of the American Folklife Center at the Library of Congress, has researched and written about these ceremonies. In the *North Dakota History Journal of the Northern Plains*, Taft described mock weddings as a form of folk drama.

The mock wedding is a parody in which members of a community dress as a wedding entourage and stage a marriage ceremony. Players have specific roles and there is a written script in which several of the players have lines. The mock wedding is a ritual within a ritual, for it most often occurs as part of the larger celebration of a couple's marriage or their wedding anniversary. In Saskatchewan, the drama usually takes place during the celebration of a couple's milestone anniversary, especially the twenty-fifth anniversary. In Nebraska, the drama seems to occur more often at the actual wedding reception of the couple, but other occasions—such as wedding and baby showers, birthdays and community benefit concerts—may also serve as excuses for performing this drama.[9]

Newspaper articles are further evidence of the existence of mock weddings throughout the United States. The following entry appeared in a November 19, 1895, *New York Times* article with the headline, "Mock Wedding at Vassar College": "The juniors at Vassar College gave a novel entertainment in Strong Hall Saturday night. Cards were sent to the seniors inviting them to 'attend the wedding of the Duke of Marlborough to Miss Consuelo Vanderbilt.' The seniors rigged themselves up in bloomers and powdered tresses and came to represent the nobility. The marriage was, of course, a farcical affair, at which a most extraordinary appearing Bishop officiated. The happy pair were congratulated and Queen Victoria then held a reception."[10]

In Oklahoma, reports of mock weddings beyond those done to commemorate Statehood Day appear in newspaper archives. Numerous stories from society pages mention mock weddings staged as entertainment at bridal showers. A March 21, 1943, *Daily Oklahoman* article described a mock wedding that went terribly wrong, at least as far as the "bride" was concerned:

An alleged mock wedding ceremony that turned out to be the real McCoy was revealed Saturday in district court records here. A petition by a local woman revealed that the "mock ceremony" took place at a time when the plaintiff "had no intention whatever of being married or getting married." But later, according to the petition, the woman discovered that someone had actually taken out a marriage license and that the wedding, which had been conducted by a minister, was apparently legal and binding. . . . [T]o show her sincerity in believing that the ceremony was not genuine, she stated further in the petition that after the performance of the rites, "the plaintiff and defendant went their respective way and never then or thereafter acted as husband and wife."[11]

Luckily for the bride in this ceremony, the court agreed and declared her status as unmarried.

A 1991 *New York Times* article discussed another kind of mock wedding, in which children perform the parts of the bride, groom, and bridal party, called "Tom Thumb" weddings. According to the article, the name comes from P. T. Barnum's General Tom Thumb, who married a dwarf named Lavinia Warren in the 1860s to wide publicity. Churches and other organizations, the article says, began holding their own Tom Thumb weddings featuring child actors after the marriage of Tom Thumb and Lavinia Warren took place (fig. 2.2).

Michael Taft explains that this kind of miniature mock wedding dates back to the Victorian era. He believes that Tom Thumb weddings may be the oldest form of this particular type of folk drama. According to the *New York Times* article, the Tom Thumb weddings had become increasingly rare in the 1970s and 1980s but were making a comeback in the 1990s.[12]

While Tom Thumb weddings began as entertainment, those performed in contemporary times seem to be scripted in an attempt to educate young people about marriage and commitment. In addition, Tom Thumb versions of the 1907 mock wedding of Miss Indian Territory and Mr. Oklahoma Territory have been performed by Oklahoma schoolchildren for the past one hundred years as a way to teach and celebrate Oklahoma's admission as a state. It is likely that newcomers to the Twin Territories brought the North American tradition of the mock wedding with them. Newspaper articles and photographs tell us that these dramas continued to be performed as entertainment in Oklahoma even after statehood.

When a mock wedding reenactment was performed as part of the state's official centennial celebration on November 16, 2007, in Guthrie, everything was done to make the production as historically accurate as possible—that is, as it had been performed in 1907. Mrs. Leo Bennett's lavender dress was re-created based on the photograph from the *Chronicles of Oklahoma* article (fig. 2.3), the attire of Mr. Oklahoma Territory was re-created, and the Oklahoma Territorial Museum made clothing patterns available so that even audience members could also dress in Edwardian clothing.

The Oklahoma Territorial Museum developed the 2007 script from 1907 newspaper accounts. The script reflects how folk drama is transformed into a retelling of the history of the Twin Territories. Here is its proposal by the groom's godfather:

Figure 2.2. Oklahoma "Tom Thumb" wedding performed at a bridal shower, c. 1940s. Photograph courtesy of Mary Jo Watson.

Figure 2.3. Mr. Oklahoma Territory and Miss Indian Territory, 2007 Statehood Day reenactment. Photograph courtesy of Malia K. Bennett.

I have been asked to perform the agreeable duty of proposing the marriage of Oklahoma to Miss Indian Territory. Permit me to say that nothing gives me greater pleasure, as the President advises us in this proclamation that the marriage will be strictly legal with regard to age or previous condition of servitude. The bridegroom is only 18 years old, but is capable of assuming all the matrimonial responsibilities of a stalwart youth. Though he was born of trouble and tribulation in the city of Washington, his life of 18 years on the plains has been one of tremendous activity and he has grown to the size of a giant. Like every well-regulated masculine individual, he has grown tired of being alone, though he was fully capable of taking care of himself. Strange to say on account of his youth and inexperience, he is possessed of unconquerable modesty and he has asked me to propose the marriage with Miss Indian Territory.

The script continues:

I present to him Miss Indian Territory, who was reared as a political orphan, tutored by federal office holders and controlled by an indifferent guardian residing 1,000 miles from her habitation. Despite these unhappy circumstances of her youth, which have cast a shade of sorrow over a face intended by nature to give back only the warm smiles of God's pure sunshine, this beauteous maiden comes to him as the last descendent of the proudest race that ever trod foot on American soil, a race whose sons have never bowed their neck to the feet of an oppressor; the original occupants of the American Continent. Although an orphan, Miss Indian Territory brings to her spouse a dowry equal in fertile fields, productive mines, and sterling, upright citizenship, to the fortunes of her wooer. To Oklahoma, into whose identity Miss Indian Territory is about to be merged forever, must be entrusted the care of this princely estate. This is not exactly a case of love at first sight. A lady by the name of Sequoyah interfered with the courtship and at one time tried to break up the match. But having failed to do so, and tired of the loneliness of single blessedness, she gracefully surrendered to the inevitable, and has ever since been in favor of the marriage.[13]

The use of this popular form of folk drama was not limited to the original Statehood Day ceremonies in Guthrie. Although details are sparse, some local historical documents reveal that other communities held versions of the mock wedding of the Twin Territories as part of their celebrations. One of these was performed in the community of Atoka. Although the theme was the same as in Guthrie, the script and costumes were different:

> The most novel and entertaining feature of the entire day was the wedding of Mr. Oklahoma and Miss Indian Territory in the bonds of Statehood. Miss Earl Smiser, dressed in a "magnificent buckskin costume with a blanket of brilliant hue," represented Indian Territory and Mr. Lou Watson, "in dandy cowboy attire with six-pistol adornment," represented Oklahoma. Each looked and acted the part splendidly.
>
> The Reverend Weston performed the ceremony, after the marriage license (the proclamation) had been delivered by "President Teddy." When Mr. J. Fred Groman appeared in khaki military suit and rough rider hat with gun in hand and followed by a squad of little boys with Teddy bears, the crowd gasped with astonishment at his resemblance to the President.
>
> With both hands clasped, Miss Indian Territory and Mr. Oklahoma vowed a state of perpetual partnership. The groom promised to refrain from making goo-goo eyes and not to ask his bride to obey him nor support him, while the bride consented, for a proper consideration, to divide her vast possessions with the groom and . . . "to build his wigwam with her lumber, light it with her oil and gas, and warm it with her coal."[14]

An article written for the sixtieth anniversary of statehood says that "Miss Norma Earl Smiser," who had portrayed Miss Indian Territory in Atoka, had turned twenty on the day of the ceremony, November 16, 1907. The article also states that the mock wedding was performed on a platform near the intersection of Court Street and Pennsylvania Street in downtown Atoka.[15]

Another mock wedding was performed on the same day in the community of Stigler in Haskell County, writes Ted Byron Hall in his history of Indian Territory. Among the participating citizens listed in an account of the event is James Benjamin Jones, who was born in 1887 in Arkansas, attended Whitefield School, and became a farmer and stockman. Dressed in traditional cowboy clothing, he played the role of Mr. Oklahoma Territory. Hall makes no mention of who played Miss Indian Territory.[16]

The marriage between the territories was also portrayed in Okmulgee as part of their official Statehood Day parade. This account is found in the *History of Okmulgee County, Oklahoma*:

The official parade began at 2 p.m. and included Dick Farr and his prancing steed. Marshal of the Day was Colonel Peacock, with Misses McCready, Skillen and Green dressed in red, white and blue respectively. The Grand Army of The Republic and Southern Confederate Veterans marched; cowboys and Indians followed on horseback. A float of states was drawn by four black horses festooned in national colors. Forty-five young ladies dressed in white represented the states, with Carrie Baker as Oklahoma. There was also "an ingeniously wrought" bridal float symbolizing the union of Indian Territory and Oklahoma.[17]

Of the four 1907 mock weddings I found described in newspaper accounts and historical works, only the Guthrie performance was held in the former Oklahoma Territory. Atoka, Stigler, and Okmulgee are all located in the former Indian Territory. However, many other communities may have held such ceremonies. Decades later, historian Edward Everett Dale wrote, "Every important town in the state also arranged for a celebration in honor of the coming of statehood. Each of these was attended by swarms of happy people coming for many miles from every part of the surrounding country."[18]

Each of the mock weddings described above contained elements described by Taft. They were folk dramas with some humorous elements, used to mark a special occasion in a community. They were also a means of creating a narrative about the events that made Oklahoma's statehood possible, and they contained elements of public performances as described by geographer Steven Hoelscher, including "ritualized choreographies of race and place, [and] gender." They put forth stories that belied the truth, ignored the loss felt by Native Americans, and celebrated circumstances that many members of the Five Tribes did not wish to accept. Dale did note this, writing, "Only one group was absent. Within the limits of the former republics of the Five Civilized Tribes many of the older Indians remained at home to mourn the passing of the old governments and the old order under which they had so long lived and which they so much loved."[19]

The concept of a mock wedding to celebrate statehood was unique, and—as contemporary critics have argued—the ceremony performed in Guthrie in 1907 was more than entertainment. It represented the dominant culture's version of events, assigning roles based on gender and race which affirmed the superior place of white males, with Native Americans portrayed as subservient, yet willing, partners. This criticism was vocalized during Oklahoma's centennial year, 2007, with performances of the mock wedding ceremony in Guthrie and Duncan. Muscogee Creek artist Richard Ray Whitman was among those interviewed by the *Oklahoma Gazette*. "Native Americans know the importance of celebration," he said. "[But] renewing the vows of Indian Territory and Oklahoma Territory, what does that entail? Have [the vows been] met? I think we've been in an abusive marriage up to this point—not the ideal relationship. It's like the dominant husband, the submissive wife. We need to . . . examine those things and say . . . what's the role of this today?"[20]

Others voicing their criticism included Clara Sue Kidwell, former director of the University of Oklahoma's Native American Studies Program, who referred to the union as a shotgun marriage—made under duress. OU history professor William W. Savage, Jr., characterized the event as "happy history," and criticized the ceremony as being both misogynistic and ethnocentric. While a spokesperson for the Oklahoma Territorial Museum said that the historical context of the mock wedding script should be considered, Savage argued that this was not an excuse for continuing to perform the ceremony. "Why not include a black participant?" he asked. "By the 1910 census, there were nearly twice as many black residents as American Indians in the state. And, why white man, native woman, rather than the other way around? It's the white man who makes the judgment about who's going to participate in the ceremony," he said. "It was a racist ceremony in 1907, it was racist again in 1982 and if we do it again, it will still be racist—and sexist."[21]

The Duncan performance of the mock wedding was held on Saturday, June 23, 2007, without any protests. Native Americans offended by the ceremony instead turned their focus to holding their own demonstration on November 16. That morning, while thousands of Oklahomans watched the reenactment of the mock wedding in Guthrie, two hundred protesters gathered just north of the State Capitol building in Oklahoma City. According to news articles, they marched toward the Capitol carrying a banner that said, "Why celebrate 100 years of theft?" and signs that said "The Land Run was Illegal Immigration."[22]

Brenda Golden, a member of the Muscogee (Creek) Nation, organized the event, saying that Native Americans wanted to explain why not everyone felt that the centennial was something to celebrate. "We want to remember where our ancestors came from and what they sacrificed," she said. "When our ancestors were moved here, they were told this was going to be Indian Territory forever." By the time the group marched to the Capitol, there were now about five hundred protesters—some in Native dress. There was also a performance of a mock wedding written in protest of the original one performed in Guthrie.[23]

Figure 2.4. "Reverse Wedding" reenactment, 2007 Statehood Day. Photograph courtesy of Vicki Monks.

The script was written by a former Oklahoman, Gerald D. Tieyah, a member of the Comanche Nation. In an interview with the *Oklahoman*, Tieyah compared asking Indians to celebrate the centennial with asking a Jew to celebrate Kristallnacht, the night of broken glass in 1938 when Jewish homes were ransacked in numerous German and Austrian cities. "Our part of the story," he said, "the part where our lands are invaded and stripped away from us, and the part where our cultures are attacked, the part where our peoples' lives are trampled and forever altered by this encroachment of land hungry invaders, is always conveniently neglected or overshadowed."[24]

Tieyah called his version of the mock wedding "The Wedding of the Century." In his script, the gender and racial roles of the bride and groom were the opposite of the Guthrie wedding. Mr. Indian Territory was the groom, and he remained gagged throughout the ceremony. Oklahoma Territory was represented by Miss Oklahoma Pioneer, with yellow hair made of yarn, and a buxom physique. During the mock wedding, the bride was given away by President Andrew Jackson, under whose administration the forced removals of the Five Tribes to Oklahoma took place. In the opening scene, a minister recounted the history that led to the joining of the territories into a single state:

Ladies and Gentlemen of the Oklahoma and Indian Territories! We are assembled here, in the presence of God, Andrew Jackson and these Sooners to join Oklahoma Territory and Indian Territory in the marriage of statehood. In the beginning this land was the land of the Indian Nations. Then White people came, taking the land as they could and slowly invading across the face of the continent. Despite legal and armed resistance to the encroachment on their lands, the Great White Father of the Groom removed many Indians from their homes in the East and forced them into the homes of Indians in the West so that his own children may occupy and live in those homes. But even this did not satisfy his children so they continued Westward, ever more invading Indian country until the last bit of Indian country was rushed upon and parceled out against the will of the indigenous people of the land so that now we have come to this wedding and the joining of these two territories.[25]

As the couple exchanged vows, the bride promised to ignore agreements made with the groom when it suited her needs and promised to turn a blind eye when it came to teaching the truth about Indian history. She also promised to abuse the sovereignty of his children when the mood should strike her. The minister asked the groom whether he would allow the pioneer woman to take him against his will and whether he would promise to forsake the truth in order to allow her to whitewash history. At the end of the ceremony, the minister gave the audience, acting as the congregation, the opportunity to voice their objections. The congregation and Mr. Indian Territory, with his gag now removed, all shouted "No!" to the impending union.

Native protesters used the folk drama form to protest the Guthrie mock wedding but also to express their views about the treatment of Native Americans from the forced removal to the forced "union" with Oklahoma Territory. And they were not alone. Though receiving less media attention than other centennial events held that day, Oklahoma blacks, who were not a part of the official mock wedding ceremony or the protest ceremony, held their own observance in Guthrie that included a play about their history in the region.

Whites, Indians, and blacks were all a part of what historian Murray Wickett called the "contested territory" that became the state of Oklahoma. One hundred years later, they offered competing views of how history should be interpreted and how the centennial of statehood should be marked.[26]

Mock weddings have been part of North American folk culture since the Civil War era, and they are still performed today, although a ceremony celebrating or commemorating the joining of Oklahoma Territory to Indian Territory, a land in which the Five Tribes had hoped to retain their sovereignty, is unique. The Native protest of 2007, however, echoes other events.

As the state celebrated the centennial of the 1889 Land Run, Jerald C. Walker, former president of Oklahoma City University, shared his inner conflict: he had both white and Indian ancestry, and those ancestors must have had very different views on the run. He discussed how some public officials were attempting to help Oklahoma "come to terms with its past as an Indian land" and wrote:

> The tensions and conflicts in the Walker family over the last eighty years mirror the complex history of what came to be known as Oklahoma. My father's family, joined by several related families, moved to Indian Territory from the mountains of East Tennessee to buy "surplus land" in the Creek Nation. It was, of course, surplus land only in the minds of federal officials and non-Creek land seekers. The "surplus" land eagerly sought by the Walker family and their relatives was seen as land stolen from its rightful owners by my mother's clan. . . . They, like many of my mixed-blood relatives, worked toward acceptance of their neighbors no matter what they thought of statehood and the demise of the five Indian republics. But one thing was clear then and now: these folk never forgot or forgave the loss of the Cherokee republic. Many of their descendants hold exactly the same unreconstructed view in the present.[27]

One hundred years after the Land Run, Walker believed that Oklahoma had made significant progress toward gaining a better understanding and respect for its Native roots and heritage, and he gave much credit to then-governor Henry Bellmon and state senator Enoch Kelly Haney for this. Haney, an artist who left the senate in 2002 and was later elected chief of the Seminole Nation, said that there were both "symbolic" and "concrete" ways in which Oklahoma could come to terms with its beginnings as Indian land. Walker wrote that Haney's examples of concrete actions included legislation making it a felony to desecrate Indian graves in Oklahoma, as well as legislation that for the first time acknowledged the federally recognized Indian tribal governments within the state.[28] One positive sign was the 1989 dedication of Apache artist Alan Houser's sculpture *As Long as the Waters Flow* outside the State Capitol building. This thirteen-and-one-half-foot bronze statue reminds observers of the promise President Andrew Jackson made to the Native Americans that this land should always belong to them. The figure of a woman in traditional native attire is complete with the sacred symbol of the eagle feather fan.[29]

Since the 1989 Land Run centennial there have been many other state actions to acknowledge Oklahoma's Native American heritage. In 2002 the Oklahoma City skyline was changed by the completion of the Capitol dome topped by Enoch Kelly Haney's statue, *The Guardian*. The seventeen-foot bronze depicts an Indian holding a lance, which pierces through his legging and into the earth, something Haney said that warriors would do in times of battle. Haney explained, "He is standing his ground. He refuses to be moved. . . . He stands strong in the face of adversity."[30]

The Oklahoma legislature has also begun to work toward rectifying previous legislative discrimination. In 2008 Senate Concurrent Resolution (SCR) 49 denounced Oklahoma's Jim Crow laws of times past, and Senate Concurrent Resolution (SCR) 74 supported a U.S. congressional measure acknowledging official depredations and ill-conceived policies regarding Native American peoples.

Some called the initial passage of SCR 74 a "historic first step toward recognizing the true history of Oklahoma" and said that "an apology could lead toward a new non-combative attitude in this state toward indigenous residents."[31] Still, while this sort of action represents an important shift in how the state of Oklahoma views its relationships with Indian tribal groups, there are emotional wounds that may never completely heal.

In decades to come it will be interesting to see what changes occur in attitudes of citizens and elected officials regarding the state's efforts to reconcile past mistreatment of Native Americans. Clearly the mock wedding of the Twin Territories has been embraced as part of a traditional celebration, and it is undeniably a part of Oklahoma's history. No doubt there will be those who will continue to support performances of the mock wedding as part of Oklahoma's Statehood Day tradition. Perhaps one day, though, the ceremony will be relegated to history books.

Notes

1. *Oklahoma State Capital*, November 17, 1907, p. 1, Oklahoma Newspaper Collection, Oklahoma Historical Society.

2. Ibid.; Muriel H. Wright, "The Wedding of Oklahoma and Miss Indian Territory," *Chronicles of Oklahoma* 35, no. 3 (1957): 255–58.

3. W. David Baird and Danney Goble, *The Story of Oklahoma* (Norman: University of Oklahoma Press, 1994), 336.

4. *Daily Oklahoman*, November 16 and 17, 1957. Journalists were fond of portraying Oklahoma Territory as a cowboy and Indian Territory as an Indian princess. See Charles M. Harger, "Oklahoma and the Indian Territory as They Are Today," *American Review of Reviews* (February 1902): 178–81, and Clinton O. Bunn, compiler, *Constitution and Enabling Act of the State of Oklahoma, Annotated and Indexed* (Ardmore, Okla.: Bunn Brothers, 1907), 123. By 1957 Oklahoma historian Muriel Wright had accurately portrayed the Statehood Day wedding based on an interview with William A. Durant, who had presented the "bride" on that day. See Linda W. Reese, *Women of Oklahoma, 1890–1920* (Norman: University of Oklahoma Press, 1997) 75–77.

5. "Uncle Sam Marries Them," *Daily Oklahoman*, April 10, 1938.

6. Emily Jerman, "Shotgun Wedding," *Oklahoma Gazette*, June 20, 2007.

7. Henry Morris, "Irish Wake Games," *Béaloideas* 8, no. 2 (December 1938): 124, www .jstor.org/stable/20521993 (accessed June 4, 2010).

8. Patricia Lysaght, National Folklore Collection of Ireland, personal communication by email to author, April 14, 2010.

9. Michael Taft, "Folk Drama on the Great Plains: The Mock Wedding in Canada and in the United States," *North Dakota History: Journal of the Northern Plains* 56, no. 4 (1989): 17.

10. "Mock Wedding at Vassar," *New York Times*, November 19, 1895.

11. "Woman Finds Mock Wedding Real Thing, Asks It Be Voided," *Daily Oklahoman*, March 21, 1943.

12. "Tom Thumb Weddings: Only for the Very Young," *New York Times*, June 16, 1991; Taft, "Folk Drama," 20.

13. John Estus, "Territories Tying the Knot, Centennial Mock Wedding in Guthrie Tries to Match Grandiose Atmosphere of Original Ceremony," *Oklahoman*, November 11, 2007, 114; "Mock Wedding" script, Oklahoma Territorial Museum, Guthrie, 2007.

14. *Tales of Atoka County Heritage* (Atoka, Okla.: Atoka County Historical Society, 1983), 35.

15. "Atoka's Wedding," photo and article, Atoka County Historical Society, November 16, 1976.

16. Ted Byron Hall, *Oklahoma Indian Territory* (Fort Worth, Tex.: American Reference, 1971), 588.

17. Heritage Society of America, *History of Okmulgee County, Oklahoma* (Tulsa: Tulsa Historical Enterprises, 1985), 164.

18. Edward Everett Dale, "Two Mississippi Valley Frontiers," *Chronicles of Oklahoma* 26 (Winter 1948–49): 381.

19. Steven Hoelscher, "Making Place, Making Race: Performances of Whiteness in the Jim Crow South," *Annals of the Association of American Geographers* 93, no. 3 (September 2003), 657; Dale, "Two Mississippi Valley Frontiers," 381.

20. Jerman, "Shotgun Wedding," 11.

21. Ibid., 12.

22. "American Indians Protest Oklahoma Centennial," MSNBC.com, November 16, 2007, www.msnbc.msn.com/id/21841853/print/1/displaymode/1098 (accessed December 28, 2012).

23. JoKay Dowell, "Hundreds Oppose Centennial Celebration at Capitol," *Cherokee Phoenix*, November 2007, www.cherokeephoenix.org/Tools/19424/Article.aspx (accessed December 28, 2012).

24. Johnny Johnson, "Where Is Our Side of History: Indians Plan to Protest State Centennial Events," *Oklahoman*, November 6, 2007, 11.

25. Gerald D. Tieyah, "Wedding of the Century," unpublished manuscript, 2007.

26. Murray Wickett, *Contested Territory: Whites, Native Americans, and African Americans in Oklahoma, 1865–1907* (Baton Rouge: Louisiana State University Press, 2000).

27. Jerald C. Walker, "The Difficulty of Celebrating an Invasion," in *An Oklahoma I Had Never Seen Before*, ed. Davis D. Joyce (Norman: University of Oklahoma Press, 1994), 15–17.

28. Ibid., 25.

29. Malia K. Bennett, "Finally a Dome," *State Legislatures* 27, no. 10 (December 2001), 24–27; "As Long as the Waters Flow, by Alan Houser, Oklahoma Arts Council," www.arts .ok.gov/Art_at_the_Capitol/Capitol_Collection/Houser/As_Long_as_the_Waters_Flow .html (accessed February 20, 2013).

30. "As Long as the Waters Flow," Oklahoma Arts Council, www.arts.ok.gov/ (accessed December 28, 2012).

31. American Tribes forum,
http://forum.americanindiantribe.com/ (accessed 2008; posting discontinued December 28, 2012).

CHAPTER 3

"The Land We Belong To Is Grand!"

ENVIRONMENT AND HISTORY IN
TWENTIETH-CENTURY OKLAHOMA

Sterling D. Evans

Historian Muriel Wright began *Our Oklahoma* (1939) with a colorized lithograph of children singing the state's first anthem, belting out the lyrics "Oklahoma, Oklahoma, fairest daughter of the West, / Oklahoma, Oklahoma, 'tis the land I love best."[1] Choosing lines that dealt with the love of the land was a telling way to preface her book, since hers and nearly every other text on the state's history starts with a background narrative of Oklahoma's geography and climate. Entitled "Geography and Natural Features," "The Country," "The Natural Setting," "Geography," "The Land," and "The Land and Its Influences," these introductory chapters offer students different levels of analysis of the physical makeup of Oklahoma and its variegated ecological regions.[2] As for the anthem, when the legislature officially changed the state song in 1953 to Rodgers and Hammerstein's "Oklahoma!" proud residents sang even more heartily about the land they loved, its climate, and its promise of natural resources—familiar lyrics and fitting categories here in which to explore the state's environmental history in the twentieth century.

The framework that environmental history offers in which to view these issues is useful for understanding much of the history of Oklahoma since statehood in 1907. From its origins as a means to study U.S. conservation history in the late 1960s, and as one of the subdisciplines tied to the so-called new western history of the 1980s, environmental history has become an important field for historians of all North America, the entire globe, and for all time periods.[3] As historian Donald Worster has defined it, it concerns "the role and place of nature in human life." Its goal, Worster maintains, is "understanding how humans have been affected by their natural environment through time and, conversely, how they have affected that environment."[4]

But does this notion bow to environmental determinism that suggests that a region's natural environment dictates its historical outcome, including its economic development? The theory arose in the late nineteenth century, especially with geographers, as a spinoff of natural selection and evolution, arguing for "geographical explanations of cultural difference" and that "mechanisms for cultural behavior were to be found in the environment."[5] The problem is that this ideology downplayed human agency by saying that geography determined all. David Baird and Danney Goble alluded to this in *Oklahoma: A History*, writing that "the state's physical features have influenced—and sometimes determined—the course of history." The key word here is "sometimes." The environment surely did foster certain forms of economic development (agriculture and fossil fuel extraction, for example), but as Baird and Goble point out, "the natural environment . . . is just the beginning of Oklahoma's history." Equally important factors are "time and change."[6]

"Brand New State, Brand New State!"

Statehood in 1907 not only joined the culturally diverse Indian and Oklahoma Territories under its first red, white, and blue flag, but also created a state that became identified by its rich red dirt. (The current blue flag with the Osage shield was adopted in 1925.) The soil is red from hematite (from the Greek word for blood), iron oxide deposited in the Permian Period three hundred million years ago. Books like Bonnie Lynn-Sherow's *Red Earth: Race and Agriculture in Oklahoma Territory* and Roxanne Dunbar-Ortiz's *Red Dirt: Growing Up Okie* reflect this sense of place related to soil. Lynn-Sherow captures the essence of this with her depiction of Canadian County: "Bloodred earth. Caked on my car tires and splashed across my windshield, the red muck is lurid in the bright light of an April morning sun after a drenching rain. . . . Red lines transect the green horizon in great gashes and cuts. . . . The red earth peeks out under a lush gray-green palette of grama-bluestem. . . . Thin ribbons of red dirt road empty into the pink sides of gentle hills and crimson 'canyons.'"[7]

Even the regional musical tradition known as Red Dirt music—a uniquely Oklahoman blend of folk, country, and rock that emanated from Stillwater's live music scene—seems to answer Woody Guthrie's call to "write what you see."

It is informed by Guthrie's place-based folk traditions and invokes the state's agricultural roots. Music critic Thomas Connor has called the genre "country-roots music with a decided storytelling folk ambition and a classic-rock edge."[8]

But red soil was not the only identifying geographical aspect of the new state. The "wedding" of Indian and Oklahoma Territories joined several distinct ecosystems that geographers later identified (see map 3.1). Bonnie McDonald's *Oklahoma: A Land of Contrasts* is thus appropriately titled, with ten regions having their own sections in the book.[9]

Only three other states (Alaska, California, and Texas) have as many or more ecosystems within their borders. The hilly areas (the Wichita, Ouachita, Arbuckle, and Glass Mountains, Sugar Loaf Mountain, Rainy Mountain, and the Antelope and Gypsum Hills) resulted from great tectonic action three hundred million years ago that caused uplifts to form out of sea floors. These regions are often surprising to people outside the state who entertain misconceptions of a totally flat Oklahoma.

"Where the Wind Comes Sweepin' Down the Plain"

Oklahoma and wind—the subject of one of the most recognized lines in the state song—illustrate that extreme weather is a key factor in Oklahoma's environmental history and identity. It is no coincidence that the National Weather Center's Severe Storms Laboratory is on the campus of the University of Oklahoma, America's leading school for the study of meteorology.

Although Oklahoma's climate is classified as "temperate," it is characterized by wide variations and sudden fluctuations. Rainfall varies from a yearly average of fifty-two inches in the Ouachita Mountains and decreases westward with altitude and aridity to fifteen inches a year in the Black Mesa area of the Panhandle. The variation is due to Oklahoma being situated where three climatic regions (humid, subhumid, and semiarid) join, and where the north–south effects of cooler, dryer conditions blowing from Canada meet with moister and hotter conditions blowing from the Gulf of Mexico. In the United States, only two other states, Texas and Kansas, can make the claim of having as much climatic zone differentiation.[10]

In his book *The Way to Rainy Mountain*, Kiowa scholar N. Scott Momaday—winner of the 1969 Pulitzer Prize for Fiction and 2008 Oklahoma poet laureate—revives the memory of how his ancestors described Oklahoma's weather. The Kiowas understood there to be a storm spirit that controlled the volatile climate. "At times the plains are bright and calm and at times they are black with the sudden violence of weather. Always there are winds."[11] But few

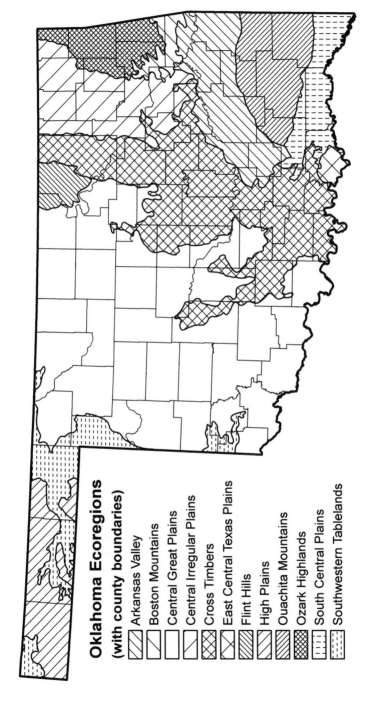

Oklahoma Ecoregions
(with county boundaries)

- Arkansas Valley
- Boston Mountains
- Central Great Plains
- Central Irregular Plains
- Cross Timbers
- East Central Texas Plains
- Flint Hills
- High Plains
- Ouachita Mountains
- Ozark Highlands
- South Central Plains
- Southwestern Tablelands

Map 3.1. Oklahoma ecoregions, Oklahoma Forestry Service. Map courtesy of Wenonah Van Heyst, Department of Geography, Brandon University.

phenomena anywhere equal the power and violence of the region's tornadoes. In Kiowa lore, Man-ka-ih was responsible: "But it was a terrible, terrible thing. It began to writhe, slowly at first, then faster and faster until there was a great commotion everywhere. . . . Great trees were uprooted, and then the buffalo were thrown up into the sky. . . . Even now, when they see the storm clouds gathering, the Kiowas know what it is: that a strange wild animal roams on the sky. It has the head of a horse and the tail of a great fish. Lightning comes from its mouth, and the tail, whipping and thrashing . . . makes the . . . wind of the tornado."[12]

Man-ka-ih's power places Oklahoma in the center of Tornado Alley. Weather data show that since 1950 the state has endured an average of fifty-three twisters a year, causing billions of dollars of damage and the tragic deaths of an average five persons per storm. The year 1999 especially stands out, not only for the Category F-5 tornado that damaged much of Moore and Oklahoma City, but also for the record-setting 73 other tornadoes that day, with a total of 146 for the year.[13]

A different kind of climatic disaster in the 1930s—drought—combined with especially hot, dry winds in western Oklahoma helped to create one of North America's worst ecological calamities of the twentieth century. Then it was not just the wind that came sweeping down the plain; it was great walls of dirt in a series of storms that made the region become known as the Dust Bowl. The severe drought and high winds were common to the region that experienced cyclical dry periods. The difference this time was the blowing top-soil that denuded farmland and covered fields and towns with gigantic dunes of dirt in much of northwestern Oklahoma.[14]

But all that good ol' Oklahoma wind has had its upsides too. Besides keeping the air pure and clean (not to be taken for granted), the wind was harnessed by farmers and ranchers for drawing water from underground aquifers. Before electricity was used to pump water, the Oklahoma landscape was dotted with windmills that provided livestock with water in the dry prairies. More recently, wind has been considered an advantage as a clean and renewable source of energy to generate electricity with the massive turbines that are now scattered in "wind farms" throughout the western part of the state. Growing numbers of the turbine towers (213 feet high, with blades 110 feet long), especially near the communities of Woodward, Weatherford, and Lawton, are, as one study puts it, "transforming wind energy into electrical energy, but without pollutants or use of nonrenewable resources like natural gas, oil, and coal."[15] The turbines have, however, changed the prairie landscape and scenery in these locations, and some ornithologists and environmentalists wonder about bird mortality from the rotating blades. But overall the wind farms are adding to Oklahoma's energy industry in a relatively clean and useful way.

"Flowers on the Prairie Where the June Bugs Zoom"

Oklahoma is blessed with unusual botanical diversity. It is home to approximately 2,500 species of flowering plants, 330 species of trees (130 native), mostly deciduous but with a number of evergreens and shrubs, 3 species of cacti, 13 fern species, hundreds of species of forbs (leafy annual, biennial, or perennial plants), 51 species of grasses, and nearly 1,000 species of wildflowers—ranking third in the country after California and Texas in wildflower speciation. And it retains some of the last remnants of the tallgrass prairie.[16]

Oklahoma's richly forested lands lent themselves to economic development for an incipient timber industry in the nineteenth and early twentieth centuries. There are hardwood forests in the eastern part of the state and the Cross Timbers environment runs a north–south swath in central Oklahoma—a unique zone of post oaks and blackjack oaks that grow so thick that that they create a barrier between the western plains and eastern hills. Visiting writer Washington Irving and other early travelers to the region found the Cross Timbers nearly impossible to cross, with Irving calling the area "forests of cast iron." Indians, Texan drovers on the cattle trails to Kansas, and builders of railroads and major highways, especially in the early days of automobile travel, stayed either west or east of the forested barrier. So were communities developed mostly outside of the region. Only a limited number of relocated Indian and Anglo-American farmers chose to try agriculture in the Cross Timbers, most of whom had a tough go of it, becoming impoverished in the process. The eastern hardwood forests were open to commercial logging, yet today about 20 percent of Oklahoma remains forested.[17]

As for other "flowers on the prairie," Oklahoma has suffered from an epidemic of exotic species—noxious weeds and nonnative plants that damage rangelands, forests, and riparian areas (stream beds). The greatest problems have been caused by two Asian invasive species, Chinese bush clover and salt cedar, and the native but noxious eastern red cedar. Bush clover, an aggressive perennial legume introduced in the late nineteenth century as livestock forage, has severely displaced native vegetation and altered grasslands and forests throughout the state. Salt cedar, a riparian shrub that grows in thickets, consumes vast quantities of water and chokes out local plants. Eastern red cedar (actually a juniper) has expanded at dangerously high rates due to the suppression of prairie fires. Between 1950 and 2000, it spread from dominating

1.5 million acres to 6 million acres, taking over landscapes at an estimated rate of 720 acres per day. It sterilizes soil, causes severe erosion below its canopy where grasses cannot grow, decreases grazing lands for livestock, and greatly reduces habitat for wildlife such as bobwhite quail and the endangered prairie chicken. As a heavy pollinator, it has caused dramatic increases in allergies, especially in early spring. Prescribed burns and mechanical removal seem to be the only options for red cedar control, with ongoing projects conducted by Oklahoma State University's Range Ecology and Management Program and the state's chapter of The Nature Conservancy.[18]

"And Watch a Hawk Makin' Lazy Circles in the Sky"

Originally Oklahoma was home to far more wildlife species than were around by the twentieth century, including vast populations of bison, elk, bears, wolves, mountain lions, bighorn sheep, white-tailed and mule deer, pronghorn antelope, prairie dogs, and even peccaries. There were also a great variety of birds, including some of the largest flocks of wild turkeys, prairie chickens, and quail in North America. Although the last sighting of a passenger pigeon in the area was in Osage County in 1890, at the time of contact with Europeans their numbers were so huge as to "darken the sun when in flight."[19] There was high demand for the pigeons as a cheap source of meat, often for slaves in the South. In the mid-nineteenth century commercial hunters working in Indian Territory killed tens of thousands of the birds, sending four thousand in one single shipment from Muskogee in 1879.[20] Hunters in the nineteenth century also wiped out Oklahoma's population of bison that roamed in all parts of the state, and significantly reduced populations of deer, upland game birds, beavers, bears, antelope, and even alligators in the southeastern part of Indian Territory. Habitat conversion to farming severely reduced the immense populations of prairie dogs in the high plains. Few scholars, especially historians, were writing on those issues in the early twentieth century, even though the ecological consequences were taking place around them at the time. That analysis did not come until the late twentieth century, by then too late for many species that had disappeared from the state.

Of course, species extinction was not unique to this time period, as millions of years ago Oklahoma and the southern plains were home to dinosaurs and an amazing array of sea creatures, the paleontological evidence of which is cataloged, interpreted, and displayed at the Sam Noble Oklahoma Museum of Natural History in Norman. More recently, only thousands of years ago, the region was home to other megafauna species that have subsequently gone

extinct. Some two hundred genera of large mammals, including giant arma-
dillos, large rodents, ancient species of deer, antelope, and giant bison, and
the enormous mastodons and woolly mammoths disappeared from the
region during the Late Pleistocene (eighteen thousand to eleven thousand
years ago) due to climate and environmental changes and perhaps to over-
kills by Native hunters.

Despite these extinctions, Oklahoma remains one of the most biologically
diverse states, and its wildlife speciation is greater than most areas of equal size
in the country. It is home to nearly 400 hundred species of birds, 113 species of
mammals (including 20 of bats and 29 of mice and rats), and it is third in the
nation in reptiles and amphibians with 80 species.[21] The state also has a large
speciation of insects and spiders, including the Oklahoma tarantula. Ecologists
attribute this biodiversity to the intersection of Oklahoma's many geographical
regions that created the variety of habitats. And twentieth-century conservation measures have been successful in restoring populations of deer and upland
game birds, although bison and elk now exist only in wildlife refuges.

"We Know We Belong to the Land"

No one singing "Oklahoma!" is more deserving of "belonging to the land" than
the state's American Indians. Wright used the term "wilderness" to describe
Oklahoma before contact with Europeans—a word that has different connotations today (roadless, "untrammeled" areas on public lands) than it did when
she wrote. Then it referred to an empty or virgin land, a place without civilization, despite descriptions of Indians who inhabited the forests and prairies of
Oklahoma. In their discussions of how the European explorers perceived these
places, Wright and most historians since have left out of textbooks how Native
peoples understood their relationship with the natural world, and how many
continue to do so today.

To understand "belonging to the land," we should keep in mind the the-
ories and beliefs regarding when Native peoples started to inhabit Oklahoma.
Most anthropologists agree that the Americas were the last place to be inhabited in a long history of human movement around the world. As people dispersed from Africa and the Middle East, some migrated over thousands of
years to northern Asia. As various ice ages evolved, some groups crossed a
land and ice "bridge" across the Bering Strait to Alaska, into the rest of North
America, and eventually to Central and South America. The theory holds
that humans came into the area of Oklahoma around eleven thousand years
ago. But as many Native groups maintain, it is reasonable to believe that some

peoples originated in the Americas—they may have always been here, or came from other places at earlier times, a theory corroborated by archaeological evidence that predates the Bering Strait crossings.[22] Whichever the belief or theory, these prehistoric peoples of the southern plains survived by hunting big game, gathering roots, nuts, berries, and seeds, and—for some—becoming small-scale agriculturalists, farming along rivers and creeks and trading with other groups for game.

However, assumptions that early Native groups lived in a kind of harmony with nature with only minimal impacts on ecosystems do not correspond with archaeological evidence. Early humans in the southern plains, like indigenous peoples anywhere, were agents of change—they used brainpower and skills to adapt to surroundings, altering local environments. As historians Richard White and William Cronon argue, "Depictions of Indians as savages wandering in the wilderness or as innocent children living gratefully off nature's bounty are cultural artifacts of Europe; they have little to do with the actual lives of Native Americans."[23] Instead, evidence shows that some groups overhunted food species, leading to a so-called Pleistocene overkill—a theory that suggests that some megafauna species went extinct due in part to overhunting.[24] Great hunts at times included the driving of bison over cliffs known as buffalo jumps, resulting in the deaths of hundreds of bison—far more than could be used by a village at the time.

Gatherers left their own impacts, especially with the use of fire. They learned they could alter habitats with controlled burns to favor different annual plants, and to clear forested areas to encourage the growth of food plants or grasses for bison grazing. Native people on the Great Plains used controlled fires to hinder the growth of trees, woody brush, and forbs that interfered with the grassland ranges of bison.[25] Burning became an important tool to help them go from simple adaptation and subsistence to active management of environments.

Thus it is worthwhile to consider the traditions and ideas of Oklahoma Indians in the twentieth century regarding their understandings of the natural world. The Wichitas believe that their ancestors originated from the tops of the Wichita Mountains, holding them in reverence—exemplifying what it means to be native to a place. In a provocative essay with the very title "Being Native to This Place," Raymond Pierotti (Comanche) and Daniel Wildcat (Yuchi) have written, "Being native to a place requires one to live with nature. It is built on a worldview directly opposite to the dominant Western worldview, which assumes humans live above, on, separated [from], or in opposition to nature." They relate how Western concepts of evolution, ecology, biological "connectedness," and the "idea of a cycle, or circle, of life" were all understood by Native peoples far in advance of the development of evolutionary biology as a scientific field. Thus American Indian understandings of wildlife, the hunt, eating meat as a way of gaining an animal's strength, and offering gifts back to nature in reciprocity are all aspects of being truly native to a place.[26]

Scott Momaday claims, "I don't think that anyone has clearly understood yet how the Indian conceives of himself in relation to the landscape." He writes that it is "a matter of the imagination" and that American Indians' "heritage has always been rather closely focused, centered upon the landscape as a particular reality." Humans have "two visions of nature," he explains. One is physical; the other imaginative. The Native American experience of the natural world also includes appropriateness, both morally, and naturally."[27] In *The Way to Rainy Mountain*, he writes of the Kiowas' relation to the landscape of western Oklahoma. Referring to his people's migration from the northern Rockies to the southern Plains, he talks about their "love and possession of the open land," how they "reckoned their status by the distance they could see," where "the sun is at home on the plains." It was there—northwest of the Wichita Range—that Rainy Mountain became the center point for the Kiowa sense of place: "To look upon that landscape in the early morning, with the sun at your back, is to lose the sense of proportion. Your imagination comes to life, and this, you think, is where Creation was begun."[28] Similarly, native Oklahoman Suzan Shown Harjo (Cheyenne, Pawnee, Creek), a poet and activist, advised, "We can no longer be polite about the agents . . . that would sacrifice our mother, the earth, on the altar of materialism. We have an obligation . . . to protect our future generations, not just our personal blood line or our relations, and not just humankind, but all the beings of the universe."[29]

"Pasture for the Cattle . . . Plen'y of Room to Swing a Rope"

Cattle ranching has been important to Oklahoma's identity and economy and has brought environmental changes, although admittedly fewer than other forms of agricultural development. From the Texas cattle trails to the historic 101 Ranch near Ponca City (that at one time stretched across 135,000 acres before its demise in 1932) to the famous Terry Don West rodeo school in Henryetta, ranching and rodeo culture have gone hand in hand in Oklahoma. This has not been accidental; the state's grasslands, especially in the central and western plains, are ideal for grazing. The native grasses include bunch grass, bluestem, and goldentop of the tallgrass region, and the sparser short-stemmed buffalo and grama grasses out west—both of which were essential to the bison that once roamed the region and later for cattle. Both regions' grasslands adapted to climatic conditions. The short-stemmed grasses were, as Thoburn and Wright described them, "exceedingly hardy and persistent" and "furnish excellent pasturage for livestock under range conditions" and during the dry season "retain most of their nutritive properties."[30]

At statehood, the cattle industry had already settled into fenced ranches and had moved away from the wiry livestock descended from old Spanish stock. Ranchers started replacing longhorns with English breeds, especially Herefords, that did well on the Plains and when fed corn during the winter months produced marbled meat popular with consumers. Ranchers out in the Panhandle switched to Herefords by the 1910s, with stock growers in other prairie sections raising them soon after. By the 1930s, however, with the double jeopardy of drought and depression, the state's livestock industry declined. As ranchers raised more cattle, the prices for beef fell, as many of the grasslands in western Oklahoma were blowing away or were too sparse to sustain many head. The New Deal's stock reduction program was not popular with Oklahomans, but reflected the need to curb cattle numbers. With better rainfall and the demand for beef during World War II, ranching returned to some of its former glory and has continued apace ever since. In the Panhandle, livestock remains a significant industry, with enormous ranches (the largest, in Beaver County, with over 87,000 acres). Cimarron County alone has 650,000 acres in pasturage.[31] Thus Oklahoma remains one of the country's leading beef producers.

The industry faces big challenges. Overgrazing is an environmental concern in some areas, and the Range Ecology and Management Program at Oklahoma State University provides expertise on this and on rangeland conservation in general. The worsening problem of invasive species overtaking natural grasses threatens the long-term viability of ranching in some parts of western counties. Likewise, enormous feedlots, especially in the Panhandle, are replacing rangelands grazing. Swift's plant in Guymon opened in 1967 and processes around 200,000 head a year, making the region one of the largest beef-producing areas in the country.[32] But shifting consumer demands are raising valid public concerns about feedlots, especially their need for increased production of irrigated row crops (corn silage and sorghum) for feed, the hormones and antibiotics given to the animals as a part of feedlot processing, and the considerable waste generated at feedlots and slaughtering plants. A return to natural grass-fed beef became more popular in the late twentieth century.

Finally, while neither sung about in state anthems nor having a place in cowboy lore, the significant increase in the state's pig farms has greatly affected the livestock landscape of Oklahoma, especially in the Panhandle. Near Guymon the first large-scale pig farm began in 1972, with most hogs shipped in from Arkansas. The industry expanded in the 1990s, growing by a whopping 900 percent as world demand for pork rose. The region became "plastered with proliferating pork palaces," as one study complained, with many of the farmers in the region devoting some of their land to hog sheds. By 1996, the region was producing four million hogs annually, or about 4 percent of the national total. To process so much meat, Seaboard Farms, a multinational corporation with its out-of-place name for the region, opened a plant near Guymon in 1995 capable of processing one thousand hogs an hour or two million a year. Some of the hogs slaughtered come from south of the state line in Perryton, Texas, where a Japanese firm raises five hundred thousand pigs annually for processing at Seaboard and then ships to markets in Japan. Likewise, the pig farms and processing plants have employed thousands of Mexican and other immigrants, a labor dimension that has changed the regional demography and cultural landscape. Critics of the industry claim the water and feed demands strain local resources and that the waste "lagoons," in which the industrial wastewater evaporates quickly in the Panhandle sun, leave a steady stench over the region.[33] Thus the pork industry in Oklahoma continues to be controversial on social and ecological levels, and the waste lagoons remain a significant environmental concern.

"The Wavin' Wheat Can Sure Smell Sweet"

Agriculture has always been central to Oklahoma's culture and history, and it continues to be an important industry in the state's economy. It has also been one of the largest contributors to environmental change. Agricultural expansion into Indian Territory led to the region becoming a major producer of cotton—a commodity that relocated Five Tribes (especially Choctaws) and later incoming southern immigrants farmers brought. The climate in Indian Territory, more like that of the Southeast than of the Great Plains and with warmer weather and more rainfall, lent itself well to cotton production. By the 1920s farmers grew cotton on nearly 5.4 million acres—representing more than one-fourth of all the cropland in the state, with only Mississippi and Texas producing more of the fiber than Oklahoma. Planters cleared forests and valleys for cotton fields, displacing some of the native vegetation and landscape, but most of the area's hills remained wooded. Ninety percent of the growers were tenant farmers who did not own the farms they worked. Thus when cotton prices plummeted in the 1930s and 1950s, many tenant farmers were forced to leave the state or seek employment in cities. Still, cotton was a mainstay agricultural industry for many years and continues to be on a lesser scale into the twentieth-first century.[34] The Oklahoma Cotton Exchange, a landmark high-rise in Oklahoma City, remains a monument to cotton's role in the state's agricultural history.

In the dense Cross Timbers of central Oklahoma, only limited agriculture was possible in small intermittent meadows, and there the sandy soil eroded quickly when plowed. Except for family gardens and some poultry and livestock, farming was relatively unproductive, leaving most people impoverished. Baird and Goble note that the environment was responsible in determining many of the social and political trends that emanated there: "This heritage of broken dreams partly explains why many of Oklahoma's radical political and religious traditions have centered in the Cross Timbers . . . [which] gave birth to an army of socialist sympathizers like Woodie Guthrie, as well as a host of faith-healing evangelists like Oral Roberts."[35]

Over in Oklahoma Territory, the land runs and subsequent theft of Indian lands were all for expanding the wheat and ranching frontiers. German Mennonites had perfected Turkey Red wheat that thrived well in the southern plains climate and soils, and became the grain of choice for most of Oklahoma's wheat farmers. From 1900 to 1930, agriculture was the dominant economic activity in the state, especially as steam engines and tractors greatly aided the breaking of sod, and inventions like the twine binder facilitated harvesting crops. To subsidize some of the farmers' expenses, in 1916 the state legislature approved establishing a twine factory at the penitentiary in McAlester, importing fiber from Mexico and using convict labor to produce less-expensive twine than the implement corporations were making.[36] Nearly five million acres of prairie land in northern and western Oklahoma and the Panhandle were converted to wheat fields in those years, making Oklahoma third in national wheat production (behind Kansas and North Dakota), producing over sixty million bushels a year.[37] Farmers prospered from the weather conditions and excellent prices for wheat in the 1910s and '20s.

Tractors and harvesting implements (binders and combines) allowed for the rapid spread of wheat into previously unbroken grasslands across the Great Plains, especially during the era of World War I and its aftermath when there were heightened demands for grain and high prices paid to farmers. But expansion into that region, characterized by periodic drought cycles, led to the Dust Bowl conditions of the mid-1930s in the southern plains. By 1935, the wind, drought, and dust storms were so severe that over thirty-three million acres (51,500 square miles) was void of plant life, and mountains of powdery dust replaced what had been farm fields.[38]

Severe drought and dust storms in north central and northwestern Oklahoma affected approximately thirteen million acres (20,000 square miles) in the early 1930s. In 1933 alone, no fewer than *forty* highly destructive dust storms hit the Panhandle with disastrous results. Reports, as cataloged by historian Richard Lowitt, reflect the plight: "cattle dying, almost no wheat in areas that previously harvested 4 to 6 million bushels, 90 percent of the poultry dead in one Panhandle county because of sand storms, milk cows turned onto highways to starve. . . . Winds soon carried away soil from plowed lands and piled it in mounds on highways, along fences, and around buildings. Fields never touched by plows were swept clean down to the hard dirt." And, as Lowitt relates, as "deplorable as conditions were in 1933, they would get worse when vegetation disappeared from sandy soils." New problems included "serious erosion," sand drifts "filling yards and covering farm implements, tanks, troughs, woodpiles, shrubs, and young trees." Likewise, the Dust Bowl significantly changed the demography of the region, driving many farmers off their land due to foreclosures on over fifteen thousand acres of land by 1935 (but not necessarily away from the state, as occurred more with tenant cotton farmers elsewhere in the state during the Great Depression). From 1930 to 1935 the Panhandle lost over thirteen thousand people.[39]

Most environmental historians agree that the great plow-up of the 1910s and '20s caused the Dust Bowl. Famed ecologist Aldo Leopold's reference to the disaster as "wheating the land to death" was indicative of what Donald Worster has called investors', farmers', and millers' "exploitative relationship with the earth" in that region.[40] But Franklin Roosevelt's New Deal introduced a variety of conservation measures aimed at avoiding similar environmental and agricultural disasters in the future. The government encouraged farmers to practice listing (making small "dams" in furrows to collect water), to plant shelterbelts to stave off wind damage around farmyards and fields, to convert crop fields in dryer areas to grasslands for grazing, and to increase the variety of crops to avoid wheat monocropping. But planting row crops like corn and sorghum (milo) or field crops like alfalfa required greater amounts of water and a steady supply of it. Thus drilling to tap the region's Ogallala Aquifer and using expensive center-pivot sprinkling became the norm from the 1950s on. The Ogallala is an enormous underground "lake" containing what has been estimated to be $25 billion worth of water.[41] Center-pivot sprinkling, more efficient and less expensive and wasteful of water than ditch irrigation, especially for alfalfa, nonetheless has its own set of environmental implications. It requires fossil fuels or electricity to run the pumps, it caused the near depletion of the aquifer by the 1990s, and the landscape changes inherent in the round center-pivot fields, as new ground was broken to increase agriculture, should also be factored into the irrigation equation. As Lynn-Sherow explains, this was a big part of "the displacement of Oklahoma's complex ecology of grasses, legumes, and forbs for commercial monocultures of wheat, corn, alfalfa, and cotton."[42]

"Plen'y of Hope"

Farming and ranching, while historically important to Oklahoma's identity and economy, have been overshadowed in the state's economic history by other natural resources. Timber, coal, minerals, oil, natural gas, and water have had their own significant roles in the state's economic development—providing "plenty of hope" for Oklahomans needing jobs and for the state treasury needing revenue. But they have also had environmental impacts.

Timber was one of the first natural resources in Indian Territory, especially as much of it was naturally forested with hardwoods (hickory and post oak) and softwoods (such as longleaf pine). Although much of the logging was first done to clear forests to create farm fields and for firewood, there was a market for some of the wood, especially for railroads and construction. Clear-cutting was the common practice, and hence most of the forests in eastern Oklahoma now are second- or third-growth. Now, however, the industry uses more selective cutting practices and pumps $1.8 billion into Oklahoma's economy annually.[43] Oklahoma has about ten million acres of forested land, of which only 6 percent are on public lands (national forests), which do allow leases for harvesting wood under multiple-use management guidelines.

Under a crescent-shaped swath of that land covering twelve thousand square miles lies the state's "swamp treasure." There, where ancient tropical forests turned into bituminous coal, an important industry for the state developed. Cherokees and other Native Americans in the region knew of coal and referred to it as the "rock that burns," but it took newcomer James McAlester, who moved to Indian Territory in the 1860s, to start mining the coal, especially when he learned the Missouri, Kansas, and Texas Railroad (the MK&T, or Katy) was completing its line through the area en route to Texas, knowing it would need the coal. Thus he not only began mining in 1872 and selling to the MK&T; he also used the railroad to ship coal to other markets back east. Katy itself became one of the largest mining firms, operating the Osage Mining and Coal Company for many years. The Curtis Act of 1898 allowed private investors to lease land for coal mining from Choctaw and Chickasaw Indians, which while decreasing the Indians' own development of the mines,

Figure 3.1. Coal mining with a water drill, c. 1915. Courtesy of the Western History Collections, University of Oklahoma Libraries, Division of Manuscripts.

did provide them with millions of dollars in leases which they used for education and other benefits. Early mining in the region was primarily hard-rock, or underground, but by 1915 surface mines developed, and since 1967 all of Oklahoma's coal has come from strip mines.[44]

Production advanced quickly. In 1880 the coal earned $120,000 but by 1920 it peaked at $4.8 million before declining during the Depression. Between 1872 and 2006 a total of 283 million tons of coal were mined, providing about 64 percent of the state's electrical production. The Arkoma Basin has a reserve estimated to be 1.6 billion tons, which generates $12 billion for the state annually, employs fifty thousand workers, and provides $800 million in revenues.[45]

The environmental impacts of strip mining are staggering. Mined areas are stripped of vegetation—all plants and whole forests—with waste fill going into valleys or low areas that bury streams and alter watersheds. This causes permanent loss of ecosystems and subsequently affects plant and animal biodiversity. The waste fill, called overburden, is infertile and does not reactivate biological regeneration. The sludge used in fill is often tainted with mercury, diesel fuel, and chemicals that seep into groundwater, increasing metal contaminants in water used for drinking. Strip mining also affects air quality, first by removing vegetation, and then by adding dangerous particulate matter to the air like arsenic and lead that can be absorbed in people's respiratory systems or through the skin. Heavy machinery belching out diesel fumes and particulates detracts from the air quality.[46]

State and federal policies, however, have been enacted to stem these impacts. In 1968, the state legislature passed the Open Cut Land Reclamation Act to deal with forty thousand acres of unreclaimed underground mines and thirty-two thousand acres of surface mines. The law required leveling of spoil ridges and mandated the creation of "a rolling topography." Still, policy makers in Oklahoma and other coal-producing states believed that reclamation was larger than states could do by themselves and lobbied the federal government for assistance. Help came with the Surface Mining Control and Reclamation Act of 1977, advanced by President Jimmy Carter and administered by the Office of Surface Mining, which mandated reclamation and established a nationwide system for controlling surface effects of coal mining. The law established the Abandoned Mine Land (AML) Trust Fund, paid for by a tax on active coal mines, which assists states in restoring the land around closed mines. In the late 1970s, Governor David Boren designated the Oklahoma Conservation Commission to be responsible for the reclamation of abandoned mines, and his successor, George Nigh, signed legislation implementing the AML in Oklahoma—one of the few states to use conservation districts for the reclamation program.[47]

More hope for economic development was aroused with the discovery of oil and natural gas. Much has been written on these industries (for example, see chapter 4), but a few words here are in order, especially in terms of environmental considerations of the industry. There are five major geological provinces responsible for twenty-six oil fields in the state. Oil was first discovered accidentally in 1859 near Salina while drilling for salt and then sold for a few years to burn in lamps, but it was not until thirty years later that the first intentional well was drilled near Chelsea, the oil from which was primarily used for dipping cattle for ticks. In 1896 the giant Bartlesville-Dewey Field was discovered, which created the first oil boom and—along with other oil discoveries—prompted talks of statehood for Indian Territory. Ten years later Oklahoma oil accounted for 59 percent of the world's total, and by the 1920s the state was the number-one oil producer in the world, with a production record of 278 million barrels in 1927.[48]

Since then there have been a total of five hundred thousand oil wells drilled in Oklahoma, with the peak year of 1984 (one hundred thousand wells) producing nearly fifteen billion barrels. Each year fluctuates, but by 2000 around fifty thousand wells were active, pumping sixty million barrels a year—3 percent

Figure 3.2. Oil wells on the Oklahoma Capitol grounds, c. 1940s. Courtesy of the Western History Collections, University of Oklahoma Libraries (Phillips, 2172).

of the nation's total. Oil is produced in sixty-six of Oklahoma's seventy-seven counties, and geological estimates suggest there could be as much as twenty-five billion more barrels available.[49] Such production has come with environmental costs. The U.S. Geological Survey and the Environmental Protection Agency (EPA) found that wells in Osage County (a top producer, with thirty-nine thousand wells whose rights are owned by the Osage Nation) have caused detrimental impacts on soils and on surface water and groundwater, due to improperly disposed volumes of saline water produced from oil and gas production and from improperly sealed abandoned wells. The agencies also found inorganic salts, trace metals, and radionuclides in water in the Osage area. More visible were salt scars, tree kills, soil salinization, and petroleum contamination from brine pit leaks. Some of this pollution is extending into Skiatook Lake on the Osage Reservation.[50]

Natural gas has had its own boom and has become almost as important as oil to Oklahoma's economy. Production has increased in recent years with the search for clean burning fuels; natural gas emits fewer pollutants than other fossil fuels. Gas is produced across the state, although most heavily in the northwest and the Panhandle. The first wells were drilled soon after discovery in 1903, and since then the state has produced 9.3 trillion cubic feet of gas from thirty-five thousand wells. The Hugoton Field under the Panhandle is considered the largest natural gas field in the world. By 1958 there were nearly fourteen hundred gas wells drilled in Texas County alone, and geologists estimated that there were trillions of feet of gas reserves remaining. Oklahoma today supplies 8 percent of the nation's total natural gas, making it the number-three producing state (behind Texas and Wyoming), with an annual production of nearly 1.75 million feet.[51] Concomitant environmental impacts include ones ranging from the process of drilling itself to the harmful effects of by-product methane emissions.

The search for alternative energy, especially during the oil crises of the 1970s, prompted the promotion of wind power making use of the constant winds in western Oklahoma, and wind-power generation has since expanded remarkably, especially since the 1990s. But it was the nuclear power industry that attracted nationwide attention to Oklahoma in the 1970s, when union activist Karen Silkwood exposed the dangers of working with plutonium fuel rods. A chemical technician who made plutonium pellets at the Kerr-McGee nuclear plant near Crescent, just west of Guthrie, and a member of the Oil, Chemical, and Atomic Workers Union, Silkwood discovered numerous health and safety violations at the Kerr-McGee plant, and she herself became contaminated with radiation. Ready to blow the whistle on the company to the *New*

York Times and to officials in Washington, Silkwood died in a mysterious car accident in 1974. Her death, and the larger dangers of nuclear power, prompted the creation of the Sunbelt Alliance, an organization that worked to stop construction of nuclear reactors in Oklahoma. Its efforts, along with the publicity of the Silkwood case (and the Hollywood movie *Silkwood*, starring Meryl Streep, Kurt Russell, and Cher, and nominated for five Academy Awards), were successful in halting further nuclear development in the state.[52] Other groups, such as state chapters of the Sierra Club, the Audubon Society, the National Wildlife Federation, and The Nature Conservancy, have also worked for environmental protection on various issues around the state.

Also tragic, and more reflective of the environmental and health hazards involved with extractive industries, is the case of the lead and zinc mining at Picher in the northeast corner of the state. There the Tar Creek mines produced the metals needed for the manufacture of ammunition since World War I, especially for making bullets in World War II. With decreasing demand and increasing environmental concerns, the mines closed in 1970, leaving mountains of lead-laced waste outside the town. The contaminated piles covered an incredible twenty-five acres. Soon acid mine water was polluting Tar Creek, turning it red, and causing sinkholes to open in the piles, seriously threatening anyone who ventured near, including children who played in the area. The EPA did not declare Tar Creek a Superfund site for cleanup until 1981, and residents did not start leaving Picher until 2006 when houses, churches, and the local school were about ready to cave in. At forty square miles, the toxic area remains one of the EPA's largest Superfund sites.[53] Adding to the problem, in May 2008 a violent F-4 tornado struck Picher, destroying twenty-four city blocks and causing the deaths of six people. Despite the contamination, at the time of the storm there were still twenty thousand people living there, but soon after, most residents left thanks to a government buyout program for their homes.[54] The wisdom of Suzan Harjo once again applies:

> tomorrow we will worry about a way to find water that is free of tetanus
> on the next tomorrow we will worry about how the air will be rationed
> then, on the day after that tomorrow, who will have compassion
> for my sleeping one, this gift of the sun?[55]

A final natural resource hope has been with water. Controlling the state's rivers has been serious business with developers and politicians in the twentieth century, but no project has been greater than the River and Harbor Act of 1946 that created the Arkansas River Navigation System. Developed by the

Figure 3.3. Picher lead and zinc mines. Courtesy of the Western History Collections, University of Oklahoma Libraries, Division of Manuscripts, 209.

U.S. Army Corps of Engineers, the plan connected Tulsa by navigable water with the port of New Orleans and created three reservoirs (Eufala, Keystone, and Oolagah), becoming at the time the second-largest water project ever conceived in the United States after the Panama Canal. It provided flood control, water supply, hydroelectricity, and expanded trade using barges and tugboats. But many people's farmlands and homes were inundated in the process, and, as Thomas Connor has written, "It was a promising economic venture for the state and a severe economic hardship for those forced off their land."[56] There has been little written on the environmental effects of the immense project, but such an interpretation could consider the destruction of farmlands, the human manipulation of waterways, and the ecological changes involved with landscape transformation. Combined, the reservoirs cover nine hundred square miles and their shorelines exceed the length of the entire coastline from Maine to Texas.[57]

Less grandiose are Oklahoma's nearly twenty-one hundred other flood-control structures. Each could tell its own story of storage and diversion, but one—the Optima Dam in the Panhandle—represents a telling environmental history. Optima today is one of Oklahoma's national wildlife refuges, but it started as a project of the federal Flood Control Act of 1936 to solve water worries for Panhandle farmers by damming the Beaver River. The project got delayed until the 1950s when U.S. Senator Robert S. Kerr played an influential role in resurrecting it and used his authority on the Subcommittee on Flood Control and Rivers to hasten the project. Optima was to provide irrigation, flood control, municipal water, silt control, and local recreation opportunities. It was completed in 1966, costing over $46 million—more than double the original estimate, but the dam is a failure. The reservoir never filled with water and the benefits never materialized. As historian Richard Lowitt has written, it was "a $46 million pipe dream."[58]

"Plen'y of Air and Plen'y of Room"

Finally, a discussion is in order of conservation in twentieth-century Oklahoma. Efforts to preserve natural wonders, forests, and prairies—those areas with "plenty of air and plenty of room"—are important in Oklahoma's recent environmental history. Preserving those spaces has been the work of federal, state, and private entities. There are three areas managed by the National Forest Service, six national wildlife refuges, two national recreation areas, fifty state parks, a variety of other state conservation areas, and the Tallgrass Preserve managed by The Nature Conservancy. There are also several national historic sites, including the Santa Fe National Historic Trail, the Trail of Tears National Historic Trail, and the Oklahoma City National Memorial (Murrah Federal Building bombing site), that are in the domain of the National Park Service.

The first official conservation area in Oklahoma was the Wichita Mountains National Wildlife Refuge near Lawton. Like other federal lands, the refuge of fifty-nine thousand acres was not suited for agriculture (beyond grazing) and thus became earmarked for conservation. President William McKinley established it as the Wichita Forest Reserve in 1901, President Theodore Roosevelt renamed it the Wichita Game Preserve in 1905 as a refuge for endangered bison and elk, and Congress declared it a national refuge in 1936 (administered by the Bureau of Biological Survey, the predecessor of the U.S. Fish and Wildlife Service that manages refuges today). In 1970 Congress designated fifty-seven hundred acres of the refuge as the Charon Wilderness Area—a roadless section in which motorized or mechanical vehicles are off limits as outlined in the Wilderness Act of 1964.

The refuge illustrates the significance of biological and cultural preservation. In 1907 the Forest Service shipped in fifteen bison from the Bronx Zoo, capitalizing on the relatively unspoiled grasslands. The herd went on to produce ten thousand bison in the twentieth century, most of which were sold to private breeders or removed to other areas in the West. In 1911 the Forest Service did the same for Rocky Mountain elk, importing five from Jackson Hole, Wyoming. Elk originally inhabited the region but had been gone for eighty years (with the legend of the last being shot by General William Sheridan in 1881 on the mountain named in his honor). Game wardens today maintain a population of around eight hundred elk in the Wichita Mountains National

Wildlife Refuge.[59] More unusual was the introduction of longhorn cattle in 1927 to stave off extinction of the breed. It was Ranger Earl Drummond's belief that longhorns represented a vital aspect of regional cultural history that convinced Congress, along with some private funding, to search South Texas for longhorns for the Wichita Mountains, where a herd of three hundred head continues to be managed.[60] The refuge also protects black-tailed prairie dogs and over 40 other species of mammals, 240 species of birds, 64 species of reptiles and amphibians, 36 species of fish, and over 800 species of plants.[61] Other national wildlife refuges in the state include Sequoya, Deep Fork, Tishomingo, Washita, Salt Plains, and Optima, all of which protect wetlands important for migratory birds. In addition, Oklahoma maintains four state wildlife areas and three fish hatcheries.

Although there are no national parks in the state, one of the oldest of the state's conservation units, what is today Chickasaw National Recreation Area near Sulphur, actually began as Sulphur Springs Reserve in 1902 with an arrangement devised by the Chickasaw Nation that owned the land. It became Platt National Park a few years later (oddly named for Senator Oliver Platt, a member of the Dawes Commission entrusted to assimilate Indians), lasting until 1976. Home to thirty natural springs containing sulfur, bromide, and mineral salts, the pools were popular with locals and visitors who frequented them for health purposes. At fewer than ten thousand acres, it was the smallest national park yet remained the "Playground of the Southwest" for seventy years until it was folded into the Chickasaw National Recreation Area when the Bureau of Reclamation created Lake of the Arbuckles. Along with Winding Stair National Recreation Area, it is administered by the National Park Service.[62]

Another early conservation unit was the Arkansas National Forest, established in 1907, which became the Ouachita National Forest in 1926. The Ouachita (meaning "good hunting grounds" in Caddoan languages), about one-fifth of which is in Oklahoma and the rest in Arkansas, was the first national forest in the South. In Oklahoma, the forest encompasses the Ouachita and the Winding Stair mountain ranges and is characterized by dense mixed forests of post oak, hickory, and longleaf pine. A local effort in the 1920s to change the status of the area into a national park failed with President Calvin Coolidge's veto, ensuring that the unit would remain under multiple-use management allowing timber harvests, grazing, and recreation opportunities. State Highway 1 includes the Talimena Scenic Drive that runs along the ridge tops of the Winding Stair Mountains. The federal government declared it a national scenic byway in 2005. Important for the preservation of the forest's old-growth post oaks and hickories, as well as a large population of black bears and other wildlife, was Congress's designation of two wilderness areas within the Ouachita Mountains in 1984: the Black Mountain Wilderness Area (mostly in Arkansas) and the Upper Kiamichi Wilderness (within Oklahoma) that protects ten thousand acres of old-growth forest that are off limits to logging, mining, and vehicles.

Managed by the National Forest Service, but not forested, are large sections of two national grasslands in western Oklahoma. The largest, Black Kettle National Grassland (named after the Cheyenne chief), which laps over into the Texas Panhandle, includes thirty-one thousand acres of grazing land and cropland near the town of Cheyenne. In the 1930s the federal government purchased the land from private owners in response to Dust Bowl conditions and turned the area over to the Soil Conservation Service (of the Department of Agriculture) to manage as untilled grazing lands. In 1953 the land became a unit of the Cibola National Forest and it was designated a national grasslands in 1960. In the southwest corner of the Panhandle is a strip of fourteen thousand acres, the Rita Blanca National Grasslands, most of which is in Texas. Its history is similar to most national grasslands in the southern plains: conserved to retain soil cover with grazing allotments as better management than farming. Like other national "forest" lands, both of these units are managed for multiple use that includes livestock grazing, oil and gas development, and recreation.[63]

Not designated a national grassland, the Tallgrass Prairie Preserve on the Osage Reservation near Pawhuska is a unique conservation unit managed by The Nature Conservancy. There, thirty-nine thousand acres of remnant tallgrass prairie with dark, deep soils in a relatively warm and wet climate produces the bluestem and goldentop grasses that grow to five feet or higher. It was part of an ocean of grass that originally spread across the Midwest and the Canadian prairies, an area in Oklahoma that Washington Irving described as "an immense extent of grassy, undulating . . . country with here and there a clump of trees, dimly seen in the distance like a ship at sea."[64] There is only about 10 percent of this ecosystem left, and the Tallgrass Prairie Preserve is the largest area protecting it in North America.[65] Part of the preservation effort was serendipitous as the region was never tilled for crops, only grazed by cattle that did not destroy the ecosystem. The Nature Conservancy acquired the land in 1989 and manages it using over twenty-five hundred free-roaming bison and a prescribed burning system known as "patch burn"—burning one-third of the preserve each year, which according to rangelands researchers at Oklahoma State University "offers huge rewards for biodiversity."[66]

Finally, Oklahomans can be proud of their fifty state parks conveniently located throughout the state. Most are located on reservoirs, but others protect such things as the world's largest gypsum cave (Alabaster Caverns), sand dunes on the plains (Beaver Dunes, Little Sahara), high plains sagebrush topography (Black Mesa), salt plains (Great Salt Plains), various mountainous areas (Gloss Mountains, Quartz Mountain), waterfalls (Natural Falls), rocky outcrops and canyons (Roman Nose, Red Rock Canyon), cultural and historic places (Heavener Runestone, taken over by the city of Heavener in 2011; Robbers Cave), and other features. Together they cover nearly seventy thousand acres.

Many of these parks, refuges, and forests were the sites of important work projects during the Great Depression, when President Roosevelt's New Deal created public works programs for unemployed men. The Works Progress Administration and the Civilian Conservation Corps created 116,000 jobs for park development, trail maintenance, and construction of bridges, pavilions, and other structures on these public lands.[67] Many of the structures remain today and stand as monuments not only to a needed employment strategy in time of economic malaise, but also as important reminders of the importance of public lands and conservation to the state.

In Conclusion: "The Land We Belong to Is Grand!"

In *Red Earth*, Bonnie Lynn-Sherow concluded, "While much has been lost, Oklahoma's unique combination of prairies, shrublands, and forests . . . is still intact. It is not yet too late to fulfill the promise of the red earth."[68] That promise is associated with how Oklahomans have been connected to the land in a variety of ways, from Indians being native to places within the state, to agriculture, ranching, mining, natural resource development, and conservation. Many people work and play in the remarkable diversity of natural settings here, but the Dust Bowl, Karen Silkwood, and the tragedy of Picher remind us that the land we belong to is fragile and that ecological disasters usually spell economic and human health disasters. Thus conservation and responsible management of the land and resources is hardly extreme environmentalism—it is good stewardship and economics. This land we belong to is grand and thus should be respected for future generations and the future well-being of the environment. Sustainable agricultural practices and well maintained and expanded conservation areas remind us of what Oklahoma has been—and offer a promise of what it yet can be.

Notes

1. Muriel H. Wright, *Our Oklahoma* (Guthrie, Okla.: Co-operative Publishing, 1939), front matter. On Wright's career, see Patricia Loughlin, *Hidden Treasures of the American West: Muriel H. Wright, Angie Debo, and Alice Marriot* (Albuquerque: University of New Mexico Press, 2006); and Linda W. Reese, "'Petticoat' Historians: The Foundation of Oklahoma Social History," in *Alternative Oklahoma: Contrarian Views of the Sooner State*, edited by Davis Joyce (Norman: University of Oklahoma Press, 2007), 12–15.

2. Joseph B. Thoburn and Muriel H. Wright, *Oklahoma: A History of the State and Its People* (New York: Lewis Historical Publishing, 1929); Wright, *Our Oklahoma*; Arrell Gibson, *Oklahoma: A History of Five Centuries* (Norman: University of Oklahoma Press, 1965); Wayne Morgan and Anne Hodges Morgan, *Oklahoma: A Bicentennial History* (New York: W. W. Norton, 1977); David Baird and Danney Goble, *Oklahoma: A History* (Norman: University of Oklahoma Press, 2008).

3. See Richard White, "American Environmental History: The Development of a New Historical Field," *Pacific Historical Review* 54, no. 3 (August 1985): 297–335; Donald Worster, "Doing Environmental History," in *The Ends of the Earth: Perspectives on Modern Environmental History*, edited by Donald Worster (Cambridge: Cambridge University Press), 289–307; Richard White, "Environmental History: Watching a Historical Field Mature," *Pacific Historical Review* 70, no. 1 (Feb. 2001): 103–11; and J. R. McNeill, "Observations on the Nature and Culture of Environmental History," *Environment and History* 42, no. 4 (December 2003): 5–43.

4. Worster, "Doing Environmental History," 290–91, 292.

5. Don Mitchell, *Cultural Geography: A Critical Introduction* (Oxford, UK: Blackwell Publishers, 2000), 17.

6. Baird and Goble, *Oklahoma*, 12.

7. Bonnie Lynn-Sherow, *Red Earth: Race and Agriculture in Oklahoma Territory* (Lawrence: University Press of Kansas, 2004), 1; Roxanne Dunbar Ortiz, *Red Dirt: Growing Up Okie* (Norman: University of Oklahoma Press, 2007).

8. Thomas Connor, "Getting Along: Woody Guthrie and Oklahoma's Red Dirt Musicians," in *Alternative Oklahoma: Contrarian Views of the Sooner State*, edited by Davis Joyce (Norman: University of Oklahoma Press, 2007), 91–92.

9. Bonnie McDonald, *Oklahoma: A Land of Contrasts* (Atlanta: Claremont Press, 2007), 31–39. Another source, TraveklOK.com ("Oklahoma's Diverse Ecoregions," www.travelok.com/article_page/oklahomasdiverseecoregions) describes eleven ecosystems. The official twelve regions are from Oklahoma Forestry Services ("The Ecoregions of Oklahoma," www.forestry.ok.gov/ecoregions-of-oklahoma); and Oklahoma Department of Wildlife Conservation ("Ecoregions of Oklahoma," www.wildlifedepartment.com/facts_maps /ecoregions.htm).

10. Thoburn and Wright, *Oklahoma*, 7; Baird and Goble, *Oklahoma*, 8–9.

11. N. Scott Momaday, *The Way to Rainy Mountain* (Albuquerque: University of New Mexico Press, 1969), 48–49.

12. Ibid., 48. For an artist's rendition of Man-ka-ih, see p. 51.

13. Gary England, *Those Terrible Twisters and the Weather of Oklahoma* (Oklahoma City: Globe Color Press, 1987); Baird and Goble, *Oklahoma*, 8.

14. See Donald Worster, *Dust Bowl: The Southern Plains in the 1930s* (New York: Oxford University Press, 1979); Matthew Bonnifield, *Dust Bowl: Men, Dirt, and Depression* (Albuquerque: University of New Mexico Press, 1979); R. Douglas Hurt, *The Dust Bowl: An Agricultural and Social History* (Chicago: Nelson-Hall, 1981); Brad Lookingbill, *Dust Bowl, USA: Depression America and the Ecological Imagination* (Athens: Ohio University Press, 2001).

15. Baird and Goble, *Oklahoma*, 8.

16. Bruce Hoagland, "Oklahoma Is a State to Cherish," *Norman Transcript*, April 22, 2010; R. John Taylor and Constance Taylor, *An Annotated List of the Ferns, Fern Allies, Gymnosperms and Flowering Plants of Oklahoma* (Durant, Okla.: Southeastern State University Biology Department, 1991); F. L. Johnson and B. L. Hoagland, "Catalog of the Woody Plants of Oklahoma: Descriptions and Range Maps," Oklahoma Biological Survey, www.biosurvey.ou.edu/shrub/shrubndx.htm (accessed December 31, 2012); "State Plant Listings, Oklahoma," Federal Highway Administration, www.environment.fhwa.dot.gov/ecosystems/vegmgmt_rd_ok.asp (accessed February 18, 2013); Doyle McCoy, *Oklahoma Wildflowers* (Oklahoma City: D. McCoy, 1987).

17. Irving quoted in Baird and Goble, *Oklahoma*, 3.

18. Lynn-Sherow, *Red Earth*, 148–49. See also "The Nature Conservancy in Oklahoma," Nature Conservancy, www.nature.org/.

19. Thoburn and Wright, *Oklahoma*, 8–9.

20. Baird and Goble, *Oklahoma*, 11.

21. "Mammals of Oklahoma," American Society of Mammalogists, www.mammalsociety.org/mammals-oklahoma (accessed December 31, 2012), "Reptiles and Amphibians," *Encyclopedia of Oklahoma History and Culture*, Oklahoma Historical Society, http://digital.library.okstate.edu/encyclopedia/entries/R/RE029.html (accessed December 31, 2012).

22. See Vine Deloria, Jr., "Low Bridge—Everybody Cross," in *Red Earth, White Lies: Native Americans and the Myth of Scientific Fact* (New York: Scribner, 1995), 67–92.

23. Richard White and William Cronon, "Ecological Change and Indian-White Relations," in *Handbook of North American Indians, Vol. IV: History of Indian-White Relations*, edited by William C. Sturtevant (Washington, D.C.: Smithsonian Institution, 1988), 417. See also David Waller, "Friendly Fire: When Environmentalists Dehumanize American Indians," *American Indian Culture and Research Journal* 20 (1996), 107–26.

24. P. S. Martin, "Prehistoric Overkill," in *Pleistocene Extinctions: The Search for a Cause*, edited by P. S. Martin and E. H. Wright, Jr. (New Haven: Yale University Press, 1967), 75–120; James E. Mosimann and Paul S. Martin "Simulating Overkill by Paleoindians," *American*

Scientist 63 (May/June 1975): 304-13. For debate, see Donald K. Grayson and David J. Meltzer, "A Requiem for North American Overkill," *Journal of Archaeological Science* 30 (2003): 585-93.

25. Clive Ponting, *Green History of the World: The Environment and the Collapse of Great Civilizations* (New York: Penguin Books, 1991), 33; I. G. Simmons, *Environmental History: A Concise Introduction* (Oxford, UK: Blackwell, 1993), 5.

26. Raymond Pierotti and Daniel R. Wildcat, "Being Native to This Place," in *American Indians in American History, 1870-2001: A Companion Reader*, edited by Sterling Evans (Westport, Conn.: Praeger Publishers, 2002), 3, 6-10. See also Christopher Vecsey and Robert W. Venables, eds. *American Indian Environments: Ecological Issues in Native American History* (Syracuse: Syracuse University Press, 1980).

27. N. Scott Momaday, "Native Americans Attitudes to the Environment," in *Stars Above, Earth Below: American Indians and Nature*, edited by Marsha C. Bol (Niwot, Colo.: Roberts Rinehart, 1998), 3-4, 6.

28. Momaday, *The Way to Rainy Mountain*, 4, 5, 7.

29. Suzan Shown Harjo, "Western Women's History: A Challenge for the Future," in *The Women's West*, edited by Susan Armitage and Elizabeth Jameson (Norman: University of Oklahoma Press, 1987), 308.

30. Thoburn and Wright, *Oklahoma*, 8. Classic studies of cattle in Oklahoma include Edward Everett Dale's *The Range Cattle Industry* (Norman: University of Oklahoma Press, 1930) and *Cow Country* (Norman: University of Oklahoma Press, 1965); Jimmy M. Skaggs, *Ranch and Range in Oklahoma* (Oklahoma City: Oklahoma Historical Society, 1978); and Michael Wallis, *The Real Wild West: The 101 Ranch and the Creation of the American West* (New York: St. Martin's, 1999).

31. Richard Lowitt, *American Outback: The Oklahoma Panhandle in the Twentieth Century* (Lubbock: Texas Tech University Press, 2006), 94.

32. Ibid., 97.

33. Ibid., 99-102.

34. Baird and Goble, *Oklahoma*, 95-96, 194-95.

35. Ibid., 10.

36. See Sterling Evans, *Bound in Twine: The History and Ecology of the Henequen-Wheat Complex for Mexico and the American and Canadian Plains, 1880-1950* (College Station: Texas A&M University Press, 2007), 124-30.

37. U.S. Department of Agriculture, *Wheat: Acreage Yield Productions by States, 1866-1943*, Statistical Bulletin no. 158, February 1955 (Washington, D.C.: USDA and Agricultural Marketing Service, 1955).

38. Worster, *Dust Bowl*, 94.

39. Lowitt, *American Outback*, 43-45.

40. Aldo Leopold, *A Sand County Almanac* (New York: Ballantine, 1990), 15; Worster, *Dust Bowl*, 93.

41. Lowitt, *American Outback*, 93. See also John Opie, *Ogallala: Water for a Dry Land* (Lincoln: University of Nebraska Press, 1993).

42. Lynn-Sherow, *Red Earth*, 147.

43. Baird and Goble, *Oklahoma*, 10.

44. Gibson, *Oklahoma*, 261–71; Baird and Goble, *Oklahoma*, 4–5, 123.

45. Baird and Goble, *Oklahoma*, 4–5.

46. M. A. Palmer, et al., "Mountaintop Mining Consequences," *Science* 327 (January 8, 2010): 148.

47. "Abandoned Land Mine Program," Oklahoma Conservation Commission, www.ok.gov/conservation/Agency_Divisions/Abandoned_Mine_Land_Reclamation_Division/AML_Background_Information (accessed December 31, 2012).

48. Dan Boyd, "Oklahoma Oil: Past, Present, and Future," *Oklahoma Geology Notes* 62 (Fall 2002), 97–100. See also Brian Frehner, *Finding Oil: The Nature of Petroleum Geology, 1859–1920* (Lincoln: University of Nebraska Press, 2011).

49. Boyd, "Oklahoma Oil," 104, 113; Baird and Goble, *Oklahoma*, 4.

50. Yousif K. Kharaka and James Otton, eds. "Environmental Impacts of Petroleum Production: Initial Results from Osage-Skiatook Petroleum, Environmental Research Sites, Osage County, Oklahoma," Water-Resources Investigations Report 03-4260, U.S. Geological Survey, 2003, http://pubs.usgs.gov/wri/wri03-4260.

51. Lowitt, *American Outback*, 83–84; Baird and Goble, *Oklahoma*, 4; "Top Natural Gas Producing States, 2007," U.S. Energy Information Administration, www.eia.doe.gov/neic/experts/natgastop10.htm (accessed December 28, 2012).

52. Elizabeth D. Barlow, "Nonviolent Civil Disobedience in Oklahoma: The Campaign against Nuclear Power," in *Alternative Oklahoma: Contrarian Views of the Sooner State*, edited by Davis Joyce (Norman: University of Oklahoma Press, 2007), 122–33.

53. Oklahoma Department of Environmental Quality, "Oklahoma Plan for Tar Creek," http://inhofe.senate.gov/superfund1.pdf (accessed February 16, 2013).

54. Orval "Hoppy" Ray, the "last man standing," made national news in 2009 when he vowed not to leave Picher. See John D. Sutter, "Last Man Standing at Wake for a Toxic Town," June 30, 2009, www.cnn.com/ (accessed December 28, 2012).

55. Harjo, "Western Women's History," 309.

56. Connor, "Getting Along," 89.

57. See William A. Settle, Jr., *The Dawning: A New Day for the Southwest: A History of the Tulsa District Corps of Engineers* (Tulsa: U.S. Army Corps of Engineers, Tulsa District, 1975).

58. Lowitt, *American Outback*, 80.

59. See Matthew A. Pearce, "Bringing Back the Big Game: The Reintroduction of Elk to the Wichita Mountains," *Chronicles of Oklahoma* 88 (Fall 2010), 260–87.

60. Arthur F. Halloran and Claud A. Shrader, "Longhorn Cattle Management on Wichita Mountains Wildlife Refuge," *Journal of Wildlife Management* 24 (April 1960), 191.

61. See "Wichita Mountains," U.S. Fish and Wildlife Service, www.fws.gov/southwest/refuge/Wichita_Mountains (accessed December 28, 2012).

62. See "Platt National Park Maps and Brochures," National Park Service, www.nps.gov/chic/historyculture/plattnp-brochures.htm (accessed December 28, 2012).

63. Francis Moul, *The National Grasslands: A Guide to America's Uncovered Treasures* (Lincoln: University of Nebraska Press, 2006), 100–107.

64. In Baird and Goble, *Oklahoma*, 10–11.

65. See John Madson, *Where the Sky Began: Land of the Tallgrass Prairie* (Iowa City: University of Iowa Press, 1995).

66. In "Results Released for 2012 Bison Roundup at Tallgrass Prairie Reserve," The Nature Conservancy, November 27, 2012, www.nature.org/wherewework/northamerica/states/oklahoma/preserves/tallgrass.html (accessed December 31, 2012). See also "Four Seasons of the Osage," *Oklahoma Today* (March/April 2010), 46–59.

67. See Neil M. Maher, *Nature's New Deal: The Civilian Conservation Corps and the Roots of the Modern Environmental Movement* (New York: Oxford University Press, 2008).

68. Lynn-Sherow, *Red Earth*, 149.

CHAPTER 4

Oil and Natural Gas: Putting Oklahoma on the Map

Dan T. Boyd

Oil and natural gas are formed by the alteration of microscopic organisms deposited with sediment that eventually turns into sedimentary rock. These sediments, and the organic remains that are buried with them, are thickest where they accumulate in large, gradually subsiding depressions called geologic basins. Within these basins there is enough temperature and pressure, resulting from increased burial depth, to convert these remains over millions of years into oil and natural gas. The resulting organic compounds consist mostly of hydrogen and carbon, and so are called hydrocarbons.

Nature smiled on Oklahoma. The state's prominent place in the oil industry is the fortunate result of the prolific Anadarko, Arkoma, and Ardmore-Marietta geologic basins and their associated platforms. Hydrocarbons are produced throughout most of the state, with the only relatively unproductive areas located on the corners. Natural gas production is concentrated in the Anadarko and Arkoma Basins and areas adjacent to them, with most oil located along their flanks and on the Cherokee Platform (see map 4.1). The bulk of Oklahoma's hydrocarbon production occurs in rocks deposited during the Pennsylvanian geologic period (290–323 million years ago), but reservoirs range in age from the Cambrian to the Cretaceous (roughly 520 to 100 million years old).

Oil and natural gas have been an integral part of the economy of Oklahoma throughout the twentieth century. Nationally the state ranks sixth

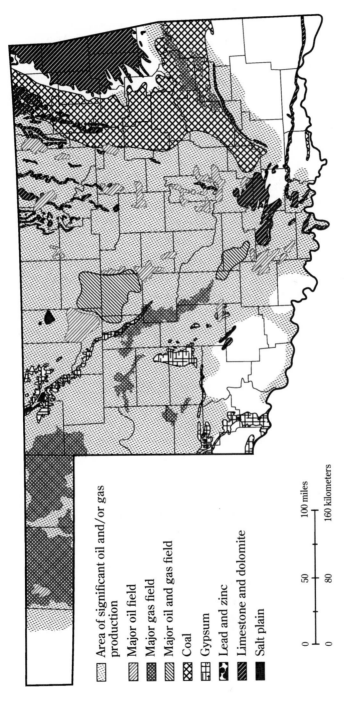

Map 4.1. Oklahoma oil and gas production. Map adapted from W. David Baird and Danney Goble, *The Story of Oklahoma*, rev. 2nd ed. (Norman: University of Oklahoma Press, 2013), p. 25.

Area of significant oil and/or gas production

Major oil field

Major gas field

Major oil and gas field

Coal

Gypsum

Lead and zinc

Limestone and dolomite

Salt plain

0   50   100 miles

0   80   160 kilometers

in oil production, behind Texas, Alaska, California, Louisiana, and North Dakota, and third in gas production, behind Texas and Wyoming (EIA 2009). Cumulative production, all told from day one, is about 14.8 billion barrels of crude oil and 101 trillion cubic feet of natural gas (OCC 2008), with 2008 production generating over $1.5 billion in state tax revenues (OTC 2009). With a history that now stretches over a century, oil and natural gas will clearly still be central to Oklahoma's economy well into the twenty-first century.

Oklahoma Oil

Oil put Oklahoma on the map. This is true both figuratively and literally, as oil was the driving force behind turning the Oklahoma Territory into the state of Oklahoma in 1907. Oil seeps had been recognized in Oklahoma long before the arrival of European settlers. To Native Americans they were often called "medicine springs," and some were mined by settlers for asphalt. The first subsurface oil was recovered in 1859, by accident, from a well drilled for salt near present-day Salina (in Mayes County)—the same year that Edwin L. Drake made the first commercial U.S. oil discovery, in Pennsylvania. The small amount of oil produced from this Mayes County well was sold for use in lamps. The first intentional Oklahoma oil find came from a well drilled in 1889 in an area of seeps near Chelsea (Rogers County). This well produced a half barrel of oil per day, and was used as "dip oil" to treat cattle for ticks (Franks 1980, 284).

Oil exploration in Oklahoma began before there was any real understanding of why and where it might occur, although long before statehood it had been known to exist in the subsurface: the drilling of water wells sometimes led to water contaminated by crude oil. Early wells seeking oil were usually drilled near seeps, with the first commercially successful one drilled adjacent to a seep near Bartlesville in 1897. Operators of the Nellie Johnstone No. 1 discovered the Bartlesville-Dewey Field and ushered in the oil age to the Oklahoma Territory, a period in which annual crude production went from 1,000 barrels in all of 1897 to 43.5 million barrels—about 120,000 barrels per day—in 1907, the year of statehood. In the ten years following the discovery, Oklahoma became the world's largest oil producer, with Tulsa claiming the title "Oil Capital of the World" (Franks 1980, 284).

This was just the beginning: the boom continued with a steady stream of enormous discoveries. These included the Cushing (1912), Burbank (1920), Seminole District (1923), and Oklahoma City (1928) oil fields, each of which would ultimately produce more than five hundred million barrels of crude.

Figure 4.1. Early-day "gusher" oil well, Yale, Oklahoma. Courtesy of the Western History Collections, University of Oklahoma Libraries, Cunningham Collection, 607.

In addition to these giants, twenty-one other fields with recoveries that would eventually yield more than one hundred million barrels were also discovered. Combined these fields pushed Oklahoma oil production to a peak rate of 762,000 barrels per day in 1927 (see fig. 4.2). It was in this era that the economic underpinnings of the state were laid, with numerous companies of all sizes founded to help produce the oil bounty. Some of the larger companies that were born in Oklahoma at this time include Sinclair Oil Company (1905), Marland Oil Company, which would become Conoco (1910), Cities Service Oil Company (1912), Champlin Petroleum Company (1916), Phillips Petroleum Company (1917), Halliburton Oil Well Cementing Company (1920), Noble Drilling Company (1921), and Anderson and Kerr Drilling Company, later known as Kerr-McGee Oil Industries (1929).

Oklahoma's pre–World War II oil came mostly from its medium-to-large fields during their primary phases of production. Primary production occurs when natural reservoir energy is the main driver in forcing oil from the ground. The increase in production after the war, and the flattening of production at a relatively high level through the early 1970s, largely represents the period when oil fields were water-flooded. This secondary recovery procedure involves forcing saltwater into a reservoir and, in so doing, pushing oil through pores into adjacent wells. In many oil fields in Oklahoma the secondary recovery volume can equal the primary.

Many smaller-scale rises and falls in Oklahoma's oil production are superimposed on these larger trends. Increases came through discoveries of new fields, increased "production allowables" (during periods of higher prices)—the amount of oil a field was allowed by the state to produce per month—large secondary recovery projects, and price-driven surges in drilling activity. Falls in production have been caused by curtailment due to low prices, reduced drilling activity, and the natural, long-term decline in field production (see fig. 4.2).

Typically as the number of wells increases in a given area, more and more significant reservoirs and their structural and stratigraphic-trapping styles (called "geologic plays") are identified. These reservoirs are exploited through a combination of random or trend drilling and prospecting driven by science and technology. Trend drilling is drilling along what is termed a "play fairway," which is a geologically controlled line of wells that follow a structure, a paleo-shoreline or channel system that deposited the productive reservoir. Regardless, as drilling continues, the average discovery size becomes progressively smaller: it is more difficult to find large fields in the progressively smaller areas yet to be explored. In every petroleum province the large fields,

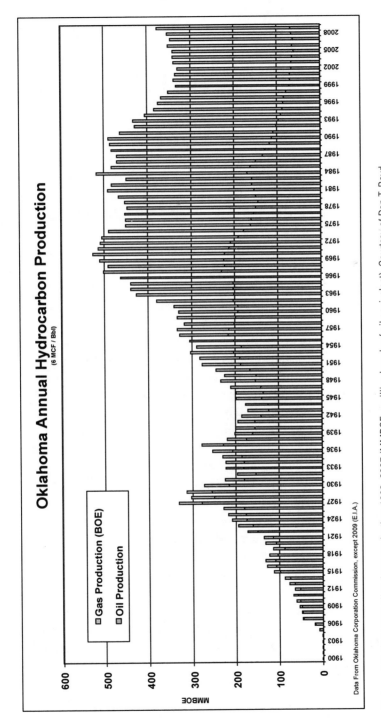

Figure 4.2. Oklahoma oil and gas production, 1902–2007 (MMBOE = million barrels of oil equivalent). Courtesy of Dan T. Boyd.

which are usually discovered early on, account for a disproportionate share of total production, and this is true in Oklahoma. Twenty of the state's twenty-five major fields (which would produce more than one hundred million barrels) were discovered before the end of World War II, with the last, Postle Field, found in Texas County in 1958. Although the major fields represent only about 1 percent of the nearly two thousand oil fields that have been found in Oklahoma, they account for about two-thirds of the total oil produced.

As the average size of newly discovered fields decreases, a point is reached where the potential reward no longer justifies the risk and expense of large-scale exploration by major oil companies, and the focus of their activity moves elsewhere. As this occurs, smaller companies with more modest overhead begin to account for a larger proportion of drilling activity. For Oklahoma this point was reached in the late 1960s after the price of crude oil had remained flat for decades and discovery sizes had fallen dramatically. Far from curtailing drilling activity, these conditions opened the door for thousands of smaller companies to find and develop many of the state's smaller fields. Because these are often shallow, and hence relatively inexpensive to drill, they are ideal for the small operator.

As can be seen from statistics for well completion (see fig. 4.3), Oklahoma has had three major drilling booms. The first, which occurred just after statehood, lasted through 1930 and was most active from 1913 through 1920. This boom was driven by tremendous exploratory success and the development of these initial large discoveries and brought national recognition of Oklahoma as a major oil producer. The drilling lull that followed, lasting through most of World War II, was followed by a second boom, which reached its peak between 1953 and 1956. This mostly entailed the development drilling necessary to begin secondary recovery projects in existing fields. This drilling phase also gradually declined, reaching lows from 1971 through 1973.

The first Oklahoma drilling boom had been driven by the number and size of discoveries made early in the century, and the second followed increased demand for petroleum products during conversion to a peacetime economy. The third and most recent boom, which set all-time records in state drilling activity, was caused by a rapid increase in the crude oil price beginning in 1974, during what became popularly known in the United States as "the energy crisis," with high consumer gasoline prices precipitated by the embargo proclaimed by OPEC—the Organization of Petroleum Exporting Countries. At this time political leaders and oil executives alike were increasingly aware of the growing dependency of oil-consuming nations on Middle Eastern oil sources represented by OPEC.

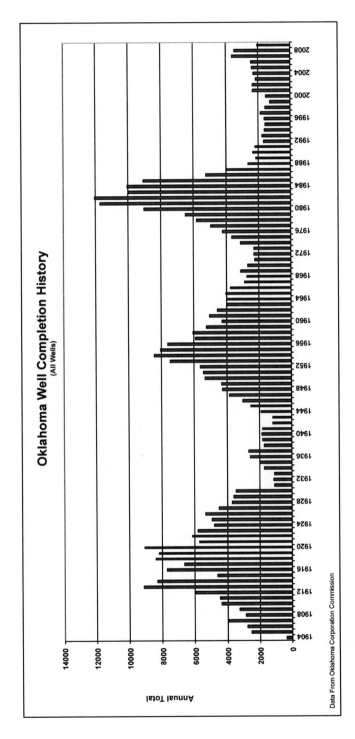

Figure 4.3. Oklahoma well completion history, 1904–2007. Courtesy of Dan T. Boyd.

The near-doubling of Oklahoma crude prices—from $3.78 per barrel in 1973 to $7.18 in 1974—had the effect of doubling the value of every oil well's production, as well as the value of the oil still in the ground. It also halved the reserves necessary for a well to make money, thereby making progressively smaller projects economically viable. This is what pushed drilling activity to record levels.

Drilling during this third boom gave rise to the last major increase in Oklahoma's oil production. However, when prices fell, drilling activity fell sharply and production quickly followed. By the late 1980s the decline that had characterized oil production in the state in the early 1970s was firmly reestablished. Today the bulk of the state's oil production is from over eighty thousand low-rate, "stripper" wells (producing less than ten barrels per day), located mostly in fields that have been producing for decades. The maturity of the industry is highlighted by an average per-well production rate that is now down to about two barrels per day.

Because over five hundred thousand wells have been drilled in the state, in every potentially oil-producing region, the possibility of finding new conventional fields large enough to stop or reverse the long-term production decline has nearly vanished. Undrained accumulations continue to be found, but these are usually small and contained within or adjacent to existing fields. Because discoveries are no longer a significant component of new oil production, future reserve additions must come through improvements to recovery from existing fields. Recent research, however, indicates that significant producible oil remains in many fields in Oklahoma (Boyd 2008). Efforts are now under way to aid operators in identifying these potential opportunities and the most beneficial production enhancement techniques.

Even if the rate of decline in Oklahoma oil production continues, the state's remaining oil reserves are still significant. Although extraction of these will be produced in ever-declining volumes over the next several decades, increasing prices are expected to offset much of the economic impact. State oil production in 2007 was about 166,000 barrels per day, which is comparable to what was being produced in 1913. However, its average price of $69.01 per barrel made that production worth about $4.2 billion and brought the state $293 million in gross revenue from production taxes. With long-term prices projected to rise, oil should remain a major component of the state's economy well into the twenty-first century.

Oklahoma Natural Gas

Throughout much of history, natural gas has been an enigma. Where it seeped from the subsurface it was sometimes ignited by lightning and became a burning spring—a phenomenon perceived as evidence of supernatural forces. Often springs became religious centers, a famous example being the spring associated with the Oracle of Delphi in ancient Greece.

Gas is almost always associated with oil, as it represents the lighter chemical fraction (shorter molecular chain) formed when organic remains are converted into hydrocarbons. Therefore, in addition to being found underground in discrete gas reservoirs, much natural gas is also found dissolved in subsurface oil. As this oil is brought from reservoir to the surface and its pressure is reduced to atmospheric levels, this dissolved gas comes out of solution much like the carbonation from a soft drink. Natural gas that comes from produced oil is classified as "associated gas."

Large discoveries and high demand made oil far more significant than gas in the early history of the state. Large-scale natural gas production in Oklahoma began much later than oil due to initial lack of a market. The earliest years of the Oklahoma gas industry were sustained by the associated gas produced from shallow oil fields on the Cherokee Platform. It is estimated that over three trillion cubic feet of associated natural gas were vented or flared in Oklahoma prior to World War II. This practice led to oil recoveries that were often substandard (Boyd 2008).

Natural gas is especially important to Oklahoma because it alone maintains a positive state energy budget that would otherwise be strongly negative. Despite ranking sixth nationally in oil production, oil consumption in Oklahoma is still about twice that produced. The state's coal is an important energy-generating resource, but to meet strict sulfur-emission requirements, 90 percent of the coal burned in the state comes from Wyoming (Boyd and Cardott 2001). In marked contrast, gas production is still three times state consumption, with over one trillion cubic feet per year sold in the interstate market.

As with oil, Oklahoma's prominent place in the natural gas industry is a result of its geology. In this case the key regions are the Anadarko and Arkoma Basins and their adjacent platforms. As with oil, the sedimentary rock from which the bulk of Oklahoma's gas comes is Pennsylvanian in age, with productive reservoirs ranging in age from late Cambrian to early Cretaceous. However, many of the state's source rocks and reservoirs are, or were in the geologic past, located below the depth at which oil is stable. Deep sedimentary basins and gas-prone source rocks have made large parts of Oklahoma almost exclusively gas-producing (see map 4.1).

Oklahoma's primary production in terms of energy equivalence shifted in 1963 from oil to gas, a change that occurred despite the fact that oil production in that year was still well over five hundred thousand barrels per day. It was not until the year 2000, however, that the state's cumulative natural gas production exceeded that of oil for the first time in terms of millions of barrels of oil equivalent. Although these are important milestones, the critical point is that, despite Oklahoma's perennial image as an oil producer, natural gas has been the state's primary energy resource for nearly half a century and today represents roughly 80 percent of both total hydrocarbon production and drilling (OCC 2008).

Most of the oil discovered in Oklahoma was found during a time when natural gas, especially that seen in association with oil, was viewed mainly as a nuisance or drilling hazard. Early wells were drilled with cable tool rigs that, unlike modern rotary rigs, operate without drilling mud and therefore any mechanism to control fluid flows. A discovery meant a blowout, with gas in the air and oil on the ground. The gas was vented and earthen dams were used to collect the oil. If a well encountered a large gas flow, it would be vented, sometimes for days, to determine if there was oil beneath. If oil eventually flowed into the well, the oil was produced and the gas flared. If not, the well would be plugged and the operator would move elsewhere (Franks 1980).

Most of the state's largest gas fields were discovered in the first half of the twentieth century through unsuccessful oil exploration. However, because associated gas production was easily able to satisfy demand, these fields were not developed and their size appreciated until much later, when demand—and therefore gas-targeted drilling—increased. Initial gas activity (drilling) in Oklahoma was restricted to the northeastern part of the state. It began in 1894 when Cudahy Oil Company drilled two wells in the Muskogee area, each economically producible, but neither well was produced for lack of a local market. However, in 1901 gas from two wells completed in the Red Fork Formation sand was sold to a brick plant in Tulsa, marking the first commercial use of natural gas in the state. After this milestone, associated gas production was added from five fields: Bartlesville-Dewey (1904), Glenn Pool (1905), Hogshooter (1906), Boynton (1910), and Cushing (1912) (Koontz 1962).

In 1906 the Oklahoma Natural Gas Company, today the state's dominant supplier, was formed to deliver gas to the Oklahoma City market (Moore 1962). At the time, gas fields were near the towns they served, but as demand climbed and nearby wells were depleted, the industry was forced to rely on more distant sources. Despite a rapid increase in gas drilling and reserve additions due to a series of discoveries in the late 1920s, it was not until the Anadarko and Arkoma Basins and adjacent shelves (including the Panhandle) were exploited in the middle of the twentieth century that production began to grow exponentially (see fig. 4.2).

Delayed development due to the lack of a market caused Oklahoma gas production to peak sixty-three years later than oil. Over most of the twentieth century Oklahoma's gas production rose steadily, with exploitation beginning in earnest after World War II. There were especially strong growth spurts in the early 1960s and the late 1980s, with peak gas production for the state occurring in 1990. Although production has declined since that time, discoveries and development drilling have been able to help slow the decline, unlike oil, and in recent years production has even increased.

Oil production and reserve additions come almost exclusively from improved recovery from previously defined fields, but the discovery of significant new or incompletely drained gas reservoirs is still common. Recent activity directed toward finding and producing natural gas has succeeded in both conventional and nonconventional settings. Conventional accumulations occur in discrete reservoirs (mostly sandstones, limestones, and dolomites) that are relatively permeable and of limited aerial extent (small on a map). These represent the vast majority of Oklahoma's gas fields and reserves. An example of an important conventional gas discovery in Oklahoma is the Potato Hills Field, which was found in 1997 in a geologically complex area in the southeastern part of the state.

As gas prices have risen, there has also been a concerted effort to recover gas from the state's many nonconventional reservoirs. Such gas accumulations do not occur in discrete traps, but in low-permeability reservoirs that tend to cover large areas. These include the natural gas found in coal-bed, "tight" (impermeable) sandstones, and shale. Although the intensive drilling of coal and shale did not start until recently, they are now the most active geologic plays in the state, accounting for about one-third of all gas drilling in recent years (IHS 2009). The six thousand coal-bed methane and one thousand shale gas producers in Oklahoma produce about six hundred million cubic feet per day, or 14 percent of state gas production. Horizontal drilling technology has been the key factor in making both of these inherently poor reservoirs economically viable. Although their stabilized production rate is typically low, geologic risk is minimal due to the ubiquitous nature of the reservoir. The major risk associated with these plays is the long-term gas price.

Coal beds are an important gas resource, because as plant material is heated and compressed into what will eventually become coal, methane is released. The generation of methane turns coal into a source rock from which gas sometimes migrates into adjacent, permeable rock (such as sandstone), where the gas can be produced as a conventional accumulation. More often, the gas has no means of escape and stays locked within the coal bed itself. Although horizontal drilling improves productivity, because coal is inherently impermeable, its quality as a reservoir depends on the spacing and interconnectivity of the fractures (cleats) that are formed during the coalification process, the process that turns plant remains to coal. Production of coal-bed methane is unique: rather than producing from reservoir pores, the gas desorbs from the coal itself. Coal-bed methane play in Oklahoma is about fifteen years old and continues to be quite active. Shallow, low-cost, coal-bed methane wells are suited to the small operators that dominate in Oklahoma. Areas that produce coal-bed methane in Oklahoma include parts of fifteen counties on the eastern margin of the Cherokee Platform and the northern half of the Arkoma Basin (map 4.1).

The other major gas play is shale gas, which in Oklahoma targets the Woodford Shale. Concerted Woodford gas drilling began in the first decade of the twenty-first century, and while recent declines in price have reduced activity, its potential is large. Because shale is impermeable, Woodford gas production comes mainly from horizontal wells, where the amount of the formation that is intersected by the wellbore is maximized. Unlike coal-bed methane wells, shale wells are fracture-stimulated in a process that forces sand onto the formation in order to form cracks and keep them open so that gas can flow from the shale into the wellbore.

Although the Woodford Shale has only about one thousand gas producers, or one-sixth the number of wells producing coal-bed methane, in 2008 it eclipsed coal-bed methane both in terms of production and drilling activity. Since 2005 Woodford gas production has gone from negligible to about 450 million cubic feet per day. Like coal-bed methane, because of its especially high initial declines, which can see production in a typical well fall 60–80 percent in its first year, future Woodford production will be dependent on drilling activity, which in turn will be dependent on the price of natural gas. Woodford Shale wells are scattered throughout the state, but most are concentrated in the far western part of the Arkoma Basin.

In 2008 Oklahoma's cumulative natural gas production since its inception (including associated gas) reached a staggering 101 trillion cubic feet (TCF). Daily production of about 4.5 billion cubic feet per day now comes from thirty-nine thousand active wells contained within about fourteen hundred named fields (OCC). In 2007 Oklahoma's natural gas production was 1.64 trillion cubic feet, which is about 25 percent less than the peak year of 1990, in which 2.26 TCF was produced. However, because the average gas price in 2007 ($6.48 per million cubic feet) was more than four times that in 1990 ($1.57 per million cubic feet), its gross value of $10.6 billion far exceeded 1990's $3.5 billion.

Natural gas production in Oklahoma generally moves up or down by a few percentage points each year, while fluctuations in price can be hundreds of times greater. This illustrates how, like oil, the value of natural gas to the state depends far more on its price than the volume produced. However, unlike oil, the price of which is closely tied to the global economy, another major driver of natural gas demand, and hence price, is the severity of winter weather. Notoriously difficult to predict with any degree of certainty, the winter months mark the period of greatest demand for natural gas.

The natural gas price is by far the most critical variable affecting the Oklahoma economy. It is a major driver in employment and income tax and in 2007 contributed about $750 million to the state through gross production taxes alone. Gas is environmentally friendly compared to coal or oil (releasing fewer environmentally harmful contaminants) and still relatively abundant, and its infrastructure can support substantial growth in demand. Oklahoma's location and geology, estimates of its remaining gas reserves, the state's pipeline system, and the energy industry's strong history together indicate that natural gas will be a key component of the state's economic future well into the twenty-first century.

The Future

If oil and natural gas production are combined, the 1927 peak in Oklahoma oil production can be seen as only an intermediate high in overall hydrocarbon production. The state actually reached its all-time production high of 527 million barrels of oil equivalent (MMBOE) in 1970, and was able to reach nearly the same level in 1984 when 518 MMBOE were produced. Overall hydrocarbon production today is roughly the same as 1927; the difference is that now natural gas is carrying most of the load. From this perspective it can be seen that, although clearly past its peak, energy production in the state will remain strong for decades.

Because sizable oil discoveries are a thing of the past, Oklahoma production will continue to decline, however, unless a systematic effort is made to enhance recovery in existing fields. A resurgence of oil production is possible because potentially large volumes of producible oil are waiting in thousands of existing fields. Although finding this oil will not be easy, the target is large with over 80 percent (sixty-eight billion barrels) of the state's original oil still in the ground. A review of the geologic literature has shown that many examples of low recovery can be addressed relatively simply, through waterfloods, modified waterfloods, dewatering (a process in which large volumes of water are produced to reduce reservoir pressure to the point that the gas that is dissolved in subsurface oil bubbles out of solution and drags oil along with it to the producing wellbore), new wells, and the recompletion of existing wells into new reservoirs (Boyd 2008).

Drilling success shows that there is a great deal of natural gas left to produce in the state, both conventionally and nonconventionally. The gas industry is strong and will continue to be.

Success in finding abundant (and hence relatively cheap) oil and natural gas, much of it from Oklahoma, has helped make these, with coal, the world's primary energy sources. This energy has been a key factor in the unprecedented prosperity and technological advancement that humanity enjoyed in the twentieth century. However, it has also brought a dependency on fuels that carry environmental consequences. The transition from fossil fuels to more environmentally friendly energy sources will take decades to accomplish and undoubtedly be bumpy. Oklahoma oil and natural gas will be vital in providing a secure bridge to the sustainable energy sources that will carry the human race into the future.

Note

Oil-production figures have changed since 2008, when this article was written, as a result of the increased drilling and completion of unconventional reservoirs using the technique commonly called fracking.

References

Boyd, D. T. 2008. "Oklahoma: The Ultimate Oil Opportunity." *Shale Shaker: Journal of the Oklahoma City Geological Society* 58, no. 6: 205–21.

Boyd, D. T., and B. J. Cardott. 2001. *Oklahoma's Energy Landscape*. Information Series 9. Norman: Oklahoma Geological Survey.

EIA. 2009. "U.S. Petroleum and Natural Gas Information." Energy Information Administration. http://www.eia.doe.gov/ (accessed June 2009).

Franks, K. A. 1980. *The Oklahoma Petroleum Industry*. Norman: University of Oklahoma Press.

IHS Energy. 2009. Data supplied by Petroleum Information/Dwights LLC dba IHS Energy Group, May 1.

Koontz, Terry. 1962. "History of Natural Gas in Oklahoma." *Tulsa Geological Society Digest* 30: 146–49.

Moore, Leland E. 1962. "Natural Gas in Oklahoma." *Tulsa Geological Society Digest* 30: 116–20.

OCC. 2008. "2007 Report on Crude Oil and Natural Gas Activity within the State of Oklahoma." Oklahoma Corporation Commission, Documents.OK.gov, http:// digitalprairie.ok.gov/cdm/compoundobject/collection/stgovpub/id/2077/rec (accessed February 19, 2013).

OTC. 2009. Oklahoma Tax Commission, Delores Flowers, personal communication, February.

CHAPTER 5

Petroleum, Planning, and Tribal Property

OIL FIELD DEVELOPMENT ON THE OSAGE
RESERVATION, 1896–1950

Houston Mount

In December 1949 the *Oil and Gas Journal* reported a remarkable conservation project unfolding on the Osage Reservation in Oklahoma.
The various companies that held leases in the extensive North Burbank
oil field had agreed to set aside their private rights and to cooperate in
a plan that would pump water through select wells into the subsurface
reservoir. By increasing pressure, these measures would ensure greater ultimate production from the field. It meant avoiding waste that had occurred in
other Oklahoma reservoirs, where countless barrels of crude had been trapped
in the ground due to rapacious production methods. Writing in the *Journal*,
Kenneth Barnes hailed the North Burbank agreement as the largest conservation project of its kind in the vast Mid-Continent Region. But it was only
the most recent of a number of such plans successfully put into action on the
reservation.[1]

More than a triumph of planned operation, the activities on the Osage
Reservation stood as a tribute to the vitality and, in this case, potential superiority of Indian tribal property. The project almost certainly would have failed
had the companies faced the multitude of conflicting property interests that
typically characterized Oklahoma oil fields. Indeed, the success of conservation efforts on Osage lands contradicted the logic of federal Indian policy that
had been embodied in the Dawes Act, which presumed that individual private

ownership went hand in hand with economic efficiency. Instead, conservation on Osage lands indicated that tribal property arrangements could sometimes offer distinct advantages over the dominant American system of private ownership, even in the context of modern economic life.

The development of oil fields in Oklahoma and throughout the nation took place in a legal environment where private ownership of petroleum was the norm. This was a legacy of the common law tradition inherited from Britain. Under common law, the ownership of land included rights in both the surface and the minerals below it. Mineral rights could be transferred, independent of the surface itself, through sale, gift, or other transaction.[2]

For most minerals, this rule of thumb proved sufficient to determine the rights of property owners, but petroleum presented certain problems in practice. Most troublesome was the fact that crude oil could migrate underneath the soil that lay above it. Because of this characteristic, it was possible to drill a well on one's own property and pump oil out from under a neighbor's land. Understandably, those who found themselves the unfortunate neighbors in a scenario like this were not pleased with the arrangement and asked courts to protect their property rights.

In the early years of the nineteenth-century oil industry, courts struggled to create reasonable rules governing the exploitation of the viscous new resource. The plight of the unfortunate neighbor was compelling, but there were few tools available to determine the extent of damages. How could a neighbor demonstrate the value of his or her loss due to drainage from an oil well on another's property? It was simply unknown. Furthermore, rules that placed obstacles in the way of drilling wells or hampered potential profits might kill the incentive to drill a well in the first place. These practical concerns gravitated against penalizing the driller and helped lead courts to formulate a legal principle that favored developers—the so-called "rule of capture." The rule of capture likened underground petroleum to a wild animal that wanders from place to place. Through this principle, the developer who first "captured" the petroleum by pumping it out of the land obtained full ownership rights in it.[3]

For the vast majority of oil fields, the rule of capture directed the course of the early petroleum industry in the United States. Initially the creature of a few state courts, it was nationally entrenched by the beginning of the twentieth century thanks to the U.S. Supreme Court decision in *Brown v. Spilman*.[4] The rule of capture made ownership rights in subsurface petroleum an inherently slippery concept. Just when did an oil producer really become the "owner" of the crude that flowed from his wells? Some states, such as West Virginia, Texas, and Kansas, viewed oil and gas deposits as the property of the estate owner, subject to loss by escape to adjacent lands. Other states, including Oklahoma, refused to acknowledge any title in the oil and gas beneath the surface. Only actual extraction could establish ownership rights. In either case, the insecurity of oil rights encouraged owners to develop their mineral estate before their neighbors could do so.[5]

Generally speaking, the owner of the mineral estate did not personally direct or even fund the drilling or operation of oil wells on her land. Relatively few landowners had the technical knowledge or the capital to drill for oil on their own property. The legal solution to this unhappy situation was the oil and gas lease. Instead of pursuing development on their own, the majority of landowners leased the mineral estate of their land to entrepreneurs who were given development rights in exchange for rent, royalties, bonuses, and other benefits. In most cases, it was the entrepreneur who sought out the landowner and solicited the lease agreement. The lease system added another layer of property interests and rights on top of those held by the landowner. It also complicated the process of development.[6]

Among other obligations that the oil lessee owed to the owner, he was required to protect the value of the estate that he had leased. If a well were drilled on a neighboring property, the developer was required to "offset" with a new well roughly mirroring the placement of the neighbor's well. Thus the landowner was assured of recovering a fair share in royalties based upon the oil under his land. If the developer refused to offset, the landowner was entitled to cancel the lease and seek another developer.[7]

Private ownership, the rule of capture, and the obligations of the leasing system created incentives for the rapid development of the nation's oil fields. During the second half of the nineteenth century, the entrepreneurial forces that these incentives unleashed made the United States the world's largest oil producer and called into being the modern petroleum industry. But there were problems with the system, most of which were related to an experience repeated in new fields opened to development—the "rush to pump."

The rush to pump characterized the early years of the petroleum industry in practically all American oil fields. In the nineteenth century the petroleum industry was still young and the science behind oil extraction was only dimly understood. But as the years passed it became evident that the development patterns fostered by the rule of capture were wasteful and destructive.

There were a variety of disadvantages of the rush to pump. Typically it promoted overproduction of petroleum. Overproduction in turn caused a host of difficulties. Most disconcerting to producers was the market effect—it depressed prices. Additionally over-drilling sapped subterranean oil pressure and ultimately reduced the amount of oil that it was feasible to remove from the ground. Once removed from below, pumped petroleum created other problems. Production in boom fields typically outpaced the ability of infrastructure to transport the oil. Companies that had sufficient resources at hand might cope by constructing storage tanks for their surplus. More often, financially strapped operators would simply dig large holes and allow petroleum to lie exposed to open air. In some cases, even these crude facilities could be exhausted, with the black gold flowing off the land and into local rivers, streams, and ponds. As both fire hazard and toxic pollutant, feral petroleum was a threat to local communities and wildlife. The negative consequences were apparent to all, but solutions were elusive.[8]

Throughout the vast majority of American oil fields, including in Oklahoma, the rule of capture dictated similar results. Almost all of the Indian tribes in Oklahoma would experience private allotment under the Dawes Act and similar legislation.[9] Allotment broke up tribal lands into parcels that were distributed to individual Indians, likewise dividing the mineral interests among a multitude of individual tribal members. It was an outcome that was consistent with the dominant legal culture of the United States. It also represented the triumph of a viewpoint that equated private ownership with the superior efficiencies of modern economic life. Therefore most Indians who had the good fortune to benefit from the oil fields in Oklahoma did so as individual, private owners.

There was a glaring exception to this rule in the Osage tribe. In accepting allotment, the Osages explicitly reserved their mineral rights as a tribe.[10] It was a decision that would have a far-reaching impact upon the Osages as a people as well as the land that they called home. The unusual ownership arrangement on the Osage Reservation resulted in the atypical development of its oil fields and ultimately offered possibilities for implementing the kind of conservation plans that were impeded on lands where private ownership predominated.

The development of the oil industry in Oklahoma took place in a complex and often confusing legal context. During the twentieth century, state and federal officials increasingly turned to regulation to ameliorate the worst consequences of the rule of capture. In Oklahoma, conflicting federal, state, and tribal jurisdictions complicated this process. As Kenny Franks, historian of the Oklahoma petroleum industry, has observed: "For the most part, the early efforts at regulation of the oil business within present-day Oklahoma could be described as a maze of often conflicting tribal, federal, territorial, and state actions which, in many cases, overlapped and were almost always a source for confusion to the oilmen."[11]

The early ineffectiveness of regulation meant that market incentives, informed by the rule of capture, dictated the development of the first Oklahoma oil fields. Typical of the familiar pattern of overdevelopment and overproduction was the fabulous Glenn Pool. Discovered in 1905, the Glenn Pool was located on lands of the Creek Nation, which had allotted lands to tribal members. With tribal ownership passing to individual landowners, the federal government proved generally willing to approve oil leases on Creek lands. Here the form that the final allotment settlement had taken would shape the development of the field.[12]

The Dawes Act of 1887 had established the principle of breaking up tribal reservations into individual lots.[13] In the case of the Creeks, this approach resulted in the fragmentation of the mineral as well as surface estates of the land. A Creek allotment thus included its mineral estate and in most cases could be leased or even sold on an individual basis after a probationary period.[14] In the Glenn Pool, this property arrangement combined with the legal principle of the rule of capture to create a classic case of waste and premature field exhaustion.

A multitude of developers rushed to the field in the weeks following the initial strike in the oil field. Ultimately the field stretched to two miles in length and less than one mile in width. Within that space, oil companies fought with one another to secure leases with a variety of allotment holders. Very quickly the field grew out of control. The failure of the federal, tribal, and ultimately state governments to establish spacing rules for the wells resulted in rampant over-drilling. Many operators failed to seal or at least control the flow of natural gas, resulting in a rapid decline in gas pressure. As pressure declined, so did productivity. Without the natural "engine" that gas pressure provided, large amounts of petroleum were effectively lost—trapped below the ground with no apparent means to get it out. Production peaked in 1908, just three years after the field was opened, at over twenty million barrels of oil. In five years the annual total would fall to under half that amount.[15]

Premature exhaustion of the Glenn Pool was not the only problem connected with property arrangements and the rule of capture hampering the rational development of the field. Competition among producers and landowners created problems on the surface as well as below the ground. Anxieties over losing subsurface oil to the competition drove oil companies at the Glenn Pool into a frenzy of reckless production. Once above ground, title to the oil was assured and oil companies and royalty owners alike could look forward to sales proceeds. But the glut of petroleum flowing from the fields presented financial as well as technical difficulties. Above all, companies suffered from price depression due to the enormous output of the field. Such an event should have been foreseen. Production gluts and price collapses had been a regular feature of the industry since its inception in Pennsylvania almost a half-century earlier. Nevertheless, many producers were not adequately prepared for the disappointment.[16]

Bitter experiences with the perils of overproduction such as occurred at the Glenn Pool were a key to later demands for regulation and to the establishment of groups like the Independent Producers League. More disturbing were the technical problems associated with overproduction. By the peak year of 1908 it was clear that production in the Glenn Pool was outstripping the ability of pipelines and railroads to accommodate output. Concerned oilmen arranged a voluntary reduction of petroleum production, but the fantastic yield of many of the wells proved too great a temptation. Overflow from inadequate storage containers burned, creating billowing towers of smoke. A local creek caught fire frequently and flames often traced its banks for miles. As a result of gratuitous overproduction, approximately five thousand barrels of petroleum were lost in the field each day.[17]

Despite the disastrous waste, Glenn Pool opened the way for the intensive development of petroleum fields in Oklahoma. The influx of vast amounts of capital, the construction of an extensive network of petroleum pipelines, and the arrival of a crowd of entrepreneurial oilmen ensured the swift exploitation of the state's reservoirs. Unfortunately the same legal arrangements that encouraged rapid exploration also undermined rational development of many of these fields.[18]

In contrast to the outcome of the Creek allotment, unitary tribal ownership of the mineral estate remained untouched on Osage land. In 1906 the congressional act that implemented allotment for the Osages explicitly stated that "the oil, gas, coal, or other minerals covered by the lands . . . are hereby reserved to the Osage tribe for a period of twenty-five years from and after the eighth day of April, nineteen hundred and six."[19] Although the surface of the Osage Reservation was effectively dismantled through the allotment process, the mineral estate remained uncompromised in what one historian has called the Osage "underground reservation."[20]

Tribal retention of the mineral estate was a triumph in a long-standing battle by Osage leaders against the U.S. government to preserve as many as possible of its tribal institutions. This struggle dated back to 1825, with the establishment of the first "permanent" Osage reservation in Kansas. The cession of these lands in 1865 raised the specter of tribal dissolution, but under the leadership of Chief Joseph Paw-ne-no-pashe they succeeded in acquiring new tribal lands in Oklahoma. These lands were held in tribal rather than individual title, and preserving tribal title became the primary business of the new Osage constitutional government that was formed in 1881. Six years later, the passage of the Dawes Act ensured that this task would be difficult indeed. It is a measure of the success of the Osage government that allotment was resisted for almost twenty years, but federal abolition of the constitutional government in 1901 convinced most Osages that some form of allotment was inevitable. Still, pressure to expedite the move toward statehood in Oklahoma gave the Osages some leverage in their negotiations with the government. The greatest concession that they won was their retention of the mineral estate.[21]

The arrangement was certainly atypical. Rather than parceling out the mineral estate based upon surface ownership, tribal members were entitled to a "headright" interest in petroleum royalties and benefits received by the tribe (a right to receive funds distributed from the tribal mineral estate).[22] Though originally subject to renewal, the tribal mineral reservation was extended "in perpetuity" in 1978.[23]

Despite this unusual property arrangement, the early development of many Osage oil fields would resemble the pattern of reservoirs elsewhere in Oklahoma due to leasing practices. From the earliest days of oil exploration, the Osage Reservation played an important role in the growth of the petroleum industry in Oklahoma. In the years before statehood, the Osage people owned their reservation in Indian Territory as a tribal entity. Unlike the case of the Five Tribes, the Osage did not face allotment until statehood. As a result, leases were concluded directly with the tribe, rather than through individual Osages. As early as 1896, the tribe granted Edwin B. Foster a lease to explore for oil that included 1.5 million acres of Osage lands. The Foster "blanket" lease was truly vast, though of dubious value, but one year later Foster's Phoenix Oil Company struck oil on the reservation. Although the well proved to be a poor producer, it did establish with certainty that there was petroleum on Osage land.[24]

The initial discovery of oil was followed by a series of disappointments. A number of "dry holes" discouraged development for the remainder of the nineteenth century. It was not until 1902 that several successful strikes resulted in intensive exploration. In the meantime, Foster had reorganized his venture under the aegis of the Indian Territory Illuminating Oil Company. With unified control of the mineral estate by the Osage Nation, and unified rights to development secured under Foster, the Osage fields might have been structured and exploited in a rational, measured fashion. But despite this auspicious beginning, lease arrangements on Osage lands gradually fragmented, creating conditions like those found elsewhere.

Figure 5.1. Bartlesville oil field, Indian Territory, 1905. Courtesy of Oklahoma Historical Society Research Division.

It was a matter of money. The Indian Territory Illuminating Oil Company lacked capital sufficient to the task at hand and therefore reacted as any reasonable business would have. It cashed in on the value of its lease by selling off a series of subleases to a variety of would-be developers. By the end of 1904, the company had subleased 687,000 acres. Eager to develop their leases, the new petroleum companies quickly drilled a number of wells, discovering the Okesa Pool, the Osage City Pool, the Avant Pool, the Wiser Pool, and the Boston Pool by 1905. The subleases executed by the Indian Territory Illuminating Oil Company began the process of fragmentation that would lead Osage oil fields in the direction that development had taken in other areas, such as the Glenn Pool.[25]

The division of lands based upon subleases hindered the advantage offered by unified ownership. More trouble was on the way. In 1906 even the limited unity provided by the Indian Territory Illuminating Oil Company was compromised when its lease on the western half of the reservation was not renewed. Then in 1912 the tribe opted to open even more lands to exploration. Far from promoting any unitary leasing interest, the tribe actually encouraged the division of its remaining lands into small leaseholds. Parcels were leased by auction but companies were limited to a maximum of twenty-five thousand acres total.[26]

The expiration of the blanket lease in 1915 stirred the industry into a whirlwind of debate over future development. On the one hand, the Indian Territory Illuminating Oil Company sought to renew its profitable leasehold in Osage lands. On the other hand, independent operators were anxious to lease directly from the tribe and avoid the additional cost of dealing with an intermediary. Although powerful interests, including the governor, supported renewal of the blanket lease, the small companies won in the end. In July 1915 the Department of the Interior refused to renew the lease held by the Indian Territory Illuminating Oil Company. This ended the possibility of any unified leasehold of Osage lands. The Foster lease was divided into 160-acre plots with companies limited to a maximum forty-eight-hundred-acre leasehold. The old Indian Territory Illuminating Oil Companies sublessees were allowed to keep their subleases if they did not total more than forty-eight hundred acres. The dissolution of the Foster lease completed the process of fragmentation that had begun with the subleases of the early 1900s.[27]

The multiplication of Osage oil leases facilitated the rapid location and exploitation of the remaining undiscovered fields. In 1916 alone, three new fields were discovered: the Myers Dome, Barnsdall, and Hominy Pools. The entry of the United States into World War I spurred further exploration and coincided with the founding of the Pershing Pool, the Dome Pool, the Nelagoney Pool, the Wynona Pool, and the Almeda Pool. The Pettit, Pearsonia, Pawhuska, X686, and Y686 oil fields opened following the armistice. Yet it was not until 1920 that one of the most productive fields of the region, the Burbank, was discovered. Pioneered by wells from the Carter Oil Company and the Marland Oil Company, the Burbank Field became the site of another major rush and ushered in the Roaring Twenties. The discovery of oil in the Burbank Field further multiplied the leaseholds on Osage land. Located in western Osage county, the region had drawn scant attention before 1920. Petroleum companies bid sky high on leases held for auction underneath the already famous "million dollar elm" outside the Osage Council House in Pawhuska. One expensive plot went for $1,990,000—a high price for the privilege of developing 160 acres of land.[28]

It was a golden age for the state, characterized by high hopes and extravagant spending. It also marked a turning point as the Osage Nation, the oil companies, the state, and indeed the entire country began to come to grips with the senseless overdevelopment and waste of petroleum reserves. As the extent of that waste became apparent, some began to question the existing system. Even President Calvin Coolidge, a noted supporter of industry, stated in December 1924, "It is evident that the present method of capturing oil is wasteful to an alarming degree."[29]

The president was not the only person concerned over the course of oil field development. A driving force for reform in the 1920s was Henry L. Doherty, founder of Cities Service Oil Company. A pioneer in the science of petroleum engineering, Doherty was responsible for promoting research into the relationship between natural gas and petroleum in the exploitation of oil fields. Employed by Doherty, researcher Charles Beecher established the role of natural gas as a motive force in oil production. This discovery inspired Doherty in his quest to promote the rational development of oil fields through the institution of a legal regime known as "unitization."[30]

Unitization aimed at establishing unitary management of entire oil reservoirs. This was necessary to take advantage of what Doherty's researchers had discovered about the way oil fields work. Depending upon the type of geological formation, the presence of natural gas could serve as a propellant in an underground petroleum reservoir. These formations were and are often stratified, with natural gas tending toward the upper level and water at lower levels, with petroleum somewhere in between. Doherty's researchers had discovered that the presence of pressurized gas exerted force upon petroleum to facilitate extraction once wells were drilled. Later, waterflood projects proceeded on the basis that increased water pressure could also serve as a propellant.

The problem that fragmented ownership and the rule of capture presented to this scheme is that drilling wells everywhere tended to undermine the natural "engine" of the oil fields. Reducing the gas pressure undermined the productivity of neighboring wells and ultimately left much oil trapped under the surface. Unitization offered a solution to competitive drilling by pooling the interests of owners and lessees in order to develop the field as a whole. Former owners and developers might receive a predetermined share of proceeds based upon the extent of their interest in the field. In this manner, unitization would rationalize oil production to an extent impossible under a fragmented estate governed by the rule of capture. But when Doherty first advocated government-sanctioned unitization to the Federal Oil Conservation Board in 1926, his ideas were too advanced for acceptance within the industry.

Nevertheless, Doherty laid the groundwork for a more rational approach to reservoir development. In addition to controlling abuses during the initial development of a field, unitization also opened the door to so-called secondary recovery methods. Secondary recovery involved the artificial enhancement of reservoir pressure after natural pressure had been exhausted during the period of primary production. This might involve the injection of natural gas or water into a reservoir at strategic locations and extraction of petroleum from designated wells. As oil field production declined, companies showed increasing willingness to contemplate these measures. But operators who were open to unit operation faced a number of obstacles in implementing such a plan. Up until the 1940s, voluntary agreement among royalty owners and leaseholders was the only viable option if unitization was to take place. One observer noted problems involved in achieving such accord:

- Sometimes some men are unreasonably stubborn.
- At other times some men are selfish and try to drive unconscionable bargains.
- Royalty owners are frequently without adequate understanding of the problems or of the reasonableness of the solutions suggested, and are reluctant to make any new agreement.[31]

As oil producers came to realize the advantages that could result from unitization, they started to address some of these difficulties through clauses in leases they signed with landowners. For example, a lease might provide that a company could enter a plan for unit operation, thereby bypassing the need for approval from the owner of the mineral estate. But such provisions were uncommon at the midpoint of the twentieth century.[32]

In 1945 another option opened for operators eager to unitize. That year Oklahoma passed the nation's first comprehensive compulsory unitization statute. If operators of 50 percent or more of an area sought to enter a unit plan, then the state could compel others in the area to join the plan. Still, there were significant limitations. If companies holding leases on 15 percent or more of the area objected, then the order was invalidated. Even if all operators were agreed, mineral estate owners had a right to appeal the decision. In addition to these possible challenges, producers were reluctant to petition for a compulsory unitization order because of concerns in giving a government agency power over company property rights.[33]

On Osage lands, the challenges in implementing a unit operation plan were significantly reduced by tribal ownership of an undivided mineral estate. For this reason, the Osage Reservation still presented unusual possibilities for implementing conservation and secondary recovery methods despite the multiple leaseholders operating on tribal land. Developers attempted and sometimes succeeded in unitization where private ownership was the rule. Yet a multitude of royalty interests inevitably complicated these attempts. Developers not only had to come to an accommodation with one another, but might go to great lengths in order to convince royalty owners that unitization was in their interest as well. Industry observers took note on unusual occasions when developers succeeded in executing a cooperative plan without arousing opposition from mineral royalty owners.[34]

These obstacles to rational development were absent on the Osage Reservation. Because the tribe retained unitary ownership of the mineral estate, coordination of a variety of owners under a unitization plan would be unnecessary. Instead the greatest challenge would be harmonization of the leasehold developers under a single plan. As production in the fields tapered, such harmonization seemed more and more possible. In the early 1930s a number of secondary recovery projects were implemented in the Burbank Field on the Osage reservation—already one of the most profitable petroleum deposits in the United States.[35]

The Burbank Field was identified and mapped based upon the presence of the "Burbank sand." Describing parts of the same geological formation, developers divided the Burbank sand into the North Burbank, South Burbank and ultimately, Mid Burbank Fields. These divisions reflected stages of discovery and development. The North Burbank was the oldest field, discovered in 1920. South Burbank was not discovered until 1934, with Mid Burbank developed in 1934 and expanded in 1936. As a result of its age, the older North Burbank suffered more than the other two from early abuse.[36] The greater Burbank suffered from overdevelopment as much as any other reservoir had suffered. Indeed, one historian of the industry identified this field, among others, as witness to "madcap operations and profligate waste."[37]

Initial conservation efforts focused upon gas repressurization aimed at enhancing petroleum production. The North Burbank began repressurization in 1932 with planning started for the South Burbank almost immediately after its development in 1934.[38] In their analysis of the prospective repressurization of the South Burbank, consultants I. L. Dunn and James Lewis stressed the importance of leasehold consolidation: "Complete consolidation of all properties in the pool is so desirable that we strongly recommend that every effort be made to attain as near unitization as is practicable."[39] They were aware of the potential rewards of cooperative field management. Dunn and Lewis were also optimistic about the advantages offered by the unusual property regime in Osage County. Consolidation of leaseholds was all the more desirable on Osage lands because the mineral interests were already consolidated: "The fact that the royalties are already pooled in Osage County will make consolidation simpler and operation of the unit more effective than elsewhere."[40] The benefits that would accrue to developers as a result of unitization would be significant. More oil, less overhead, and, above all, greater revenues would be the result.[41]

Although Dunn and Lewis's plan was complex in detail, the basic concept was simple. Natural gas repressurization involved the injection of natural gas into the oil reservoir at strategic locations selected to feed into the subterranean reservoir. The more gas injected, the more pressure would be exerted on the petroleum, forcing it upward through selected producer wells. In the case of the South Burbank Field, this would mean the injection of over one million cubic feet of gas daily within the first year of production, with plans to raise this by an additional five million cubic feet per day soon thereafter.[42]

Developers submitted the plan for the South Burbank Field to the Osage Agency in 1935 where it was approved. In his response to the repressurization project, oil and gas inspector William Ash Waid dwelt on the benefits of unitization and expressed regret that these measures had come so late: "I only wish this idea could have filtered through some executive skuls [sic] when we started the old Burbank field in 1920. . . . 70% of the oil now lays [sic] dormant in the sands. . . . The law of capture theory prevailed. It is fundamentally wrong, it is disastrous to the conservation of one of the Nations [sic] great resources. For the old Burbank pool, I see nothing ahead but re-pressure, re-pressure with gas or gas and air mixture and finally some form of water flood. It is in the offing."[43]

Waid's remarks proved prescient. Gas repressurization benefited production in the Burbank Field after its initiation in the 1930s. It was a success story of which the industry did not fail to take note. Describing the South Burbank unit as an "example of efficient development," *Oil and Gas Journal* reporter and petroleum engineer L. G. E. Bignell acknowledged the role of tribal property in facilitating the operation: "This plan of operation is made possible because this is the only completely unitized pool in Oklahoma and not only have the oil and gas rights been covered by the unitizing plan but the royalty rights are also protected as they all belong to the Osage Indians and can be treated as one interest."[44]

Eased into action through the unusual property regime on the Osage Reservation, the plan was remarkably effective. Yet it was not enough. Although these efforts helped to slow the decline of the Burbank fields, gas repressurization alone proved insufficient to maintain productivity at desired levels. As a result, William Ash Waid's prophecy that waterflood would be the destiny of the Burbank Pool was fulfilled by the late 1940s.

Waterflood recovery was based upon the same principle as gas repressurization. By pumping water below the surface, increased pressure would help propel petroleum upward through select production wells. The North Burbank Field was the site of the pilot waterflood project. Added expenses associated with implementing the new conservation plan meant renegotiation with the Osages. Because the mineral estate was owned as a community, a majority vote of headright interests ratified the new unit operation plan. Company officials were well aware of their good fortune in dealing with the tribe. If the mineral estate had been held privately then the assent of royalty owners in the pool would have been necessary to implement an effective plan. Three or four

Osage tribal Council who approved H.V. Foster lease in 1896
Chief Bigheart, back now 3rd from left.
1916

Figure 5.2. Osage Tribal Council, 1916. Courtesy of the Western History Collections, University of Oklahoma Libraries, City Service Collection, 399.

stubborn royalty owners might be sufficient to undermine waterflood operations. Under a fragmented, private-ownership regime, something close to unanimity rather than a simple majority would be required. Fortunately for the Burbank developers, this was not the case on Osage lands.[45]

At the time that it was instituted in 1949, the waterflood project in the North Burbank Field was one of the largest secondary recovery efforts in the history of the petroleum industry.[46] The waterflood project ultimately coordinated twenty leaseholders through unitization of their interests in the North Burbank Field.[47] Their cooperation was facilitated by the simplicity of dealing with the undivided mineral estate of the Osage Nation and helped sustain the commercial productivity of a declining reservoir. By 1950 similar efforts were underway in the South Burbank Field, where the Phillips Petroleum Company also initiated waterflood recovery.[48] Ultimately such efforts, combined with the sheer magnitude of the reservoir, made the Burbank Field one of the most lucrative in the history of the petroleum industry and a bonanza for the Osage people. The continued success of the field during its later years owed much to the cooperative management of the reservoir.[49]

The legal regime under which the petroleum industry was born shaped its early development in ways that encouraged exploration and exploitation, but also promoted gross and reckless waste of resources. The rule of capture, combined with fragmented property conditions, virtually guaranteed over-drilling and overproduction in the early fields. Although rational development on the Osage reservation was compromised by fragmentation of leaseholds, the perpetuation of the tribal mineral estate left the door open for later remedial action. The broad institution of conservation plans on Osage land owed much to retained tribal ownership and demonstrated the flawed logic that had informed the Dawes Act and private allotment. Tribal property could not be dismissed out of hand as a relic of a more "primitive" way of life. The success of conservation projects on the Osage Reservation demonstrated that in some cases tribal ownership could be more economically efficient than private ownership, even in the context of the very modern oil industry.

Notes

1. Kenneth B. Barnes, "Biggest Water Flood: Phillips to Begin North Burbank Secondary-recovery Project Immediately on 1-year, Pilot Plant Basis," *Oil and Gas Journal* 48 (December 1, 1949): 37.

2. Eugene Kuntz, *A Treatise on the Law of Oil and Gas*, vol. 1 (Cincinnati: Anderson Publishing, 1987), §2.1; W. L. Summers, *The Law of Oil and Gas*, vol. 1 (Kansas City, Mo.: Vernon Law, 1954), §§11, 21.

3. Kuntz, *Law of Oil and Gas*, vol. 1, §4.1.

4. *Brown v. Spilman*, 155 U.S. 665 (1895), 669–70.

5. Kuntz, *Law of Oil and Gas*, vol. 1, §2.4.

6. For a summary of basic lease characteristics, see W. W. Thornton, *The Law of Oil and Gas*, vol. 1, 5th ed., revised by Simeon S. Willis (Cincinnati: W. H. Anderson, 1932), §§74, 75.

7. Kuntz, *A Treatise on the Law of Oil and Gas*, vol. 5 (Cincinnati: Anderson Publishing, 1991), §61.1.

8. Daniel Yergin, *The Prize: The Epic Quest for Oil, Money, and Power* (New York: Simon and Schuster, 1992).

9. "General Allotment Act of 1887," *U.S. Statutes at Large* 24 (1887): 388–91.

10. "An Act for the Division of the Lands and Funds of the Osage Indians in Oklahoma Territory, and for Other Purposes," *U.S. Statutes at Large* 34 (1907): 543.

11. Kenny Franks, *The Oklahoma Petroleum Industry* (Norman: University of Oklahoma Press, 1980), 56.

12. Ibid., 41–46; Kenny A. Franks, *The Rush Begins: A History of the Red Fork, Cleveland and Glenn Pool Oil Fields* (Oklahoma City: Oklahoma Heritage Foundation, 1984), 62–72.

13. "General Allotment Act of 1887," *U.S. Statutes at Large* 24 (1887): 388.

14. "An Act to Ratify and Confirm an Agreement with the Muscogee or Creek Tribe of Indians, and for Other Purposes, *U.S. Statutes at Large* 31 (1901): 861–73.

15. Franks, *Oklahoma Petroleum Industry*, 44–45; *The Rush Begins*, 73–86, 132.

16. Franks, *Oklahoma Petroleum Industry*, 44.

17. Ibid., 46.

18. Ibid.

19. "An Act for the Division of the Lands and Funds of the Osage Indians in Oklahoma Territory, and for Other Purposes," *U.S. Statutes at Large* 34 (1907): 543.

20. Terry P. Wilson, *Underground Reservation: Osage Oil* (Lincoln: University of Nebraska Press, 1985).

21. Terry P. Wilson, "Scarred Earth, Scarred People: The Osages and Oil on Allotted Lands," in *Native Views of Indian-White Historical Relations*, edited by Donald L. Fixico (Chicago: Newberry Library, 1989), 94–96.

22. *U.S. Statutes at Large* 34 (1907): 544.

23. "An Act to Amend Certain Laws Relating to the Osage Tribe of Oklahoma, and for Other Purposes," *U.S. Statutes at Large* 92 (1980): 1660.

24. Gerald Forbes, "History of the Osage Blanket Lease," *Chronicles of Oklahoma* 19 (March, 1941): 70–72; Franks, *Oklahoma Petroleum Industry*, 14–15.

25. Forbes, "Osage Blanket Lease," 72–73; Franks, *Oklahoma Petroleum Industry*, 57–59.

26. Forbes, "Osage Blanket Lease," 75, 78–79; Franks, *Oklahoma Petroleum Industry*, 60–61.

27. Forbes, "Osage Blanket Lease," 79–81.

28. Franks, *Oklahoma Petroleum Industry*, 64, 101–102.

29. Quoted in Carl Coke Rister, *Oil! Titan of the Southwest* (Norman: University of Oklahoma Press, 1949), 372.

30. For an overview of Doherty's ideas about unitization, see Daniel Yergin, *The Prize: The Epic Quest for Oil, Money, and Power* (New York: Simon and Schuster, 1992), 220–22; Franks, *Oklahoma Petroleum Industry*, 146–47.

31. Robert E. Hardwicke, "Unitization Statutes: Voluntary Action or Compulsion," *Rocky Mountain Law Review* 24 (December 1951): 37.

32. Ibid., 42.

33. Oklahoma, *Official Session Laws, 1945* (Guthrie, Okla.: Cooperative Publishing, 1945), 162–69; Hardwicke, "Unitization Statutes," 37, 40–41; K. E. Barnhill, "Oil and Gas—Compulsory Unitization," *Rocky Mountain Law Review* 24 (December 1951): 129.

34. Louis F. Burns, *A History of the Osage People* (Tuscaloosa: University of Alabama Press, 1989), 539; Leigh S. McCaslin, "Preplanned Program with Royalty Owners Followed in Newest Unit Project . . . Gas Injection Expected to Double Recovery," *Oil and Gas Journal* 46 (April 8, 1948): 64.

35. James McIntyre, "Osage County Is Producing over All-time Average," *Oil and Gas Journal* 36 (June 10, 1937): 38.

36. C. H. Riggs, *Water Flooding in the Burbank Oil Field: Osage County, Oklahoma* (Washington, D.C.: U.S. Department of the Interior, 1954), 1–2, 11, 13, 15; J. Arthur Sohn, "Unitization vs. Competition," *Oil Weekly* 83 (September 21, 1936), 22.

37. Rister, *Oil! Titan of the Southwest*, 369.

38. Burns, *A History of the Osage People*, 541; I. L. Dunn and James O. Lewis, "Oil Producers and Engineers, Report on Feasibility, Pressure Maintenance, South Burbank Field, Tulsa, December 15, 1934," stack A, row 27, compartment 54, shelf 3, Repressurization (322.761), Classified Files, 1920–1960, Records of the Oil and Gas Division, Records of the Osage Agency, Records of the Bureau of Indian Affairs, Record Group 75, National Archives Southwest Regional Archive Building, Fort Worth, Texas.

39. Dunn and Lewis, "Oil Producers and Engineers," 3.

40. Ibid., 20.

41. Ibid., 2.

42. L. G. E. Bignell, "Unitized Block in the Osage Nation Is Example of Efficient Development," *Oil and Gas Journal* 34 (September 12, 1935): 42.

43. William Ash Waid, "Memorandum Report, May 3rd, 1935," stack A, row 27, compartment 54, shelf 3, Repressurization (322.761), Classified Files, 1920–1960; Records of the Oil and Gas Division, Records of the Osage Agency, Records of the Bureau of Indian Affairs, Record Group 75, National Archives Southwest Regional Archive Building, Fort Worth, Texas.

44. Bignell, "Unitized Block," 42. See also Sohn, "Unitization vs. Competition," 22.

45. Riggs, *Water Flooding*, 3. "Resolution of the Tribal Council No. 17-119, Minutes, Regular Meeting, Osage Tribal Council, June 14, 1948," stack A, row 28, compartment 38,

shelf 6, box 6, pp. 25–27, Osage Council Minutes and Proceedings, Records Relating to the Osage Tribal Council, Records of the Osage Agency, Records of the Bureau of Indian Affairs, Record Group 75, National Archives Southwest Regional Archive Building, Fort Worth, Texas. "Remarks by Councilman Dave Ware and Operator Representative H. H. Kaveler, Minutes, Regular Meeting, Osage Tribal Council, January 10, 1949," stack A, row 28, compartment 38, shelf 6, box 7, p. 13, Osage Council Minutes and Proceedings, Records Relating to the Osage Tribal Council, Records of the Osage Agency, Records of the Bureau of Indian Affairs, Record Group 75, National Archives Southwest Regional Archive Building, Fort Worth, Texas.

46. Kenneth B. Barnes, "Biggest Water Flood: Phillips to Begin North Burbank Secondary-recovery Project Immediately on 1-year, Pilot Plant Basis," *Oil and Gas Journal* 48 (December 1, 1949): 37; Burns, *A History of the Osage People*, 541.

47. Barnes, "Biggest Water Flood," 37.

48. Kenneth B. Barnes, "Osage Revival: Modern Well-completion and Water-flood Techniques Again Make Osage Nation a Happy Hunting Ground for Oil Men," *Oil and Gas Journal* 49 (August 24, 1950): 95.

49. Franks, *The Oklahoma Petroleum Industry*, 104.

CHAPTER 6

Butchers against Businessmen

THE 1921 PACKINGHOUSE STRIKE AND THE OPEN SHOP MOVEMENT IN OKLAHOMA CITY

Nigel A. Sellars

A s the sun rose on Oklahoma City three days after Christmas 1921, it revealed glass and debris strewn along Exchange Avenue from Western Avenue to the gates of the county stockyards. The glass came from the windows of cars that had carried mostly poor, African American strikebreakers to the Morris and Wilson meatpacking plants on the previous day, December 27. A small riot had broken out just outside the entrance gates to the Packingtown industrial district, where striking workers had attacked the cars with stones and brickbats, and smashed automobile windows and headlights. The driver of one car had accused Oklahoma City police of forcing him to slow down so that strikers could attack his vehicle. The next day Oklahoma County sheriff's deputies patrolled both the stockyards and the area outside the plants. Governor James B. Robertson warned county and city officials to control the situation or he would send in the National Guard. The ferocious strike, however, lasted for almost another month.[1]

The intensity of the Oklahoma City meat cutters' strike demonstrated how sharply divided business and labor were in the city. The strike marked the last episode in a yearlong war in which Oklahoma City's healthy, pre–World War I labor movement fell victim to a concerted, well-financed anti-union crusade that used both patriotism and economic unrest to achieve its goals.

The Amalgamated Meat Cutters and Butcher Workmen of North America had called its 1921 national strike—which affected Oklahoma City and twelve other cities—to halt the plans of the major meatpacking corporations to cut hourly wages and establish an "open shop" system, a forerunner of so-called right-to-work laws, that denied the union the right to require all plant employees to join the union. The Butcher Workmen, however, stood little chance of defeating the packers' unified efforts.[2]

With thirty-five active labor organizations, Oklahoma City's labor movement had entered the twentieth century in relative strength. At statehood, Oklahoma City and Tulsa claimed the bulk of the state's 21,280 unionized workers in 303 different unions. Oklahoma City had its share of serious labor unrest. A bitter 1911 streetcar strike led the city council there to approve an anti-picketing ordinance, which the state court of criminal appeals overturned following a 1917 theatrical workers' strike. After World War I, the state and the city witnessed national strikes in the coal and the railroad industries. In summer of 1921 the city's printers joined a nationwide walkout.[3]

Oklahoma City's chamber of commerce established an aggressive open shop division in 1920. Led by attorney John H. Shirk, the division pressured Oklahoma City companies to end the "closed shop" practice of hiring only union members or requiring employees to belong to a union. From early June to mid-July 1920, the chamber purchased seven four-column ads in the *Daily Oklahoman*. By July 18, 1920, the open shop division claimed twenty-five hundred members, half of its goal of five thousand. It soon joined fifteen local open shop organizations in New Mexico, Arkansas, Texas, Oklahoma, and Louisiana to establish the first regional open shop organization, the Southwestern Open Shop Association.[4]

The open shop movement found fertile soil in both Oklahoma City and Tulsa, but especially in Oklahoma City. Its organizers promoted the idea that employment was an individual contract between employer and employee, saying that labor unions and collective bargaining interfered with the "sanctity" of this contract. The chamber of commerce's *Open Shop News* declared that the crux of the fight was the employer's right to "employ and discharge." The publication claimed that the power of the unions meant that employers no longer controlled their own workers. The open shop movement asserted a nonunion worker's right to work where he or she chose, regardless of whether belonging to a union. The goal of most open shop associations was to eliminate trade unions completely. Addressing the Oklahoma City Chamber of Commerce, J. H. Miller, president of Tulsa Open Shop Square Deal Association, urged his audience to "go after the unions" and destroy them. To do so, open shop groups would come to rely less on the championing of business owners' "rights" and more on appeals to patriotism. By waving the U.S. flag and speaking of its program as "the American Plan," they could brand labor unions un-American. To make this point clear, the Oklahoma City open shop division logo bore the phrase "A Square Deal for All" and—in capital letters—the word AMERICANISM.[5]

The open shop drive of 1920–21 additionally distilled wartime anti-German sentiment and anticommunism into its ruthless anti-union offensive. To show support for the war effort, the city's unions—like those nationally—had avoided strikes when possible. Employers, meanwhile, used "patriotic" wartime lock-outs, in which the company management refused to allow employees, even if willing to work, onto company premises until the workers reject their "disloyal" union. Lockouts often included changing all the locks and placing hired security guards around the plant. Sometimes management went so far as to fine employees who reported to work or to deny them the right to clock in. The official organ of the Oklahoma Employers' Association, *The Employer*, claimed in December 1919 that unions had replaced the sacrifice and patriotic zeal of the war with strikes, riots, violence, chaos, and un-American calls for revolution. "Would Hindenburg and Ludendorff do less evil to the country than [union leaders John L.] Lewis and [William Z.] Foster?" the publication asked. In a letter to H. H. Anderson of the Kansas City Employers' Association, attorney John Shirk, chair of the Oklahoma City Chamber of Commerce open shop division, sentimentally declared, "The stars and stripes form a net-work around my heart and at every pulsation I fancy one of the stars in the field of blue takes on a brighter hue."[6]

The patriotism of men like Shirk ran second only to their antipathy to labor unions. While the stars and stripes of the U.S. flag might form a network around Mr. Shirk's heart, labor journalist Leon Goodelman wrote, employer associations formed a red, white, and blue network meant to strangle the very life from American workers and their unions.[7]

Oklahoma City unions responded to the chamber of commerce in 1920 by boycotting and picketing nonunion merchants. One target was the Witt Clothing Company, a new member of the chamber's open shop division. On November 22, six pickets wore sandwich boards that read: "This store built and made rich by Union Labor. They now believe in the open shop and Sweat Shops." The retailer's managers, however, proved less hostile than most open shop supporters. In fact, the store took advantage of the situation with good-natured, humorous newspaper ads saying that shoppers should note the polite and well-dressed picketers, who "will remind you to look in our windows and see the values" in clothing and furnishings. Witt employees avoided offending the picketers and offered them assistance when needed. When the weather turned cold, rainy, and windy, one Witt employee gave a new raincoat to one poorly clad picketer. After a week, the unions admitted that they could not counter the ads, which had increased Witt's sales by 10 percent. "You have jollied us out of it," one picketer told the store's advertising manager.[8]

The city's chamber of commerce had a particular interest in promoting the open shop when it came to packing plants. Beginning in 1908 the chamber made a concerted effort to interest the "Big Five" packers—Armour, Swift, Cudahy, Morris, and Schwarzschild and Sulzberger (known after 1916 as Wilson and Company)—in locating a plant in Oklahoma City. Its officials kept their negotiations quiet so as to prevent other communities in gaining leverage to lure the packers elsewhere. Eventually the Edward Morris Company, impressed by the city's excellent railroad connections, sent its executive vice president, Thomas E. Wilson, to meet with city business leaders such as newspaper publisher Edward King Gaylord, chamber president Sidney Brock, Anton Classen, and John Shartel. Wilson laid out his company's almost extortionate conditions for building a plant: a $300,000 cash "inducement" up front; tax-exempt status for the stockyards area for five years; sewer connections from the plant to the North Canadian River; streetcar lines extended to the plant; and construction of a railroad belt line to connect the plant with existing trunk lines. The chamber of commerce accepted the demands and secured 575 acres of county land about two miles southwest of downtown. The plant itself was to occupy 120 acres bounded by Exchange and Central Avenues on the north and south, and Agnew Street on the east. City business leaders subscribed $427,000 toward financing construction.[9]

The Morris plant officially opened on October 3, 1910, and the company soon organized much of the remaining county land around it as the Oklahoma National Stockyards Company, an outlet for buying and selling livestock. The company expanded rapidly. In June 1911 Sulzberger & Sons Company offered to build its own plant immediately west of the Morris facility. Sulzberger's demands resembled those of Morris: a $300,000 inducement; sewer, water, and gas connections; a fire station near the site; and 350,000 gallons of free water daily for five years. The new plant opened on October 11, 1911. By the year of the strike, 1921, the Morris plant took in 315,113 cattle, of which 202,352—about 64.2 percent—were slaughtered. Morris and Sulzberger & Sons soon made Oklahoma City one of the ten largest meatpacking centers in the United States. With a total public investment of about $3.5 million, the two plants and the adjacent stockyards generated twenty-four hundred new jobs and constituted the heaviest concentration of labor in a city with a 1910 population of sixty thousand.[10]

While the plants created jobs, they also created slums. Housing conditions in Packingtown for plant workers were wretched. In 1919 the Oklahoma Public Health Survey noted a community of mostly overcrowded, dilapidated, one-story, single-room shacks, inadequately lighted and poorly ventilated. Often two or three families shared such a shack, with only transparent curtains separating them. "Under such conditions," the survey's authors reported, "privacy is impossible and modesty becomes greatly diminished." Packingtown also contained numerous open toilets, and a single pump might supply drinking water for as many as twenty families. Single, unmarried workers frequented so-called boarding houses and hotels where, the health inspectors noted, the beds sat side by side, with little space between them. One such "hotel," unusually dirty, lacked both drinking water and washing facilities.[11]

Packingtown had few sanitary sewers. A twenty-four-inch sanitary sewer at Walker Avenue and Ash (now Central) Street discharged effluent from the packing plants that had an offensive odor and posed serious public health problems. Two individuals hired by the city collected Packingtown's garbage every night from businesses—and twice a week from residents. The men disposed of the garbage at two nearby pig farms, where it was used to feed hogs. One pig farm, located on the road to Packingtown, had three to four acres of garbage and manure piled nine feet high. Naturally the decaying rubbish attracted flies, mosquitoes, and other disease-carrying insects.[12]

Despite these deplorable conditions, unions made little effort to organize the plants' workers. This seems odd at first because the Amalgamated's first Oklahoma City chapter had been organized before statehood. Founded in 1900 by H. C. Schilling, a former Knights of Labor member, the fifteen-member Local 92 only represented skilled butchers working in local meat markets. That the local only included skilled workers partly explains why it failed to organize the packing plant workers. The American Federation of Labor (AFL) rarely bothered to recruit African American workers and common laborers, who were generally unskilled and often worked on a payment-by-piece basis—piecework. It took little training to do such slaughterhouse jobs as "knockers" did (they stunned cattle with sledgehammers) or as "stickers" did (they severed an animal's carotid artery so that it bled to death). Oklahoma City packinghouse workers finally organized after 1917, but only after the Chicago Federation of Labor (CFL) had successfully organized all of Chicago's packinghouse workers under its Stockyards Labor Council. The CFL succeeded by organizing the workers by industry rather than by craft or trade, and by thus including both skilled and unskilled and the African American workers who comprised much of the stockyard workforce.[13]

Figure 6.1. Entrance to Packingtown, Oklahoma City, 1914. Courtesy of the Research Division of the Oklahoma Historical Society.

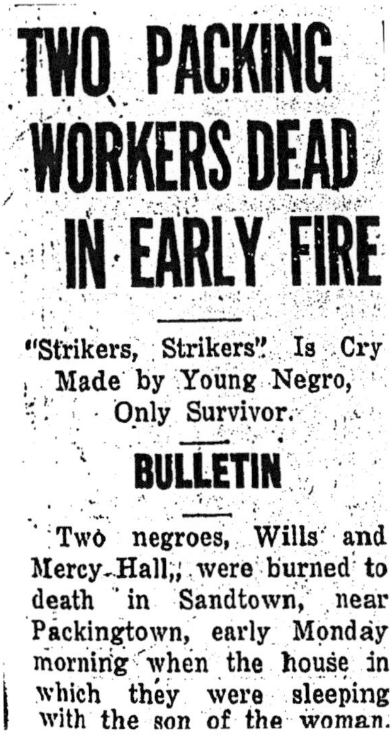

TWO PACKING WORKERS DEAD IN EARLY FIRE

"Strikers, Strikers" Is Cry Made by Young Negro, Only Survivor.

BULLETIN

Two negroes, Wills and Mercy Hall, were burned to death in Sandtown, near Packingtown, early Monday morning when the house in which they were sleeping with the son of the woman.

Figure 6.2. "Two Packing Workers Dead in Early Fire," front-page story, *Daily Oklahoman*, January 23, 1922. Reprinted by permission of the Oklahoman.

By judicious use of strike threats, the Amalgamated Meat Cutters won concessions from the Big Five firms in 1916. Thanks to the War Labor Board, the Amalgamated gained federal mediation in 1918. The union sought an eight-hour day and a dollar-a-day increase for all workers. Federal judge Samuel B. Altschuler—after hearing nearly a month of testimony—awarded the union an eight-hour day with ten hours' pay: time and a quarter for the first two hours of overtime. He also granted pay increases of four and a half cents an hour for workers earning thirty cents or less and hour, four cents an hour for those earning between thirty and forty cents an hour, and three and a half cents an hour to those earning more than forty cents an hour. While the judge's decision spurred the unionization of packinghouse workers, it became a major bone of contention for the meatpacking industry, which was already dealing with federal antitrust investigations. On November 30, 1920, the Justice Department asked the Supreme Court to end the packers' control of the stockyards and to appoint trustees to sell them. Under a consent decree in 1920, the packers divested their interests in stockyards, terminal railroads, cold storage warehouses, and retail meat markets.[14]

Stung by the divestiture, the packers found an opportunity to defy Altschuler during the postwar depression of 1919–21. Numerous factors produced the economic collapse. Reduced loans to European countries lowered European orders for U.S. goods. Lowered government spending and inflationary price trends were also among factors that denied investors an expected return on funds. Industrial production fell and employment dropped with it. Between 1919 and 1921, wage-earning jobs in manufacturing dropped almost 25 percent, a loss complicated by over two million jobless returning veterans. As labor historian Joseph Rayback has noted, 1921 was "a propitious time for launching an anti-labor campaign."[15]

The Big Five packers also felt the sting of the economic downturn, suffering heavy losses on the devaluation of their inventories. Armour faced a $31.7 million deficit by the end of 1921, while Swift suffered net losses of $8 million. Morris was on its way to failure and acquisition by Armour. The corporations blamed their condition on Judge Altschuler and the union. The judge's War Labor Board administration was to end in February 1921, and the corporations planned wage cuts and a quick return to the open shop system.[16]

The depression deeply affected Oklahoma. The state's oil and agricultural industries had profited from the war, but the depression reversed those gains. Cotton prices plunged from thirty-nine cents a pound in early 1919 to just nine cents a pound by December 1920, causing some landowners to evict their tenants and turn their land over to cattle grazing. Working days in state coal

mines dropped from 197 in 1918 to 141 in 1921. The severe downturn put an end
to most community economic development and created a shortage of capital. Oil companies headquartered outside Oklahoma drained what little profits
came and declined to reinvest in the state. Although workers in the state struck
thirty times in 1919 and twenty-two times in 1920, growing unemployment
undermined their actions. In September 1921, the State Labor Commission
estimated that Oklahoma City had 3,210 unemployed workers.[17]

Confrontations between unionists and anti-union forces increased during
this time. On November 25, 1920, Oklahoma City's pro-labor mayor, John C.
Walton, addressing the state convention of the National Association of Letter
Carriers, called open shop demands a vital question that every worker would
have to defeat with the ballot. Walton also successfully encouraged unionization of the city police force, which the mayor directly controlled. The *Daily
Oklahoman* argued that the unionized police would sympathize with strikers.
Police, the newspaper declared, should be nonpartisan, "free to enforce the law
against anyone and everyone." In 1921 an anti-Walton coalition of Republican
business leaders, the chamber of commerce, and the Gaylord and Harlow
newspapers attacked the mayor's control of the police as unconstitutional and
demanded an end to the AFL-affiliated police union. The state supreme court,
however, overruled the opposition and returned power to Walton.[18]

By that time the city's chamber of commerce and some local business
leaders confronted Oklahoma City's unionized print-shop workers and pressmen, and the local newspapers gave their support to the Open Shop Division.
Both E. K. Gaylord's *Daily Oklahoman* and Victor Harlow's paper, *Harlow's
Weekly*, took antilabor positions and regularly extolled the open shop philosophy. A strike by the printers would hurt the newspapers and block a valuable
channel for disseminating open shop propaganda. On April 28, 1921, twenty-
three print shop owners took out an ad in the *Daily Oklahoman* demanding an
open shop for printers and denouncing calls for a 44-hour workweek by the
International Typographical Union and International Printing Pressmen and
Assistants' Union. Harlow lashed out at organized labor in his paper, and he
increased his attacks after binders and pressmen struck his own printing plant.
Harlow vowed he would reorganize the plant as an open shop. The open shop,
Harlow editorialized, was "fundamental in the reorganization of industry in
such a way as to assure a renewed prosperity for our state and nation."[19]

All Oklahoma City pressmen and printers struck on May 21, 1921. The
strike was contentious, with violent incidents that included a strikebreaker
shooting and wounding a union picket outside an open shop printing business. After that incident the open shop Employing Printers Association took

Figure 6.3. Oklahoma City mayor John C. Walton, 1923. Courtesy of the Western History Collections, University of Oklahoma Libraries, Nancye Good Collection.

out a four-column ad in the August 23, 1921, *Oklahoman*. Ignoring that a strikebreaker was the shooter, the ad accused the pickets of harassment and of "fomenting anarchy." "How long is the citizenship of Oklahoma City going to tolerate lawlessness?" the ad demanded. Union members felt let down by their employers and willingly made sacrifices to continue the strike. In the end they proved a match for the printing companies, and they won their demands.[20]

By contrast, the packinghouse workers proved an easy mark for their employers. February 1921 brought to a close Judge Altschuler's adminis-tration of the packers through the War Labor Board, and on March 8 Swift and Armour announced wage cuts and plans for "industrial democracy" in the form of their own company "unions." Armour went so far as to hold a "union" election exactly a week later. Wilson had a similar plan that applied to its Oklahoma City plant. Under the Wilson plan, employee committees could present grievances to management. The plan, however, lacked any means for arbitrating disputes, in part because the packers did not expect any. By May 1921, the other packers, except for the ailing Morris, followed suit.[21]

The Amalgamated reacted quickly to the creation of the company unions. The international immediately took a strike vote, and ten other unions with members in the packinghouses placed themselves at the disposal of the Amalgamated should a strike occur. Only the actions of the secretaries of labor, commerce, and agriculture managed to avert a strike. With apparent reluctance, the packers on March 23 agreed with the unions to extend the Altschuler ruling until September 15. It quickly became evident that this agree-ment was an uneasy truce and that the Big Five had no intention of going along with it. In December 1920 the packers had already cut the wages of unskilled workers by two cents an hour, and in March 1921 they had again reduced wages despite their March 23 agreement with the unions. In June the packers pressed Altschuler to order further wage cuts, but he refused, citing the continued high cost of living.[22]

The packers then elected to press forward with their plans for "employee representation." The Amalgamated's secretary complained to Altschuler that managers of the firms were coercing employees to join the new company unions. But the Amalgamated position rapidly deteriorated. The depression and the company unions hurt the international, which saw its membership drop from forty thousand at the end of 1920 to about half that number in September 1921. Of that twenty thousand or so, about ten thousand came from west of the Mississippi, which included Oklahoma City. With the expiration of the Altschuler agreement, the union also had no real means of represent-ing its membership.[23]

On September 15, 1921, the Big Five packers—again minus Morris—announced that they had adopted the open shop system. The packers declared that they would not discriminate in hiring and that all men and women were eligible for employment whether union members or not. They also declared that no outside person or agency could represent their employees in grievance matters, which effectively barred unions from negotiating contracts. Employees were to elect their representatives—who had to be U.S. citizens—and only those representatives could negotiate wages and work conditions.[24]

In response, the Amalgamated called on the packers to reinstate the Altschuler agreement for one year. The packers refused to talk with the union. AFL officials expected wage cuts to follow. AFL secretary Frank Morrison called the packers' action "stone-age" and charged that they denied their employees the right of counsel in decisions that affected workers' lives. In October, the Amalgamated executive board authorized a strike vote but delayed issuing a strike order. In Oklahoma City, almost 99 percent of the local's 250 members voted to strike. The Oklahoma City local had the full support of the Oklahoma State Federation of Labor (OSFL), which placed Armour, Cudahy, Swift, and Wilson on its "unfair" list and urged shoppers to patronize merchants and wholesalers not supporting the open shop system and to patronize only unionized merchants and retailers.[25]

At its September 22 state convention in Shawnee, the OSFL had affirmed its commitment to oppose the open shop system. It had attacked the Oklahoma City Chamber of Commerce and praised Mayor Walton for his "fair and impartial stand" in Oklahoma City labor disputes. The OSFL also chose this time to organize the Farmer-Labor Reconstruction League and announce its support for Walton in the following year's gubernatorial election. An October 1921 *Oklahoma Federationist* editorial argued that the "American plan" (of open shops) was thoroughly *un-American* because it deprived workers of the traditional Jeffersonian right of the consent of the governed. "Under the 'open shop' alleged utopia the workers are not asked as to their consent. . . . The workers are told by the boss where they get off, and being unorganized, they 'get off' where told." The editorialist declared that union members would never submit to losing their freedom and optimistically claimed the open shop movement was "about at the end of its rope. Dissolution is near."[26]

The editorial's prediction proved wrong. By October the Open Shop Division of the chamber of commerce was issuing letters and bulletins urging shoppers to buy from nonunion "home merchants," thereby associating the unions with interests outside the community. The unions responded by urging its members to buy from mail order stores rather than deal with nonunion merchants. The chamber had continuing support from the press, especially *Harlow's Weekly*. Victor Harlow, once a liberal reform crusader, now embraced conservative values with a vengeance. His editorials regularly lambasted the AFL, as well as the fledgling Farmer-Labor Reconstruction League. Drawing on rhetoric rendered moot under the 1914 Clayton Anti-Trust Act, Harlow contended that unions were illegal combines that intimidated unorganized workers and "starved" them of employment. Harlow called it effrontery for unions to claim they represented both union and nonunion employees. When Edgar Fenton, state AFL president, criticized the city's superintendent of schools, R. H. Wilson, for abetting the open shop movement by letting students debate the question, Harlow attacked Fenton. "Has organized labor reached the point where it is afraid to permit its fundamentals to be presented to the public?" he asked. Harlow, however, was disingenuous. He knew the OSFL complaints were well founded because the open shop Oklahoma Employers' Association had sponsored and funded the high school debates and an accompanying essay contest.[27]

The only newspaper supporting the unions—other than from the labor and socialist press—was the *Oklahoma News*, a Scripps-Howard newspaper. Press baron Edward Willis Scripps, a self-proclaimed "crank," saw himself as an advocate for labor and delighted in irritating his fellow capitalists. Unsurprisingly the *News* drew the ire of the city's chamber of commerce and praise from unions when it charged that the packers were part of a nationwide war waged by employers' associations. If the unions were smashed, the newspaper said, "It will make a difference to all of us. If the open shop triumphs generally, followed as eventually it must be by reductions in wages and increases in working hours, the prosperity of the entire community will be affected. . . . The merchant will suffer because low wages can't buy as often or as much as high wages." The reduced purchasing power, it continued, would eventually hit the doctor, the dentist, the lawyer, and other professionals. "The open shop works its greatest benefit to those corporations which fatten on the misery of the mass," the *News* argued.[28]

The city's unions responded to the open shop movement attacks by withdrawing their support for a $7 million municipal bond issue. Labor leaders said they would only support the measure if union labor were employed with the funds and if the chamber ceased its open shop advocacy. The bond issue failed to pass by one hundred votes. Even Victor Harlow admitted that the unions' actions defeated the measure. "[T]he activity of labor leaders during the election indicates that union labor mustered as many votes as those by which the bonds were defeated."[29]

Tensions remained high when the wage cuts the Amalgamated feared came in November. This time Morris immediately joined the other four packers. On November 20, 1921, Morris's Oklahoma City manager, H. L. Binyon, announced a wage reduction identical to the rest of the industry, effective November 28. Hourly workers earning forty-seven and a half cents an hour and more received a cut of three cents an hour; those earning from forty-three to forty-seven cents an hour were reduced five cents an hour; workers earning forty-two and a half cents an hour and less lost seven cents an hour. In addition, wages for piecework shrank 25 percent. "The reduction has been required by the cut in prices made by competitors, and, after being given the consideration of the employees' conference [that is, the company union], was deemed advisable," Binyon announced. He made no mention of the collusive nature of the Big Five's action.[30]

Slashed wages would devastate many employees, local union officials argued, because the cost of living in Oklahoma City had not decreased. For many workers, the officials said, it was the second wage cut of the year, and the reductions pressed hardest on those with families. The dire effects of the cuts were demonstrated by two wage surveys made that fall, the first by state labor commissioner Claude Connally, and the second by OSFL secretary Victor Purdy. Despite some obviously pro-labor bias on the part of both men, their findings clearly showed that unskilled packinghouse workers earned little more than subsistence wages. Purdy randomly interviewed twenty Wilson employees—nine men and eleven women—and nineteen Morris employees—eighteen men and one woman. Anna Braddock, who worked in Wilson's sausage department, had her wages go from thirty-one cents to twenty-five cents an hour, while a Morris ice-dock hand, J. H. Canary, saw his hourly wages reduced from forty-one and a half cents to thirty-four cents. Canary told Purdy that company officials had warned him that if he went on strike he could only return to work as a "new" hand at twenty-five cents an hour.[31]

Connally found similar conditions. Mack Evans, an African American skilled butcher with seven years at Morris, had his wages drop from $24.40 per week to $18.40. "This man has a family of thirteen to support; eleven children, six of whom are of school age, the oldest being fourteen years and the youngest two months. This family lives in three very small rooms." For the unskilled, the reductions made life almost impossible. Mrs. Annie Thompson, a widow, lived with her six children in a two-room basement in the Capitol Hill area. She told Connally she had earned $15 a week at Morris but that her wages had been cut to $12.[32]

Faced with the reality of wage reductions, the union's national leadership agreed to strike all the Big Five's plants but only after it made a final, futile attempt to negotiate. Rather than issue an immediate strike order, however, the leaders instead surveyed rank-and-file sentiment in a series of mass meetings on November 27, the day before the cuts took effect. The union's members demanded a strike. The strike order was issued December 1, to take effect Monday, December 5.

The strike order came at a bad time, as historian David Brody has noted. The weather was wintry, strike funds low, and the union could rely on little support from the public or any branch of government. Postwar Red Scare fears made picketing and boycotting, previously effective tools, less acceptable. The packers, on the other hand, were acting in a unified manner, could call on large financial reserves, and had a pool of unemployed workers willing to cross picket lines for jobs.[33]

The packers, though, underestimated worker anger at the corporate leaders' cynicism and stinginess with wages. Oklahoma City packinghouse workers enthusiastically supported the strike order. Fred Kemp, the secretary of the Oklahoma City local of the Amalgamated, claimed that some workers had seen their wages cut to twenty-nine and a half cents an hour, and that Morris and Wilson had systemically discharged some workers earning more than forty-seven and a half cents an hour. Kemp declared that a thousand workers would walk out of the plants. Binyon and J. F. McMahon—the superintendent for Oklahoma City's Wilson plant—branded Kemp's statements lies. Both declared that neither Morris nor Wilson had ever recognized the union— which was untrue—made any contracts with it, or compromised with it in any way. They vowed the plants would remain open as usual and said that plenty of unemployed men would fill strikers' jobs.[34]

At 6:00 A.M. on December 5, at least five hundred workers walked out of the packing plants. Despite the packers' and chamber's claim that the union represented only two hundred or so workers, many nonunion workers responded to the strike call and seemed as determined as the union members to win the strike. A similar trend occurred nationwide, which surprised the packers. Strikers and sympathizers crowded Stockyard City's business district, with about four hundred persons gathered at the entrance gates to the Morris and Wilson plants. Police and deputy sheriffs patrolled the streets, but they did little to stop the numerous fights and disturbances between strikers and strikebreakers. Pickets injured two strikebreakers severely enough to send them to local hospitals. The next day a third strikebreaker was injured.[35]

While the packers declared operations were at 50 percent of normal capacity, union officers claimed 90 percent of the workers were on strike and charged plant officers with forcibly holding some workers in the plants. Representatives for the strikers said they would settle the strike on two conditions: that the wage cuts be rescinded or reduced and that wage reductions be put to arbitration, with old wages restored pending a decision.[36]

The local press with one exception, siding with the packers, argued that the strikers were violating precepts of peaceful picketing. *Harlow's Weekly* said the legislature needed to take action to outlaw "peaceful" picketing and argued that Oklahoma permitted picketing only because of a 1917 criminal court of appeals ruling, "which is strictly a court decision and not a legislative enactment." The *Daily Oklahoman* contended picketing was a form of violence "contrary to all principles of American citizenship." Its editorial writer called the open shop movement merely a protest against "unreasonable, unjust and expensive union regulations." Even the cross-state *Tulsa World* weighed in, calling peaceful picketing "the same thing as bloodless murder, fireless arson, honest larceny and virtuous rape." The *Oklahoma News*, however, defended the strikers and argued that it was the open shop system that was un-American. "The open shop works its greatest benefit to those operations which fatten on the misery of the hungry," wrote the paper's editorial writers. But the open shop advocates contended that the newspaper's owners catered to "union labor and socialists."[37]

The editorializing on both sides had little effect on the violence, which continued almost daily. City police continued to do little to stop the altercations, in part because the packinghouses were located on county land, therefore outside police jurisdiction. In fact, the main gate to the Packingtown area lay on the municipal boundary line at the west end of Exchange Avenue. While Packingtown was indeed outside their authority, the city police and Mayor Walton sympathized with the strikers as fellow unionists. Walton went so far as to speak at a strikers' meeting December 8 and told them they were winning the fight. Throughout the strike the mayor secured supplies for the strikers, who by then had set up camps around the plants. Despite Walton's pro-labor position, the packers at one point requested police protection. Besides reiterating the jurisdictional question, the mayor replied that additional police would strain the city budget. Wilson and Morris representatives said that they had provided funds for additional officers and charged that city officials had pocketed some of the money. Walton replied that he had payroll receipts for every penny.[38]

The violence escalated on both sides. On Christmas Day, company guards used revolver butts to beat three picketers unconscious. The three men were war veterans who had been gassed at the front in Europe. As it happened, the three were also "Wobblies," members of the Industrial Workers of the World.

The IWW was an international union that proved to be very successful in the American West. Although membership numbers fluctuated, at its height in the 1920s it was estimated to have about forty thousand members. It stood for the unification of all workers into "one big union," and the abolition of capitalism and wage labor. Nationally, the AFL, the federal government, and the general public feared them as violent radical socialists. While the chamber viewed the men as dangerous radicals or anarchists, the strikers saw them as victims and responded in kind. Two days after Christmas, a small riot erupted just outside the entrance gates in Packingtown as strikers attacked cars carrying strikebreakers to the plants, as described earlier. Walton responded by increasing the number of patrolmen in the area from sixteen to seventy-five. That decision left a total of two officers to patrol the downtown business district. Those seventy-five remained until ten thirty that night, when police officials decided a smaller number could handle the situation. Walton, fearful that militia would be called in, ordered the officers to stay inside city limits. Oklahoma County sheriff Ben Dancy then took action, increasing the number of his deputies in the area to twelve, while the county attorney filed ten complaints of assault and battery against strikers.[39]

Open Shop Division head Shirk accused strikers of stoning the home of a woman whose husband was a strikebreaker. Mrs. I. L. Hayes reportedly told chamber officials that strikers had threatened "that her home would be blown to atoms if her husband didn't come out of the plant and put on a union button." Another individual alleged that police had stood by as strikers attacked a nonunion worker trying to enter the Wilson plant. Shirk called the attacks "dastardly" and praised Mrs. Hayes because, "moved by her mother instinct, her first thought was to protect her babe while the mob outside was hurling stones against the house."[40]

The following day, Governor Robertson sent letters to Walton, Dancy, and Oklahoma County Attorney Forrest Hughes. The governor said he had observed the situation at Packingtown since the strike had begun and that he was convinced local authorities could not cope with the state of affairs. "[U]nless rioting and disturbances are under absolute control within twenty-four hours from this time I will have to take a hand in the situation." Robertson never carried out his threat. This seems odd as the governor had shown little reluctance in using the National Guard in 1919 to quell a telephone operators' strike in Drumright and a coal miners' strike in the southeastern part of the state. Perhaps he believed that with both city and county law enforcement on duty, the situation could be controlled. Shirk sent a telegram to President Warren G. Harding asking that he refrain from arbitrating the strike, as the

Amalgamated had requested. OSFL secretary Purdy denounced Shirk, alleging that open shop advocates feared arbitration because it would reveal how underpaid the workers were. They preferred industrial strife, Purdy argued. "By his action, Mr. Shirk shows the 'open shop' agitator in his true light," he said. "The mask is off. We might as well fight it out here as further up the road."[41]

Despite the violence, nonunion workers continued to cross the picket lines and keep the packers in operation. Commissioner Connally, in his report, noted that a large percentage of the strikebreakers were very young men and that plant foremen did active duty as workers. More significantly, in one plant Connally had seen a large department composed entirely of African American strikebreakers. The use of blacks as strikebreakers was not new: the packers had hired them in strikes in 1894 and 1904. During the 1921 strike the Chicago Urban League actively recruited African Americans in the South for the companies. Generally blacks proved especially useful against unions that refused to accept them as members, and they were important in every city during the 1921 strike (Oklahoma City was one of thirteen localities where meat cutters were striking), although the Amalgamated was one of the few unions then admitting African Americans. For many blacks at the time, the choice to become a scab was between having a job or no job at all. Many accepted the low-paying, unpleasant tasks demanded in the packinghouses—and crossed picket lines to work. The inherent racism of AFL policies damaged unions in the eyes of African-Americans. As labor historian Philip Foner noted, "The unwillingness of the AF of L national unions to accept blacks as white workers were accepted only strengthened the hand of the employers and their agents, who could present black workers with real reasons for resisting unionization." Though they were a minority of all strikebreakers, African Americans became the likeliest targets for violence. During World War I, race riots had occurred in Chicago, East St. Louis and Omaha, all spurred by white workers' fears of increased black hiring by the meat packers and other employers. Racial tensions remained high in Oklahoma in the 1920s. Tulsa experienced racial bloodshed when white gangs invaded the prosperous all-black neighborhood following a reported rape attempt of a white woman. Homes and businesses were burned to the ground and hundreds of black citizens murdered. While a race riot did not develop in Oklahoma City, racial violence manifested itself in a more brutal and primitive form—lynching.[42]

Despite the action on the streets, the larger struggle seemed to be favoring the packers. Officials at both the Morris and Wilson plants reported December 28 that cattle and hog buying and killing were at normal levels. The packers, however, had now resorted to using armored cars to deliver strikebreakers to their plants. One striker told the press that the vehicles were clearly a necessity for the packers. "It's a dangerous business without it," he said. Strikers also boarded city streetcars to discourage strikebreakers riding the cars. Other pickets patrolled the North Canadian River to prevent nonunion hands from crossing it. Disturbances, including fights and near-riots, continued almost daily until January 14, 1922. About nine o'clock that night eight armed men took a twenty-six-year-old African American strikebreaker named Jake Brooks from his home in the city's predominantly black northeast side and hanged him from a tree in Capitol Hill, south of the North Canadian River. A passing motorist found the body.[43]

The *Oklahoma News*—under the headline "Lynched by the I.W.W.?"—reported that county attorney Forrest Hughes had accused the Wobblies of the crime. Hughes later denied that he had accused the IWW and said that the organization's members were safe in Oklahoma City as long as they obeyed the laws. Regardless of what Hughes actually said, the Open Shop Division used the claim of Wobbly involvement to its advantage. On January 18, chamber of commerce president W. J. Pettee issued a call for the chamber's entire membership to meet the next morning and appoint a committee to request a martial law order from Lieutenant Governor Martin Trapp. Trapp was at the time acting governor, with Governor Robertson away from the state, in Waco, Texas. Shirk personally called for martial law, saying that Brooks's only crime had been to anger the strikers because he had wanted to earn a living for his family. Speakers at the Thursday morning meeting said that "the better citizens"—meaning the chamber members—might have to arm themselves if state protection was not forthcoming. Emotions grew so extreme that the chamber, E. K. Gaylord, and his managing editor, Walter Harrison, pressured county attorney Hughes to arrest all IWW members in the city. Other than the three picketing members who had been beaten, the IWW had absolutely no connection with the strike or the lynching, but that hardly mattered to the open shop leaders. Oklahoma City police arrested most of the Wobblies on vagrancy charges and told them to leave town.[44]

With tensions continuing, Walton charged that Shirk and his aides, "having killed the city, are intent on burying it." The mayor accused the chamber of railroading through resolutions calling for martial law. In response to the chamber, Walton organized a mass meeting that same night of January 19 for persons opposed to martial law. More than three thousand people met at the city's district courthouse and appointed a committee of eight to meet with the governor that Friday. After meeting with both this group and a chamber of commerce group, Governor Robertson said he would take the matter under advisement, but he never issued an order one way or the other—he simply did not call out the National Guard.[45]

With the chamber clamoring for martial law, city police had already detained twelve men in connection with the lynching. On January 19, one suspect, a black worker named Robert Allen, had confessed to participating in the murder. The twenty-seven-year-old Allen, who was Brooks's cousin, implicated seven other men. One was an African American worker named Nathan Butler, whom Allen said had named Brooks as a strikebreaker to union officials. In a detailed confession, Allen described how the eight had met at the Amalgamated union hall in Packingtown, then driven to Brooks's home and abducted him. The eight had all taken an oath of silence about the affair.[46]

After the confession, Governor Robertson quickly appointed George F. Short, the assistant state attorney general, to head the prosecution. Robertson said he believed that the heavy Oklahoma County docket would make it difficult for the county attorney to handle the case. Short's appointment was probably unnecessary, however, as most of the men pleaded guilty and received life sentences. One man later changed his plea, but he was convicted at trial and also received a life term. One investigator for the governor remarked that the entire incident, from lynching to sentencing, had probably set a national record for speed.[47]

Although the union tried to distance itself from the incident, the damage had been done. While most area newspapers asserted that the lynching had resulted from the strikers' radicalism and from lax law enforcement, the *Daily Oklahoman* claimed—without evidence—that Brooks's death was actually part of a conspiracy. It urged that the "master mind or minds . . . should be routed from cover and given the extreme penalty, no matter who they are."[48]

Public opinion turned against the strikers, but the union also faced other serious problems, including dwindling funds. The strikers also never seriously threatened city meat supplies as the packers' use of strikebreakers assured that production remained at nearly normal levels. Gradually strikers returned to the plants, hoping to secure their old jobs. The defeat was so thorough for the Oklahoma City union that membership fell to the point where the local gave up its charter to national headquarters.[49]

Nationally too the strike failed, and the reasons for this are easily understood. The strike's violence alienated many potential sympathizers. The Amalgamated failed to gain support from the Teamsters and other unions, and the meat cutters were internally divided. Because most plants were only partially unionized, some workers opposed to the strike remained on the job, and the packers could draw from a pool of strikebreakers—black and white—made desperate for work by the depression. The Amalgamated's failure to organize the retail meat markets meant that it found little help from that sector, even though the National Wholesale Grocers Association, which feared the packers' power over the entire food industry, had sided with the union. The final blow came January 23, 1922, when three federal mediators informed Dennis Lane, the Amalgamated's general secretary, that the Department of Labor would not intervene. While a January 26 vote supported continuing the strike, the vote only involved one-quarter of the original strikers. Locals in all of the other cities had already given up the ghost and returned to work under open shop conditions. Sensing the inevitable, on February 1, 1922, the Amalgamated's executive office ordered the strike to end "in the name of justice to the loyal strikers and their families."[50]

The lessons of the strike were clear. The balance of political and economic power lay with the packers, united in their resistance to trade unions. Unions on their own could not hope to organize the meatpacking industry and would have to rely on some form of government intervention. Throughout the 1920s, packinghouse workers depended on corporate ideas of employee representation, occasional relief payments, and the dubious benefits of the "open shop." For Oklahoma City, the strike produced two specific effects. First, John Walton's pro-labor stands and his battles with the chamber of commerce so impressed the OSFL and the new Farmer-Labor Reconstruction League that they endorsed him for governor. It placed Walton at the forefront for the Democratic nomination and undoubtedly contributed to his electoral victory that fall. Second, the open shop system ruled in the city throughout the 1920s until the Great Depression, which brought renewed union organizing.[51]

Notes

1. *Oklahoma News* (Oklahoma City), December 28, 1921.

2. David Brody, *The Butcher Workmen: A Study in Unionization* (Cambridge, Mass.: Harvard University Press, 1964), 102.

3. Federal Writers' Project of Oklahoma, *Labor History of Oklahoma* (Oklahoma City: A. M. Van Horn, 1939) (hereafter *Labor History of Oklahoma*), 22–23; *Harlow's Weekly* (Oklahoma City), September 23, 1921.

4. Harlow, Rex F., and Victor E. Harlow, *Makers of Government in Oklahoma* (Oklahoma City: Harlow, 1930), 579; *Daily Oklahoman* (Oklahoma City), June 6, June 20, June 27, July 15 and July 18, 1920; "Shirk Rites Set for Today," *Daily Oklahoman*, September 19, 1942; W. S. Mosher, "The Open Shop in the Southwest: Address of W. S. Mosher, Mosher Manufacturing

Company, Dallas, at Convention of National Founders Association, Hotel Astor, New York, November 18, 1920," *Open Shop Review* 18, no. 3 (March 1921): 120.

5. *National Labor Digest* 4, no. 1 (January 1921), 18; Joseph G. Rayback, *A History of American Labor*, rev. ed. (New York: Macmillan, 1966), 291–92; Philip Taft, *Organized Labor in American History* (New York: Harper and Row, 1964), 364–65; Samuel Zimand, *The Open Shop Drive* (New York: Bureau of Industrial Research, 1921), 5; Philip S. Foner, *History of the Labor Movement in the United States, Vol. 8: Postwar Struggles, 1918–1920* (New York: International, 1987), 178; Robert W. Dunn, *The Americanization of Labor: The Employers' Offensive against the Trade Unions* (New York: International, 1927), 22.

6. Dunn, *Americanization of Labor*, 18–19, 22; "Report of General Organizer [James J.] Sheehe," *Plumbers, Gas and Steam Fitters Journal* (Chicago) 23, no. 1 (January 1918): 18; Leon Goodelman, *Look at Labor: The Story of Industrial War and Peace* (New York: Modern Age Books, 1940), 121.

7. Goodelman, *Look at Labor*, 121.

8. *Harlow's Weekly*, December 10, 1920; "Union Pickets' Licked with Kindness," *Law and Labor* (League for Industrial Rights & American Anti-Boycott Association, New York) 3, no. 2 (February 1921), 41–42.

9. Carol Holderby Welsh, "Cattle Market for the World: The Oklahoma National Stockyards," *Chronicles of Oklahoma* 60 (1982), 42–55; Roy Stewart, *Born Grown: The Story of Oklahoma City* (Oklahoma City: Fidelity National Bank/Metro Press, 1974), 140; Lucyl Shirk, *Oklahoma City: Capital of Soonerland* (Oklahoma City: Oklahoma City Board of Education, 1957), 217; W. F. Kerr and Ina Gainer, *The Story of Oklahoma City* (Chicago: S. J. Clarke, 1922), 313–17, 326–27. Each of these sources, all basically booster histories, called the payment to the packers a "bonus" or, at best, an "inducement."

10. Kerr and Gainer, *The Story of Oklahoma*, 313–17, 326–27; Rudolf Alexander Clemens, *The American Livestock and Meat Industry* (New York: Ronald Press, 1923), 256–57. Clemens was editor of the packers' journal *The National Provisioner* and generally defends the packers' business practices. On the other hand, his work contains a large amount of useful information on the industry in the early twentieth century.

11. Murray Philip Horowitz and Jules Shevitz, *The Oklahoma Public Health Surveys: Oklahoma City* (Oklahoma City: Oklahoma Tuberculosis Association, 1919), 51–52, 57, 68.

12. Ibid., 16–24.

13. Members' certificates of Local 92 in H. C. Schilling Papers, vertical file "Unions," Oklahoma Historical Society Research Center; Jimmy M. Skaggs, *Prime Cut: Livestock Raising and Meat Packing in the United States, 1607–1983* (College Station: Texas A&M University Press, 1986), 125–28. Skaggs's book includes a good, clearly detailed description of each job on the assembly line; Brody, *The Butcher Workmen*, 76–77; William Z. Foster, *Pages from a Worker's Life* (New York: International, 1939), 153–59.

14. Brody, *The Butcher Workmen*, 79–82; Foster, *Pages from a Worker's Life*, 153–56; *New York Times*, December 1, 1920; *Packer Consent Decree*, document no. 219, 68th Congress, 2nd

sess., serial 8413 (Washington, D.C.: Government Printing Office, 1924–1925); "Statement of Edward Morris, President of Morris & Company," in *Hearings before the Committee on Interstate and Foreign Commerce of the House of Representatives, Sixty-Fifth Congress, Third Session, on HR 13324, January 21 to January 30, 1919, Part 4; Government Control of Meat-Packing Industry* (Washington, D.C.: Government Printing Office, 1919), 1025.

15. Rayback, *A History of American Labor*, 291.

16. Brody, *The Butcher Workmen*, 96, 97–104; Skaggs, *Prime Cut*, 160; Theodore V. Purcell, *The Worker Speaks His Mind on Company and Union* (Cambridge, Mass.: Harvard University Press, 1953), 50; Clemens, *The American Livestock and Meat Industry*, 720n; Taft, *Organized Labor in American History*, 366–67.

17. Gary Nall, "King Cotton in Rural Oklahoma," in *Rural Oklahoma*, edited by Donald Green (Oklahoma City: Oklahoma Historical Society, 1977), 46–47; John Thompson, *Closing the Frontier: Radical Response in Oklahoma 1889–1923* (Norman: University of Oklahoma Press, 1986), 169–70, 172; "Strikes and Lockouts," *Monthly Labor Review*, May 1922, 182; *Harlow's Weekly*, September 16, 1921.

18. *Postal Record: A Monthly Journal of the National Association of Letter Carriers* 34, no. 1 (January 1921), 7; *Harlow's Weekly*, April 15, 1921; Kerr and Gainer, *The Story of Oklahoma City*, 496; Stewart, *Born Grown*, 205.

19. *Daily Oklahoman*, April 28, 1921; *Harlow's Weekly*, May 6, 1921.

20. *Daily Oklahoman*, May 21, August 10, and August 23, 1921; Selig Perlman and Philip Taft, *History of Labor in the United States, 1896–1932, Vol. IV: Labor Movements* (New York: Macmillan, 1935), 498–99.

21. Brody, *The Butcher Workmen*, 99-100; Perlman and Taft, *History of Labor*, 499–500.

22. Brody, *The Butcher Workmen*, 99–100; Perlman and Taft, *History of Labor*, 499–500; Clemens, *The American Livestock and Meat Industry*, 720n.

23. Brody, *The Butcher Workmen*, 101.

24. *Oklahoma Federationist* (Oklahoma City), September 16, 1921; *Daily Oklahoman*, September 16, 1921.

25. *Oklahoma Federationist*, September 16, October 1921. With the October issue, the *Federationist* went from weekly to monthly publication.

26. *Oklahoma Federationist*, September 23, October 1921.

27. *Daily Oklahoman*, October 1, 1921; *Harlow's Weekly*, September 16, October 7, October 28, 1921; January 13, 1922.

28. Reprinted as "The Open Shop—An Analysis," in *The Mixer and Server* 31, no. 1 (January 15, 1922) 35–36. This was the Cincinnati-based monthly journal of the Hotel and Restaurant Employees International Alliance and Bartenders' International League of America.

29. *Harlow's Weekly*, December 15, 1921.

30. *Daily Oklahoman*, November 21, 1921.

31. Both Connally's "Report by the Commissioner of Labor on Effects of the Packing Industry and the Strike of Packinghouse Workers in Oklahoma City, December 31, 1921"

and Purdy's report are cited in Ellis Donham, "Labor," unpublished manuscript in vertical files "Unions," Oklahoma Historical Society Research Center, 25, 32–33. Donham's manuscript was intended as a portion of the *Labor History of Oklahoma* but the material that did appear in that book seems severely edited.

32. Donham, "Labor," 25–26.

33. Brody, *The Butcher Workmen*, 101–102; Henry Pelling, *American Labor* (Chicago: University of Chicago Press, 1960), 141–42.

34. *Oklahoma City Times*, December 2, 1921.

35. The figure of one thousand comes from Donham, "Labor" (p. 30) and *Labor History of Oklahoma* (p. 48). Some argument remains over just how many workers left the plant. Albert McRill says only five hundred walked out, as does Roy Stewart (*Born Grown*, 206). But McRill cites no sources and Stewart merely quotes McRill. It is clear, however, that if the union represented only about 200 to 250 workers, then a majority of the strikers were non-union workers. See Albert McRill, *And Satan Came Also* (Oklahoma City: Britton, 1955), 192.

36. Donham, "Labor," 27.

37. All editorials cited verbatim in *Harlow's Weekly*, December 15, December 30, 1921.

38. *Oklahoma City Times*, December 8, 1921; William McBee, *The Oklahoma Revolution* (Oklahoma City: Modern Publishers, 1956), 24–25.

39. *Industrial Solidarity* (IWW-Chicago), January 7, 14, 21, 1922; Melvyn Dubofsky, *We Shall Be All: A History of the Industrial Workers of the World* (Champaign: University of Illinois Press, 2000); *Oklahoma News*, December 28, 1921; *Daily Oklahoman*, December 28, 1921.

40. *Daily Oklahoman*, December 29, 1921.

41. Donham, "Labor," 33–35; *Labor History of Oklahoma*, 48.

42. Donham, "Labor," 28; Walter Fogel, "Blacks in Meatpacking: Another View of the Jungle," *Industrial Relations* 10 (1981), 341–43, and *The Negro in the Meat Industry*, Report no. 12, Racial Policies of American Industry (Philadelphia: Wharton School of Finance and Commerce, University of Pennsylvania, 1970), 34–38; Philip S. Foner, *Organized Labor and the Black Worker 1619–1981*, 2nd ed. (New York: International Publishers, 1982), 143; Scott Ellsworth, *Death in the Promised Land, The Tulsa Riot of 1921* (Baton Rouge: Louisiana State University, 1992).

43. *Daily Oklahoman*, December 29, 1921, January 18, 1922; *Labor History of Oklahoma*, 49; Donham, "Labor," 25, 37.

44. *Oklahoma News*, January 18, 1922; *Oklahoma City Times*, January 18, 1922; Donham, "Labor," 37–38.

45. Donham, "Labor," 38–39; McBee, *The Oklahoma Revolution*, 24–25.

46. *Oklahoma City Times*, January 19, 1922; Donham, "Labor," 40.

47. *Daily Oklahoman*, January 25, 1922. McRill (*And Satan Came Also*, 192) wrongly claims that nine white union members alone made up the lynch mob. Roscoe Dunjee's

Black Dispatch, an African American newspaper that sympathized with the strikers, seemed less concerned that a black strikebreaker was lynched than that African Americans made up part of the lynch mob.

48. Cited in *Harlow's Weekly*, January 27, 1922.

49. Donham, "Labor," 41; *Labor History of Oklahoma*, 49.

50. Purcell, *The Worker Speaks His Mind*, 51; Brody, *The Butcher Workmen*, 105.

51. Brody, *The Butcher Workmen*, 158; *Daily Oklahoman*, September 19, 1942.

CHAPTER 7

"Spirited Away"

RACE, GENDER, AND MURDER IN
OKLAHOMA IN THE 1920s

Christienne M. McPherson

On August 8, 1922, Wellington ("Wellie") Adair, a young wife and mother of two children, was found murdered in the front yard of her home in rural Mayes County, Oklahoma. She had been severely beaten and stabbed multiple times while her two young children watched helplessly from inside the house. The violent attack struck fear into the community, and authorities searched for a motive and a murderer. The police quickly found a suspect, an orphaned, thirteen-year-old African American boy named Elias Ridge, who lived on the Adair property with his tenant farmer uncle.[1] The circumstances surrounding Mrs. Adair's murder and the trial of Elias Ridge reflect the precarious state of race relations in Oklahoma in the 1920s and shed light on how Oklahomans were deeply attuned to national politics of gender, race, and law and order.

Following the Civil War, African Americans looked to Oklahoma, then known as Indian Territory (divided into Indian Territory and Oklahoma Territory from 1890 to 1907), as a potential haven from the racial prejudice and economic and political oppression of the South. In addition to its agricultural economy, African Americans were drawn to Oklahoma because of its territorial status—and with a mind to its probable statehood. For a U.S. territory to become a state meant creating a state constitution and legal code, and this held enormous promise for racial equality. Numerous African

American towns developed across the territory, many with their own news-papers and growing economic strength, but the actual population of African Americans within the territory remained small. African Americans made up less than 4.1 percent of the population in 1889, and though their popula-tion had doubled by 1910, they still made up less than 10 percent of the gen-eral population.[2]

A small but active and vocal group of African Americans arose at the turn of the twentieth century and fought for their rights. One of Oklahoma's most influential African American professionals, W. H. Twine, Sr., of Tulsa, led a significant statewide campaign to keep racial segregation out of the Oklahoma Constitution. The debate over racial segregation in the constitution almost caused the territorial government to dissolve, but eventually the state con-stitution was written without any segregation clauses, and African American Oklahomans felt empowered.[3]

Oklahoma held enormous potential for African Americans, but it also held an equal or greater amount of adversity that had to be faced and over-come for true racial progress to be made. Numerous Jim Crow laws were quickly written into the state's legal code.[4] These racist laws were founded on two basic principles. The first was that African Americans were not individu-als capable of either success or failure, good or evil, being civically upstanding or scandalous—they were a deviant and inferior race, a criminal and ignorant people intent on harming the white race and thus requiring segregation. The second principle behind Jim Crow laws was that whites, because of their moral and cultural superiority, had the right to separate themselves from African Americans and to limit their upward mobility. Jim Crow laws in Oklahoma segregated nearly all aspects of life into white and colored. Separate facilities were the least of black Oklahomans' worries in Jim Crow America, however.[5]

With Jim Crow laws based on the premise of African American inferior-ity creating racial separation, crime and race became intricately intermingled, and many saw vigilantism as a necessary check on black criminality. Lynching and race riots became very effective means of maintaining the political, eco-nomic, and social subordination of African Americans throughout the coun-try. Lynching peaked in the United States in the 1890s but it continued to be a substantial threat to African Americans well into the 1920s.[6]

In April 1902, in Oklahoma Territory and Indian Territory, mobs of whites forced African American townspeople to flee their homes in Law-ton and Shawnee. Similar incidents of violence or threatened violence forced African Americans to relocate in Sapulpa, Braggs, Holdenville, and Clare-more. In Oklahoma between 1882 and 1927 there were 141 persons lynched.

Only forty-two were black, but this statistic is somewhat deceiving. Until 1900 most of the victims of lynch mobs in Oklahoma were white men accused of murder or a crime related to cattle rustling, but after that year lynching in the state took on a racial agenda, and racial violence did not decrease after Oklahoma achieved statehood. From 1908 to 1927 there were at least forty-one reported lynchings; thirty-two of these were of African Americans.[7]

Oklahomans' open acceptance of lynching was common knowledge to the rest of the country.[8] This was not just an Oklahoma phenomenon or even just a Southern phenomenon, however. While most lynching did occur in the South—up to 95 percent of lynchings in the 1920s occurred there—the only states in which a lynching was not reported were Massachusetts, Rhode Island, New Hampshire, and Vermont.[9] Between 1882 and 1927, at least 4,951 individuals were lynched in the United States, and 71 percent were African American.[10] Lynching was not an individual instance of a spike in vigilantism. Lynchings were community events that often took on festive tones, with men, women, and children watching, participating, and even taking souvenirs. Photographic records of these lynchings were reproduced commercially for white communities to commemorate their execution of justice.[11] According to historian Amy Louise Wood, "Mobs performed lynchings as spectacles for other whites. The rituals, the tortures, and their subsequent representations imparted powerful messages to whites about their own supposed racial dominance and superiority. These spectacles produced and disseminated images of white power and black degradation, of white unity and black criminality."[12] Because of the cultural significance of lynching, and the fact that leading community members, including judges, police, and future jurors, were often participants, members of a lynch mob were rarely prosecuted.[13]

Full-fledged race riots, where African American communities were attacked en masse, arose from even small threats of racial intermixing or racial violence. Between 1900 and 1930, race riots broke out across the country. Not atypical, in August 1904 during a riot in Statesboro, Georgia, an African American boy was beaten, based "on general principles."[14] Atlanta, Georgia, and Brownsville, Texas, both experienced race riots during the summer of 1906, while sites of such riots in 1917 included Houston, Texas; Dewey, Oklahoma; and East St. Louis, Illinois. Twenty-six race riots occurred in U.S. municipalities within the course of a single season in 1919, called afterward "the Red Summer," including clashes in Longview, Texas; Washington, D.C.; Chicago; Omaha; Knoxville and Nashville, Tennessee; Elaine, Arkansas; and Charleston, South Carolina. Most of these riots developed out of a combination of increased economic competition between poor whites and African

Figure 7.1. 1921 lynching near Mannford, Oklahoma. Courtesy of the Research Division of the Oklahoma Historical Society.

Americans, racial stereotypes, inflammatory newspaper reports, and individual incidents of alleged or real transgressions of social boundaries.[15]

Oklahoma found itself host to one of the worst race riots in the history of the nation during the summer of 1921 in Tulsa. Tulsa had a booming African American district called Greenwood by the 1920s. African Americans often called the neighborhood "Dreamland" after one of the black theaters there. Whites sometimes called it "Black Wall Street" or a number of other, less appealing nicknames.[16] Greenwood was home to two theaters, four hotels, dozens of restaurants, grocery stores, barbershops, a YMCA, a roller rink, two newspapers, and a variety of professional offices. The neighborhood also claimed a number of churches, two schools, a branch of the public library, and an African American hospital.[17] It was a shining example of black economic mobility in the United States. The approximately thirty-five square blocks of Greenwood were home to most of the African American citizens of Tulsa.[18]

A rough-and-tumble oil town, Tulsa up to this point had never seen the lynching of an African American. It had, however, quite a reputation for its violence and crime. The Prohibition Era and Oklahoma's youth as a state were the perfect mixture for a robust life of bootlegging, gambling, prostitution, and general crime.[19] Tension in the city escalated in 1921 when Tulsa civic leaders began aggressively fighting the town's reputation as a vice city. The *Tulsa Tribune* was a major proponent of a law and order campaign, and in May the newspaper began running articles claiming that race was the cause of the city's high crime rate. Articles blamed African Americans porters for rampant prostitution in the city and uncovered interracial dancing at a roadhouse, publishing tales assured to shock white Tulsans into action.[20]

A seemingly insignificant event that occurred on Memorial Day, May 30, set the city ablaze. Dick Rowland, a nineteen-year-old African American shoe shiner, and Sarah Page, a seventeen-year-old white elevator operator both worked in downtown Tulsa. There was a no "colored" bathroom in the shoe shining shop were Rowland worked, so his employer arranged for the black employees to use the only "colored" bathroom in downtown Tulsa, on the fourth floor of the Drexel Building where Page worked. On this particular day, Rowland went to the Drexel Building for just this reason. As he got into the elevator, something happened that caused Page to scream and Rowland to flee the scene. The most likely event is that the elevator jerked as Rowland was entering it. Rowland then stumbled and grabbed her arm. Page "said later she thought she stumbled against him herself, and was nervous, so she screamed."[21] Whatever the events that took place inside the elevator, outside a white clerk heard her scream, saw Rowland fleeing, and called the police.[22]

The police conducted a very low-key investigation, and the next day, May 31, Dick Rowland was arrested for assault. Later that day the *Tulsa Tribune* printed a front-page story: "Nab Negro for Attacking Girl in an Elevator," which claimed that Rowland had viciously attacked Page, tearing her clothing and scratching her face. It painted Page as an innocent, hard-working, and down-on-her-luck girl.[23] Later the chief of police alleged that her character was more than questionable.[24] It is also believed that an editorial was run the same day, also in the *Tulsa Tribune,* with the headline "To Lynch a Negro Tonight." The original editions of that day's paper have since been destroyed, so the editorial's existence and content still continue to be a matter of conjecture.[25]

Riled by the media accounts, hundreds of white men and women gathered on the lawn of the courthouse after work. The sheriff had received an anonymous call earlier that day warning of a lynching. As darkness fell, the crowd began calling for the release of Rowland into its hands, but the newly appointed sheriff, Willard M. McCullough, refused. Several African American World War I veterans and prominent businessmen who had heard of the crowd amassing at the courthouse believed that the men of Greenwood needed to organize to protect Rowland. Several men argued against the action, but by 9:00 P.M. a group of twenty-five armed African Americans went to the courthouse, where they were turned away by the sheriff. The audacity of these men to show up armed to prevent a lynching outraged many whites in the crowd. The throng began to grow, reaching numbers as high as two thousand men, women, children, curious citizens, and threatening would-be lynchers. Not even local white leaders could force the group to disperse. One white eyewitness later described the scene, saying, "a great many of these persons lining the sidewalks were holding a rifle in one hand, and grasping the neck of a liquor bottle with the other."[26]

Several small groups of African American men returned to the courthouse to protect Rowland, and Sheriff McCullough again turned them away. As they were leaving, one white man apparently tried to take away a black veteran's gun. This created a struggle, causing the gun to go off. The whites began to open fire on the African Americans on the courthouse lawn. The African American men retreated to Greenwood. At this point, the mob was no longer concerned with Dick Rowland and his innocence, guilt, or whereabouts. Whites clamored that a "Negro uprising" was underway. The police began deputizing hundreds of white citizens, giving them badges or ribbons for identification purposes. These "special deputies" were supposed to work in conjunction with the police department to restore order, but they reportedly had been told by low-ranking officers to "get a gun and get a nigger."[27] These so-called deputies were one of the most destructive elements in the mob.

The fighting continued into the early hours of June 1 as whites and blacks exchanged fire on the outskirts of Greenwood along the Frisco railroad tracks. Several small groups of whites ventured into the Greenwood district, shooting into random houses and setting fires. More than twenty businesses burned down. When the Tulsa Fire Department sent a crew into Greenwood to fight the blazes, it was turned away by a white mob.[28] While some citizens of Greenwood took up arms to defend themselves and their community, the majority of African Americans decided to flee the area. By 2:00 A.M. the white attackers appeared to have tired and the fighting died down. The residents at Greenwood sighed in relief, believing that the fray was over and that they had successfully held their own and protected most of their community. This was not the case, however. The whites reassembled in downtown Tulsa and brooded over their disgust and outrage at the "Negro uprising." Within an hour, rumors circulated that five hundred African American men from Muskogee had commandeered a train and were coming to Tulsa, and that a group of African American men had killed a white woman in a white Tulsa neighborhood. Members of the group began organizing a new attack to take place at daybreak. [29]

As it got closer to dawn, somewhere between five thousand and ten thousand whites began to reassemble in small groups around Greenwood. At approximately 5:00 A.M. on June 1, the second invasion of the neighborhood began. A whistle blew and whites entered Greenwood in a coordinated manner.[30] Whites went building by building, forcing the occupants out into the streets where they were arrested by National Guards and police or other uniformed men, who were supposedly there to protect them from the mob. The mob then looted and set more buildings on fire. Some Greenwood residents who resisted or were found with ammunition or weapons were summarily shot. National Guards and police both fired upon community residents. Thomas Higgins, a white man who was visiting Tulsa at the time from Wichita, was shocked by the events. He reported, "I saw men of my own race, sworn officers, on three occasions search Negroes while their hands were up and not finding weapons, extracted what money they found on them. If the Negro protested, he was shot."[31]

Oklahoma City National Guard units arrived around 9:15 A.M. Sometime after noon martial law was declared, and then the state troops moved into Greenwood, disarming the whites that were left, and clearing the district. By eight that evening the riot had officially ended. Those blacks who had been detained by police and National Guards were released over the next week, but they returned home to little but ashes. The official death count stood at 39, but newspapers reported death tolls of 75 to 175, and the Red Cross estimated up to 300 deaths, nearly all of them African Americans.[32] Several African Americans faced charges related to the riot, but these were quickly dropped, and no whites were ever charged for any crime committed during the events of May 31 and June 1. Months later Dick Rowland was released from jail because Sarah Page refused to testify at his trial.[33]

It was in this atmosphere of racial tension, violence, and vigilantism that the fate of Mrs. Wellie Adair and young Elias Ridge became intertwined a year later. As already described, on August 8, 1922, in rural Mayes County, approximately sixty miles from Tulsa, Mrs. Adair was murdered in the yard of her home while her two children watched from inside the house. Her husband was working the family's fields at the time. According to later newspaper reports, Wellie Adair had been brutally bludgeoned and also stabbed numerous times in the neck and upper body. Authorities believed that the assault had transpired for almost twenty minutes before she succumbed. Her children had been found locked in the house.[34]

Soon after police initiated their investigation, they focused on an African American tenant farmer, Hardy Smith. Smith informed police during an interrogation that he had witnessed his orphaned nephew, thirteen-year-old Elias Ridge, committing the crime. Ridge resided with his uncle and aunt on the Adair property. Police officers arrested Ridge and began to interrogate him. Smith was then arrested for being an accomplice to the murder. Once Smith had implicated Elias Ridge, the boy had little hope of escaping the prejudiced legal system of Oklahoma, despite the evidence. Described in court documents and newspaper accounts as being five feet tall and weighing 105 pounds, Ridge was small compared to the victim, who weighed approximately 180 pounds and was described as a healthy and robust woman.[35]

Elias's aunt either chose not to be present or was not allowed to be present during his interrogation. Either way, Elias was questioned without any adult representative present. During the relentless questioning, which unfolded over a considerable number of hours, Elias confessed to the murder. He claimed that his uncle had instructed him to kill Mrs. Adair, for which Elias was supposed to receive a pig in payment. Police pushed Ridge hard because he claimed to have no idea why Hardy Smith wanted the woman dead. His confession was full of inconsistencies regarding how he had committed the murder.[36]

After his confession, Ridge was taken out of the county to the Craig County Jail in nearby Vinita, Oklahoma. There, in spite of having been removed to the Craig County facility to avoid local mob hostility, he was twice almost lynched. "Preparations had been made for a shoe-string party," according to the *Tulsa*

Daily World. "The rope had been secured, the tree selected and everything was in readiness."[37] The local sheriff, Ridenhour, however, admirably stepped in to protect his prisoner. He personally kept a mob at bay the first time, and for the second attempted lynching he was better prepared. He positioned armed guards around the jail and on all of the roads leaving the town. He then disguised Ridge as a farmer, hiding him behind a door, and invited the mob to inspect the jail. While the mob searched for Ridge, the sheriff slipped him outside and into a taxi, which "spirited him away" about thirty miles to Pryor, the seat of Mayes County, and the jail there. The next morning the vigilantes learned of the sheriff's successful ruse and began looking for the taxi driver, but he too had fled town.[38]

Having escaped vigilante justice, Ridge then faced Oklahoma's legal justice system. At the start of the business day on September 12, 1922, Ridge was brought to the juvenile court of Mayes County in Pryor, where he stood before the juvenile judge, T. L. Marteney. Marteney deemed Ridge capable of understanding the immorality and severity of the crime and decided that he should be tried as an adult for the murder. Ridge's case was immediately transferred to the county's district court. At his initial appearance in front of the magistrate of Mayes County, Ridge was appointed counsel, public defender A. H. Fisher. Fisher advised him to waive his right to a preliminary hearing. His case was then moved forward immediately. Less than ninety minutes later, the district court trial commenced. Fisher advised Ridge to plead guilty and waive his right to a trial by jury. The attorney then announced to the court that Ridge wanted to do so, without Ridge ever having personally spoken a word to the court. With the guilty plea, no witnesses were called for either side. Fisher then waived Ridge's right to separate hearings for conviction and sentencing. Thus by the end of the day on September 12, 1922, the district judge for Mayes County, Oklahoma, A. C. Brewster, had presided over the trial, convicted Ridge of the murder, and sentenced him to death by electrocution. This boy, barely a teenager, was sentenced to be stripped of his life within the bounds of the Oklahoma legal system, with no adult guardian having been present at any point, and all this was accomplished within less than ninety minutes.[39]

Wellie Adair's murder and the successful prosecution of Elias Ridge was celebrated by the local press and made headlines across the state and eventually in national newspapers. Having already acknowledged the racial problems of Oklahoma evidenced by the race riot in Tulsa, African American leaders saw the celebration of the conviction and pending execution of such a young black boy as disturbing—and potentially as a serious case of malicious prosecution and injustice. Dr. Baxter A. Whitby, the president of the Oklahoma

Figure 7.2. Ku Klux Klan gathering in Oklahoma, 1923. Courtesy of the Western History Collections, University of Oklahoma Libraries, Blue Clark Collection, 13.

branch of the National Association for the Advancement of Colored People (NAACP), was outraged by the events surrounding the case, especially the attempted lynching of Ridge while he was in jail. Whitby urged the NAACP to fund Ridge's appeals and to find the best possible lawyer to take on the case. He believed that Ridge was the victim of the racially charged atmosphere of the area. Whitby professed, "The whole state is a network of K.K.K. and seething with prejudice. It is almost next to impossible to get a fair decision in court, even for a white man, without the [support of] the Klan."[40] To counter the Klan's influence, Ridge fortunately found great support from Whitby and the NAACP.[41]

Whitby arranged for the Oklahoma chapter of the NAACP to take on the case, but the national office informed him that it would be unable to provide funds for an appeal. Whitby then turned to surrounding black communities for support, and he managed to gather enough in donations for the first appeal, a total of $90. He then persuaded W. H. Twine, Jr., an experienced attorney in racial and constitutional law (and the son of a civil rights activist in Oklahoma during the founding of the state), to take the case at no charge. Father and son had devoted much of their lives to fighting racial injustice, and this case was another example of the injustice that threatened the security of all African Americans in the state.[42]

W. H. Twine, Jr., played a significant role in fighting for the freedom and life of Elias Ridge, and in maintaining national attention on his plight. Twine's first step was to have W. D. Matthews, the state commissioner of charities and corrections, appointed as Ridge's guardian. Matthews actively participated in the appellate efforts and used his state authority to benefit Ridge whenever he could. Twine then began combing through the record, constructing an appeal.[43]

Twine did not set out to prove Ridge's innocence, although Elias claimed adamantly after his conviction that he was indeed innocent. Instead Twine fought for the appeal based on the fact that the original trial had been unconstitutionally hasty, and his belief that Ridge lacked the capacity to assist in his own defense or to waive his right to trial by jury. If the court would not or could not go so far as to set Ridge free, he was at least deserving of a new trial.[44]

Twine's appeal rested foremost on his contention that Elias Ridge was mentally incapable of understanding the seriousness of the crime or the charges against him because of his youth. In cases involving minors, the prosecution had the burden to prove that youths between the ages of seven and sixteen had the mental capacity to understand their actions and the consequences of those actions to the same degree that adults would. Twine argued that there was no positive evidence that Ridge had that degree of mental capacity, and that he should have been tried in juvenile Court instead of the district court. He also argued that a jury should have been called to determine if the prosecution had enough evidence to meet that burden. The defense claimed that Ridge, contrary to the findings of the juvenile court magistrate, was of below average intelligence, functioning at the level "of an ordinary child of the third or fourth grade in school."[45] This was most evident by his written confession, which showed a lack of grammatical skills. Twine also held that, as a child— especially one of below-average intelligence, Ridge was not capable of countering his attorney's insistence that he waive the right to a trial by jury without a parent or legal guardian present.[46]

Twine also argued that the defense attorney had seriously failed Ridge by rushing the case through without allowing him to speak, by encouraging him to plead guilty, and by waiving the boy's right to a trial by jury. He also argued that Fisher had been deficient and "made no objections . . . through fear of the mob."[47] Twine and the NAACP believed that the timing and the racial climate of the area had influenced the participants in the case, whether intentionally or not, all the way from the lowest-level officials to the judges. For evidence they cited the fact that the attorney general, days prior to the trial, had stated that 99 percent of the people in Mayes County were calling for the death of Ridge for the murder.[48]

In addition to Ridge's age and lack of intelligence and the mob atmosphere that surrounded the case, Twine raised two other major issues in Ridge's appeal. He argued that it was irrational for Ridge to be sentenced to death by electrocution inasmuch as the same court had sentenced Hardy Smith, an adult and the alleged mastermind of the crime (if one believed Ridge's confession), to a lesser punishment. Several days after Ridge had been convicted in September 1922, Smith was had also been charged and quickly convicted for his role in the murder of Wellie Adair. He was convicted on a murder charge, not the lesser charge of being an accomplice to murder, yet he, a grown man, had been sentenced to life in prison. Twine also censured the Mayes County Sheriff's Department and county solicitor because all of the evidence from the original trial had been destroyed directly after the trial concluded. Twine hinted that this had been done intentionally to either cover up improprieties or to prevent any attempt by Ridge to mount an appeal. Regardless of the motive, Twine maintained that since the evidence was not properly preserved, any attempts the defendant might make to appeal were prejudiced. In addition, because of the haste with which the trial was held, little to no evidence could have been collected anyway, especially in support of the defense. In fact, by the time W. H. Twine took over as Ridge's defense attorney for his appeals at the end of 1922, not only was the evidence gone, the original court transcripts had been destroyed as well. Twine argued that not only was the defense thus hindered, but also that the prosecution would be unable to mount a new case persuasive beyond a reasonable doubt, and that the conviction should be overturned and any further prosecution barred.[49]

The Oklahoma Appellate Court agreed, decided that trying Elias Ridge under such circumstances would not be a faithful representation of the true function and spirit of the legal system. Specifically the Appellate Court charged that Ridge's having been brought before Juvenile Court, magistrate hearing, and district court all within an hour and a half had infringed on his rights to due process. The Appellate Court also acknowledged that Ridge had the right to a trial by jury in the juvenile court, and the appellate decision stated that the court had erred in allowing Ridge to waive rights that as a juvenile were not his to waive. In their response to the appeal, the attorney general and other prosecuting attorneys admitted that Ridge should not have been sentenced to death and that his youth should have been taken into consideration before he was allowed to relinquish his rights within criminal procedure. Thus the Appellate Court declared, "the circumstances must be inquired of by a jury and the infant [Ridge was] not to be convicted upon his confession."[50] On December 18, 1923, the Appellate Court reversed Ridge's conviction, and new charges were filed against him in the District Court of Mayes County. He would be retried for the murder of Wellie Adair the year before.[51]

Ridge's second trial reaffirmed African Americans' belief that blacks accused of criminal activities, especially murder, were not likely to get a fair trial, at least not in Oklahoma. During the trial, however, Twine found an important ally, Charles N. Harmon, a white attorney practicing with ex-governor J. B. A. Robertson. After hearing about the case, Harmon offered his services free of charge to defend Ridge. While the jury and community might not approve of a white attorney representing a black defendant accused of murdering a white woman, they would be less openly hostile to Harmon than they would be toward an African American attorney like Twine.[52] And hostility would dominate the second trial. Facing threats of violence, Twine was forced to reside in the county jail for the course of the trial to protect his own safety. A mob atmosphere swirled around Pryor, where the trial was held, but no organized attempts were made to lynch Twine or Ridge.[53]

In the retrial, Ridge was once again tried as an adult but his right to trial by jury was granted. Twine and Harmon conceded that Ridge participated in the murder, but they argued that he had not acted alone or as the primary assailant. There is little information available about the evidence presented by either the state or the defense in the second trial. The first motive for the crime offered by witnesses for the state was that Ridge had murdered Mrs. Adair because he had wanted to rob her of a large diamond ring she wore regularly. However, the coroner testified that the ring had been removed from her body after her death during examination. Another suggested motive for the murder was Mrs. Adair's strong prohibitionist ways. The likelihood that a thirteen-year-old boy would kill Mrs. Adair for her belief in temperance was critiqued by the defense, though, and neither Ridge nor his uncle could be linked in any way to bootlegging. During his testimony, Ridge returned to the motive he had given in his confession: that his uncle had coerced him to participate in the murder, and that he had been promised a pig as payment for his compliance. He also continued to deny knowing his uncle's motive for murdering Mrs. Adair. The inconsistencies in Ridge's original confession continued to plague his courtroom testimony, and the defense argued that this was evidence that Hardy Smith had been the primary assailant and bore the majority of responsibility for the act.

The jury was apparently unmoved by the defense's reasoning. On April 11, 1924, an all-white jury in the district court of Mayes County convicted Elias Ridge of murder and sentenced him to death by electrocution.[54]

Twine and Harmon wasted no time mourning. They immediately wrote to the Oklahoma City *Black Dispatch*, the largest African American newspaper in the state, asking for financial aid to help fund a second appeal. The editor of the *Black Dispatch* described Twine's valiant efforts to save the youth and the racial opposition he had met in defending the case: "Twine has twice faced alone the mob spirit of this cut-law town Pryor, where men violate the spirit of our Constitution in condemning a helpless child to the gallows. Twine has gone [into] this hell hole of prejudice, single handed and alone, demanding justice and a square deal at the risk of his life."[55]

Even the *Tulsa World*, the major white newspaper for the region, acknowledged the culture of violence that surrounded the case. One article reported, "[The women of Mayes County] are now keeping shotguns just inside their doors. We must have some protection . . . against mob violence and the only way is this boy's execution."[55] Of course, the *Tulsa World's* version of the mob atmosphere reflected the white community's fear that African Americans would retaliate for Ridge's conviction, rather than the actual threats of vigilante violence leveled by local whites against Ridge and his black attorney. The NAACP's continued involvement, the mob atmosphere, and the white community's celebration of a black youth getting the death penalty made the story very enticing for the national media. The *St. Louis Argus*, *New York Times*, *Chicago Tribune*, and other major urban newspapers reported on the case. The national attention brought donations and support from across the country to help Ridge's second appeal. Most donors, black and white, were touched by the defendant's age. If executed, Ridge, then fourteen, would have been the youngest person executed in Oklahoma.[56]

The defense took a similar position in the second appeal that it had argued in Ridge's first appeal, although this time focusing solely on commuting his death sentence to life imprisonment. This tactic of settling for a lesser sentence, whether black defendants were truly innocent or not, was adopted by many defense attorneys in the South. They realized that chances were slim that any black defendant accused of assaulting or murdering a white person, especially a white woman, would be acquitted. They believed that strategically it would be much easier to fight for a lesser sentence than a not-guilty plea. Defense attorneys, for example, adopted this strategy in the much-publicized Scottsboro cases of the 1930s, where nine African American boys were accused of raping two white girls. The lawyers believed that conviction was guaranteed for black youths accused of raping white girls in the United States, in spite of any overwhelming evidence in favor of the defense.[57]

Twine, in the second Ridge appeal, also emphasized the racial unrest of the state and the undeniable influence the atmosphere of racial hatred had played in Ridge's second conviction. This time, however, the court of appeals decided that the second trial was fair and impartial and that the jury was correct in its belief that Ridge had a degree of understanding in relation to the crime. Despite losing the first argument, Twine successfully proved that according to legal precedent the death penalty was uncommonly stringent and did not match the nature of the crime, primarily because of Ridge's youth.[58] Thus the Oklahoma Court of Criminal Appeals commuted the sentence of Elias Ridge to life imprisonment, while saying, "The record shows that this boy is possessed of only ordinary intelligence, coupled with degenerate criminal tendencies, making it unsafe to ever again give him his liberty. For the safety of society he should be kept in the penitentiary at hard labor."[59]

The defense had accomplished its final hope, saving Elias Ridge's life. However hollow the victory might have been, it was by then the most that could have been hoped for in a case where an African American defendant had at one point confessed and pled guilty to a crime against a white woman. Even at the level of the Oklahoma appeals court, prejudice seems evident in its suggestion that a fair trial could be held despite the racially charged location and times.

Later in 1924 Hardy Smith brought his case to the Oklahoma court of criminal appeals. That court decided that there was not enough evidence to link Smith to the crime and that his case should never have gone to trial. The only evidence that the prosecution could use to tie Smith to the murder was the confession of Elias Ridge. The appeals court found that the confession was not reliable, since it could not be corroborated with any material evidence, and that it should not have been used. Thus Hardy Smith's conviction was reversed, and he was released, based on the same evidence that had convicted Ridge and been used to sentence him to death.[60]

The facts of the case aside, and Ridge's innocence or guilt aside, the truth remains that a thirteen-year-old boy was conceived to be competent to waive his constitutional right to a trial by jury at the advice of a court-appointed attorney whom he had known less than one day. He was arrested and tried in two separate courts within an hour and thirty minutes. His attorney in a retrial was forced to seek refuge in the local jail to avoid becoming the target of vigilante violence. The racist violence behind the destruction of an entire African American community in Tulsa in 1921 had definitely influenced the

Ridge case. Mrs. Adair's murder in 1922 had taken place less than sixty miles away from Tulsa. There was no way for Ridge to receive a fair trial in the 1920s in Oklahoma given the crime charged. Being African American was enough to convict him of the crime. In Ridge's second trial there was little more than his race as evidence—the evidence and the transcripts from the first trial had not been preserved.

While it is important to remember that Elias Ridge was an individual and that the unique circumstances of his case led to its outcome, it is also important to recognize that Ridge and his case are part of a larger story of racial inequality and injustice in Oklahoma and elsewhere. The racial tension, vigilante mentality, and notions of African American criminality that dominated Oklahoma during the early 1920s as Ridge fought for his life in the justice system were not unique to the state. This atmosphere reflected national trends of racially targeted violence and vigilantism.

All African American men lived with the reality that if charged with a crime against a white person, especially a white woman, they would likely forfeit their lives, regardless of the evidence supporting their guilt or innocence. If they made it to trial without being lynched, they were typically convicted and sentenced harshly. It was not uncommon for African Americans to plead guilty in hopes of escaping the death penalty, whether or not they had committed a crime.

African Americans had looked upon Oklahoma as a place to break ground, become self-supporting, and even reach a level of success. The state, with its mining and oil and rich agricultural opportunities, had a lot to offer, but even when blacks achieved success it was tenuous. White Oklahomans used Jim Crow laws, lynching, race riots, and their control of the justice system to limit African American achievement. They also reminded blacks that any transgression of the color line, any inappropriate relationship with a white woman or any attack against a white person, would be met with swift justice, legal or not, and severe punishment. The clear message of the times was that white Americans were dominant and superior, and African Americans should remain in their place, at their mercy.

Notes

1. *Tulsa Daily World*, August 9, 1922, and *Ridge v. State of Oklahoma*, 1923 OK CR 25, Okla. Cr. 396, 220, p. 390, and rehearing 1924 OK 28, Okla. Cr. 150, 229, p. 649 (court file on microfilm, Mayes County, Oklahoma, district court collection).

2. Arkansas Colored, Canadian (Colored) Town, Foreman, Gibson Station, Homer, Huttonville, Langston City, Lee, Mabelle, Marshalltown, North Fork Colored, Overton,

Rentie, Sanders, Tullahasee, Wiley, and Wybark were African American towns founded in Indian Territory. Black towns established later, under the Oklahoma territorial government just before it became a state, include Bailey, Boggy Bend, Boley, Bookertee, Brooksville, Chase, Cimarron City, Clarksville, Clearview, Columbia, Emanuel, Douglas, Ferguson, Grayson, Iconium, Lewisville, Liberty, Lima, Lincoln City (Lincoln), Macedonia, Melvin, Oberlin, Pleasant Valley, Redbird, Rentie, Rentiesville, Summit, Taft, Tatums, Udora, Vernon, Wellston, Yahola, and Zion. The African American population remained at around 7 percent of the general population in Oklahoma well into the 1930s before it began to rise again. Arthur Lincoln Tolson, "The Negro in Oklahoma Territory, 1889–1907: A Study of Racial Discrimination" (master's thesis, University of Oklahoma, 1996), 2, 11, 21, 59–60, 108; Larry O'Dell, "All-Black Towns," in *Encyclopedia of Oklahoma History and Culture*, Oklahoma Historical Society, http://digital.library.okstate.edu/encyclopedia/entries/A/AL009.html (accessed January 4, 2013); "All-Black Towns of Oklahoma," map, Oklahoma Historical Society Research Center; Gene Aldrich, *The Black Heritage of Oklahoma* (Edmond: Thompson Book and Supply, 1973), 29.

3. Tolson, "The Negro in Oklahoma Territory," 108.

4. Ibid.

5. Marlon B. Ross, *Manning the Race: Reforming Black Men in the Jim Crow Era* (New York: New York University Press, 2004); Glenda Elizabeth Gilmore, *Gender and Jim Crow: Women and the Politics of White Supremacy in North Carolina, 1896–1920* (Chapel Hill: University of North Carolina Press, 1996).

6. Stewart E. Tolnay and E. M. Beck, *A Festival of Violence: An Analysis of Southern Lynchings, 1882–1930* (Urbana: University of Illinois Press, 1995), 30.

7. Walter White, *Rope and Faggot: A Biography of Judge Lynch* (New York: Arno Press, 1969), 230–32, 257; Tolson, "The Negro in Oklahoma Territory," 37, 40–46.

8. Jimmie Lewis Franklin, *Journey toward Hope: A History of Blacks in Oklahoma* (Norman: University of Oklahoma Press, 1982), 129.

9. W. Fitzhugh Brundage, ed., *Under the Sentence of Death: Lynching in the South* (Chapel Hill: University of North Carolina Press, 1997), 4; Robert A. Gibson, "The Negro Holocaust: Lynching and Race Riots in the United States, 1890–1950," Themes in Twentieth Century American Culture, Yale–New Haven Teachers Institute, 1979, www.yale.edu/ynhti/curriculum/units/1979/2/79.02.04.x.html (accessed January 4, 2013).

10. There are many contradictory accounts as to exactly how many lynchings occurred each year since they began being recorded in 1882. The Tuskegee Institute has a conservative record. Others, such as the *Chicago Tribune* and the NAACP, have independent calculations. However, it is very likely that many lynchings occurred and went unreported or unpublicized. Therefore it is safe to say that all estimates of lynchings in the United States during this period are conservative. Walter White, *Rope and Faggot*, 230–32; National Association for the Advancement of Colored People, *Thirty Years of Lynching in the US, 1889–1918* (New York: Negro Universities Press, 1969); Jimmie Lewis Franklin, *From Slavery to Freedom: A History of American Negroes* (New York: Alfred A. Knopf, 1947).

11. Often clothing, personal items, and even body parts (such as ears) were taken from a lynching victim. Ann Louise Wood, *Lynching and Spectacle: Witnessing Racial Violence in America, 1890–1940* (Chapel Hill: University of North Carolina Press, 2009), 21, 29; Sherrilyn A. Ifill, *On the Courthouse Lawn: Confronting the Legacy of Lynching in the Twenty-first Century* (Boston: Beacon Press, 2007), 57–73; William D. Carrigan, *The Making of a Lynching Culture: Violence and Vigilantism in Central Texas, 1836–1916* (Urbana: University of Illinois Press, 2004).

12. Wood, *Lynching and Spectacle*, 2.

13. Ifill, *On the Courthouse Lawn*, 74–104; Carrigan, *The Making of a Lynching Culture*.

14. This "general principles" reasoning was a common justification for racial violence. For more on the justifications whites used to excuse racial violence see Clark, "A History of the Ku Klux Klan in Oklahoma;" Ida B. Wells, *The Red Record*; Southern Poverty Law Center, *A Hundred Years of Terror: A Special Report*; Franklin, *From Slavery to Freedom*, 433.

15. James Weldon Johnson was the first to call it "The Red Summer." Gibson, "The Negro Holocaust," 5–7; Richard Wormser, *The Rise and Fall of Jim Crow: The African American Struggle against Discrimination, 1865–1954* (New York: Franklin Watts, 1999), 99; *The Tulsa Race Riot: A Report by the Oklahoma Commission to Study the Tulsa Race Riot of 1921* (Oklahoma City: Oklahoma Commission to Study the Tulsa Race Riot of 1921, 2001), iv; Franklin, *From Slavery to Freedom*, 433–75.

16. *The Tulsa Race Riot*, 38–39; Hannibal B. Johnson, *Black Wall Street: From Riot to Renaissance in Tulsa's Historic Greenwood District* (Austin, Tex.: Eakin Press, 1998), vii.

17. *The Tulsa Race Riot*, 22–23.

18. Ibid., iv.

19. Carter Blue Clark, "A History of the Ku Klux Klan in Oklahoma" (PhD diss., University of Oklahoma, 1976), 11.

20. *The Tulsa Race Riot*, 55.

21. Frances W. Prentice, "Oklahoma Race Riot," *Scribner's Magazine*, no. 90 (August 1931), 151–56.

22. *The Tulsa Race Riot*, 57; Johnson, *Black Wall Street*, 199.

23. *The Tulsa Race Riot*, 58.

24. Reports by the police chief following the riot mentioned the possibility that Page was of a disreputable nature and had recently left her husband in Kansas City and moved to Tulsa. He then filed for divorce. This is discussed in more detail in Jonathan Larsen, "Tulsa Burning," *North Tulsa*, 1997, www.northtulsa.com/tulsa_burning .html (accessed January 7, 2013).

25. *The Tulsa Race Riot*, 59.

26. "The Questions that Remain: Timeline," *Tulsa World*, www.tulsaworld.com/special-projects/news/race-riot/timeline.aspx (accessed February 10, 2013); *The Tulsa Race Riot*, 64.

27. Laurel G. Buck, a white bricklayer, testified to this statement in court. For more information, see Attorney General's Civil Case Files, Case 1062, State Archives Division, Oklahoma Department of Libraries. See also *The Tulsa Race Riot*, 64–65.

28. *The Tulsa Race Riot*, 65–66.

29. Ibid., 64–70.

30. The origin of the whistle is still unknown. However, it is noted in almost all of the accounts of the riot, including National Guard reports. It served as a signal of coordinated attack on Greenwood. *The Tulsa Race Riot*, 157.

31. Ibid., 72–78.

32. Johnson, *Black Wall Street*, 201.

33. *The Tulsa Race Riot*, 82, 167.

34. *Tulsa Daily World*, August 9, 1922; *Ridge v. State of Oklahoma*, first appeal, Mayes County, Oklahoma, District Court file.

35. Ibid.

36. *Smith v. State of Oklahoma*, 1924 OK CR 27, Okla. Cr. 206, 226, p. 390.

37. *Tulsa Daily World*, August 11, 1922.

38. *Tulsa Daily World*, August 14, 1922.

39. The Juvenile and District Court files are contained together on microfilm. However, only partial records have been maintained. The majority of filings and court decisions have been retained by the courthouse archives but the court transcripts and evidence lists have been lost or destroyed. Mayes County District Court did not put transcripts or evidence listings on microfilm for cases that occurred prior to the 1970s. *State v. Ridge*, Juvenile Court of Mayes County, Oklahoma, contained in District Court file; *Ridge v. State of Oklahoma*, first death warrant and first appeal, Mayes County District Court file; *Ridge v. State of Oklahoma*, 1923 OK CR 25, Okla. Cr. 396, 220, p. 965.

40. Correspondence between A. Baxter Whitby and Walter White, April 20, 1924, Elias Ridge NAACP file, 1922–1925, NAACP Collection, Library of Congress.

41. First appellate brief sent to national office, 1922, Elias Ridge NAACP file.

42. Walter White, correspondence between national office and all Oklahoma branches, December 27, 1922, Elias Ridge NAACP file; Tolson, "The Negro in Oklahoma Territory," 108.

43. Correspondence between A. Baxter Whitby and Walter F. White, December 21, 1922, Elias Ridge NAACP file.

44. First appellate brief sent to National Office, 1922, Elias Ridge NAACP file.

45. This information was contained in the second appellate case decision, *Ridge v. State of Oklahoma*, 1924 OK CR 28, Okla. Cr. 150, 229, p. 649.

46. First appellate brief sent to national office, 1922, Elias Ridge NAACP file.

47. Ibid.

48. Ibid.; *Black Dispatch*, October 30, 1924.

49. *Ridge v. State of Oklahoma*, 1924 OK CR 28, Okla. Cr. 150, 229, p. 649; first appellate brief sent to national office, 1922, Elias Ridge NAACP file; *Ridge v. State of Oklahoma*, 1923 OK CR 25, Okla. Cr. 396, 220, p. 965.

50. *Tulsa Daily World*, December 19, 1923.

51. *Ridge v. State of Oklahoma*, 1923 OK CR 25, Okla. Cr. 396, 220, p. 965.

52. Robertson, who believed that Ridge was guilty and deserving of his given sentence, disagreed with Harmon's offer to aid Twine and Ridge. Soon after, Harmon and Robertson dissolved their partnership and began practicing law separately. Rumors began immediately, claiming that the Ku Klux Klan might have had something to do with Robertson's avid denunciation. Correspondence between A. Baxter Whitby and Walter White, n.d., Elias Ridge NAACP file; *Black Dispatch*, May 1, 1924.

53. *Tulsa Daily World*, September 14, 1922; *Black Dispatch*, October 30, 1924.

54. *Tulsa Daily World*, September 14, 1922; *Black Dispatch*, October 30, 1924.

55. *Black Dispatch*, October 30, 1924.

56. Article from *Tulsa World* reprinted in its entirety in *Muskogee Cimeter*, December 8, 1923, in Elias Ridge NAACP file. The national articles were quite less dramatic in tone, stating that a thirteen-year-old black boy had been sentenced to electrocution for murdering a white woman and that the case was going to its second appeal. Memorandum to the Board of Directors, April 14, 1924, Elias Ridge NAACP file; correspondence to Walter White, July 25, 1924, Elias Ridge NAACP file; *Oklahoman*, June 5, 1921.

57. For more on the well-known Scottsboro case, see Dan T. Carter, *Scottsboro: A Tragedy of the American South* (New York: Oxford University Press, 1969).

58. *Ridge v. State of Oklahoma*, 1924 OK CR 28, Okla. Cr. 150, 229, p. 649.

59. Ibid.

60. *Smith v. State of Oklahoma*, 1924 OK CR 27, Okla. Cr. 206, 226, p. 390.

CHAPTER 8

Native American Art in Oklahoma

AN INTERPRETATION

Alvin O. Turner

From beginnings in the last quarter of the nineteenth century, Oklahoma artists and institutions played a major role in defining and promoting the development of a unique form of Native American art that became known as either the Bacone or the Oklahoma style of painting. Many aspects of that story have been presented in museum catalogs and scripts or in studies of individual artists, usually written by anthropologists or art historians. This chapter collates information from these sources while adding a broader historical framework for understanding both the role of Oklahoma individuals and institutions in the development of this art form and the subsequent relative decline of Oklahoma influence. At the same time, it suggests other interpretations to enhance a wider understanding of Native American art history.[1]

The story of Native American art in Oklahoma begins in prehistory and continues today. The earliest forms evolved over millennia as diverse populations adapted to the geography, climate, and resources of the land. The oldest known example dates to at least nine thousand years ago: a bison skull on which is painted three lines resembling lightning patterns. Thousands of years later, the Kenton cave dwellers decorated the walls of their dwellings with the first known examples of pictorial art found in the state. Still later, the rich lode of decorated pottery and copper left by the Spiro mounds culture (AD 500–1300) included ornate and highly stylized depictions of humans, snakes, and varied predators.[2]

Together these and similar sources document the continuing use of art in religious and ceremonial functions and for decorative purposes by Native peoples. Baskets, pottery, clothing, and even weapons were adorned with paints, shells, feathers, beads, ribbons, and other materials. The continuing importance of diverse arts may still be seen among numerous tribal people in Oklahoma today. However, these artists have never received the widespread recognition gained by generations of painters from the 1870s to the 1950s.

By the nineteenth century the Plains tribes were noted for the art that adorned their brightly decorated tepees, parfleches, and robes. Typically the women painted a variety of geometric forms on household goods while the men painted vivid pictorial figures of hunts, battles, and similar events or visions. A related development was the creation of a kind of pictographic lingua franca permitting communication among diverse groups. Sioux and Kiowa calendars were built on these practices to maintain chronological records of major events in tribal history.

Many of the prevailing artistic forms and traditions were established as early as the beginning of the century, while others reflected tribal encounters with different groups, changing trade patterns, and new technologies. For example, tribal calendars were painted initially on hides, but native artists began to employ new materials from cloth to paper as the century drew to a close. Tendencies toward adaptation and blending of experiences accelerated after the Civil War as many of these peoples were forced into ever-shrinking domains in Oklahoma and elsewhere.[3]

Despite these adaptations, military conquest and other pressures on the tribes could have led to the virtual disappearance of tribal painting traditions except perhaps for a few tribal calendars. Instead whites and Indians alike began to value Native American painting in new forms. The first giant step toward that development was the ironic by-product of the first systematic effort to "destroy the Indian and save the man" that came in the aftermath of the Red River Wars, the last major outbreak of warfare on the southern plains.[4]

With the ending of hostilities in 1875, the U.S. Army isolated seventy-nine warriors from the Kiowa, Comanche, Cheyenne, and other tribes that had participated in the conflict and removed them to Fort Marion (Castillo San Marcos), Florida, under the command of Captain Richard Henry Pratt. Their imprisonment was intended only to keep them from stirring new conflicts, but Pratt soon introduced a wide variety of reforms and experiments he believed could lead to the prisoners' eventual assimilation. These included extensive commercial and other contact with residents and tourists at nearby St. Augustine. One of his most important innovations was issuing colored pencils and sketchbooks and encouraging the prisoners to sell examples of their pictographic drawings to curiosity seekers. Often called ledger book drawings, many were completed in sketchbooks or on other kinds of paper, but that term has been used since to describe most nineteenth-century Native American painting.[5]

Many art historians and other cultural historians define the Fort Marion experience as the beginning of a distinctive style of Native American painting that reflected "rapport with innovations from the white man as well as tribal traditions."[6] At least twenty-six of the prisoners produced art during their time at Fort Marion, selling books of drawings for as much as two dollars each. Sale of their art created a motive for their continuing interaction with the white economy while creating bridges to the larger culture. That process was always bidirectional, with artists responding to white tools, techniques, and concepts as they defined new forms of art for white audiences. Artists were required to adapt in response to two cultures, neither surrendering to one nor retreating to the other but instead finding a path between tradition and assimilation.

Many of the former prisoners abandoned drawing for sale after they returned to Oklahoma where there was almost no market for those efforts. There they would often work as agency and school employees, scouts, teamsters, missionaries, and farmers. Yet others followed some art-related pursuits at Hampton Institute and then Carlisle Institute, where Pratt continued his assimilationist programs, assisting him in recruiting and teaching tribal youth. In turn those schools and their counterparts that spread on the reservations of the Great Plains introduced yet more students to many of the experiences and tools that had stimulated the artists at Fort Marion.[7]

A few individual artists from Fort Marion continued to produce drawings and paintings in subsequent years. As early as 1880 Howling Wolf (Cheyenne) created a book of drawings illustrating his tribe's history for Captain John Gregory Bourke. In 1898 Kiowa artists Zotom and Ohtetoint completed a number of miniature tepees for James Mooney for an exhibit of the Smithsonian Institution held in Omaha that year. Mooney would also employ those artists, as well as Carl Sweezy, an Arapaho, who had not been at Fort Marion, to illustrate the research he conducted among the plains tribes in Oklahoma. Squint Eyes (Cheyenne) completed yet other projects for the Smithsonian and illustrated a ledger book for Major John Dunlap while at Fort Supply.[8]

Despite the fact that most of the Kiowa artists never completed additional drawings of the kind they had done at Fort Marion, their presence along with other forces stimulating cultural change undoubtedly affected their families and other Kiowas. Further, some scholars depict Ohtetoint as a key figure linking the Fort Marion experience to the next stage for Native American painting in Oklahoma. That is based on the assumption that Ohtetoint influenced his brother Silverhorn, who became one of Mooney's favorite illustrators. In turn, some scholars credit Silverhorn, who also maintained the traditional Kiowa calendar, as a principal teacher of his nephew, Stephen Mopope, one of the Kiowa Five. Mopope would bring national and even international attention to Native American painting.

Mopope identified his uncle as one of his teachers but there are disagreements about the degree of Silverhorn's influence, and that debate may obscure the larger story.[9] Silverhorn's own career and that of other Indian artists during the early twentieth century demonstrate that there were many influences that fostered changes in artistic forms of expression in Native American communities in Oklahoma and elsewhere. The work of anthropologists, the impact of education, and contact with books and photography and other such influences all affected emerging artists. For instance, Carl Sweezy attributed his earliest influence to an unidentified schoolteacher. Similarly, Ernest Spybuck, a Shawnee painter, was encouraged to develop his abilities by M. R. Harrington, an anthropologist who produced a number of studies using Spybuck's illustrations. The work of Standing Bear among the Sioux, and Alfredo Montoya and Crestencio Martinez from the San Ildefonso Pueblo in New Mexico, further illustrate broad-based influences shaping the emergence of Native American painting.[10]

At first glance, this conclusion seems to contradict the vehement present-day criticism of the assimilationist practices of schools influenced by Pratt's ideas. In fact, such schools often sought to destroy Indian identity. However, not all did, and even those where such values dominated, there was increased student exposure to print media, and pencils and paper, if not painting. Moreover, some schools encouraged some degree of Indian identity, while individual teachers taught art to their students and facilitated their efforts in other ways. The best Oklahoma example of this was the Anadarko Indian School. Originally established and named St. Patrick's by the Benedictine order in 1892, it became part of the federal Indian school system in 1911, but still retained the Catholic faculty. One of these was Sister Olivia Taylor, a Choctaw, who by 1914 was teaching art to her Kiowa charges including those who would soon be recognized as the Kiowa Five. Mopope would credit Taylor as his second teacher after his uncle Silverhorn.[11]

Susie Peters, a field agent among the Kiowas, then supplemented Taylor's instruction and became convinced that five of her charges deserved further attention. These were Mopope, Spencer Asah, Jack Hokeah, Monroe Tsatoke and Lois Smoky. James Auchiah would join the group after Lois Smoky withdrew. In 1927 J. A. Buten, the Kiowa agent, responded to Peters's urging and introduced the Kiowa Five to Oscar Jacobson, the head of the art department at the University of Oklahoma. Hired in 1915, Jacobson had developed a vigorous program and was already noted for his promotion of art in Oklahoma, and of western American art on the national scene.

Jacobson's own artistic pursuits introduced him to the emerging Native American art communities in New Mexico and other western states, which convinced him that there was potential for similar developments in Oklahoma. His experience, ability, and interests made him the best possible person to foster that goal, while the Kiowa Five held the ideal combination of abilities and commitment levels necessary to bring Native American art from Oklahoma to prominence. Jacobson immediately arranged to create studio classes for the five as they had not completed the level of education that would have made them eligible for admission to the university. He also arranged for their financial support and then supervised much of their instruction, delegating the remainder to OU faculty member Edith Mahler.[12]

Jacobson insisted that the students should paint in the "Indian way," drawing inspiration from their own traditions and culture, and he worked to prevent their "contamination" by Euro-American artistic styles and techniques. At the same time he was actively promoting their acceptance in the art world defined by those standards, and among the general public. Those goals were not always compatible, but they would dominate education of Indian artists in Oklahoma and elsewhere during the next thirty-five years.[13]

James Auchiah joined group during 1927 after Lois Smoky returned home under pressure from her Kiowa counterparts to stop working in forms considered the prerogative of young men. By this time the artists had already gained regional attention from a series of exhibits that year. Significantly, they frequently accompanied their exhibits with dance demonstrations, thereby increasing the audiences they drew and complementing the appeal of their paintings. International fame came in 1928 after Jacobson sent examples of the work of the five artists to an exhibit at the International Education Association held in Prague. Many critics acclaimed the paintings of the Indian artists as the most significant American contributions to the exhibition. Leading art magazines devoted pages and praise to the paintings, and visitors sometimes had to wait as long as three days to view the paintings because of crowds.

Acclaim for the Kiowa Five grew during the next few years, especially after a French publisher arranged to publish a portfolio of their work in 1930. In addition they had numerous showings of their work, culminating with

Figure 8.1. Oscar Jacobson (in suit) with the Kiowa Five: (from left to right) Monroe Tsatoke, Jack Hokeah, Stephen Mopope, Spencer Asah, and James Auchiah, 1929. Courtesy of the Western History Collections, University of Oklahoma.

the National Exposition of Indian Arts in 1931. That exhibition then traveled the United States for the next two years, firmly establishing Native American painting as an accepted art form. The work of Kiowa Five defined its qualities. Their painting maintained the limited-perspective characteristics and flat appearance of ledger art, but gave finer attention to detail and used highly stylized drawings. In turn scholars and the public alike associated these works with what became known as the Oklahoma or Bacone School.[14]

Broadening the bases for cultural acceptance was a major step, but Oklahoma could not achieve status as a center for Native American art until it offered stronger markets for established artists and expanded educational opportunities for younger ones. The need for markets can be seen in the fact that income from painting never supported any of the Kiowa Five for more than a few years. Some of this was due to the beginning of the Great Depression, which devastated all art markets. Oklahoma was particularly hard hit, but the Depression also led to the creation of two federal art programs that provided income for some of the Kiowa Five for a short time.

Mopope was chosen to create the majority of the paintings completed under the short-lived Public Works of Art Project in Oklahoma. He was also prominent among painters who received important commissions from the Section of Painting and Sculpture of the U.S. Treasury Department. During the same period, Tsatoke completed four murals in the Wiley Post Building in the State Capitol complex in Oklahoma City, finishing them shortly before his death from tuberculosis in 1937. Two years later Mopope and Auchiah were among a group of Native American artists selected to paint murals for the Department of Interior Building in Washington, D.C.[15] Hokeah completed studies and painted murals for the Santa Fe Indian School during this period as well.

After 1939 Mopope was the only artist from the Kiowa Five who painted regularly for any reason. Personal or cultural factors added to economic causes. Religious influences explain Auchiah's decision to abandon painting, a decision he honored for the rest of his life. The only exception was a short period when he sketched some of the drawings he found at Fort Marion while serving in the U.S. Navy during World War II. Further, the artists' achievements were not particularly valued among their fellow Kiowas. For example, Mopope and Tsatoke received more honor among their people for their dancing and storytelling than for their paintings.

Economic factors would continue to limit Native American artists in Oklahoma, though that changed to some degree after World War II. The artists had few opportunities to sell their work in Oklahoma, and the existing markets rarely attracted significant numbers of buyers. The history of the American Indian Exposition at Anadarko illustrates one dimension of the problem. An American Indian fair began there in 1931 and evolved into the American Indian Exposition in 1935. Annual weeklong celebrations regularly attracted representatives from most of the Southern Plains tribes for dancing contests, parades, princess elections, and similar events, plus the sale of tribal arts and crafts.[16]

In any given year these events offered a unique opportunity for purchase of authentic Native arts and crafts in the Southwest. Yet the expositions never drew the kind of crowds necessary to sustain a community of artists. In contrast, exhibitions in New Mexico and elsewhere were held at locations that offered more-varied attractions and that often had year-round sales venues for artists. In addition locations such as Santa Fe benefited from decades of marketing whose aggressiveness the Anadarko Fair never approached. The few Oklahoma art galleries that dealt in Native American art during the 1930s and after faced difficulties similar to those of the fairs and exhibitions. The Colonial Art Gallery in Oklahoma City sold some Indian art, but primarily to a very limited clientele, as did Nettie Wheeler, who maintained a kind of salon and gallery for Indian artists at the Sugar Bowl tearoom in Muskogee. Wolf Robe Hunt's Arrowood Trading Post in Muskogee and the Mohawk Lodge in Clinton benefited from the beginnings of travel along Route 66, but most of the tourists who stopped there were more interested in trinkets than in authentic arts and crafts. Even if there had been that kind of interest, those travelers were more likely to be displaced sharecroppers en route to California than the relatively prosperous tourists who traveled to western vistas by rail.[17]

Something more would be needed before Oklahoma would gain recognition as a center for Native American art. A giant leap toward that achievement began at Bacone College in 1936. The college had been founded by the American Baptist Convention in 1880, with other funds provided by cooperating tribal governments. It had fallen into decline until Reverend B. D. Weeks became president and began to promote the college by focusing on its history as the only college exclusively for Indians.

Weeks increased recruiting for Indian faculty members, which brought Mary Stone McClendon to the college in 1927. She was a Chickasaw who was also known as Princess Ataloa, a title she had claimed as a musician and performer of Native American legends and lore. She was hired to teach English and philosophy and also began actively promoting Native arts and crafts. McClendon collected examples of Native America arts and crafts from across the United States in order to use them as illustrations for teaching. By 1932 the collection had grown enough in size and significance to justify construction of what would become known as Ataloa Lodge in order to house the objects. In 1936 the collection became the focus of a new program at Bacone, one to teach Native American art.[18]

An article in the *Bacone Indian* that February predicted, "In the years ahead it may very well be that when the subject of Indian art is mentioned the name of Bacone College will automatically leap to mind."[19] The prophecy was well on the road toward fulfillment by the time it was written. It was contained in a story about the work of Acee Blue Eagle (Alex McIntosh) who launched the college's new art program in 1935. The next few years would place the little college at the forefront of American Indian art education, and by the end of the decade most Indian schools would be offering art programs based on Bacone's experience and teaching model.

The Bacone program filled a gap for the many promising artists who could not meet the standards of the University of Oklahoma, or who sought a smaller school where their Indian heritage would be less problematic. Oscar Jacobson continued to work with some students at the university during the next few years, and he insulated them from some of the racism they feared. He could not, however, continue studio classes of the kind he had offered the Kiowa Five, and he welcomed the Bacone program, recommending Blue Eagle to head it.

Blue Eagle was undoubtedly the man for the times and the program as he brought both a growing reputation as an artist and the flamboyance and skills of a promoter. He had attended Haskell Institute (the Indian training school), the Chilocco Indian Agricultural School, and Bacone before completing his bachelor of fine arts at the University of Oklahoma under Jacobson's direction. Even before completing his college work he had gained significant attention as a dancer and artist. He represented Oklahoma Boy Scouts on a national tour in 1929, painted murals for the Public Works of Art Project in Oklahoma, and toured the United States lecturing on the "Life and Character of the American Indian."[20]

By 1937 regional newspapers were heralding a "Renaissance in Indian Painting," one claiming that "it will be a very long time before there is another of the significance of Blue Eagle."[21] The benefits to the college were seen with three hundred new Indian students who enrolled there that year. Most had come to study subjects other than art but were clearly drawn by the attention the program had given the college. Blue Eagle taught relatively few students before he resigned to pursue other opportunities in 1938, but his students included Fred Beaver and Willard Stone, each of whom would soon earn national reputations.[22]

Bacone then hired Woodrow Wilson ("Woody") Crumbo, one of the first Indian artists to complete studies at the University of Oklahoma following the end of the special classes Jacobson had offered to the Kiowa Five. Crumbo's Kiowa classmate Woodrow Wilson ("Woody") Big Bow also soon gained recognition as an artist. Big Bow is probably best known as the creator of the Thunderbird insignia for the Forty-fifth Infantry Division. Crumbo was Potawatomi but had spent some of his childhood in Anadarko where Susie Peters had encouraged his artistic development. As Blue Eagle before him, Crumbo had already earned a national reputation when he arrived at Bacone, and his tenure there was short.

Crumbo worked to build a department that would be "a cultural center for Indian arts and crafts." He personally worked with student weavers, creating designs for their works, and he hired Vernon McNeil, his college friend, to create a silversmithing program. Crumbo also changed the course of study for painters, adding classes in figure drawing and design his first year and others the next two years. Another of his innovations was to introduce students to wider cultural influences by bringing exhibits of non-Indian art to Bacone.[23]

Crumbo departed Bacone in 1942 to work for Cessna Aircraft in Wichita, Kansas, but he had nevertheless made a number of important improvements in the art program while maintaining its national prominence. He would

Figure 8.2. Artists Woody Crumbo and Charles Banks Wilson judge the first national exhibition of Indian painting, 1949. Courtesy of the Philbrook Museum of Art Archives.

return to Oklahoma after the war and then play a key role in creating a market for Oklahoma artists. Before those developments, Bacone hired Walter Richard ("Dick") West to replace him. West had finished a year's vocational training at Haskell Institute before completing a course of study at Bacone in 1938. At Bacone he had been noted for his participation in a men's singing group. He then earned a bachelor of fine arts degree from the University of Oklahoma in 1941, and he went on to complete an master of fine arts degree there in 1951.[24]

West continued the broader educational emphases Crumbo had introduced and worked to make Bacone's studios a home away from home for his students. The years of his tenure at Bacone are recognized by most as the golden era in Native American art in the state, a period when Oklahoma artists and art education institutions were in the ascendant nationally. West's artistic reputation, teaching skills, and student relationships did much to foster that era, but the real key was the symbiotic relationship that soon grew between Bacone's program and the National Exhibition of American Indian Painting (the Indian Annual) at the Philbrook Museum of Art.[25]

The Indian Annual evolved from two interrelated developments. In 1936 the Tulsa Arts Association began an annual Indian week featuring dancing, exhibits, and other displays of tribal culture. Philbrook was established two years later with the donation of the Villa Philbrook mansion and an endowment by oilman Waite Phillips and his wife, Genevieve. Philbrook's first collections were devoted to art from the Renaissance and Baroque periods, but it also soon inherited the Tulsa Art Association's educational programs and a small collection of Indian art. Indian week, however, fell by the wayside.[26]

In 1945 Crumbo returned to Tulsa to assist Thomas Gilcrease in the creation of his massive collection of western American and Native American art. At the same time he began urging Philbrook to fill the vacuum left by the loss of Tulsa's Indian week. The next year Bernard Frazier, Philbrook's director, proposed the Indian Annual to be held July through September for "all painters of traditional American [Indian] subject matter." The Indian Annual was an immediate success, enhancing recognition of the museum as well as Native American art. The show also offered both established and emerging artists the opportunity to sell their works, the final component needed to establish the state's leadership in Native American art. At last Oklahoma had a market to complement the talents of its artists and the art programs at Bacone and other schools in the state. And, as the first museum-sponsored show open to Indian artists nationwide, the Indian Annual drew ever more artists and art students to the state.[27]

The annual awards demonstrated the integrity of Philbrook's jury process, as the first winners of the grand award were Fred Kabotie, an Arizona Hopi, and Oscar Howe, a Yankton Sioux, but Oklahoma artists were always prominent among category winners. Many Oklahomans would claim the grand award in subsequent years, beginning with Dick West in 1949 (he won again in 1955). Other Oklahoma claimants were Allan Houser (four times), Acee Blue Eagle, Albin Jake, Fred Beaver, Blackbear Bosin (twice), Solomon McCombs, Willard Stone, and David Williams.[28]

All of those artists except Houser and Bosin had been educated at Bacone. Houser, an Apache from Apache, Oklahoma, received his education in New Mexico and has been identified primarily with that state.[29] Bosin attended Anadarko Indian School and then Haskell Institute, which had begun teaching art by the time he was attending. Beaver, Blue Eagle, Bosin, Stone, and West together won at least ten awards in individual categories during the first twenty-five years of the exhibition. Joan Hill, Chief Terry Saul, and Al Momaday, fellow Bacone alumni, also won individual awards.[30]

As important as the awards were, the artists especially valued the chance to sell their paintings. More than forty paintings were sold the first year of the show, including twenty-three purchased by Philbrook, and sales grew rapidly thereafter. In addition, carryover interest from the shows also stimulated gallery sales across the state for the next two decades, with the Kiowa Five, Woody Crumbo, Woody Big Bow, and an assortment of Bacone artists as best sellers.[31]

Sometimes an award at the Indian Annual catapulted an artist to international acclaim. The best example of this occurred with the Blackbear Bosin's "Prairie Fire," which received a first purchase award from Philbrook in the 1953 plains tribal category. In March 1955, Dorothy Dunn used that painting as one illustration for an article in *National Geographic*. The painting was then used for the cover of the National Geographic Society's *Indians of the Americas*. Requests for reproductions arrived at Philbrook from all over the world and continue to this day.[32]

Philbrook's growing reputation reached new heights as the Indian Annual entered its second decade. By that time the artists had begun to pressure Philbrook to broaden the original categories. The museum responded by adding a category for sculpture in 1958 to unanimous support from the art world. The 1959 replacement of competition categories based on an artist's tribal heritage with one based on the subject matter of a painting was also well received.

Most artists supported a second change in 1959, but critics and other defenders of the Oklahoma style reacted sharply, even linking the action to concerns about subversive influences on American culture. This change was the creation of a category for "non-traditional paintings," in accordance with a recommendation from Jeanne Snodgrass, Philbrook's Native American art curator. Her goal was to recognize the emergence of a new generation of artists who sought to depict their cultures through the use of a more "sophisticated palate." At the same time she expected submissions to continue to be distinctly Native American. Thus "an abstract of a city skyline or a still life would not be acceptable."[33]

Artists who showed at the Indian Annual had called for such changes from its beginning. In 1946 Bernard Frazier had apologized to Yeffe Kimball because the judges had rejected her painting as "untraditional." He then arranged to have the work displayed in a room adjacent to the exhibition. Her submission the next year won an award, but was clearly less interpretive than the painting the judges rejected. There were similar instances in subsequent years as the judges employed increasingly flexible standards. Blackbear Bosin's "Prairie Fire" is probably the best example of that trend as its images are much more vibrant and vivid than those found in the most traditional paintings. However, it was still flat and representational. In contrast, the judges for 1958 rejected a submission by Oscar Howe, deploring his "use of symbols that are not used by the artist's own tribe."[34]

Howe, who had claimed his second grand prize from Philbrook in 1954, the same year he completed his MFA at the University of Oklahoma, fought back, insisting that his innovations were rooted in traditional Sioux art. Many of the concerns he identified were then met by the new category for the Indian Annual. He had also argued, however, that prevailing definitions of traditionalism were rooted in the white culture and the marketplace, rather than in historic Native American cultural practices. In one sense, Howe's charges echoed widespread debates that had characterized the art world for decades. Concerns about the impact of commercialism or the place of abstraction in art were not confined to Indian art circles. Likewise, many critics of western American art focused on an artist's claim to authenticity. In the case of Indian art, though, the debate had enormous implications for the Oklahoma School. Howe's challenge meant that the Oklahoma style was now associated with a suspect and dated set of standards, even equated condescendingly with "Bambi art," defined primarily by nostalgia and sentimentality.

Howe's arguments and the addition of the nontraditional category in the Indian Annual marked the beginning of the end of dominance by the Oklahoma School, but they were responses to change rather than causes. As Snodgrass had asserted, a new generation had emerged. The seventy-three submissions entered in the nontraditional category in its first year proved that assertion, but there were also other causes for the decline of the Oklahoma School.

The prevalence of the Bacone style had always rested on a shaky foundation. Oklahoma Indian artists had been defending their art from its inception against widespread beliefs that Oklahoma's Indians were too far removed from their cultural traditions to create authentic tribal art.[35] Jacobson's concerns about the potential contamination of the Kiowa Five reflected one aspect of that concern. Acee Blue Eagle probably best summarized the Oklahoma answer. He acknowledged that the kinds of paintings done by the Kiowa Five and himself were the product of recent developments, but he maintained that they retained the essential characteristics of an older Indian art after a process of "natural evolution." Nettie Wheeler, his patron and copromoter of Bacone's programs, took that claim a step further, insisting that Indian artists carried traditional Indian art in their subconscious. Dorothy Dunn defended similar views at the studio in the Santa Fe Indian School during the same period.[36]

Blue Eagle and his successors employed three other means to add authenticity to their works. First, they highlighted their Indian names: thus, Alex McIntosh became Acee Blue Eagle, and Dick West added his Cheyenne name to all of his paintings. West also urged his students to claim an Indian name if they did not already have one. The second method required attention to research, so that the artists could justify every element included in a painting. This led to a tension for the definition of Indian art and for the artists who were supposed to represent a tradition that was rooted in their genes, but which required research, often in sources created by white anthropologists. In the third method, artistic training and abilities were deemphasized in the name of authenticity or the "blood quantum" test of the artist. Thus one had to step away from the prevailing definition of Indian art to recognize the design emphases in Blue Eagle's paintings, the art nouveau influences in Willard Stone's carvings, Dick West's early adaptations of abstract and modernist emphases, and numerous comparable examples in the works of many of the leading artists from the Bacone School.[37]

The event heralding a new definition for Indian art took place in March 1959, even as Philbrook was completing plans to add the nontraditional category to the Indian Annual. This was the Rockefeller Foundation's conference on "New Directions in Indian Art," held in Tucson, Arizona. The conference was attended by a variety of interests, including tribal representatives, museum professionals, and academics. Attendees heard a wide range of opinions from the traditional views of Dorothy Dunn to advocacy of full-blown modernism that urged young Indian painters to "leave the past in the museum."[38]

The modernists received the most attention at the conference, but their impact mushroomed with the Southwest Indian Art Project, a series of workshops launched by the University of Arizona the next year. The workshops ran for three years and were then institutionalized with the creation of the Institute of American Indian Arts (IAIA) in 1962, by the Bureau of Indian Affairs. Ironically built on the site of Dorothy Dunn's studio at the Santa Fe Indian School, physically supplanting it, the institute opened with 350 Native American students representing fifty-eight tribes from twenty-five states.[39]

The collective force of these developments soon pushed Oklahoma's art institutions to the periphery nationally. Even before that the Department of Art at the University of Oklahoma had abandoned Indian art programs in its own drive to get rid of the old and bring in the new. The museum Jacobson had established at the university continued to work with Indian student groups on campus and to circulate the works of the Kiowa Five, but the emphasis had shifted. Bacone continued its art programs under the leadership of Dick West until 1970, when he left to head a new program at Haskell Junior College. Chief Terry Saul proved an effective replacement for West, but the program was already struggling by the time of his death in 1976. Competition from the IAIA and declining interest in junior college art programs largely explain that decline. Leadership in the art program fluctuated for the next three years until the appointment of Ruthe Blalock Jones. She brought renewed continuity to the program, but many of the most promising students continued to bypass Bacone for the IAIA or university programs.

The corresponding decline of Bacone's and other Oklahoma influences on Indian painting can be seen in a comparative study of the educational background of major Oklahoma artists. Nearly all of those born before 1940 were educated at either Bacone or the University of Oklahoma, and many attended both colleges.[40] In contrast, only four from a group of twelve born after 1940 attended one of those schools. The remainder completed their education at schools as diverse as Oklahoma State University at Okmulgee, the Cleveland Engineering Institute in Ohio, Southwestern Oklahoma State College, and assorted others.[41]

The same forces that account for Bacone's declining influence also contributed to the demise of the Indian Annual in 1979. Although Philbrook had earned acclaim for both the beginning of the annual exhibition and its decision to recognize nontraditional art, the luster had departed from the show by the 1970s. Both the number and quality of submissions had begun to decline as artists found a boom market in expanding exhibitions and galleries. The artists' movement away from the Indian Annual then accelerated as the museum responded to pressure from the Association of Art Museum Directors to drop the sale exhibitions that had once drawn so many artists.

Other pressures came from a proliferation of competing exhibitions in the state during this period, while new museums such as the Five Civilized Tribes Museum and others were offering a regular schedule of Indian art exhibits. In this area as well as others, Philbrook's successes had spawned competitors. The final blow came when a new director at Philbrook began to push for blockbuster exhibits that would draw a sustained flow of people, in contrast to the declining attendance that usually followed the Indian Annual's opening weekend.[42]

Most of the state's Indian artists benefited from the overall expansion of markets during this period, but they still often found it necessary to move to New Mexico or at least spend a significant amount of time there during the year.[43] Oklahoma had at least five vital galleries selling Indian art in this period, but that number was exceeded on many single blocks in Santa Fe or Taos. Worse, the Oklahoma galleries lost a significant portion of their business with the bust of the oil boom in 1982. Besides causing the loss of the business of freewheeling customers typical of the boom at its height, the sharp decline in oil prices also caused many collectors to dump the art they had collected, saturating the market. Oklahoma galleries were now often competing with garage and church rummage sales.[44]

Oklahoma galleries weathered that storm, but the state did not have a major event-related market for artists again until 1987 with the beginning of the Red Earth Festival in Oklahoma City and the Tulsa Indian Art Festival. The Red Earth Festival declined after its first ten years and it moved from downtown Oklahoma City, but a return to its original location in 2006 produced sharp gains in attendance. Subsequently the state has seen a proliferation of new tribal exhibitions and museums.

These developments, along with the addition of Kelly Haney's "Guardian" statue atop the State Capitol, suggest that state institutions will continue to offer important support for Indian art and artists in Oklahoma. Current activities even suggest the likelihood of future growth. In 2008 there were five major Native American art exhibits on display or in planning in the state's museums.[45] Plans for the completion of the American Indian Museum and Cultural Center in Oklahoma City, the addition of a concentration in Native American art in the doctoral program in art history at the University of Oklahoma, and the impact of the Eugene B. Adkins collection at the Fred Jones Jr. Museum of Art, as well as Philbrook Museum, all support that assessment. Nevertheless, the golden age for Oklahoma art has passed. A unique combination of individuals and institutions spawned a vital stage in the evolution of Native American art. New definitions for Indian painting, the spread of Indian art museums, and broad economic and cultural changes all affected the prominence of Oklahoma as the leading environment for the nurture of Native American art. There is not likely to ever be another comparable concentration of resources and influences in Oklahoma or elsewhere.

Notes

1. The author acknowledges significant contributions from Thomas Young, librarian, Philbrook Museum of Art; Frances A. Donelson, librarian, Bacone College Library; Linda Greever, Tulsa Indian Art Market; Willard Johnson, Colonial Art Gallery; and Leslie Zindl, Tribes 3 Gallery.

2. Daniel C. Swan, "Traditional Arts, American Indian," Leland C. Bement, "Cooper Site," and Mary Jo Watson, "American Indian Art," in *The Encyclopedia of Oklahoma History and Culture*, Oklahoma Historical Society, http.digital.library.okstate.edu/encyclopedia (hereafter *Oklahoma Encyclopedia*).

3. These developments are discussed in varied sources, including Lydia L. Wycoff, "Visions and Voices, A Collective History of Native American Painting," in *Visions and Voices* (Tulsa: Philbrook Museum of Art, 1996), 19–20; Dorothy Dunn, "America's First Painters," *National Geographic*, March 1955, 349–50; Norman C. Feder, "European Influences on Plains Indian Art," in *The Arts of the North American Indian*, edited by Edwin L. Wade (Tulsa: Philbrook Art Center, 1986), 93–104; and Gloria S. Young, "Aesthetic Archives: The Visual Language of Plains Indian Art," in *The Arts of the North American Indian*, edited by Edwin L. Wade (Tulsa: Philbrook Art Center, 1986), 45–63.

4. Richard H. Pratt, "The Advantages of Mingling Indians with Whites," in *Americanizing the American Indians; Writings by the "Friends of the Indians," 1880–1900* (Cambridge, Mass.: Harvard University Press, 1973), 270–71. Pratt first used the phrase to justify his assimilationist program but it has also become the catchphrase for subsequent criticisms of these efforts.

5. Karen Daniels Petersen, *Plains Indian Art from Fort Marion* (Norman: University of Oklahoma Press, 1971), 5, 15–17, Brad D. Lookingbill, *War Dance at Fort Marion* (Norman: University of Oklahoma Press, 2006); Alvin O. Turner, "Journey to Sainthood," *Chronicles of Oklahoma* 70, no. 2 (Summer 1992), 121–26.

6. Petersen, *Plains Indian Art*, 73.

7. Turner, "Journey to Sainthood," 121; Lookingbill, *War Dance at Fort Marion*, 174–98.

8. Turner, "Journey to Sainthood," 121; Lookingbill, *War Dance at Fort Marion*, 174–98; Moira Harris, *Between Two Cultures: Kiowa Art from Fort Marion* (St. Paul: Pogo Press, 1989), 131–36; Wycoff, "Visions and Voices," 22–23. Basic biographical data on all artists discussed herein may be found in Patrick D. Lester, *The Biographical Directory of Native*

American Painters (Tulsa: SIR Publications, 1995); additional information on Oklahoma artists may be found in Suzanne Silvester, *Directory of Oklahoma Artists* (n.p.: Melton Art Reference Library, 2007).

9. Lester, *The Biographical Directory of Native American Painters*; Arthur Silberman, *100 Years of Native American Painting* (Oklahoma City: Oklahoma City Museum of Art, 1978), 15–16; Robert G. Donnelley, Candace Greene, and Janet Catherine Berlo, "Transforming Images," in *The Art of Silverhorn and His Successors* (Chicago: University of Chicago Press, 2001), 16–19, 24, 88, 90; Wycoff, "Visions and Voices," 23.

10. Dunn, "America's First Painters," 349–52; Harris, *Between Two Cultures*, 132–35; Lisa K. Neuman, "Painting Culture: Art and Ethnography at a School for Native Americans," *Ethnology* 45, no. 3 (2006), 176–77; "Carl Sweezy" and "Ernest Spybuck", *Oklahoma Encyclopedia*; Ruthe Blalock Jones, "Like Being Home," *Gilcrease Journal*, Fall 1995, 11.

11. Silberman, *100 Years of Native American Painting*, 16; Wycoff, "Visions and Voices," 23–26; "Kiowa Five," *Oklahoma Encyclopedia*.

12. Edwin J. Deighton, "Oscar Brousse Jacobson: Oklahoma Painter," Oklahoma University Museum of Art, 1990, unpaged exhibit brochure; Jeanne d'Ucel, "Oscar Jacobson Biographical Notes," 77–79, and "About Indians," 1–26, in box 4, file folder 1-3, Oscar Jacobson Collection, Archives, Oklahoma Historical Society.

13. "About Indians," 6–8; Neuman, "Painting Culture," 177.

14. "About Indians," 6–10; Wycoff, "Visions and Voices," 24–26; Ruthe Blalock Jones, "Like Being Home," 11–13.

15. Their work was supervised by Olle Nordmark, whose students also included Allan Houser, Woody Crumbo, Gerald Nailor, Charles Loloma, Oscar Howe, Dick West, and Archie Blackowl. Unfortunately there has been very little written about Nordmark and his influence on Native American art other than Wycoff, "Visions and Voices." This list was developed from that article.

16. Neuman, "Painting Culture," 178–79; Edwin L. Wade, "The Ethnic Art Market and the Dilemma of Innovative Indian Artists," in *Magic Images*, edited by Edwin L. Wade and Rennard Strickland (Norman: University of Oklahoma Press, 1981), 11–14; Carol Thomas Smith, *The Empowerment of Oklahoma Indian Artists and the Southern Plains Indian Museum* (master's thesis, University of Oklahoma, 2004), 9–13; *Oklahoma Encyclopedia*, "American Indian Exposition"; author's interview with Laverne Cape, January 20, 2009.

17. Author's phone conversations with Willard Johnson, Colonial Art Gallery, 2008; Neuman, "Painting Culture," 179.

18. Frances A. Donelson, "Ataloa Lodge and Mary Stone McClendon," Princess Ataloa Scrapbook, Bacone College Library vertical files. Ruthe Blalock Jones, "Bacone College and the Philbrook Indian Annuals," in *Visions and Voices*, edited by Lydia L. Wycoff (Tulsa: Philbrook Museum of Art, 1996), 51–53; John Williams and Howard Meredith, *Bacone Indian University* (Oklahoma City: Oklahoma Heritage Association, 1980), 75, Neuman, "Painting Culture," 175–76.

19. *Bacone Indian*, February 5, 1936.

20. Frances A. Donelson and Acee Blue Eagle scrapbooks, Bacone College Library vertical files.

21. *Dallas Journal*, April 6, 1937.

22. Acee Blue Eagle scrapbooks.

23. Frances A. Donelson and Woody Crumbo scrapbooks, Bacone College Library vertical files.

24. Frances A. Donelson and Richard "Dick" West scrapbooks, Bacone College Library vertical files.

25. Ibid.; Wycoff, "Voices and Visions," 33, 38–39; Jones, "Bacone College and the Philbrook Indian Annuals," 55; "Master Pueblo Painters, 1900–1930," press release for exhibit of same name, Museum of Indian Arts and Culture, Santa Fe, New Mexico, http://www.tfaoi.com/aa/2aa/2aa107.htm. The Crumbo-McNeil friendship led to another noteworthy result. McNeil made improvements in a traditional Kiowa flute owned by Crumbo and his design was used in most Indian flutes thereafter. McNeil left Bacone during World War II to work in aviation and later for the Atomic Energy Commission. He returned to Bacone and his silversmithing program for a five-year stint in 1975. John Williams, coauthor of *Bacone Indian University: A History*, indicated that some of the attention given West stemmed from his personal friendship with Ed Shaw, publicist for the American Baptist Convention, who promoted his friend as he publicized the college; author's phone conversation with John Williams, October 14, 2008.

26. Philbrook Museum of Art, script for "The American Indian Annual Exhibition: A Historical Perspective," Library and Archives, Philbrook Museum of Art (hereafter Indian Annual script). Philbrook's founding coincided with the growth of a collection of western American art that was amassed near Bartlesville by Waite's older brother Frank, the founder of Phillips Petroleum, and that would form the nucleus for Woolaroc Museum a few years later.

27. Philbrook, script for "The American Indian Annual Exhibition"; undated proposal regarding establishment of the Indian Annual, Library and Archives, Philbrook Museum of Art; Jeanne Snodgrass King, "Foreword," in *Visions and Voices*, edited by Lydia L. Wycoff (Tulsa: Philbrook Museum of Art, 1996), 11–13; Wycoff, "Visions and Voices," 40–42; Neuman, "Painting Culture," 179.

28. Robert D. Hay, "Oklahoma Awards Won by Indian Artists of the United States, 1946–1972," and Jeanne M. Snodgrass, "Annual American Indian Painting and Sculpture Competition at Philbrook Art Center," unpaged, 1963, Library and Archives, Philbrook Museum of Art (hereafter: Snodgrass Annual Summary); Indian Annual script; Wycoff, "Visions and Voices," 39–42.

29. Houser retained close ties to the Apache community in Oklahoma and completed a set of four dioramas for the newly constructed Southern Plains Indian Museum in

Anadarko. A major exhibition of his and his sons' sculpture was exhibited at the Oklahoma History Center in 2008. His sculpture "Sacred Rain Arrow" is now represented on the standard Oklahoma passenger car license plates.

30. Hay, "Oklahoma Awards"; author's compilation of biographical data from artist biographies found at *Oklahoma Encyclopedia*; Silvester, *Directory of Oklahoma Artists*; and Lester, *The Biographical Directory of Native American Painters*.

31. Wycoff, "Visions and Voices"; Snodgrass Annual Summary; Bacone College and the Philbrook Indian Annuals, 56; Willard Johnson notes.

32. Wycoff, "Visions and Voices"; Dunn, 375; Snodgrass Annual Summary.

33. Jeanne Snodgrass, Report regarding Proposed Changes to the Indian Annual, July 1958, Library and Archives, Philbrook Museum of Art.

34. Neuman, "Painting Culture," 181; Bill Anthes, *Native Moderns: American Indian Painting, 1940–1960*, Duke University Press, 2006, 125–28 and 161–69. Ironically Philbrook's acceptance of Yeffe Kimball as an Indian artist did much to lead authenticity to her fraudulent claim to Indian ancestry. This matter is discussed extensively in Anthes, as above. The author also established that she had not attended East Central State College of Oklahoma as she had claimed and where her sister attended. There is also no record of her father's reported Osage ancestry in those tribal records.

35. One indication of this belief was seen in Edward S. Curtis' decision to delay attention to Oklahoma tribes until 1927 and then making mostly portraits rather than cultural depictions for his photographic study, *The North American Indian*.

36. Wycoff, "Visions and Voices," 44; Neuman, "Painting Culture," 181–84; Acee Blue Eagle Scrapbook and Dick West Scrapbook, Bacone Library; Wheeler owned a Muskogee gallery and would later promote the creation of the Five Civilized Tribes Museum in that community; she was also a major force stimulating the career of Jerome Tiger.

37. Wycoff, "Visions and Voices," 43, 44; Neuman, "Painting Culture," 181–84; Acee Blue Eagle Scrapbook and Dick West Scrapbook. Ironically, the synthesis which emerged after 1959 would retain only the original shibboleth, the claim that Native American art could be done only by Indians, but that argument's renewed strength was now as much about economics as racial beliefs.

38. Anthes, *Native Moderns*, 171–81; report by Jeanne Snodgrass regarding "Directions in Indian Art Conference," March 1959, Library and Archives, Philbrook Museum of Art.

39. Anthes, *Native Moderns*.

40. The most notable exceptions to that rule were Archie Black Owl (who also studied with Olaf Nordmark) and Doc Tate Nevaquayah, both of whom completed some of their education at the Ft. Sill school.

41. Figures compiled from data available on Mirac Creepingbear, Jerome Tiger, Merlin Little Thunder, Ben Harjo, Wayne Cooper, Virginia Stroud, Kelly Haney, Harvey Pratt, Troy Anderson, Bill Rabbitt, David Kaskaske and Connie Seabourn in Silvester, *Directory of*

Oklahoma Artists; and Lester, *The Biographical Directory of Native American Painters*. The list does not include all Oklahoman artists for the period, and some authorities might want to add others, but this would not likely to change the direction of my conclusions.

42. Marcia Manhart e-mail to the author, December 5, 2008.

43. For instance, Jerome Bushyhead told me during the early 1980s that he made more money selling art in Taos and Santa Fe in a few months than he would in Oklahoma during the rest of the year.

44. Besides the venerable Colonial Art Gallery, these were the Tulsa Indian Art Market, the Oklahoma Indian Art Gallery in Oklahoma City, Thunderbird Gifts and Antiques in Muskogee, and the Galleria in Norman, soon to be replaced by the Tribes Gallery in that town. The loss in business was offset to some extent by a boom in Indian art prints during the 1980s, but that growth led to the inevitable bust as well as other effects. While some artists reaped great substantial gains, there is some evidence that the explosion of limited edition prints actually depressed the value of paintings.

45. "Unconquered: Allan Houser and the Legacy of One Apache Family," Oklahoma History Center, Oklahoma City; "American Indian Mural Painting in Oklahoma and the Southwest," National Cowboy and Western Heritage Museum, Oklahoma City; "Between the Lines: Cheyenne and Arapaho Ledger Art from Fort Reno," Gilcrease Museum, Tulsa; artwork from the Kiowa Five at the Mabee-Gerrer Museum of Art, Shawnee; and interrelated exhibitions at the Fred Jones Jr. Museum of Art, University of Oklahoma, Norman.

CHAPTER 9

Let Us Help You Help Yourselves

NEW DEAL ECONOMIC RECOVERY PROGRAMS AND THE FIVE TRIBES IN RURAL OKLAHOMA

James Hochtritt

The Institute of Government Research released the Meriam Report in 1928, officially titled The Problem of Indian Administration. It documented the inability of the Office of Indian Affairs to address adequately the needs of American Indians under its control, but it also chronicled the impoverished and desperate conditions that prevailed among Cherokees, Chickasaws, Choctaws, Creeks, and Seminoles who lived in Oklahoma. The findings indicated chronic disease, illiteracy, malnutrition, and poverty, particularly in the isolated communities of the more conservative or tradition-oriented Indians. Along with the Survey of Conditions of the Indians in the United States, a transcription of 1929 hearings before a U.S. Senate subcommittee of the Committee on Indian Affairs, the Meriam Report detailed how the systematic separation of restricted members of these five nations from their lands had left them demoralized, living in "squalid homes" and continually "menaced by famine." "Restricted" Indians were those allotted individuals who possessed half or more Indian blood. Their restricted status meant that the federal government would hold their allotted land in trust for twenty-five years, at the end of which time the restricted individuals would gain outright title to their allotted land and then have the legal right to sell the land. As a result, land ownership among more traditional Indians was relatively high, and the overwhelming majority of these more traditional Indians were full-blood.[1] Even as late as the 1940s, historian Angie Debo reported that rural Five Tribes communities suffered from "appalling social and economic degradation." Apparently, rural Indians of these Five Tribes were mired in a downward spiral of physical and spiritual decay. But contrary to both government reports and some historians, nothing was further from the truth. Moreover, not only did the effort to aid rural Indians of the Five Tribes during the Great Depression garner mixed results, the Indian response to government programs proved perplexing to those outsiders who sought to improve their condition.[2]

The goals that the Indian Office set for itself in the 1930s in its efforts to improve the lives of these rural Indians were straightforward and well intended. The commissioner of Indian affairs, John Collier, wanted to expand and strengthen extension work, undertake more extensive relief efforts, and increase Indian employment opportunities both outside of and within the Office of Indian Affairs. Collier also wanted bureau employees to be better educated and more respectful of Indian culture. Lastly, as part of its economic policy, the federal government incorporated anthropologists so that it could design programs that might best serve the economic and cultural needs of rural Indian communities. Indian cooperatives, credit associations, and small-scale, family-managed, Indian agricultural projects formed the heart of the bureau's rehabilitation plan. The federal government intended to help rural Cherokees, Chickasaws, Choctaws, Creeks, and Seminoles become self-supporting, productive citizens.[3]

This mission ultimately proved futile because it remained at odds with the cultural orientation of the people Collier hoped to serve. It did not mean, however, that cultural stasis defined rural Indians. Nor did these Indians oppose government efforts to improve their lives or refuse to embrace the amenities of modernity. But they chose carefully what aspects of twentieth-century American society they allowed into their communities. When confronted with the economic advice, expertise, and aid the federal government offered, they accepted and rejected this assistance on their own terms.[4]

From 1933 to 1934, New Deal agencies such as the Public Works Administration (PWA), the Civil Works Administration (CWA), and the Indian Emergency Conservation Work (IECW) program provided the greatest employment opportunities for the Five Tribes. In 1934 the PWA allotted the Five Tribes Agency $100,000 for Indian road work, for example. Not only did this project bring income to needy Indians, it also built roads and bridges designed to benefit Indian communities. In most instances counties furnished the heavy equipment and tools while the government-appointed superintendent of the

Five Tribes maintained a roster of eligible Indians. Married men with dependents received preference, then single men with dependents. Indians who had worked on CWA or IECW projects were prohibited from employment on any PWA project. The agency rotated qualified laborers so that as many Indians as possible benefited.[5]

Rural Indians also took advantage of other federal work relief programs. From 1933 to 1942, the Civilian Conservation Corps operated camps in Oklahoma. An average of 323 members per year from the Five Tribes participated in a special Indian division of the CCC. The Works Progress Administration (WPA), created in 1935, also provided Indians with jobs. Cherokees, Chickasaws, Choctaws, Creeks, and Seminoles found employment constructing auditoriums, drainage works, dipping vats, roads, streets, and sewage and water conservation facilities. In addition, the WPA-sponsored Federal Art Project employed Indians from the Five Tribes as artists. To benefit Indian women, the WPA organized sewing rooms and Household Service Demonstration Project centers. The sewing rooms ranged in size from huge plants employing hundreds of women to small venues employing ten to twelve women. This project allowed Indian women to earn supplemental income for their families and at the same time provided clothes for the needy. The Household Service Demonstration Project trained Indian women as domestics for employment in urban households. Instruction was given in food preparation, ironing, washing, and other in-home duties. Similar in scope to the PWA, the WPA concentrated much of its work in and around urban centers such as Tulsa or Okmulgee. As a result, it had little effect on the more isolated, rural Indian areas.[6]

In addition, the Five Tribes Agency distributed chickens, beef, mutton, and pork to needy Indian families and organized lunch programs and 4-H clubs for children. For adults, the agency conducted agricultural workshops that introduced Indians to innovative techniques in both farming and animal husbandry, but these attracted relatively few Indians. From 1935 to 1940 the Indian Office organized, on average, 330 farming method demonstrations per year among rural Cherokees, Chickasaws, Choctaws, Creeks, and Seminoles. The number of Indians in attendance, however, averaged only about twelve per meeting. Some extension agents went so far as fraud to convince their superiors at the Five Tribes Agency and the Indian Office that their programs had an impact. They staged phony agricultural fairs where they displayed healthy-looking fruits and vegetables that agency workers claimed had been grown by Indian farmers. Moreover, they paid both Indians and whites to stand alongside bounties of harvested produce for the purpose of taking fraudulent

Figure 9.1. Members of the Civilian Conservation Corps–Indian Division building a flood control structure near Stilwell, Oklahoma. Courtesy of the Carl Albert Congressional Archives, University of Oklahoma, Wilburn Cartwright Collection, 884.

photographs purporting to show the productivity of the Indian agricultural extension program.[7]

At the same time, although not engaging in such hoaxes to cover up their lack of success, the efforts of the Home Economics unit of the U.S. Agriculture Department's Extension Service also produced similar, dismal results. For example, of its seventy-six meetings held in the Choctaw Nation in 1939, only 744 women attended out of a female population of roughly 12,000. Designed to instruct women in the latest methods and trends in home economics, these "kitchen chautauquas" catered more to white farm women than Indian women. The Extension Service never generated much enthusiasm among the Indians it attempted to help. Moreover, it remained drastically underfunded and understaffed, which limited the amount of husbandry, agricultural, and home economics projects it was able to manage.[8]

In April 1936 the Indian Office undertook an even more ambitious farming project. An offshoot of the experimental Indian farming projects begun in 1935, the Indian Relief and Rehabilitation (IRR) program consisted of four main farming cooperatives in the Cherokee Nation, three within the Chickasaw and Choctaw Nations, and one each in both the Creek and Seminole Nations. The bureau oversaw the construction of model homestead units designed to enable Indian families to become self-supporting. In this instance, becoming "self-supporting" did not mean becoming subsistence producers, but rather people who cultivated surplus crops for market.[9]

The Indian Relief and Rehabilitation program provided employment to 2,042 Indians from 1936–39. It expended roughly eighty-six dollars per family per year in the form of salaries, wages, and relief. Particularly effective in Wilburton in Latimer County, the IRR oversaw the construction of a smokehouse, root cellar, and blacksmith shop, and remodeled fifteen four-room houses that the Indian Emergency Conservation Work program had originally constructed. At the McCurtain County cooperative farming venture, the IRR constructed buildings designed specifically for canning and sewing. It also erected homes and community buildings at the Delaware, Grand River, Candy Mink, and General sites in the Cherokee Nation. Each homestead consisted of a three-room house with screened porch, a hog house and chicken coop, a a pump and pump house, a toilet, and fences around the property. The Thlopthlocco Creek project located south of Okemah in Okfuskee County was identical in nature, while the project for the Seminoles focused on the continued remodeling of Mekusukey Mission and Indian homes in the surrounding area. However, the majority of rural Indians remained ambivalent about these efforts and very few relocated to the homestead sites that the Five Tribes Agency developed.[10]

Even the most ambitious of the Indian Office projects in the 1930s, the Indian Arts and Crafts Board, generated little enthusiasm among rural Indians in the Five Tribes region. Organized under an act of Congress in the autumn of 1936, the board attempted to preserve the arts and crafts of American Indians while funneling needed income into rural Indian communities. A division within the Department of the Interior separate from the Indian Office, the board existed from 1937–41 and initiated and managed the various art projects. The intent was that the board "work itself out of a job," allowing Indians to manage the program themselves. Among Oklahoma Cherokees, Chickasaws, Choctaws, Creeks, and Seminoles, the board implemented spinning and weaving projects.[11]

The weaving programs, intended primarily for the less-acculturated female population in predominantly isolated, rural Indian communities, attempted to organize economic cooperatives. More-acculturated Indian women living outside of these communities were encouraged to participate too. More often than not, acculturated Indian women among the Five Tribes became involved as instructors, although some engaged in weaving.

Figure 9.2. Cherokee Nannie Hogner (center), leading a basket-making class. Courtesy of the Carl Albert Congressional Archives, University of Oklahoma, Elmer Thomas Collection, 1794.

The Cherokee Weavers' Association in Cherokee County operated out of the Sequoyah Orphan Training School. This school had experimented with beadwork, leather craft, pottery, and woven goods for sale as early as 1934. The Choctaw Spinners' Cooperative, established in McCurtain County, operated out of the Wheelock Academy. A Chickasaw Weaving Association was set up at Tishomingo, and Creek centers were located at Henryetta and Okmulgee. The cities of Coweta, Seminole, and Wewoka all housed Indian Arts and Crafts Board projects among the Seminoles. In addition to loom weaving, some Cherokee, Creek, and Seminole men and women produced handmade baskets. Other products included wood carvings, leather articles such as belts, pottery, and silver work.[12]

Under the supervision of the Five Tribes Agency, Cherokee and Choctaw women exhibited great enthusiasm for the spinning and weaving projects. About 107 Choctaw women in McCurtain County participated in spinning. They came from small, rural Choctaw communities such as Bokchito, Goodwater, Kullichito, Mountain Fork, and Ponki Bok. After profits from sales had been reinvested to purchase raw wool, spinners earned roughly $1.30 for a week's work. Payment was based on the apprentice system, with skilled women earning more. Individual spinners and weavers worked, on average, approximately two hours per day, two days per week. In a number of instances, the spinning became a family endeavor, with four to five members of a family involved in the process. The Five Tribes Agency marketed and sold the finished products. The agency concentrated its sales efforts out-side the state of Oklahoma. People such as Alice Marriott, a field representa-tive with the U.S. Department of Interior Indian Arts and Crafts Board, and Louis West, the director of the Indian Arts and Crafts Board, believed that Indian-made items had become "too familiar" to people in Oklahoma. Dyed and spun yarn and arts and crafts were sold in Chicago, Dallas, San Francisco, and New York City, as well as in Colorado and Michigan.[13]

A number of problems arose, however, as a result of the Indian Arts and Crafts Board programs. Despite the enthusiasm of some women, their partic-ipation proved sporadic. They worked, and relished the opportunity to earn money, but they chose to do so on their own terms. Throughout the spinning program, Indian Office personnel complained that the women were unreli-able. Indian women chafed at the rigid schedules and production quotas that project coordinators such as Mabel Morrow imposed. Morrow composed a list of rules and regulations. All Indian women who participated in the Choctaw Weavers' Association signed the agreement. The document emphasized effi-ciency, industriousness, and punctuality. These rules of protocol, designed to increase production and profit, remained inimical to the more relaxed rural Indian notions of time and work. Not surprisingly, Morrow complained that the Choctaw women failed to show up for work, or that when they did they worked too slowly to suit the supervisor. At one project site in McCurtain County, Indian women abandoned the program entirely. They left work one day and never returned. Some supervisors assumed that Indians should plan their entire day around spinning and weaving. Mass production and market-ing underscored the program.[14]

To compound these problems, many of the Choctaw and Cherokee women who participated in the arts and crafts programs distrusted Indian Office offi-cials. They complained that payments for their work often arrived late. To pro-test this, women in the Choctaw Spinners' Association deliberately decreased their output. Some Indians believed that consignment shops that sold their arts and crafts items failed to report the correct amount of sales, cheating them out of profits. A few Cherokee women refused to turn over finished goods until they first received cash payment. Some Cherokee and Seminole women took it upon themselves to market and sell their products on their own, orga-nizing arts and crafts shops outside the authority of the Indian Office. Indian women also used artwork and crafts as items of exchange with non-Indians for such things as groceries.[15]

Cherokee and Choctaw women also believed that the government and some of their own tribal members exploited them in other ways. In some cases, bureau personnel attempted to persuade the women to produce artifacts that their tribes did not traditionally make, hoping to capitalize on the demand for American Indian artifacts regardless of authenticity. In addition, more-acculturated members of the Five Tribes also pressured Indian craftsmen to produce items such as bows and arrows, for example, that the craftsmen did not normally produce, in order to meet the growing demand for these artifacts in Oklahoma and in other parts of the country. As a result of these pressures, many rural Indians dropped out of Indian Arts and Crafts Board programs.[16]

What began as a federally sponsored, volunteer self-help program under the Indian New Deal became an exploitive undertaking that prescribed regulations designed to increase productivity and profit. The weaving and spinning projects lasted only as long as government supervision prevailed. When that support and pressure ended so too did the arts and crafts programs. Rural Indians had no desire to develop the programs into business ventures. Thus the Indian Arts and Crafts Board underscored the inherent inconsistencies of New Deal Indian policy. Reformers such as John Collier wanted to protect Indian cultural integrity, yet New Deal programs often incorporated methods that undermined that goal.[17]

For many of these same reasons, and also because these traditional Indians did not embrace the market economy or ethos of profit, the Indian credit and loan programs initiated by the Oklahoma Indian Welfare Act (OIWA) of 1937 failed to arouse much enthusiasm among rural Cherokees, Chickasaws, Choctaws, Creeks, and Seminoles. Confident that rural Indians would take advantage of OIWA funding to start small businesses, cooperative farms, and credit associations, the Indian Office printed application forms, "elaborate credit manuals," brochures, and pamphlets explaining how to manage small businesses. Although a few Cherokees organized strawberry- and tomato-growing cooperatives, and three Creek tribal towns established credit associations, the majority of rural Indians in the Five Tribes region refused to participate. An Indian Office anthropologist reported that only those Creeks who were "most comfortable around whites" exhibited a willingness to embrace the OIWA credit program, while less acculturated Creeks refused to even meet with bureau representatives. As a result of Indian apathy and distrust of government programs from 1937–40 only eighteen "small groups" organized some type of cooperative association among all of the Five Tribes.[18]

Throughout the 1930s, the Indian Office and the Five Tribes Agency worked to improve the economic life of the Indians under their authority. The impact of their efforts remained limited, however, primarily because of their continued insistence on reshaping rural Indians into farmers and semiskilled laborers and because some Indian Office and Five Tribes agents lacked skills and proper training in the areas of their supposed expertise. Moreover, an inadequate number of extension agents worked in the region.[19]

More important, the involvement of most rural Indians in regimented, economic rehabilitation programs continued to be a secondary alternative to other activities. When relief employment did not interfere with the daily routines of their existence, some Indians participated in federal work programs. But social gatherings, fishing, hunting, subsistence farming, and family continued to take precedence in their lives. Rural Cherokees, Chickasaws, Choctaws, Creeks, and Seminoles relied upon a network made up of both settlement and tribal members who shared their cultural and economic ethos for both nurture and support. As Seminole Johnson Scott indicated, people worked together "like brother and sister." Although tribal governments attempted to help, often their reach did not extend into the isolated rural enclaves. More-acculturated tribal leaders seldom, and in some cases never, visited any of the settlements.[20]

Contrary to the exaggerated and misinformed reports of the U.S. Congress, the Indian Office, state social workers, and the Five Tribes Agency of Oklahoma, rural Indians in the Five Tribes region were not on the brink of utter starvation. This would have been news to most of the Indians living in the small communities in the central and eastern part of the state. Some people did struggle during this period, but evidence indicates that the majority of rural Indians withstood the economic downturn of the 1930s and continued to live as they had always lived. Historically, the Cherokees, Chickasaws, Choctaws, Creeks, and Seminoles who inhabited the isolated, rural enclaves had exhibited a high degree of resiliency and the Great Depression did little to damage that dynamic. Numerous factors allowed them to weather the dire economic conditions of the 1930s.[21]

Throughout the 1930s, in the central and eastern regions of Oklahoma, many rural Indians of the Five Tribes depended upon one another for their survival. Even more than the relatively acculturated, urban members of their tribes, these rural Indians relied on extended kin relationships to ensure their physical and cultural continuity. Unlike many rural non-Indians in Oklahoma who struggled through the economic hardships of the Great Depression, rural Indians utilized their historically dynamic systems of reciprocity to live as they had always lived—comfortably self-reliant. Within their communities and settlements, sharing signified respect, and openness with one's food and material items was expected. Those who possessed less or who were not as well off were not held accountable if they did not have much to offer. To complement their resource pooling, rural Indians combined temporary employment, barter and exchange, cottage industries, fishing, hunting, and home gardens to sustain themselves.[22]

The social permeability of rural Indian households and their settlements as well as the maintenance of traditional customs and habits bolstered a sense of communalism. Mutual obligations substantiated through sharing, visiting, and other forms of cultural exchange fostered interdependence as opposed to independence. In rural Indian enclaves, where most people were related by blood, clan, town, and tribe, strangers were virtually nonexistent. Extended families, both in a household and a community sense, reinforced citizens' connections to fellow tribal members as well as to their settlements.[23]

Social cohesion depended on the goodwill of community members. Amity fostered cooperation. The settlement shared responsibility in caring for those less independent, such as widows, the aged, and the mentally and physically handicapped. At various times, children lived with relatives, clan members, and family friends. Oklahoma Department of Public Welfare records indicate that few Indians in the Five Tribes region received either old-age assistance or aid to dependent children. In Delaware County in the years 1936 and 1937, for example, only eighty-six Indians received aid to dependent children. During the same period in Seminole County only seventeen Indians received such aid. Only ten Indians received old-age assistance in Seminole County that year. In a sense, people depended instead upon an informal welfare system.[24]

The practice of allowing friends to use land was prevalent throughout the Five Tribes region. The practice of "squatting" also reflected the communal nature of rural Indian settlements. Often people who did not own property stayed on the land of fellow Indians. Individuals and families moved into empty houses and also built their own homes on the land of community, clan, and tribal members. One unidentified full-blood Cherokee woman in the Nicut area accommodated six families on her sixty acres. The homeless also lived in the small camp houses located on Indian church lands and the stomp or square grounds. Sometimes landowners demanded rent but normally most allowed people to stay on their land free of charge. Some people compensated landowners through voluntary work. Rural Indians did not consider it disgraceful or shameful to live on the land of friends, neighbors, and relatives.[25]

Relatives regularly stayed at each other's homes for short periods of time. Widows shared homes with other widows. Nonrelated neighbors lived with one another. Nora Barberhouse, a Chickasaw, said that "the door to their place was always open to other Indians." Another Chickasaw, Mateo Stick, said that people were always "dropping by unannounced." Her family prepared sleeping pallets so visitors could spend the night. Chickasaw elder Flora Perry confirmed that "visiting took place on a regular basis."[26]

When relatives visited, they usually brought food and shared it with members of the household. Bear Heart, a Creek, said that his father stressed to him the importance of sharing food with guests. Even if a family did not have much food, they shared what they had. A Creek woman, Belle Gray Connor, also explained how her father believed that food should be shared with others in the community. At the same time, when one visited an older person's home it was proper to take them something to eat, money, or some other gift that "helped them out." Lola Maud Johnson Amerson, a Chickasaw woman, recalled the same sense of community beneficence. She said that neighbors lent money and food to one another and that "communal eats" were quite common. Groups of people got together for wild onion feeds as well as hog fries. Moreover, the more financially well-off people of rural Indian communities often assisted needy families. Anna Belle Sixkiller Mitchell explained how the men of her community had constructed her parents' house. Community members helped clothe, feed, and even educate the children of less fortunate Indians. Sometimes they gave money outright to families in need and at other times extended loans to financially struggling individuals.[27]

Cooperation also extended to labor exchange. This held particularly true during the fall and winter months. Jimmie Harjochee, a Seminole, and Joe Hogner, a Cherokee, said that community members helped one another out clearing brush, repairing homes, cutting and stacking firewood, and building and mending fences. In the early spring, settlement members tilled soil and planted crops. Minnie Wimberley Hodge, a Creek woman, said that women got together to refurbish family gardens.[28]

Rural Indian settlements also cultivated communal gardens. Usually, male members of each family contributed time and labor to provide for the settlement. The community divided the resultant crops among families according to their respective needs. Each family followed an honor system whereby they took only what they needed. People who lived too far a distance to help work on the community gardens on a regular basis paid a small amount of money each year for seed, tools, and "other expenses." Their financial contribution allowed them to receive their share of the produce. After each family in a settlement took their share, the community distributed the remaining portion among the "real needy." Widows and the elderly received shares of food without having to contribute either "labor or money." Cooperative farming existed in nearly all of the rural Indian settlements.[29]

Because a majority of the rural, restricted members of the Five Tribes still retained their restricted lands, they leased or rented portions of those allotments to non-Indians. This strategy not only brought in income, but rural Indians also negotiated land leases in exchange for food or a portion of the crops. In some cases rural Indians fortunate enough to own land that contained desirable mineral or oil deposits took advantage of this. Georgia Cooper and Lizzie Ott, Choctaw women, negotiated leases with Gulf Oil Corporation and Gypsy Oil Company respectively. The leases took in approximately $150 per month. Another Choctaw woman, Agnes Reed, negotiated a five-year timber lease.[30]

Some rural Indians also earned income through part-time work. Cherokees, for example, found work loading railroad ties into boxcars. The men also spent a considerable amount of time chopping down trees and fashioning them into ties or, in the case of Sam Hair, worked in regional sawmills. Women and children participated in this process, helping men strip the bark off trees. Cherokees also derived income from other home industries, such as the manufacture of clapboard shingles, stave bolts, and staves used for wooden barrels and kegs. Cherokees in Sequoyah County found part-time work in the sorghum mills. Creeks in Okmulgee County worked the clay, glass, and quarrying industries. Chickasaws hired on as part-time help in the cotton compress, ginning, and seed mills. They also worked in the brick, cement, and oil industries around Ada, Oklahoma. Rural Indians also worked as farmhands. Some rural Cherokees who lived in the northeastern counties made seasonal migrations out of Oklahoma. Cherokee men traveled together in groups, either in cars or in busses that farmers provided. These Indians worked in the broomcorn fields in places such as Campo, in southeastern Colorado. Cherokee women also found part-time work in the tomato canneries located in that state.[31]

Most rural Indians, however, did not work for wages. Unlike many non-Indians, rural Indians did not define themselves or measure their self-worth through their jobs. Within the small rural settlements, it was not imperative that men hold steady jobs, and people did not disrespect those who lacked employment. Moreover, wage labor did not appear to be a deciding factor in a family's ability to survive. Many families required little, if any, income. Nannie Barcus, a Choctaw woman, said that "her family never had any use for money." Instead of wage labor, the majority of rural Cherokees, Chickasaws, Choctaws, Creeks, and Seminoles survived off the land.[32]

Dave McIntosh, a rural Seminole, maintained that all of the Seminoles he knew lived on what they grew and hunted. He did not recall any "going hungry" during the Great Depression. Like families in the other four nations, almost all Seminole families maintained gardens, and many of the families preserved fruits and vegetables. Seminoles raised chickens, ducks, geese, pigs, rabbits, and turkeys both for home consumption and market. Families smoked and cured pork and stored barbecued bones to be used throughout the winter in soups and stocks. Sissy Fenton indicated that women worked the gardens and that Seminoles could always depend on food. Bettie Johnson also confirmed that families gathered to trade and "share things" such as food and clothing. She pointed out that her family raised sheep and hogs and cultivated black-eyed peas, cabbage, and other garden crops. Seminole women picked peaches and collected "possum grapes," wild grapes which they dried, then boiled down for use in dumplings, while Seminole men supplemented subsistence farming with hunting and fishing. Even though the oil industry had diminished the amount of wild game in the region, hunters still killed enough to provide food that complemented what the Seminoles grew and raised themselves. Rural Seminoles organized group hunts that supplied the whole community with wild game. McIntosh, Raymond Johnson, and other rural Seminoles said that people butchered and preserved meat together so that settlements could share in the wild game that hunters had killed.[33]

This same preference for subsistence living defined most rural Cherokees as well. Like many of their rural counterparts in the other four tribes, they prided themselves on their independence even if that meant being poor as measured by non-Indian standards of affluence. Independence in Cherokee culture meant the ability of an individual to have the autonomy to do as one pleased.[34]

Most rural Cherokees who lived in small communities relied on extended family and tribal relationships for sustenance and survival. Jennie Bell said that sharing was fairly typical within communities and between clans. As in the other four tribes, visiting among one another and utilizing the resources of neighbors was extremely common. Communal dinners such as wild onion feeds and hog fries brought together clans and settlements. Adam Bean maintained that the lending and exchange of draft animals and farm implements occurred regularly. People understood that a person wishing to borrow something needed the item more than the person who owned it. Occasionally rural Indians traded houses with each other simply for a change of scenery. Whether they were exchanging food, housing, labor, or equipment, sharing within a community reflected the notion that rural Indians lived "within themselves" but not "for themselves." Their primary responsibility was to the settlement. Cherokees referred to this as the "harmony ethic." The harmony ethic reinforced economic reciprocity and communalism.[35]

Within Cherokee communities, subsistence labor was not exclusively gender-specific. Nannie Loren Baker said that both women and men worked the fields, chopped wood, cultivated gardens, and tended to animals. Cherokee women received no special consideration. They were not expected to do any more or any less arduous labor than men. Primarily, men undertook the fishing and hunting in the area. An extensive stream system in northeastern Oklahoma provided an adequate supply of bass, catfish, crappie, and perch as well as crawfish, eel, frogs, and soft-shell turtles. Callie McNiece and others pointed out that in Cherokee settlements they shared the fish and game that male members of the community had caught or killed.[36]

The wooded areas also held game such as deer, rabbit, raccoon, quail, squirrel, and turkey. Abundant wood provided fuel for cooking and heating. Women and children collected dandelions, poke greens, hickory nuts, and walnuts. Most families ground their own cornmeal. They also ground the hickory nuts that women strained and cooked with hominy to make a dish called ca-nu-chi. Beans, berries, chicken, corn, cowpeas, locusts (insects), onions, potatoes, pork, squash, wild mushrooms, and other food items rounded out the diet. This ensured that most Cherokees did not suffer from malnutrition. One Indian woman said that her father went into town one or two times a year to obtain flour and coffee. Occasionally Indians purchased supplies from local stores that other Indians owned. They more readily obtained credit at these country markets.[37]

Anawak Chuculate Webb's family typified the living strategies that most rural Cherokees utilized. She said that her father smoked meat such as deer, hog, rabbit, and squirrel on a regular basis. Her father preferred hickory wood, and her mother tended the fire. In addition the women dried or preserved fruit and vegetables such as apples, grapes, peaches, pumpkins, and string beans, and collected wild mushrooms such as "owl head" mushrooms that they found in creek beds. Women also utilized a "purple corn" that she referred to as "squaw corn" to mix with beans for the purpose of making bread. Webb indicated that the rural Indians she knew "lived off the land."[38]

To sustain themselves, rural Indian also relied on more traditional institutions within their communities. Cherokee settlements, in particular, operated community work groups known as *gadugi*. The word means "working together." Settlements maintained gadugi or cooperative labor groups consisting of both men and women to meet settlement needs. Rural Indians managed communal treasuries to help provide for people who could not afford such things as burial or travel expenses. Community funds purchased food or medicine for the poor and the infirm. The gadugi organized work groups that

Figure 9.3. Bull Hollow Camp orchestra, CCC–Indian Division. Courtesy of the Carl Albert Congressional Archives, University of Oklahoma, Wilburn Cartwright Collection, 882.

periodically assisted families with jobs that needed to be done on their home-steads. Anna Belle Sixkiller Mitchell said that she lived in a house that had been built by the men of her community. The gadugi, moreover, served as an informal lending agency. People received money to cover funeral expenses, hospitalization, and transportation, among other things. Similar informal work cooperatives existed among the other four tribes.[39]

The degree to which rural Indians depended on one another and their communities for livelihood and emotional sustenance cannot be overstated. Unlike non-Indians and their comparatively acculturated tribal brethren, the commitment that traditional rural Cherokees, Chickasaws, Choctaws, Creeks, and Seminoles showed toward subsistence and communally oriented living was bolstered by their shared family, clan, town, and tribal cultural heritage. In the 1930s they attempted to maintain a way of life based on the traditions of previous generations. This did not mean that no change in lifestyle occurred in relation to the past or that all rural Indians among the Five Tribes adhered to a communal construct. Rural Indians creatively adapted in relation to their circumstances and continued to combine a number of economic strategies to maintain their livelihood. Indians who inhabited the small, rural settlements attempted to preserve what was culturally important to them and

accommodated the market economy and federal aid in ways that did not completely destroy the social integrity of their enclaves. They neither rejected
nor embraced completely the economic programs of the Indian Office. They
remained pragmatic, determined, and resourceful in the face of increasing pressure from both the economic hardships of the 1930s and the further
encroachment of non-Indian society.[40]

Moreover, contrary to the dire government reports that many members
of the Five Tribes lived in deplorable, famine-ravaged conditions, most rural
Indians failed to corroborate those accounts. Some suffered through hard
times, but they did not equate poverty with hopelessness. The historical and
popular image of a spiritually broken, starving Indian was more caricature
than reality. Rural Indians in all of the Five Tribes said that people depended
on one another as always, and the 1930s proved no different. Cherokees,
Chickasaws, Choctaws, Creeks, and Seminoles who lived in the isolated communities of central and eastern Oklahoma retained their social and economic
vitality as they had successfully done for decades, despite the consequences
of the Great Depression and the efforts of the federal government to help the
Indians help themselves.[41]

Notes

1. S.R. 449, 71st Cong., 2nd Sess., June 17, 1930; Lewis Meriam, *The Problem of
Indian Administration in the United States* (Washington, D.C.: Institute of Government
Research, 1928); *Survey of Conditions of the Indians in the United States* (Washington,
D.C.: Government Printing Office, 1929), xiv, 5322–24, 5351–52, 5696–5702, 5714–15, 5881–
82, 5918–23, 6035–36, 6265–66, 13697–722; Angie Debo, *And Still the Waters Run: The
Betrayal of the Five Civilized Tribes* (Princeton: Princeton University Press, 1940), 354–
57; Gerald D. Nash, *The Great Transition: A Short History of Twentieth-Century America*
(Boston: Allyn and Bacon, 1971), 217–18; *Harlow's Weekly*, October 22, November 19, and
November 26, 1932; *Daily Oklahoman*, February 16, 1933. In terms of nomenclature in
regard to the Cherokees, Chickasaws, Choctaws, Creeks, and Seminoles, I use the historical term "Five Civilized Tribes" in the notes below when referencing government agency
reports. At all other times, I use the preferred modern term "Five Tribes" or name the
nations individually.

2. Meriam, *The Problem of Indian Administration in the United States*, 484–88, 748,
756, 799–803; Oklahoma State Planning Board, *Preliminary Report, 1936* (Oklahoma City:
Oklahoma State Planning Board, 1936), 35b, 37b; Angie Debo, "The Five Tribes of Oklahoma
Report on Social and Economic Conditions," n.d., box 238, E. E. Dale Collection, Western
History Collections, University of Oklahoma Libraries.

3. Commissioner of Indian Affairs, *Annual Report*, 1930–39 (Washington, D.C.: Government Printing Office); Superintendent of the Five Civilized Tribes, *Annual Report*, 1930–1939, RG 75, National Archives at Fort Worth.

4. Superintendent of the Five Civilized Tribes, *Annual Report*, 1930–40, RG 75, National Archives at Forth Worth; Albert Wahrhaftig, "In the Aftermath of Civilization: The Persistence of Cherokee Indians in Oklahoma" (PhD diss., University of Chicago, 1975); Dr. Virgil Berry Collection, Western History Collections, University of Oklahoma Libraries; Jack Maurice Schultz, "Fulfilling the Work in the Oklahoma Seminole Baptist Church: The Interdependence of Cultural and Social Factors in the Maintenance of a Traditional Community" (PhD diss., University of Oklahoma, 1995); Leslie Hewes, "The Geography of Cherokee Country" (PhD diss., University of California, Los Angeles, 1940); Morris Opler, "The Creek Indian Towns of Oklahoma in 1937," Morris Opler Collection, Western History Collections, University of Oklahoma Libraries; Janet Etheridge Jordan, "Politics and Religion in a Western Cherokee Community: A Century of Struggle in a White Man's World" (PhD diss., University of Connecticut, 1975), 229.

5. Superintendent of the Five Civilized Tribes *Annual Report*, 1933–34, RG 75, National Archives at Fort Worth.

6. Superintendent of the Five Civilized Tribes, *Annual Report*, 1933–34, 1939, RG 75, National Archives at Fort Worth; Reid Holland, "Life in Oklahoma's CCC," *Chronicles of Oklahoma* 48 (Summer 1970), 227; William Leuchtenberg, *Franklin D. Roosevelt and the New Deal* (New York: Harper and Row, 1963), 124–25, 132; Oklahoma State Planning Board, *Preliminary Report, 1936*, 161; Dove Montgomery Kull, "Social and Economic Factors" (master's thesis, University of Oklahoma, 1940), 42, 58; Sally Bradstreet Soelle, "New Deal Art: The Section of Fine Arts Program in the Great Plains State" (PhD diss., Oklahoma State University, 1993), 141–43; Kathleen Grisham Rogers, "Incidence of New Deal Art in Oklahoma: An Historical Survey" (master's thesis, University of Oklahoma, 1974), 10–11, 52; *Report on Public Works Planning, 1938*, 21–23, 30–42, box 1, Industrial Development, Parks Department, Oklahoma Department of Libraries; *Indians at Work*, February 15, 1934; "An Exhibition of Skills of the Unemployed," WPA report, untitled, n.d., box 18, Alice Marriott Collection, Western History Collections, University of Oklahoma Libraries; William Zimmerman to Julian Schley, October 21, 1939, and H. D. Bashore to the Office of the Commissioner of Indian Affairs, August 21, 1939, Bureau of Indian Affairs, Central Classified Files, 1907–1939, reel 1, microfilm copy, Western History Collections, University of Oklahoma Libraries; Norman Cooper, "Oklahoma in the Great Depression, 1930–1940: The Problem of Emergency Relief" (master's thesis, University of Oklahoma, 1973), 68.

7. Superintendent of the Five Civilized Tribes, *Annual Report*, 1933–39, RG 75, National Archives at Fort Worth; O. V. Chandler to W. B. Pine and Elmer Thomas, box 2, Legislative Series, Elmer Thomas Collection, Carl Albert Center, University of Oklahoma.

8. O. V. Chandler to W. B. Pine and Elmer Thomas.

9. Oklahoma State Planning Board, *Preliminary Report, 1936*, 169; Superintendent of the Five Civilized Tribes, *Annual Report*, 1936–40, RG 75, National Archives at Fort Worth.

10. Oklahoma State Planning Board, *Preliminary Report, 1936*, 169; Superintendent of the Five Civilized Tribes, *Annual Report*, 1936–40, RG 75, National Archives at Fort Worth.

11. Alice Marriott to Dr. Willis Stovall, August 17, 1938, and Fountain H. Angel to the Superintendent of the Five Civilized Tribes, June 14, 1938, box 18; Edna Burney to Alice Marriott, July 12, 1940, box 10; and Alice Marriott to Louis C. West, April 8, 1937, box 16, Alice Marriott Collection, Western History Collections, University of Oklahoma Libraries; Cinda Kaye Baldwin, "The Sequoyah Indian Weavers Association: A New Deal for the Oklahoma Cherokee" (master's thesis, University of Arkansas, 1984), 4–5, 16–26.

12. Alice Marriott to Dr. Willis Stovall, August 17, 1938, and Fountain H. Angel to the Superintendent of the Five Civilized Tribes, June 14, 1938, box 18; Edna Burney to Alice Marriott, July 12, 1940, box 10; and Alice Marriott to Louis C. West, April 8, 1937, box 16, Alice Marriott Collection, Western History Collections, University of Oklahoma Libraries; Cinda Kaye Baldwin, "The Sequoyah Indian Weavers Association: A New Deal for the Oklahoma Cherokee" (master's thesis, University of Arkansas, 1984), 4–5, 16–26.

13. Alice Marriott to P. W. Danielson, April 20, 1938, box 17; Mabel Morrow to Alice Marriott, November 4, 1937, box 8; Willard Beatty to Jack Brown, February 8, 1939, box 17; Alice Marriott to Louis C. West, April 20, 1937, Z. E. Black to Alice Marriott, July 6, 1937, and Mrs. A. L. Rittman to Jane Williams, March 18, 1938, box 16; Alice Marriott to Mary Hogue, September 15, 1937, and Alice Marriott to A. M. Landman, September 25, 1937, box 7; Edna Burney to Alice Marriott, July 12, 1940, box 10; Maude Blanchard to Alice Marriott, March 10, 1939, box 17, Alice Marriott Collection, Western History Collections, University of Oklahoma Libraries.

14. Mabel Morrow to Alice Marriott, January 6, 1937, Mabel Morrow to Alice Marriott, January 15, 1938, Mabel Morrow to Alice Marriott, November 4, 1937, P. W. Danielson to Alice Marriott, November 29, 1937, box 8, Alice Marriott Collection, Western History Collections, University of Oklahoma Libraries.

15. Maude Blanchard to Alice Marriott, March 17, 1939, box 17, Alice Marriott Collection, Western History Collections, University of Oklahoma Libraries.

16. Maude Blanchard to Alice Marriott, March 17, 1939, box 17; P. W. Danielson to Alice Marriott, November 29, 1937, box 8; Minta Foreman to Alice Marriott, June 10, 1938, and Alice Marriott to Louis C. West, December 6, 1937, box 16; Alice Marriott to Louis C. West, April 8, 1937, box 10; Alice Marriott to R. C. Bane, January 9, 1939, Mrs. A. L. Rittman to Jane Williams, March 18, 1938, and Jayne Williams to Alice Marriott, March 22, 1938, box 16; Alice Marriott to Mary Hogue, September 15, 1937, and Mabel Morrow to Alice Marriott, June 8, 1938, box 11, Alice Marriott Collection, Western History Collections, University of Oklahoma Libraries; Baldwin, "The Sequoyah Indian Weavers," 16, 21, 30, 50–54.

17. Maude Blanchard to Alice Marriott, March 17, 1939, box 17; P. W. Danielson to Alice Marriott, November 29, 1937, box 8; Minta Foreman to Alice Marriott, June 10, 1938; Alice

Marriott to Louis C. West, December 6, 1937, box 16; Alice Marriott to Louis C. West, April 8, 1937, box 10; Alice Marriott to R. C. Bane, January 9, 1939, Mrs. A. L. Rittman to Jane Williams, March 18, 1938, and Jayne Williams to Alice Marriott, March 22, 1938, box 16; Alice Marriott to Mary Hogue, September 15, 1937, and Mabel Morrow to Alice Marriott, June 8, 1938, box 11, Alice Marriott Collection, Western History Collections, University of Oklahoma Libraries; Baldwin, "The Sequoyah Indian Weavers," 16, 21, 30, 50–54. The best example of John Collier's good intentions gone awry during this period involved the Navajos. The Indian Office believed that the Navajos had too many goats and sheep grazing on too little land. This caused significant soil erosion, which, if left unchecked, threatened to undermine federal water reclamation efforts in the region. Collier believed that reduction of the Navajo herds would not only benefit the Navajo in the long run, but also eliminate the impact of soil erosion on federal damming and irrigation projects. Thus Collier ordered the slaughter of Navajo livestock—goats and sheep that were economically and symbolically vital to Navajo culture. Not only did this embitter many Navajos, it forced numerous people who had been self-sufficient to seek menial wage-labor employment.

18. Superintendent of the Five Civilized Tribes, *Annual Report*, 1937–40; "Annual Report of the Extension Industry," Superintendent of the Five Civilized Tribes, *Annual Report*, 1939, RG 75, National Archives at Forth Worth; Morris Opler, "Creek Indian Towns in Oklahoma," *Papers in Anthropology* 13 (Winter 1972), 61–64, 83, 109; boxes 16, 25.1, Angie Debo Papers, Oklahoma State University; John Collier Collection, reel 12, series 1, micro-film; Bureau of Indian Affairs, Central Classified Files, 1907–1939, reel 1, microfilm; Angie Debo, "The Five Tribes of Oklahoma Report," 28–35; Bureau of Indian Affairs Report, *Survey of Indians and Arts and Crafts, 1934*, E. E. Dale Collection, box 230, Exhibit F; Walter Woelke to McCurtain County Credit Association, September 28, 1940, Jubel Wilson to the Commissioner of Indian Affairs, April 24, 1940, Minutes of the McCurtain County Credit Association, n.d., Bureau of Indian Affairs, Central Classified Files, 1907–39, reel 1, micro-film; *Indians at Work*, February 1940; Edna Burney to Alice Marriott, July 12, 1940, box 10, Alice Marriott to Louis C. West, April 8, 1937, box 16, and *Revolving Credit Fund Report as of July 1938 and Analysis of Loans to Individuals by Purpose*, box 11, Alice Marriott Collection, Western History Collections, University of Oklahoma. Libraries; Rennard Strickland, *The Indians of Oklahoma* (Norman: University of Oklahoma Press, 1984), 72–73; B. T. Quinten, "Oklahoma Tribes, the Great Depression, and the Indian Bureau," *Mid America* 49 (January 1967), 29–43; U.S. Department of Commerce, Bureau of the Census, *Fifteenth Census of the United States, Indian Population of the United States and Alaska, 1930* (Washington, D.C.: Government Printing Office, 1937).

19. Edna Burney to Alice Marriott, July 12, 1940, box 10, Alice Marriott to Louis C. West, April 8, 1937, box 16, *Revolving Credit Fund Report as of July 1938 and Analysis of Loans to Individuals by Purpose*, box 11, Alice Marriott Collection, Western History Collections, University of Oklahoma Libraries; Debo, "The Five Tribes of Oklahoma Report," 13–35, E. E. Dale Collection, Western History Collections, University of Oklahoma Libraries;

boxes 16, 25.1, 25.2, Angie Debo Papers, Oklahoma State University; Superintendent of the Five Civilized Tribes *Annual Report*, 1937–40, RG 75, National Archives at Fort Worth; Quinten, "Oklahoma Tribes," 29–43; U.S. Department of Commerce, Bureau of the Census, *Fifteenth Census of the United States, Indian Population of the United States and Alaska, 1930* (Washington, D.C.: Government Printing Office, 1937); O. V. Chandler to W. B. Pine and Elmer Thomas January 3, 1931, box 2, Legislative Series, Elmer Thomas Papers, Carl Albert Center, University of Oklahoma; Morris Opler, "Creek Indian Towns of Oklahoma," 64; "Third Annual Report of the Supervisor of Indian Education to the Commissioner of Indian Affairs for the Fiscal Year Ended June 30, 1934," mimeograph, box 9, Subject Files, Elmer Thomas Collection, Carl Albert Center, University of Oklahoma; Jimmie Harjo, interview by Billie Byrd, January 29, 1938, vol. 38, Indian Pioneer Papers, Western History Collections, University of Oklahoma Libraries.

20. Debo, "The Five Tribes of Oklahoma Report," 13–35; Arch Ray, interview by J. W. Tyner, April 30, 1969, T-426-1, John Fox, interview by J. W. Tyner, July 15, 1968, T-293-1, Johnson Scott, interview by Guy Logadon, August 17, 1969, T-510, Doris Duke Collection, Western History Collections, University of Oklahoma Libraries; boxes 16, 25.1, Angie Debo Papers, Oklahoma State University; Superintendent of the Five Civilized Tribes, *Annual Report*, 1937–40, RG 75, National Archives at Fort Worth; Quinten, "Oklahoma Tribes," 29–43; U.S. Department of Commerce, Bureau of the Census, *Fifteenth Census of the United States, Indian Population of the United States and Alaska*, 1930 (Washington, D.C.: Government Printing Office, 1937).

21. Kenneth Ernest Fink, "A Cherokee Notion of Development" (Ph.D. diss., Union Graduate School, Ohio, 1978), 10, 36; Leslie Hewes, "The Geography of the Cherokee Country" (Ph.D. diss., University of California, Berkeley, 1940), 1–3, 105b, 114, 120, 142; Janet Haskett Hutchins, "Cherokee Country: Cultural Landscape Change, 1940–1993 (master's thesis, University of Oklahoma, 1995), 219; box 3, George Nelson Collection, American Indian Institute Papers; folder 2, Madeline Czarina Conlan Collection, American Indian Institute Papers; box 5, "The Place of the Indian in Modern Society," American Indian Institute Papers; Fox interview; John Steinbeck, *The Grapes of Wrath* (New York: Viking Press, 1939); *Indians at Work*, August 15 and September 1, 1936.

22. Despite the pessimistic assessments of government reports, Indian Office personnel, and the more acculturated tribal members of the Five Tribes, to argue that the rural, mostly restricted members of the Cherokee, Chickasaw, Choctaw, Creek, and Seminole nations were on the brink of starvation is to exaggerate their condition. An overwhelming amount of evidence exists that contradicts this assessment. It might have appealed to the paternalistic instincts of those who were attempting to help these so-called poor, hapless Indians, but the Indians themselves did not view themselves in this manner. Indeed, ambivalence, bemusement, resentment, and suspicion better describes the reactions rural Indians had to not only government personnel but to many of the more acculturated members of their own nations. Fink, "A Cherokee Notion," 10, 36; Hewes, "Geography," 1–3, 105b, 114, 120, 142;

Hutchins, "Cherokee Country," 219; box 3, George Nelson Collection; folder 2, Madeline Czarina Conlan Collection; box 5, "The Place of the Indian in Modern Society," American Indian Institute Papers, Western History Collections, University of Oklahoma Libraries; *Indians at Work*, August 15 and September 1, 1936.

23. Boxes 20 and 25.2, Angie Debo Papers, Oklahoma State University; Fink, "A Cherokee Notion," 37; box 238, E. E. Dale Collection; "The Oklahoma Ozarks as the Land of the Cherokees," Leslie Hewes Collection, Western History Collections, University of Oklahoma Libraries; Loretta Fowler, *Shared Symbols, Contested Meanings: Gros Ventre Culture and History, 1778–1984* (Ithaca: Cornell University Press, 1987), 6–7; L. G. Moses and Raymond Wilson, eds., *Indian Lives: Essays on Nineteenth and Twentieth Century Native American Leaders* (Albuquerque: University of New Mexico Press, 1985), 2–4; Karen I. Blu, *The Lumbee Problem: The Making of an American Indian People* (Cambridge, England: Cambridge University Press, 1980), 164, 167, 170–71; Lee Anne Nichols, Lee Anne, "The Infant Caring Process among Cherokee Mothers" (Ph.D. diss., University of Arizona, 1994), 55, 72; Albert L. Wahrhaftig and Jane Lukens Warhhaftig, "New Militants or Resurrected State? The Northeastern County Oklahoma Cherokee Organization," in *The Cherokee Nation: A Troubled History*, edited by Duane H. King (Knoxville: University of Tennessee Press, 1979), 223–46.

24. Nichols, "Infant Caring," 55, 72; Wahrhaftig and Warhhaftig, "New Militants," 223–46; boxes 20 and 25.2, Angie Debo Papers, Oklahoma State University; Fink, "A Cherokee Notion," 37; box 238, E. E. Dale Collection; "The Oklahoma Ozarks as the Land of the Cherokees," Leslie Hewes Collection, Western History Collections, University of Oklahoma Libraries; Oklahoma Department of Public Welfare, *Annual Report*, August 6, 1936, to June 30, 1937, box 1, Oklahoma Department of Public Welfare, Oklahoma Department of Libraries; , Josiah Billy, interview by Lawrence A. Williams, July 8, 1937, vol. 8, Indian Pioneer Papers, Western History Collections, University of Oklahoma Libraries.

25. Nichols, "Infant Caring," 55, 72; Wahrhaftig and Wahrhaftig, "New Militants," 223–46; boxes 20 and 25.2, Angie Debo Papers, Oklahoma State University; box 238, E. E. Dale Collection; "The Oklahoma Ozarks as the Land of the Cherokees," Leslie Hewes Collection; Lizzie Johnson Kernell, interview by Robert Miller, April 8, 1967, T-44; John Scott interview by Lucinda Tiger, March 22, 1970, T-558; Elmer Lusty, interview by Lucinda Tiger, May 10, 1970, T-571, Mary Green Johnson, interview by Lucinda Tiger, November 28, 1969, T-536, Raymond Johnson, interview by Lucinda Tiger, November 28, 1969, T-547-2, Bettie Johnson, interview by Robert Miller, January 26, 1968, T-243, Sissy Fenton, interview by Robert Miller, May 10, 1967, T-51, Walter Billingsley, interview by Robert Miller, May 14, 1969, T-259, Doris Duke Collection, Western History Collections, University of Oklahoma Libraries; Lola Maud Amerson, interview by Anna Berry, May 28, 1937, vol. 2, Adam Bean, interview by Gus Hummingbird, May 19, 1937, Nora Barberhouse, interview by Johnson Hampton, March 2, 1938, vol. 5, Martin Blackwood, interview by W. J. B. Bigby, June 22, 1937, vol. 8, Indian Pioneer Papers, Western History Collections, University of Oklahoma

Libraries; Dorothy Milligan, *The Indian Way: Chickasaws* (Quanah, Tex.: Nortex Press, 1976), 50, 81; Wilma Mankiller and Michael Wallis, *Mankiller: A Chief and Her People* (New York: St. Martin's Press, 1993), 32–33; Flora Perry, interview with author, Ada, Oklahoma, November 18, 2005.

26. Nichols, "Infant Caring," 55, 72; Wahrhaftig and Wahrhaftig, "New Militants," 223–46; boxes 20 and 25.2, Angie Debo Papers, Oklahoma State University; box 238, E. E. Dale Collection; "The Oklahoma Ozarks as the Land of the Cherokees," Leslie Hewes Collection; Lizzie Johnson Kernell, interview by Robert Miller, April 8, 1967, T-44; John Scott interview by Lucinda Tiger, March 22, 1970, T-558; Elmer Lusty, interview by Lucinda Tiger, May 10, 1970, T-571, Mary Green Johnson, interview by Lucinda Tiger, November 28, 1969, T-536, Raymond Johnson, interview by Lucinda Tiger, November 28, 1969, T-547-2, Bettie Johnson, interview by Robert Miller, January 26, 1968, T-243, Sissy Fenton, interview by Robert Miller, May 10, 1967, T-51, Walter Billingsley, interview by Robert Miller, May 14, 1969, T-259, Doris Duke Collection, Western History Collections, University of Oklahoma Libraries; Lola Maud Amerson, interview by Anna Berry, May 28, 1937, vol. 2, Adam Bean, interview by Gus Hummingbird, May 19, 1937, Nora Barberhouse, interview by Johnson Hampton, March 2, 1938, vol. 5, Martin Blackwood, interview by W. J. B. Bigby, June 22, 1937, vol. 8, Indian Pioneer Papers, Western History Collections, University of Oklahoma Libraries; Dorothy Milligan, *The Indian Way: Chickasaws* (Quanah, Tex.: Nortex Press, 1976), 50, 81; Wilma Mankiller and Michael Wallis, *Mankiller: A Chief and Her People* (New York: St. Martin's Press, 1993), 32–33; Flora Perry, interview with author, Ada, Oklahoma, November 18, 2005.

27. Nichols, "Infant Caring," 55, 72; Wahrhaftig and Wahrhaftig, "New Militants," 223–46; boxes 20 and 25.2, Angie Debo Papers, Oklahoma State University; box 238, E. E. Dale Collection, Western History Collections, University of Oklahoma Libraries; Fink, "A Cherokee Notion," 37; "The Oklahoma Ozarks as the Land of the Cherokees," Leslie Hewes Collection; Oklahoma Department of Public Welfare, *Annual Report*, August 6, 1936, to June 30, 1937," box 1, Oklahoma Department of Public Welfare, Oklahoma Department of Libraries; Kernell interview, J. Scott interview, E. Lusty interview, M. Johnson interview, R. Johnson interview, B. Johnson interview, Fenton interview, Billingsley interview, Belle Gray Connor interview by Lucinda Tiger, October 10, 1969, T-526-1, Doris Duke Collection, Western History Collections, University of Oklahoma Libraries; Amerson interview, Bean interview, Barberhouse interview, Blackwood interview, Indian Pioneer Papers, Western History Collections, University of Oklahoma Libraries; Mary Jo Watson, "Oklahoma Indian Women and Their Art" (PhD diss., University of Oklahoma, 1993), 230; Hampton Tucker to Ben Dwight, February 13, 1931, box 11, Hampton Tucker Collection, Western History Collections, University of Oklahoma Libraries; A. M Landman to Commissioner of Indian Affairs, January 4, 1933, box S26, Seminole Nation Papers, Western History Collections, University of Oklahoma Libraries; Milligan, *The Indian Way: Chickasaws*, 50, 81; *Wewoka Times Democrat*, January 10, 1936; box 239, E. E. Dale Collection, Western History

Collections, University of Oklahoma Libraries; Bear Heart with Molly Larkin Clarkson, *The Wind Is My Mother: The Life and Teachings of a Native American Shaman* (New York: Potter Publishers, 1996),18–19, 45; Amerson interview, Indian Pioneer Papers; Dave McIntosh, interview by Robert Miller, October 10, 1967, T-210, T-211, Doris Duke Collection, Western History Collections, University of Oklahoma Libraries; Mary McKinney Frye, "Visit to an Indian Church," box 239, E. E. Dale Collection, Western History Collections, University of Oklahoma Libraries.

28. Jimmie Harjochee, interview by Billie Byrd, February 17, 1938, vol. 38, Clem Hogner, interview by Gus Hummingbird, June 26, 1937, vol. 43, Minnie Wimberly Hodge, interview by Mary Dorward, March 4, 1938, vol. 43, Indian Pioneer Papers, Western History Collections, University of Oklahoma Libraries.

29. Federal Writers' Project of Oklahoma, *Calendar of Annual Events in Oklahoma*, American Guide Series (Tulsa: Tribune Publishing, 1938), 231–33; John R. Swanton, *Social Organization and Social Usages of the Indians of the Creek Confederacy, 42nd Annual Report, Bureau of American Ethnology, 1924–1925* (Washington, D.C.: Government Printing Office, 1928), 334–35, 363, 384–85; Dr. Virgil Berry Collection, Western History Collections, University of Oklahoma Libraries; Harjochee interview, Joe Hogner interview by W. J. B. Bigby, June 20, 1937, vol. 43, and Hodge interview, Indian Pioneer Papers, Western History Collections, University of Oklahoma Libraries; Alice Marriott to Rene d' Harnoncourt, n.d., box 8, Alice Marriott Collection, Western History Collections, University of Oklahoma Libraries; Audis Neumeyer Moore, "The Social and Economic Status of the Seminole Indians" (master's thesis, University of Oklahoma, 1939), 56.

30. Box 3, George Nelson Collection, Western History Collections, University of Oklahoma Libraries; Superintendent of the Five Civilized Tribes, *Annual Report*, 1939–1940, RG 75, National Archives at Fort Worth; Hewes, "Geography of Cherokee Country," 172, 224–27, plate 25; Jordan, "Politics and Religion," 211; *A Social and Economic Survey of Six Counties in Southeastern Oklahoma* (Norman: University of Oklahoma, 1946), 36–40, 46, 48, 51, 56; Oklahoma State Planning Board, Preliminary Report, 1936, 37b; Pierce Kelton Merrill, "The Social and Economic Status of the Choctaw Indians" (master's thesis, University of Oklahoma, 1940), 48–69; Tom Aldis Hall, The Social and Economic Status of the Cherokee Indians" (master's thesis, University of Oklahoma, 1934), 41–97. "Restricted" Indians were those allotted individuals who possessed half or more Indian blood. Their restricted status meant that the federal government would hold their allotted land in trust for twenty-five years, at the end of which time the restricted individuals would gain outright title to their allotted land and then have the legal right to sell the land. As a result, land ownership among more traditional Indians was relatively high and the overwhelming majority of these more traditional Indians were full-blood.

31. Moore, "The Social and Economic Status of the Seminole," 62–106; Richard W. Chuculate, "Participation in Community Activities According to the Degree of Indian Blood of a Group of Indians Residing in Bunch Township, Adair County, Oklahoma"

(master's thesis, University of Oklahoma, 1957), 3–4, 112–50; Hewes, "Geography of Cherokee Country," plate 34; Spencer Berry, "A Social Analysis of Okmulgee County, Oklahoma," (master's thesis, University of Oklahoma, 1941), 42–76; Quinten, "Oklahoma Tribes," 29–43; Sandra Faim-Silva, "Choctaw at the Crossroads: Native Americans and the Multinationals in the Oklahoma Timber Region" (PhD diss., Boston University, 1984), 338–40; Mankiller and Wallis, *Mankiller*, 34–37; *State of Oklahoma Department of Labor Bulletin 1-A: Industrial Directory* (Guthrie: Oklahoma Department of Labor, 1932); Champ Clark Carney, "The Historical Geography of the Chickasaw Lands of Oklahoma" (PhD diss., Indiana University, 1961), 100–110; Sam Hair, interview by Faye Delph, April 11, 1969, T-412-1, and Billy Spencer, interview by Robert Miller, May 1, 1967, T-48, Doris Duke Collection, Western History Collections, University of Oklahoma Libraries; Dicey Stake Adams, interview by Jerome Emmons, May 25, 1937, vol. 1, Indian Pioneer Papers, Western History Collections, University of Oklahoma Libraries; E .E. Dale, "Why A Program," box 236, and E. E. Dale, "The Five Civilized Tribes Progress," box 236, pp. A15, A19, E. E. Dale Collection, Western History Collections, University of Oklahoma Libraries.

32. Nannie Barcus, interview by Pete Cole, September 13, 1937, vol. 5, Indian Pioneer Papers, Western History Collections, University of Oklahoma Libraries.

33. McIntosh interview, B. Johnson interview, Kernell interview, M. Johnson interview, Doris Duke Collection, Western History Collections, University of Oklahoma Libraries; Meredith Burrill, *A Socio-Economic Atlas of Oklahoma* (Stillwater: Oklahoma A&M College, 1936), 31; Bruce Gilbert Carter, "A History of Seminole County, Oklahoma" (master's thesis, University of Oklahoma, 1932), 3; Moore, "The Social and Economic Status of the Seminole Indians," 62–65, 75, 88–96; *Wewoka Times Democrat*, February 11, 1930, February 14, 1934, and January 16, 1937.

34. Hall, "The Social and Economic Status of the Choctaw," 41–97; Debo, "The Five Tribes of Oklahoma Report," 14; Noah Fish, interview by Lucinda Tiger, November 7, 1969, T536-1, Fenton interview, Johnson interview, Bell interview, Hogner interview, Bean interview, Doris Duke Collection, Western History Collections, University of Oklahoma Libraries.

35. Hall, "The Social and Economic Status of the Cherokee," 41–97; Merrill, "The Social and Economic Status of the Choctaw," 54–56; Hutchins, "Cherokee Country," 131, 152–53; Morris Opler, "Creek Towns of Oklahoma in 1937"; Brian F. Rader, "The Political Outsiders: Blacks and Indians in a Rural Oklahoma Community" (PhD diss., University of Oklahoma, 1977), 183–84; Dorothy Milligan, *The Indian Way: Cherokees* (Quanah, Tex.: Nortex Press, 1976), xi, 110; Debo, "The Five Tribes of Oklahoma Report," 14; Fenton interview, Fish interview, Johnson interview, Bell interview; Callie McNiece interview by W. T. Holland, October 19, 1937, vol. 61, Indian Pioneer Papers, Western History Collections, University of Oklahoma Libraries; C. Hogner interview and Bean interview, Indian Pioneer Papers, Western History Collections, University of Oklahoma Libraries; Hutchins, "Cherokee Country," 60.

36. Loren Barker, interview by Nannie Lee Burns, January 31, 1938, vol. 5, Indian Pioneer Papers, Western History Collections, University of Oklahoma Libraries; Hall, "The Social and Economic Status of the Cherokees," 61–68; Chuculate, "Participation," 4, 112, 153; Dorothy Milligan, *The Indian Way: Cherokees* (Quanah, Tex.: Nortex Press, 1976), 76–95; Mankiller and Wallis, *Mankiller*, 34–36; McIntosh interview, Lucinda Vann Tibbs, interview by J. W. Tyner, April 26, 1968, T-251, Sunday Bark, interview by J. W. Tyner, September 1, 1969, T-518-1, Doris Duke Collection, Western History Collections, University of Oklahoma Libraries; McNiece interview, Indian Pioneer Papers, Western History Collections, University of Oklahoma Libraries.

37. Loren Barker, interview by Nannie Lee Burns, January 31, 1938, vol. 5, Indian Pioneer Papers, Western History Collections, University of Oklahoma Libraries; Hall, "The Social and Economic Status of the Cherokees," 61–68; Chuculate, "Participation," 4, 112, 153; Dorothy Milligan, *The Indian Way: Cherokees* (Quanah, Tex.: Nortex Press, 1976), 76–95; Mankiller and Wallis, *Mankiller*, 34–36; McIntosh interview, Lucinda Vann Tibbs, interview by J. W. Tyner, April 26, 1968, T-251, Sunday Bark, interview by J. W. Tyner, September 1, 1969, T-518-1, Doris Duke Collection, Western History Collections, University of Oklahoma Libraries; McNiece interview, Indian Pioneer Papers, Western History Collections, University of Oklahoma Libraries.

38. Anawak Chuculate Webb, interview by J. W. Tyner, April 8, 1968, T-249-2, Doris Duke Collection, Western History Collections, University of Oklahoma Libraries.

39. John Witthoft, "Observations on Social Change Among the Eastern Cherokees," in *The Cherokee Indian Nation*, edited by Duane King (Knoxville: University of Tennessee Press, 1979), 204–205; box 25.2, Angie Debo Papers, Oklahoma State University; Hewes, "The Land of the Cherokee," Leslie Hewes Collection, Western History Collections, University of Oklahoma Libraries; Sharlotte Neely, *Snowbird Cherokees: People of Persistence* (Athens: University of Georgia Press, 1991), 35. Community and interdependence are cogently discussed in Conrad M. Arensberg and Solon T. Kimball, *Culture and Community* (New York: Harcourt, Brace and World, 1965); Blu, *The Lumbee Problem*; Denis E. Cosgrove, *Social Formation and Symbolic Landscape* (Totowa, N.J.: Barnes and Noble, 1984); Derek Gregory, Ron Martin, and Graham Smith, eds., *Human Geography: Society, Space, and Social Science* (Minneapolis: University of Minnesota Press, 1994); Joan Weibel Orlando, *Indian Country, L.A.: Maintaining Ethnic Community in Complex Society* (Urbana: University of Illinois Press, 1991). Raymond D. Fogelson and Paul Kutsche, "Cherokee Economic Cooperatives: The Gadugi," in *Symposium on Cherokee and Iroquois Culture*, Bureau of American Ethnology bulletin 180, no. 11 (Washington, D.C.: Government Printing Office, 1961); Howard Tyner, "The Keetowah Society in Cherokee History" (master's thesis, University of Tulsa, 1949), 128–29; Hall, "The Social and Economic Status of the Cherokee," 66–68; Addye Gunter, "Health Problems and Practices of a Group of Cherokee Indians" (master's thesis, University of Oklahoma, 1953), 97–99; Milligan, *The Indian Way: Cherokees*, 26; M. Johnson interview, Indian Pioneer Papers, Western History Collections, University

of Oklahoma Libraries; Wahrhaftig and Wahrhaftig, "New Militants," 204–205; Heart and Clarkson, *Wind Is My Mother*, 12; Baldwin, "The Sequoyah Indian Weavers," 2–4; Jordan, "Politics and Religion," 224; Hutchins, "Cherokee Country," 131, 152–53; Dr. Virgil Berry Collection and Madelina Czarina Colbert Conlan Collection, Western History Collections, University of Oklahoma Libraries; Jack Frederick, and Anna Gritts Kilpatrick, eds., *The Shadow of Sequoyah: Social Documents of the Cherokees, 1862–1964* (Norman: University of Oklahoma Press, 1965), 75.

    40. Fowler, *Shared Symbols*; *Wewoka Times Democrat* January 10, 1936, and September 3, 1937; Angie Debo, *Five Civilized Tribes Survey* (Philadelphia: Indian Rights Association, 1951), 1–9, 19, box 229, E. E. Dale Collection, Western History Collections, University of Oklahoma Libraries; Kernell interview, Dean interview, Fish interview, Johnson interview, Bonner interview, Bean interview, N. Baker interview, J. Baker interview, Barcus interview, Barker interview, Barberhouse interview, Indian Pioneer Papers, Western History Collections, University of Oklahoma Libraries; box 11, Hampton Tucker Collection, Western History Collections, University of Oklahoma Libraries.

    41. *Wewoka Times Democrat*, January 10, 1936, and September 3, 1937; Debo, *Survey*, 1–9, 19, box 229, E. E. Dale Collection, Western History Collections, University of Oklahoma Libraries; Kernell interview, Dean interview, Fish interview, Johnson interview, Bonner interview, Bean interview, N. Baker interview, J. Baker interview, Barcus interview, Barker interview, Barberhouse interview, Indian Pioneer Papers, Western History Collections, University of Oklahoma Libraries; box 11, Hampton Tucker Collection, Western History Collections, University of Oklahoma Libraries.

CHAPTER 10

The War on Poverty in Little Dixie, 1965–1974

Jennifer J. Collins

I n a tarpaper shack just outside McAlester, Oklahoma, in 1970, an elderly couple named Fred and Jessie lived a meager existence. Although the United States boasted of an affluent society, Fred and Jessie did not share in the American prosperity that pervaded the post–World War II period. Their dilapidated dwelling barely provided protection from the elements, as Fred, crippled by age, arthritis, and diabetes, found it difficult to repair the large hole in the roof and the cracks in the walls. As a result, rain, snow, and wind were often unwanted visitors inside. Fred had once collected newspapers and sold vegetables door to door to make ends meet for his wife and the infant granddaughter in their care, but his deteriorating health prevented him from continuing these jobs. Few other employment options existed for the sixty-five-year-old, for he had never attended school and could not even sign his name. Hence the couple worried about finding the funds necessary to provide adequate nutrition for themselves and their young charge. Upon visiting the couple, a local reporter noted that the scene in their home was an "awful lesson of depression and decay [and] human want at its worst."[1]

When the plight of Fred and Jessie came to the attention of three local workers at the Pittsburg County Community Action Agency, they immediately began securing food for the family from a local relief office. They then processed the requisite paperwork to have Fred classified for disability welfare, which provided the couple with funds both to buy essential medication and make payments on a refrigerator. Finally the workers connected Fred and Jessie to the local Indian agency, where the couple received help in securing a grant for a new home. For all of their efforts, Fred praised his local community action agency, noting, "I'm sure glad we found them when we did."[2]

While the War on Poverty programs of the 1960s and 1970s have been heavily scrutinized ever since Lyndon Johnson announced his "unconditional war on poverty" in 1964, the stories of people like Fred, Jessie, and their local community action workers have remained for the large part untold. Scholarly monographs on the period have focused on the origins and implementation of the War on Poverty programs at the national level, while the majority of local case studies have centered on metropolitan areas and the impact of these programs on inner-city poor people and the urban power structure.[3] Although the existing scholarship has contributed significantly to the academic understanding of the War on Poverty, it has for the most part overlooked the experiences of rural Americans in the nation's fight against poverty.

In thousands of communities much like McAlester, Oklahoma, the programs created by the War on Poverty affected the lives of local citizens in numerous ways. These programs created a record of distinct accomplishments and disappointments both similar to and different from those of their urban counterparts. Their unique experiences were no less significant, however, and must be uncovered before a definitive verdict of the War on Poverty can be made.[4]

This case study focuses on the War on Poverty in one rural area, the Third Congressional District of Oklahoma, between 1965 and 1974. Better known locally as Little Dixie, the Third District was distinguished in the 1960s by the national prominence of its representative, Carl Albert, and by its extremely high poverty rate.[5] Indeed, the House Majority Leader's home district, which spanned the southeastern corner of Oklahoma, was the most poverty-stricken region in a comparatively poor state. According to the 1960 U.S. census, over 50 percent of the families in the district had incomes below the federally established poverty line.[6] Fewer than half of all households had reliable housing and plumbing, and in some areas raw sewage ran on the ground.[7] Only two-thirds of the adult population had completed the eighth grade, while almost 3 percent had no schooling whatsoever.[8] The district had the lowest percentage of residents in the state that owned automobiles (69 percent), telephones (55 percent), and televisions (72 percent).[9] Although the phrase "pockets of poverty" seems inadequate in a region where poverty was so pervasive, some areas experienced severe destitution. Three towns in the area had unemployment rates among the highest in the United States, and in Tatums, an all-black community in Carter County, the poverty rate was over 90 percent.[10]

Heavily Democratic, the Third District had been the birthplace of many of Oklahoma's most prominent leaders. However, it had dwindled in both population and influence in the postwar period.[11] By the 1960s, Little Dixie had become a prime example of what happened when agriculture left an area and no industry replaced it. As cotton production in the region diminished, most of the rural residents of the district were forced to relocate to Oklahoma City or Tulsa to find work.[12] As a result, the population of the district declined by over 10 percent in the years between 1950 and 1960.[13]

The destitution throughout Little Dixie in this period highlights the nature of rural poverty in the 1960s. In many ways it was far different from its urban counterpart. While 80 percent of all urban housing units were in sound condition with adequate plumbing facilities at this time, only 50 percent of all rural homes met that standard.[14] Rural people on average were two years behind their city equivalents in education level, while rural communities had fewer than half as many medical professionals per 100,000 people.[15] Citizens widely dispersed in underdeveloped, rural areas also faced a dearth of job opportunities, inadequate water and sewer systems, and practically nonexistent public transportation.[16] These were the conditions in Little Dixie when the War on Poverty programs began amidst a flurry of optimism and high expectations in the summer of 1964.

The antipoverty agenda that Lyndon Johnson announced in January of that year actually had its start in the previous administration, as Kennedy had charged Walter Heller, head of the Council of Economic Advisers, with composing an antipoverty program for his 1964 presidential campaign. After Kennedy's death in November 1963, Johnson inherited the still-vague concept of a "war on poverty" and enthusiastically embraced the idea. His administration pushed ahead with what became known as the Economic Opportunity Act of 1964. The bill was met with much enthusiasm when it arrived on Capitol Hill in March 1964, and it passed both the House and Senate with margins of victory much greater than even the administration had anticipated. On August 20, 1964, Johnson triumphantly signed the War on Poverty legislation into effect, proudly proclaiming, "Today, for the first time in all the history of the human race, a great nation is able to make and willing to make a commitment to eradicate poverty among its people."[17]

However, the bill that he signed had, throughout the legislative process, become a hodgepodge of different ideas. The result of months of work on the part of a team of politicians, economists, and social scientists, the antipoverty crusade had become a confederation of different, and often incoherent, antipoverty programs. The original task force that formulated the program had developed an innovative method of mobilizing local communities, called the Community Action Program (CAP), which was designed to stimulate local communities to plan and implement their own methods of attacking poverty. The CAP was intended to encourage cities and towns across the United States to establish nonprofit community action agencies, which, with the "maximum feasible participation" of the local poor population, would serve to diagnose regional problems with regional solutions.

When Sargent Shriver was named the director of the War on Poverty task force in January 1964, his response following a briefing on the community action recommendation was that the program would "never fly."[18] Eager for immediate results, Shriver watered down the concept of local initiative by developing prepackaged programs at the national level. These programs, such as Head Start and Job Corps, emphasized traditional services, and were designed to have an immediate effect in local communities. Rushed to formulate a policy before the election and forced to avoid detailed language that might have jeopardized congressional approval, planners of the War on Poverty decided to include both community initiative and national concepts, creating dozens of complex programs without any attempt to clarify diverging attitudes toward poverty prevention. These programs were to be administered by one central agency, the newly created Office of Economic Opportunity (OEO), with Shriver at the helm.

When the War on Poverty came to the sparsely populated Third District of Oklahoma, more traditional aspects of the program received the initial emphasis. The already-existing power structure uniformly initiated the establishment of community action agencies, greatly influenced by local elected officials. Indeed, a local government agency filed most of the applications for the community action agencies in the region.[19] Once granted, most of the agencies were housed in a local government building, such as a city hall, county courthouse, or chamber of commerce headquarters.[20] Forced to choose between immediately implementing widely available, well-funded national programs or waiting to develop less-certain local initiatives, Little Dixie leaders unanimously chose the former.

The best known of these national-emphasis programs, and the most prevalent in the first months of the War on Poverty in Little Dixie, was Head Start. The largest of the programs nationwide in 1965, Head Start was also the first program introduced in almost all of the counties in Little Dixie.[21] The program was designed to provide underprivileged preschool-aged children with the necessary education, health, and socialization to begin public schools. As early as the summer of 1965, over twenty-five cities and towns in the Third District had Head Start programs, enrolling over one thousand children and bringing in over $180,000 in War on Poverty funds from the federal government.[22] Like the community action agencies, the Head Start programs were sponsored by extant local organizations, as all but one of the twenty-eight Head Start programs in Little Dixie in the summer of 1965 were applied for and administered by local school boards.[23] Most residents seemed to agree with a local school superintendent when he commented that, "of all the federal programs, Head Start is the greatest of all."[24]

A program closely related to Head Start was the Family Planning Program, as most recruits to the program in Little Dixie were Head Start mothers—and most children in Head Start had mothers involved in the Family Planning Program.[25] At Family Planning–funded clinics, women whose family income fell below the poverty line were given free medical examinations, educational materials, and information about and access to birth control.[26] Again the reliance of a local War on Poverty program on established social service agencies within the district was apparent. In 1967 six of the original thirteen counties in the Third District were served by the Family Planning Program, and all six depended upon the health department or a local nursing service as a delegate agency.[27]

Local colleges and universities also played a major role in bringing War on Poverty programs to Little Dixie. The four institutions of higher learning in the district—Eastern Oklahoma A&M College, Murray State Agricultural College, Southeastern State College, and Poteau Community College (later renamed Carl Albert Junior College)—sponsored national-emphasis educational programs such as Neighborhood Youth Corps (NYC), Upward Bound, and Work-Study as early as 1965.[28] The NYC provided vocational training and education for poor teens both in and out of school. Upward Bound, often called "Head Start for teenagers," prepared low-income high school students for university life by allowing them to spend a summer on a college campus.[29] The last of these education programs aimed at teenagers, the Federal Work Study Program, offered college students below the poverty line jobs on campus to help provide for their education. By 1966 there were ten Neighborhood Youth Corps programs, four Work-Study programs, and one Upward Bound program in the district, incorporating thousands of Little Dixie youth.[30]

The Job Corps was an additional national-emphasis program that appeared early in the Third District. The Job Corps program involved youth between the ages of 16 and 21 living in residential centers where they were provided with education and job training. The Economic Opportunity Act of 1964 had established two types of camps: urban centers, which focused more on vocational training, and rural conservation centers, which provided both job training and education for those with "more acute educational deficiencies."[31] Carl Albert's

Figure 10.1. Third District Representative Carl Albert (right) and Job Corps director Wayne Keenan of West Orange, New Jersey (left), at the dedication of the Arbuckle Job Corps Conservation Center, 1966. Courtesy of the Carl Albert Congressional Archives, University of Oklahoma, Carl Albert Collection.

district was the beneficiary of two conservation centers: the Hodgens Camp, near Heavener, and the Arbuckle Camp in Sulphur, both up and running by the end of 1965.

The region's early efforts in the War on Poverty serve as an example of local interpretation of the ambiguous concept of "maximum feasible participation" of the local poor population. A look at the composition of community action agency boards within the district in 1966 shows that most programs, whether nationally or locally inspired, fell short of the goal of development involving poor people themselves. In many ways this was not an uncommon occurrence in community action bodies. Historian Irwin Unger has noted that most of the first boards "were thrown together by local officials and inevitably represented the old order."[32] This was indeed the case in Little Dixie, as mayors, county commissioners, and school superintendents filled most of the prominent positions in local community action agencies.[33] Civic leaders were heavily involved in the formation of the War on Poverty programs in their region, even after 1965 when most county-level community action agencies in the Third District began applying directly for the federal programs themselves.

Thus the period between 1965 and 1967 in Little Dixie was marked by the active involvement of regional leaders in bringing War on Poverty programs to the area. In this respect, these new agencies were not that different from many of their counterparts in urban areas, where big-city mayors saw the War on Poverty as "merely a new mechanism to provide an expanded flow of conventional services" to the poor.[34] Indeed, for the most part, the programs that the Little Dixie officials selected were national efforts designed to provide basic health and education services to their constituents in new ways. Planned by the Office of Economic Opportunity in Washington, these programs had little local distinction. A roster of the programs operating in the district during this period reads like a list from most other regions of the country, urban and rural.

During the early years of the War on Poverty, despite the involvement of a large number of people in the Third District in federal antipoverty programs, few were occupied in local-initiative programs. This reliance on national-emphasis programs not only subverted the more innovative intent of the War on Poverty legislation but also failed to deal with uniquely rural issues such as inadequate health care and access to clean water. Rural communities in Little Dixie between 1965 and 1967 had mostly fallen short of the goal of local initiative by relying almost solely on prepackaged programs that did little to fight the unique conditions of rural poverty.

However, by the late 1960s, local leaders had developed more confidence and needed expertise in dealing with regional antipoverty issues, and their own antipoverty efforts began to emerge. One spur to community initiative in Little Dixie was the creation of the Emergency Food and Medical Service (EFMS). Designed as a national effort to "counteract conditions of starvation or malnutrition among the poor," the EFMS provided food stamps and medical vouchers for those in extreme poverty.[35] In addition the program made available discretionary funds for supplemental dietary programs, which in many ways allowed the community action agencies in Little Dixie to address one of the major problems in the region—malnutrition. These discretionary funds aided the development of local initiative projects in Little Dixie significantly.

EFMS money was used in many local efforts to provide dietary supplements to the rural poor in Little Dixie between 1967 and 1971. These so-called "self-help projects" included the establishment of hothouse tomato gardens, feeder pig and rabbitry projects, watermelon patches, and catfish farms. All were designed specifically to combat the conditions of rural malnutrition in the region.[36]

In the counties covered by the KI BOIS Community Action Foundation, an innovative garden program was implemented using the EFMS discretionary funds. The local community action agency issued seeds and tools to needy families to encourage them to plant gardens to supplement their diets.[37] Half of the family heads who took advantage of the program were retired or on disability, and thus the program allowed them to improve their diet without straining their low fixed income. Thousands of individuals in the region participated in the "Garden Program," as it was known, between 1968 and 1971.[38]

Another innovative program funded through the EFMS was the "rent-a-cow" initiative, developed by the Indian Nations Community Action Agency. The program provided cattle for low-income families to rent for three years to supplement their income. The borrower was to pay the community action agency twenty-five dollars for every calf that was born during the period so that the agency could buy more cows. Each calf then belonged to the farmer, who could sell it, slaughter it, or build a herd with it. The borrower was to provide the shelter and feed for the rented animals, while the antipoverty agency paid all medical expenses and provided advisers on "feed and protein for the cattle." By 1973 ninety calves had been born since the program's start. Conceived entirely at the local level, the program was estimated to have provided an additional $500 to $1,000 annually to its participants. It was also turning a profit for the community action agency and inspiring similar initiatives across the nation, including a rent-a-sheep program in Wisconsin.[39]

By 1970 most of the communities in Little Dixie were experimenting with programs more suited to local needs. Just as they were making gains, however, a change in the design of the War of Poverty bureaucracy dramatically altered the nature of antipoverty efforts in the district. The "Oklahoma Plan," announced in the summer of 1970, was a two-year OEO demonstration grant given to Oklahoma "to test the management capabilities of states."[40] In this experimental plan, all of the applications for community action programs within the state were to first go through the State Economic Opportunity Office (SEOO). That office was given the responsibility for evaluating local programs to decide whether or not they should be forwarded to a regional office for approval. This plan, in effect, gave the state "virtual control of all local programs."[41]

The grant came in response to growing pressure the OEO faced from its political opponents nationally, and it represented the mounting struggle between OEO proponents on the national level and opponents on the state level. Indeed, within Oklahoma there was much debate between federal and state leaders over the nature of the plan. While U.S. Senator Fred Harris insisted that he was "very much concerned" by the anticipated effects of the Oklahoma Plan on community action, Governor David Hall asserted that the plan would cure many of the problems with community action by bridging the "very distant relationship" between the federal government and local communities.[42]

While the Oklahoma SEOO touted the plan as the ultimate in local control and "decentralized government," local antipoverty leaders saw it differently.[43] To these leaders the plan actually moved the idea of "community" from the regional to the state level, destroying the idea of maximum feasible participation of the local population. One community action director insisted that control at the regional level was "the backbone of the entire poverty program."[44] Fred Tucker, the president of the Oklahoma Community Action Directors' Association and a Third District CAA director, put it succinctly when he stated, "If [the state is] going to take control of the programs, I think we're in trouble."[45]

A review of the two major War on Poverty programs in the Third District under the Oklahoma Plan shows that in many ways the fears of the district's community action directors were well founded. The new programs implemented under the plan demonstrate the growing role the state bureaucracy was playing in designing, implementing, and controlling local programs. They also highlight the vulnerability more innovative local programs had to pressures from government agencies and the local establishment.

The first of these local programs designed under the Oklahoma Plan was a cooperative pharmacy intended to fill the void left by the cancellation of the EFMS program in 1971.[46] A joint effort by the SEOO and the Little Dixie Community Action Agency, the program was put forward as a "new and innovative" approach for providing emergency medical services to the Idabel area. In the region, the average elderly person spent 20 to 40 percent of his or her income on necessary medications.[47] Thus the local antipoverty officials wanted to create a cooperative that would sell medicine to those below the poverty line at reduced costs. All profits that the pharmacy made were to be divided among the co-op members at the end of the year.[48]

The program immediately met a storm of protest from local pharmacists, who decried the program as a "direct step toward socialism." Responding to this outrage, the McCurtain County Commission threatened to withdraw the county from the Little Dixie Community Action Agency, leaving the multi-county agency below the population eligible for War on Poverty funds. The county commissioner defended his choice by insisting that the program "was in direct conflict with private enterprise."[49]

State antipoverty officials initially backed the effort even in the face of protest. However, the state government was not immune to growing political pressures from the region. In the fall of 1971, Oklahoma SEOO officials, Little Dixie Community Action representatives, area pharmacists, and a representative of the governor's office met to talk about the program. After "lengthy discussions," the formation of a cooperative pharmacy was ruled out as a viable alternative for the poor population of the Little Dixie Community Action Agency. Instead the governor's office drew up a proposal in which local druggists would continue to serve the region's poor under a "cost-plus" (discounted) basis.[50]

While the program was still aimed at providing low-cost drugs for the elderly poor of the region, it was a far cry from the program advertised as "a revolutionary way to save on prescriptions."[51] The intervention of the state government and the uproar of the local elite had diluted much of the original intent of the program. The cooperative pharmacy program illustrates how innovative programs often ran afoul of local establishments, causing their demise.

Another program designed for the region under the Oklahoma Plan was the Atoka Grape Project. Described by the Oklahoma SEOO director Rex Sparger as "probably the best and first major experiment in urban-to-rural relocation in the history of the country," the program recruited poor urban families to move to ten-acre tracts outside of rural Atoka.[52] Once there, the families were to grow grapes to supplement their income. In order to participate, a family needed to include an able-bodied adult with some type of stable income (be it welfare or Social Security), as the program was not expected to deliver a profit for three years. Temporary housing, tools, and grapevines were provided by the SEOO.

The program, tagged "orchards for the poor" by the local press, gained nationwide attention for its novelty.[54] The *Los Angeles Times* had a banner headline on the project in December 1971 that read "Oklahoma Poor Offered Farms." In the Associated Press story that followed, the effort was compared to a new land run. The article began, "If you are unemployed, but would like to earn your way and don't mind working hard, the State of Oklahoma has a proposition for you."[55]

Oklahoma newspapers also optimistically advertised the program. The *Tulsa World* printed an analysis from a grape expert who compared southeastern Oklahoma to "the Bordeaux region in France."[56] Another article in an Oklahoma newspaper anticipated that the program could even lure back Okies who had left Oklahoma during the Dust Bowl (ironic considering the dramatic rendering of the Okies' plight in John Steinbeck's novel *The Grapes of Wrath*).[57] The state antipoverty officials anticipated that although the program would start with just ten families and 160 acres, it would ultimately develop to include over 50,000 acres.[58] Eventually, the office predicted, the effort would use horticulture and hard work to break the cycle of urban and rural poverty.

The Atoka Grape Project never lived up to the high expectations set for it by state leaders. In fact, the program could probably be considered a dismal failure for the Oklahoma SEOO. The program's planners had estimated that in three years the pioneering ten families would be earning $7,000 a year from their efforts.[59] Only eighteen months later, frustrated by the slow start and effort involved in the project, most participants had given up and departed.[60] The Atoka Grape Project was dismantled and the one remaining family was given the title to all the vineyards.[61]

The Little Dixie cooperative pharmacy and the Atoka Grape Project illustrate the types of programs implemented in the Third District between 1970 and 1974. While these programs were in many ways more locally driven and innovative than their predecessors in the region were, they were increasingly subjected to interference from both local and state officials. Indeed, the period is marked by the high degree of state control in many local community action programs. These programs also highlight why many community action agencies steered clear of local projects: they were by and large risky and susceptible to pressures from the local establishment.

The nature of community action and the War on Poverty in Little Dixie had changed in many ways between 1965 and 1974. Initially focusing solely on national-emphasis programs, regional community action agencies slowly began to develop more local-initiative programs as they gained experience in the War on Poverty effort. After 1970 local leaders tried to initiate more original programs, but their efforts were often resisted by those in the region's power structure. In 1974 a list of the programs in the Third District read much the same as it had nine years earlier, with a heavy emphasis on programs such as Head Start, Family Planning, and Neighborhood Youth Corps. These national-emphasis programs had proven easier to implement, better funded, and less controversial than their more original counterparts.

By 1974 the federal government had allocated billions of dollars to fight a comprehensive battle against poverty. However, just a decade after the War on Poverty began, political changes in Washington as well as controversy and disappointment with the program as a whole led President Gerald Ford to quietly sign the Community Services Act of 1974, effectively terminating the War on Poverty. The legislation was largely ceremonial: the War on Poverty had long before been stripped of its innovation, due to funding cuts, political pressures and local difficulties. While many of the national antipoverty programs that had been created remained, they were transferred to existing bureaucratic agencies. The "unconditional war on poverty" announced in 1964 was over.

It is difficult to measure the ultimate success of the War on Poverty in the United States as well as its success in local areas such as Little Dixie. The dilemma is compounded by the lofty, and often contradictory, goals of the Johnson administration and the vague methods available for evaluating the accomplishment of these goals. The one overriding objective of the War on Poverty was, obviously, to eradicate poverty from American life. The program fell far short of this highly unrealistic goal—in Little Dixie and the rest of the United States. However, poverty did decline in the Third District between 1960 and 1970. Of the thirteen counties in Carl Albert's district, the overall poverty rate fell from 50 percent of the population to 25 percent.[62] While this impact appears significant, to rely simply on poverty statistics to prove the ultimate value of the program is risky. It is hard to measure the effect of the War on Poverty against other government initiatives, such as Medicare, and the overall strengthening of the economy in this period. Historian James Patterson has noted the "virtual impossibility of singling out the effects of OEO during a time of economic progress and equally phenomenal growth in other public services."[63]

Planners of the War on Poverty had hoped to create programs developed in large part by poor people themselves. While the phrase "maximum feasible participation" was ambiguous from the outset, it is clear that even the most conservative planners wanted the input of poor people in putting together programs. However, in Little Dixie, there was no real involvement of the poor in policy making or program development. In 1966 no one below the poverty line held the top position in any of the community action boards of the Third

District.[64] As one local resident complained to Carl Albert, "the so-called Board . . . is not representing the poor, deprived, ethnic groups or any segment as intended."[65]

The War on Poverty in Little Dixie did prove to be successful in ways that were unanticipated and distinctly rural. First, its programs provided a great deal of employment in a region where little industry existed. Programs such as Job Corps and Head Start required staffers, and most were recruited from the region's poor population. Thus, in rural areas, the War on Poverty became equated with employment. By 1973 in McAlester, War on Poverty programs constituted 19 percent of the total job opportunities in the city.[66] As public policy researchers Robert Plotnick and Felicity Skidmore have noted, this was primarily a rural benefit, however, for a similar effect was not felt in urban areas.[67]

The program's effect on the growth of the administrative structure in many small rural communities has also been overlooked. In Little Dixie the community action director became trained and experienced in applying for federal funds and dealing with the government bureaucracy, a resource that had long been lacking in the District. As one newspaper editor in the region lauded in 1967, the community action program had "provided rural areas with a planner and paper work do-er . . . to help capture federal aid projects. Heretofore only large city Chamber[s] of Commerce could boast such work staffs—and that's where the projects went."[68]

Most significantly, the War on Poverty was also successful in transforming countless individual lives in Little Dixie, and any analysis of the program must be careful not to overlook the tangible benefits the program had on everyday people struggling to subsist in depopulated, depressed areas of America. This often proves difficult, for, as Irwin Unger noted, "direct gains for specific individuals . . . do not show up clearly in the aggregate statistics and the large scale costs-benefits studies." Still, scholars must be careful not to forget individual experiences in the final analysis.[69]

While the War on Poverty failed to eradicate destitution and promote much social and institutional change in the Third District, this does not mean that it had no effect on the lives of the region's poorest citizens. It had an impact on the life of Jess Swearingen, a father of seven in Wilburton, Oklahoma, who, with the help of his local CAA, planted a garden to help provide his family with the proper nutrition that they were lacking.[70] The program also influenced the life of Ottis Kinsey, an elderly man who lived outside Tishomingo, who started a herd of cattle through the rent-a-cow program and later called the effort a "lifesaver for me."[71] The program meant something to the nearly 50 percent of needy women who visited the Atoka County Planned Parenthood clinic

Figure 10.2. Jess Swearingen and children in their garden funded by the Emergency Food and Medical Service. Courtesy of the Carl Albert Congressional Archives, University of Oklahoma, Carl Albert Collection, Box 93.

in 1966 and were diagnosed with potentially serious reproductive diseases.[72] It was also significant to the 90 percent of Head Start children in Ardmore who had never seen a dentist or a doctor before their experience in the program.[73] As President Johnson himself noted, the War on Poverty "quietly transform[ed] the lives of thousands of men and women in rural America."[74]

While one historian has called the War on Poverty a battle with "no casualties [and] no victories," in reality a bevy of small yet significant victories were won.[75] Indeed, for every rural man who could provide fresh vegetables to his malnourished family, for every rural woman who received her first comprehensive medical exam, for every rural teenager who worked her way through college, the War on Poverty left not a legacy of failure but one of accomplishment. These personal triumphs were the real story of the War on Poverty in regions such as Little Dixie, and arguably they should be the ultimate measure of its success.

Notes

1. Clyde H. Duncan, "Community Action Program Gets Right at Heart of Many Personal Problems," *Daily McAlester Democrat*, February 8, 1970.

2. Ibid.

3. Examples of community action studies focused on urban areas include J. David Greenstone and Paul E. Peterson, *Race and Authority in Urban Politics: Community Participation and the War on Poverty* (New York: Russell Sage Foundation, 1973); Ralph M. Kramer, *Participation of the Poor: Comparative Community Case Studies in the War on Poverty* (Englewood Cliffs, N.J.: Prentice-Hall, 1969); and Dale Rogers Marshall, *The Politics of Participation in Poverty: A Case Study of the Board of the Economic and Youth Opportunities Agency of Greater Los Angeles* (Berkeley: University of California, 1971).

4. As historian Allen J. Matusow noted, "No final judgment on [the community action program] will be possible until an army of local historians recovers the program's lost fragments [and brings] the elusive reality of community action into better focus." Matusow, *The Unraveling of America: A History of Liberalism in the 1960s* (New York: Harper & Row, 1984), 255.

5. For Albert's background in the region, see Carl Bert Albert, "Recollections of My Early Life," *Chronicles of Oklahoma* 52, no. 1 (Spring 1974), 30–37. For the purposes of this article, the term "Little Dixie" will be used to designate the Third Congressional District of Oklahoma. Prior to 1968 the Third District consisted of the thirteen counties in southeastern Oklahoma (Atoka, Bryan, Carter, Choctaw, Johnston, Latimer, LeFlore, Love, McCurtain, Marshall, Murray, Pittsburg, and Pushmataha). Between 1966 and 1968 the Oklahoma legislature redrew the state's congressional districts, and as a result the district expanded to include nine more counties (Coal, Cotton, Garvin, Haskell, Hughes, Jefferson, Pontotoc, Seminole, and Stephens). These counties will be included in the analysis only in events occurring after 1967.

6. *The United States Census of the Population, 1960*. The U.S. Census counted 60,239 families in the Third District in 1960, and 31,190 (or 52 percent) had incomes under $3,000, the poverty line in 1960.

7. Samuel Kirkpatrick, David R. Morgan, and Larry G. Edwards, *Oklahoma Voting Patterns: Congressional Elections* (Norman: Bureau of Government Research, University of Oklahoma, 1970), 7; Oklahoma Division of Economic Opportunity, *Oklahoma Communities in Action: A Report on the Economic Opportunity Program in Oklahoma* (Oklahoma City: Division of Economic Opportunity, 1968), 18–19.

8. *The United States Census of the Population, 1960*.

9. Bureau of Government Research, University of Oklahoma, *Oklahoma Votes for Congress, 1907–1964* (Norman: Bureau of Government Research, University of Oklahoma, 1965).

10. The three towns were Poteau, Wilburton, and Atoka. "Table II" attached to Choctaw County Application for Community Action Program, folder 20, box 2, Project Series, Carl

Albert Collection, Carl Albert Center (hereafter CAC), University of Oklahoma; "OEO Grant," 1966, folder 16, box 2, Project Series, Carl Albert Collection, CAC, University of Oklahoma.

11. For the traditional Democratic affiliation of the region, see Bureau of Government Research, *Oklahoma Votes for Congress, 1907–1964*. Of the eighteen governors of the state between 1907 and 1962, eight had come from Little Dixie. Source: Stephen Jones, *Oklahoma Politics in State and Nation, Volume I, 1907–1962* (Enid, Okla.: Haymaker Press, 1974), 61. The depopulation of the Oklahoma countryside is studied in Gerald Lage, *A Profile of Oklahoma: Economic Development, 1950–1975* (Oklahoma City: Frontiers of Science Foundation of Oklahoma, 1977), 5.

12. For the growth of these cities, see Lage, *A Profile of Oklahoma.*

13. Kirkpatrick, Morgan, and Edwards, *Oklahoma Voting Patterns*, 5.

14. "Testimony of Bertrand M. Harding, U.S. Congress, Committee on Agriculture," in *Effect of Federal Programs on Rural America, Hearings before the House Subcommittee on Rural Development, 90th Congress, 1st Session* (Washington, D.C.: Government Printing Office, 1967), 664.

15. Ibid.

16. Robert O. Coppedge and Carlton G. Davis, eds., *Rural Poverty and the Policy Crisis* (Ames: Iowa State University Press, 1977), 31.

17. Lyndon Baines Johnson, *The Vantage Point: Perspectives of the Presidency, 1963–1969* (New York: Holt, Rinehart and Winston, 1971), 81. The vote totals were 61–34 in the Senate and 226–185 in the House.

18. Matusow, *The Unraveling of America*, 124.

19. For examples, see "Atoka County Application for Community Action Program" (hereafter CAP), folder 30, box 1, Project Series, Carl Albert Collection, CAC, University of Oklahoma; "Choctaw County Application for CAP," folder 20, box 2, Project Series, Carl Albert Collection, CAC, University of Oklahoma; "Johnston County Application for CAP," folder 38, box 3, Project Series, Carl Albert Collection, CAC, University of Oklahoma; "A Report on the Economic Opportunity Program in Oklahoma," folder 10, box 59, Departmental Series, Carl Albert Collection, CAC, University of Oklahoma; "1964–1965 OEO Programs in Third District," folder 27, box 59, Departmental Series, Carl Albert Collection, CAC, University of Oklahoma.

20. For examples, see "Bryan County Poverty Plan is Expanded," *Durant Democrat*, September 30, 1966; "Community Action Gets Right," *Daily McAlester Democrat*, February 8, 1970; "Field Trip Report—Southeast," in "Field Trip Reports—Southeast" Folder, box 2, E 10, Office Files of the Oklahoma District Supervisor, 1966–1968 (hereafter E 10), RG 381, National Archives at Fort Worth.

21. Henry M. Levin, "A Decade of Policy Developments in Improving Education and Training for Low-Income Populations," in *A Decade of Federal Antipoverty Programs*, edited by Robert Haveman (New York: Academic Press, 1974), 132.

22. "OEO Release," March 17, 1966, folder 16, box 59, Departmental Series, Carl Albert Collection, CAC, University of Oklahoma.

23. Only in Tatums did a non–school board agency apply for Head Start funds. In comparison, Sar Levitan noted that in fiscal year 1965–66, 35 percent of all Head Starts had a delegate agency affiliation with a public school, 10 percent with a church, and 26 percent with a private, nonprofit organization. In 29 percent of the Head Starts in 1965–66, the community action agency ran the program independently. See Levitan, *The Great Society's Poor Law: A New Approach to Poverty* (Baltimore: Johns Hopkins Press, 1969), 150.

24. Letter to Jule M Sugerman from Walter Cooper, folder 30, box 1, Project Series, Carl Albert Collection, CAC, University of Oklahoma.

25. Oklahoma Division of Economic Opportunity, *Poverty in Oklahoma* (Oklahoma City: Division of Economic Opportunity, 1974), 57; "Bryan County CAA Report," August 1968, folder 1, box 2, Project Series, Carl Albert Collection, CAC, University of Oklahoma.

26. "Bryan County Application for CAP," folder 1, box 2, Project Series, Carl Albert Collection, CAC, University of Oklahoma.

27. In comparison, Sar Levitan estimated that in fiscal year 1968–69, only 16 percent of family planning grantees listed a health department as the delegate agency. Forty percent relied upon Planned Parenthood as the delegate, while 38 percent of the family planning programs were run by community action agencies alone. Levitan, *The Great Society's Poor Law*, 211.

28. After 1967 the district also gained East Central State University with the addition of Pontotoc County.

29. Levitan, *The Great Society's Poor Law*, 165–66.

30. "OEO Information Center Summary, as of 1 January 1966," folder 10, box 59, Departmental Series, Carl Albert Collection, CAC, University of Oklahoma.

31. Levitan, *The Great Society's Poor Law*, 274.

32. Irwin Unger, *The Best of Intentions: The Triumphs and Failures of the Great Society under Kennedy, Johnson, and Nixon* (New York: Doubleday, 1996), 152. Other scholars have also emphasized the traditional control of community action agencies. See Thomas F. Jackson, "The State, the Movement, and the Urban Poor: The War on Poverty and Political Mobilization in the 1960s," in *The "Underclass" Debate: Views from History*, edited by Michael B. Katz (Princeton: Princeton University Press, 1993), 403–39; Sanford Kravitz, "The Community Action Program in Perspective," in *Urban Poverty: Its Social and Political Dimensions*, edited by Warner Bloomberg, Jr., and Henry J. Schmandt (Beverly Hills, Calif.: Sage Publications), 322; Levitan, *The Great Society's Poor Law*, 116.

33. Lists of boards of directors in the Third District can be found in the "Evaluations" folder, E 10.

34. Matusow, *The Unraveling of America*, 246.

35. "Emergency Food and Medical Services," folder 33, box 77, Departmental Series, CC, CACCRS, University of Oklahoma; OEO Press Release, March 20, 1969, folder 26, box 4, Project Series, Carl Albert Collection, CAC, University of Oklahoma.

36. OEO Grant, INCA, June 1971, folder 10, box 93, Departmental Series, Carl Albert Collection, CAC, University of Oklahoma; OEO Grant, Hughes County, June 1971, folder 13, box 93, Departmental Series, Carl Albert Collection, CAC, University of Oklahoma; Memorandum to Governor David Hall from Rex Sparger, September 3, 1971, folder 11, box 4, S-1, RG 8, David Hall Gubernatorial Papers, Oklahoma Department of Libraries, State Archives, Oklahoma City (hereafter ODL).

37. Letter to Ed Edmondson from W. J. Beck, folder 13, box 93, Departmental Series, Carl Albert Collection, CAC, University of Oklahoma. The average garden subsidy per family was twenty-two dollars; the average value of the vegetables produced per year was over one hundred dollars.

38. Letter to Albert from Grace Carter Manos, folder 13, box 93, Departmental Series, Carl Albert Collection, CAC, University of Oklahoma.

39. "Government Rent-a-Cow Program Gives Farmers Added Income," *Ada Sunday News*, July 1, 1973.

40. OEO Release, June 3, 1970, folder 29, box 84, Departmental Series, Carl Albert Collection, CAC, University of Oklahoma; "State Control of Some OEO Programs Hit," *Washington Post*, March 10, 1970; OEO Grant Announcement, June 28, 1971, folder 19, box 93, Departmental Series, Carl Albert Collection, CAC, University of Oklahoma.

41. "State Control," *Washington Post*, March 10, 1970.

42. "'Oklahoma Plan' July 1 Date Set," news clipping, folder 24, box 187, FHC, CACCRS, University of Oklahoma; "State Poverty Fight Sets Unique Pattern," folder 27, box 69, General "A" Series, Carl Albert Collection, CAC, University of Oklahoma.

43. Oklahoma Division of Economic Opportunity, *Poverty in Oklahoma*, 4.

44. Letter to Carl Albert from Jim Hall, January 12, 1970, folder 81, box 116, Legislative Series, Carl Albert Collection, CAC, University of Oklahoma.

45. *Daily Oklahoman*, March 11, 1970.

46. "Poverty Agency to Be Cut about 10 Per Cent in '71," *McAlester News-Capital*, January 12, 1971.

47. "Discount Drugs Row Perils Little Dixie Poverty War," *Tulsa World*, September 5, 1971.

48. News clipping, folder 21, box 93, Departmental Series, Carl Albert Collection, CAC, University of Oklahoma.

49. Ibid.

50. "Discount Drugs," *Tulsa World*, September 5, 1971.

51. OEO Release, December 14, 1971, folder 21, box 93, Departmental Series, Carl Albert Collection, CAC, University of Oklahoma. This solution still created some controversy in the area. One local pharmacist complained that the welfare office provided lists of which pharmacies provided the discount and which did not. The druggist felt that this was discrimination and added, "If the OEO can tell people where to trade, then I am for abolishing OEO and other give-away programs." Letter to Carl Albert from Glenda M. Teeter,

R. Ph., April 6, 1972, folder 6, box 102, Departmental Series, Carl Albert Collection, CAC, University of Oklahoma.

52. Advertisement, *McCurtain Daily Gazette*, folder 21, box 93, Departmental Series, Carl Albert Collection, CAC, University of Oklahoma.

53. News clipping, folder 64, box 101, Departmental Series, Carl Albert Collection, CAC, University of Oklahoma.

54. "Homestead Chance Stirs Interest of Tulsa Families," *Tulsa World*, January 6, 1972; "'Orchards for Poor' Set for 10 Families," *Duncan Banner*, May 4, 1972.

55. "Oklahoma Poor Offered Farms," *Los Angeles Times*, December 20, 1971.

56. "Homestead Chance Stirs Interest," *Tulsa World*, January 6, 1972.

57. "Oklahoma Homestead Plan Has Wide Appeal," news clipping, folder 65, box 101, Departmental Series, Carl Albert Collection, CAC, University of Oklahoma.

58. "Orchards for Poor," *Duncan Banner*, May 4, 1972.

59. "State Offers Poor Free Grape Farm," *Daily Oklahoman*, 29 December 1971; "Orchards for Poor," *Duncan Banner*, May 4, 1972.

60. Many of the residents who left the program expressed frustration at the lack of air conditioning in the OEO-provided trailers, and the extensive work required for little profit. News clippings, folder 64, box 101, Departmental Series, Carl Albert Collection, CAC, University of Oklahoma. The family that remained succeeded by supplementing their fixed income by selling firewood and planting gardens. News clipping, folder 2, box 32, S-1, RG 8, ODL.

61. Newsletter of the Oklahoma Division of Economic Opportunity, June 30, 1974, folder 6, box 122, Departmental Series, Carl Albert Collection, CAC, University of Oklahoma.

62. According to the 1960 Census, 31,190 of the 60,239 families in the Third District fell below the poverty line. In 1970, the U.S. Census counted 63,330 families in the original thirteen counties of the Third District, 16,065 of which fell below the poverty line.

63. James T. Patterson, *America's Struggle against Poverty: 1900–1994* (Cambridge, Mass.: Harvard University Press, 1994), 148.

64. While no one below the poverty line served as chair on any of the boards of directors, some did serve as members, ranging from 10 percent of a board to over half in the eleven counties that noted the income status of their board of directors in 1966. Murray County included the most board members below the poverty line (eleven of their twenty) while Atoka County had the fewest (three of their twenty-six). See the board of directors lists found in the "Evaluations" Folder, box 2, E 10.

65. Letter to Carl Albert from Myrtle I. Stewart, April 29, 1968, folder 26, box 4, Project Series, Carl Albert Collection, CAC, University of Oklahoma.

66. Letter to Albert from Bill Dashner, February 14, 1973, folder 6, box 154, Legislative Series, Carl Albert Collection, CAC, University of Oklahoma.

67. Robert D. Plotnick and Felicity Skidmore, *Progress against Poverty: A Review of the 1964–1974 Decade* (New York: Academic Press, 1975), 25.

68. "Just One Man's Point of View," *Johnston County Capital-Democrat*, October 19, 1967.

69. Unger, *The Best of Intentions*, 359.

70. Swearingen later wrote to Albert, "I could not have afforded much of a garden without the help." Folder 13, box 93, Departmental Series, Carl Albert Collection, CAC, University of Oklahoma.

71. "Government Rent-A-Cow Program," *Ada Sunday News*, July 1, 1973.

72. "Atoka County Health Department O.E.O. Program," in "Atoka County CAP Form 43" folder, box 8, RG 381, National Archives at Fort Worth.

73. "Pontotoc County Head Start Program," Folder 47A, Box 68, FHC, CACCRS, University of Oklahoma.

74. Lyndon B. Johnson, "Special Message to Congress: Prosperity and Progress for the Farmer and Rural America," *Rural Opportunity* 3, no. 4 (April 1968), 1.

75. Matusow, *The Unraveling of America*, 220.

CHAPTER 11

Conservative Oklahoma Women United

THE CRUSADE TO DEFEAT THE ERA

Jana Vogt Catignani

I n March 1972 a proposed amendment to the U.S. Constitution was delivered to the states to be considered for ratification. The arrival of the Equal Rights Amendment (ERA) in Oklahoma immediately engendered doubt in the minds of at least a few women in the state who thought ratification would ravage the proper functioning of the U.S. government and society as well as obliterate the appropriate place of women and men within that society. As these protesters began objecting to the amendment, like-minded women soon flocked to the cause. Within a short time, the anti-ratification campaign became both training ground and motivating force for a groundswell of advocates embracing traditionalist causes. Politicized by the amendment debate, the majority of women ERA opponents in the state came from the ranks of fundamentalist Christian organizations. Eventually, by the end of a decade-long fight, the state's conservative women successfully defeated ratification of the amendment in Oklahoma.

Illustrating the abiding nature of cultural beliefs passed from parents to children, a gendered society flourished in the predominantly white state from territorial days forward.[1] In 1972, moreover, a functioning culture of gender division remained embedded in the minds and lives of many Oklahomans. Revised in 1976, a comprehensive, eighteen-page 1972 Legislative Council study of gender-specific laws revealed that state acts required Oklahoma women and infants to post bond if they were called to testify as material

You Can't Fool Mother Nature

STOP
ERA

Equal Rights Amendment

Figure 11.1. STOP ERA handbill, Oklahoma, 1978. Courtesy of the Research Division of the Oklahoma Historical Society.

witnesses in criminal cases, barred wives from voting and holding office in certain instances, prohibited girls under sixteen from selling newspapers, magazines, or periodicals in any street or "out-of-doors public place," and imposed limitations on the number of hours women could work, among other biased statutes.[2]

In an example of the state's gendered cultural norms during the decade of debate on the ERA, a 1975 *Tulsa World* editorial complained about the content and aim of a recently released report concerning discriminatory hiring and promotion practices within state agencies. Jointly authored by the Oklahoma Human Rights Commission and the Governor's Advisory Commission on the Status of Women, the report stated that "women and racial and ethnic minorities" were underrepresented throughout state offices. A number of Oklahomans must have agreed with the publishers of one of the state's conservative newspapers, who resented the idea of imposing "quotas" upon the state's private and public entities with "no regard to whether [employees] can do the work."

While supporting the ideal of equal pay for equal work and stating that the three minority groups, "W, R, and E," should be paid "commensurately with their ability, training and experience," the editorial also called into doubt the commitment of minorities to work, particularly the dedication of women. The editorialist argued that many women "may be in state government only for a little while to augment their husbands' incomes and may have little interest in upgrading their jobs."[3] By the early 1970s and throughout the decade, Oklahoma's cultural and political traditions thus routinely excluded women from consideration as responsible individuals and included a great number of gender-biased, discriminatory laws.

At the dawn of the ratification decade, many conservative influences shaped Oklahoma. Included among those influences were the state's recent segregationist past and a Democratic Party that remained decidedly Southern Democrat in its ideology and practices: while Oklahoma Democrats controlled state and local politics throughout the ten years of the ERA campaign, a large number adhered to conservative values and beliefs rather than the more liberal tendencies of most of their national colleagues.[4] In addition, state citizens voted for Republican presidential candidates from the 1950s through the ERA decade, thus demonstrating an affinity for nationwide GOP candidates and platforms over those of the national Democratic Party.[5]

Most telling for the ratification battle, 32.7 percent of Oklahoma's total population in 1971 belonged to conservative, fundamentalist, Protestant denominations, the third highest percentage of any state in the nation.[6] As has been well documented in the literature, and is borne out in the Oklahoma experience, religious affiliation and belief systems, especially adherence to fundamentalist doctrines, comprised two of the principal motivations for anti-ratification activism nationwide.[7] In particular, Christian fundamentalist ideology underlay numerous Oklahomans' decisions to oppose the ERA. In 1980 during the ERA drive, Oklahoma's total population was over three million, with 57.5 percent of all residents members of various religious bodies. Of that group, 65.9 percent worshipped in evangelical congregations. Viewed another way, 37.9 percent of Oklahoma's total population in 1980 attended fundamentalist religious institutions, a gain of slightly over 5 percent from 1971.[8]

In addition, followers of the Church of Jesus Christ of Latter Day Saints (LDS), popularly known as Mormons, constituted a large number of ERA opponents nationally, particularly after the church publicly opposed the amendment in early 1975.[9] In 1980 LDS members made up only 0.5 percent of the total Oklahoma population. However, they reportedly represented 9 percent of state anti-ratification supporters in the 1980 ERA campaign, "a percentage almost twenty times as large" as their proportion of all Sooner residents.[10] Including LDS members, at least 38.4 percent of Oklahoma's total population in 1980 attended religious institutions whose hierarchy either opposed publicly the ERA or whose tenets plainly ran counter to both ratification and feminist goals.

Most important, sociologist Ruth Murray Brown discovered that the greatest numbers of 1980 anti-ratification advocates came from adherents of the Churches of Christ and Baptist denominations. While, in toto, those two denominations represented 32.4 percent of Oklahoma's population, Brown's figures revealed that these two fundamentalist sects alone constituted 60 percent of the state's ERA opponents. Along with a significant percentage of LDS women, therefore, Oklahoma's Christian evangelical churchwomen successfully mobilized great numbers of activists in opposition to the ERA.

On March 23, 1972, the day after receiving the amendment from Congress, two separate resolutions for ratification were introduced into the Oklahoma senate. A slight parliamentary tussle ensued, with a number of Democrats and Republicans seemingly anxious to be a part of the ERA drive. Republican James ("Jim") Inhofe authored Senate Concurrent Resolution (SCR) 108, while Democrats Senator Bryce Baggett and Representative Hannah Atkins cosponsored SCR 110.[11] When Baggett introduced SCR 110 to a vote in the Democratically controlled senate, Inhofe objected, "contend[ing] that his resolution [SCR 108] had been placed on the desk first."[12] After the senate president pro tem overruled the objection, Inhofe "challenged the ruling . . . and requested a roll call." By a vote of twenty-four to seven, with seventeen excused, Inhofe lost his bid to be the initial primary author of the ERA in Oklahoma. Along with four other senators, at least three of whom were Republicans, Inhofe then asked to be made coauthor of the Baggett resolution. Their request was granted and the Oklahoma senate then approved the ERA with a "unanimous voice vote," sending it to the house. The senate-approved Baggett and Atkins resolution, however, died in the House Constitutional Revision and Regulatory Services committee. Within one week, a separate resolution, House Concurrent Resolution (HCR) 1093, again sponsored by Representative Atkins and Senator Baggett, failed in the house on Wednesday, March 29, 1972, by a roll call vote. Further, the Oklahoma senate did not vote on Senator Inhofe's SCR 108, and it was stricken from the senate's legislative agenda for the next day.[13] Although the measure would be reintroduced into one or the other of the Oklahoma legislative houses during each session for the next ten years, the 1972 Oklahoma senate approval of SCR 110 was the closest the ERA would ever come to official state sanction.

The Oklahoma house of representatives' defeat of the ERA in March 1972 marked the amendment's first state legislative roadblock in its national struggle.[14] That early defeat owed much to the rapid response of Oklahoma women who used their influence and personal contacts to bring about the ERA's initial rejection by the Oklahoma house. Interviewed in 1978 and 1982, conservative Ann Patterson, amendment opponent and de facto head of the Oklahoma branch of the STOP ERA movement during the decade of ERA debate, recalled that she had discussed with a female friend their questioning the state senate's initial approval of the resolution in 1972. Believing that the house also would pass the resolution the Monday following the senate's approval of SCR 110, she said that she had "called a friend on Sunday evening," a Democratic member of the house of representatives, and "we got [the member] to agree to hold it up in the Rules Committee and then on Monday we went out to the Capitol and talked to people." Further, Patterson believed that had the second resolution, HCR 1093, been put to a house vote on Monday it would have passed. Her efforts, however, had also caused the house sponsor, Hannah Atkins, to delay the vote until Wednesday in order to make certain the resolution had the needed numbers. The delay, Patterson believed, had instead enabled the cultivation of "more opposition" in the House, and the measure failed.[15] From this point forward, proponents and opponents of the amendment engaged in a contentious and impassioned ten-year campaign for the votes of Oklahoma politicians, marking the state a key battleground in the nationwide ERA struggle.

Shortly after that victory, Patterson and her colleagues formed the anti-ratification organization Women for Responsible Legislation (WRL).[16] Over the course of the next three years, the women of WRL joined with other Oklahoma political conservatives as well as with religious fundamentalists to become the elementary force behind the state's growing and increasingly articulated traditionalism. In a state that had often leaned to the right in its ideology and politics since statehood in 1907, the ten-year ERA battle gave voice to an apparent and progressively dissatisfied portion of the female electorate frustrated both by their previous silence and by what they saw as the dangerous, overtly liberal excesses of the 1960s and 1970s.

Much of the impetus to stop the ERA lay in the strong belief many state women held of the moral superiority of women. As Ann Patterson declared, the "morals of a nation depend on its women. . . . [w]omen are necessary to keep men moral."[17] Belief in female moral supremacy enjoys a long history in the United States. As historian Kim Nielsen discovered of 1920s Red Scare antifeminists, their "activism . . . was part of the lineage of eighteenth-century republican motherhood."[18] In like vein, twentieth-century ERA opponents shared this ideology both with their eighteenth-century sisters and their nineteenth-century counterparts. Specifically, historian Catherine Rymph, in part quoting historian D'Ann Campbell, argued that for the Republican Party and its conservative women, the "special [nineteenth-century] link between morality and gender roles" remained viable throughout the first half of the twentieth century and by the 1950s had "revived energetically."[19] Moreover, sociologist Rebecca Klatch described social conservative women of the New Right and social conservatism itself as "rooted in religious belief," deeming the "family to be the sacred unit of society," and "envision[ing] contemporary America in terms of moral decay."[20] Oklahoma anti-ratification supporters of the 1970s displayed their belief in women's intrinsic moral authority and imagined that they too held a superior moral position to their husbands, indeed to all men, simply by being women. Through adherence to traditional gender roles and a belief in the inherent differences between women and men, Oklahoma's socially conservative women saw themselves as saviors, battling feminists and the ERA for the survival of traditional homes and families.

Although not exclusively connected to traditionalist religions, women and men who believed in female moral supremacy found an outspoken expression of and devotion to that viewpoint within conservative churches during the ERA campaign. As noted previously, female LDS adherents constituted a disproportionate percentage of Oklahoma's anti-ratification activists. In September 1978, the president of the LDS, Spencer Kimball, delivered an address to Mormon communicants through a nationwide radio broadcast.[21] The focus of Kimball's speech was women, specifically women's place in the church, the importance of their role in the family, and their duties to society. Several women preceded Kimball in the broadcast, speaking "well and professionally," it was said by Ruth Murray Brown, on different aspects of women's current status and their obligations to society. Stating that three years had passed "since we had the first women's assembly of Salt Lake City," the female president of the LDS Relief Society noted also that women in 1978 were "struggling with new . . . roles." She further averred that women "have a responsibility for the moral climate of the community in which we live," making clear that an ethical society grew from women's guidance.[22]

Following the precepts of their churches and the self-proclaimed tradition of women's greater sense of ethics and decency, many Oklahoma anti-ERA activists of the 1970s and 1980s used the idea of women's moral authority to further their political aims.[23] The message from the anti-ratification literature of the day was loud and clear: the women of Oklahoma were fighting for what they believed to be the salvation of the state and the country. They sought victory over a developing profligate, immoral, narcissistic, and indulgent citizenry, whom the anti-ERA activists saw as being led by misguided feminists. For instance, in a 1974 letter to Oklahoma political candidates, Sally Rowan Bell, "chairman" of HOTDOG (Housewives Organized to Defend Our Girls), affirmed that the small statewide organization spoke "for Oklahoma women who are at home raising their families." HOTDOG, Bell said, "wants to preserve our social and legal order." Her letter asked candidates to ally with the organization by "speak[ing] positively FOR WOMANHOOD" and "not forc[ing] this sweeping destructive legislation [the ERA] down our state throat because of a small group of malcontents."[24] During the amendment campaign, the women of HOTDOG and their conventional Oklahoma sisters continued a long tradition of politically active women in America. The activism of conservative Oklahoma women succeeded in part because amendment opponents tapped into traditional assumptions about women's moral authority and their greater involvement with church and family. In so doing, they influenced a large voting constituency of men and women alike, all of whom were invested in the idea of women's inherent differences from men, and in keeping those differences recognized legally and adhered to culturally.

For the Christian conservatives who constituted the largest portion of Oklahoma's anti-ERA movement, the amendment contravened their fundamentalist interpretations of the Bible, by which they lived and viewed the world. The amendment challenged fundamentalist core beliefs. Many Oklahoma conservatives understood their duty as Christians to vocally and forcefully oppose the ERA. In so doing, they were carrying out God's work as well as defending their country. Most important, the state's Christian conservatives discerned a twentieth-century secularization of American society that, in their eyes, presented evidence that the nation was distancing itself from the supreme authority. They believed that preventing ratification would help halt this liberal drift and assist the country's return to, in their eyes, its origins: a moral nation ruled and guided by God.

Ads Termed 'Misleading'

Advertisements asking Oklahomans to support the Equal Rights Amendment are a "cruel deception," a leader of an ERA opposition group said.

Ann Patterson, state chairman of Women for Responsible Legislation, said the advertisement implies the proposed amendment will instantly cure social problems.

The organization said there is no alleged inequality that cannot be dealt with under the 14th Amendment, and charged in a news release that the real purpose of the ERA is to remove from state legislatures the right to make discretionary judgments in law.

Figure 11.2. "Ads Termed 'Misleading'" (Ann Patterson responds to ERA), *Daily Oklahoman*, March 2, 1977. Reprinted by permission of the *Oklahoman*.

First and foremost, God lay at the center of fundamentalists' lives, a God who was known personally but whose direction and strictures they obtained through the "inerrant" word of the Bible. Those literal biblical interpretations

led a large number of Oklahoma's anti-ratification proponents to believe that
the amendment represented the exact opposite of God's plan for humanity
and, most importantly, it was against God's law. In innumerable sources from
the decade of debate on the ERA, Christian fundamentalists left their mark.
One important example was in their decrying the "secular humanism" they
believed ran rampant throughout the state and the nation. A 1978 Oklahoma
STOP ERA PEC (Political Education Committee) newsletter, for instance, said:
"What is Humanism? It is a religious movement where God is absent, prayer is
scorned, and heaven is a joke."[25] According to historian George Marsden, "'[s]
ecular humanism' came to be the shorthand framework for [Christian fundamentalists'] understanding" of American societal and political changes taking
place in the decades since the end of World War II, particularly the liberalizing
tendencies of the 1960s and 1970s. The liberal trends opposed by fundamentalists represented a wide range of recent developments, including sex education
and the banning of prayer in schools, an increase of violence and sexual content in films and on television, acceptance of homosexuality, loosened standards on dress styles and language, an increase in the number of young people
living together outside marriage, and the proposed ERA.[26]

Many of the state's anti-ratification activists warned that the country's rapidly increasing secularism would bring about the downfall of the nation. In
June 1980, for example, a small group calling itself he Committee for a Clean
Oklahoma City avowed that "God has blessed our state and nation." The group
then cautioned, "This [blessing] can only continue if we deserve to be blessed.
The liberalism in our country is fast destroying our way of life." The organization listed a number of the ills of "liberalism" it felt needed to be reversed,
beginning with the admonition: "We *DO NOT* need the ERA. This is Anti-
God & Anti-Family."[27] In addition, references to humanism and to its destruction of the nation's morals and other detrimental effects appear frequently in
interviews sociologist Ruth Murray Brown conducted with anti-ratification
leaders. Many of those interviewed spoke of humanism as a new "religion,"
one recognized as such by the U.S. Supreme Court, and one that would sup-
plant God in Americans' lives.[28] In the words of a Bethany, Oklahoma, woman,
"Humanism means anti-God."[29]

Until the decade of ERA debate, many fundamentalist Christians had
believed direct involvement in politics to be unacceptable, particularly for
evangelical women. Concern over lax morals during the 1960s and 1970s,
however, and belief that the federal government was attempting to eliminate
traditional religion from Americans' lives, substituting a legalized, pluralis-
tic secularism, spurred numerous traditionalists to shed the convention of no

direct political engagement. According to George Marsden, the "issues of family and sexuality proved the key that unlocked evangelical potential for overt political involvement."[30] For many women traditionalists, the ERA's direct connection to just those issues pulled them out of their reticence and into the public arena, demanding that they reverse their previous practice and become politically aware and active.

ERA's perceived threat to the family particularly frightened Oklahoma's Christian evangelical women. In their minds, the continued health and welfare of their families demanded protection from the nation's growing immorality. They saw faithfulness to wholesome, family-oriented Christian values decreasing daily, replaced with secular society's lurid enticements and loose mores. Through its destruction of the family, they imagined ratification of the ERA would escalate the spread of secularization, eventually resulting in a godless state and nation. According to an anti-ratification brochure distributed by the Oklahoma City STOP ERA PEC, for example, the John Birch Society correctly opposed the amendment, in that the society "strongly supports traditional American values, including the preservation of the family unit—which E.R.A. would undermine."[31]

Many conservative Christians viewed the fight against the "anti-family Equal Rights Amendment" as a battle between good and evil, with the survival of their families hanging on the outcome.[32] In speaking of her public efforts against the ERA, one state woman quoted biblical injunctions as justification for speaking out, despite the fundamentalist history of women remaining silent. She stated that the Bible instructed women and men to "expose" the "works of darkness" and to combat "wickedness" by "put[ting] on the whole armor of God and go[ing] out [to] fight." She said that her only reason for taking a public stance against the ERA "is that I want my children to know God. I don't want anybody taking God out of their lives." For this woman and other Christian anti-ratification advocates, the essence of their fight for traditional ideologies, and the central meaning of their personal activism, could be defined in one brief statement. The conservative battle against liberalism and the ERA was "warfare between God and Satan."[33]

Of particular urgency to Christian evangelicals and other traditionalists was the issue of homosexuality. They often cloaked their personal homophobia in expressions of "protecting" their children from lesbian and gay influences (and what they saw as degeneracy and "perversion"). By 1977 ERA opponents had conclusively linked homosexuality to the amendment. Throughout the decade, both anti-ratification literature and individual statements by ERA opponents kept alive the frightening specter of a nation legally recognizing the rights of gays and lesbians, to be achieved through ratification of the ERA. The Washington County, Oklahoma, chapter of Eagle Forum, for example, distributed an oversized flyer printed in large bold letters: "WHY ARE HOMOSEXUALS SUPPORTING THE EQUAL RIGHTS AMENDMENT (ERA)?" The answer: "TO ACHIEVE THEIR GOALS." According to the flyer, "many leading legal authorities" believe that ratification "will legalize Homosexual 'Marriages' and grant them [gay men and lesbian women] the Special Rights and Benefits given by law to husbands and wives." The flyer then asked, "Will the Homosexuals also be given the rights to adopt children and to teach in the schools?"[34]

Innumerable Christian fundamentalists in the state agreed that homosexuality was immoral, particularly in God's eyes. Many stated that they would prefer that gays and lesbians not be in contact with children. In 1980, for example, one Christian evangelical woman avowed, "Homosexuality is a sin, according to the Bible." She stated that she "wouldn't want one of them teaching my child" or "adopting a child." [35] Another anti-ERA woman believed homosexuality was "a sickness and it can be unlearned and learned," voicing beliefs that many conservatives held.[36] For one fundamentalist woman, homosexuality was "even worse a sin than adultery and fornication, [while] the ERA would help [gays and lesbians'] cause and would help them get permission to marry." She also "would not want them to have any positions dealing with children, or positions of influence or power," she stated. Blind to her prejudice, this Christian woman next magnanimously conceded that, "within these restrictions," lesbians and gays "should be allowed to get a job.[37]

During the ERA decade, the subject of homosexuality elicited statements born of fear and ignorance from a significant number of evangelical Christians and other reactionary conservatives. Linked to ratification of the amendment, the issue of the rights of gays and lesbians swelled the ranks of ERA-opponent organizations, leading them to enlarge their use of inflammatory, homophobic language and fear mongering. As one Oklahoma Christian antifeminist leader told Ruth Murray Brown, the leader began her speeches "with the emotional issues" in order to "get people to listen" to arguments against the ERA. Brown then asked which issues she meant. The woman's succinct reply: "Homosexuality."[38]

As mentioned earlier, anti-ratification materials connected the destruction of the social order, as advocated by feminists, to the wholesale destruction of the United States. By advancing the dissolution of traditional gendered roles for men and women, feminists were seen as weakening the U.S. political system and its principles. During the decade of ERA debate, many conservatives believed that the political liberals of the time, including feminists and others who backed the amendment, undermined the nation's anticommunism. Preserving the United States from communism became a rallying point for scores of Oklahomans, impelling them into the anti-ratification movement.

Such sentiments appear in the Oklahoma house of representatives' interim hearings on the ERA in late 1972. Men and women at the hearings raised their voices in concern over the perceived threat of the ERA to the security of the nation. A warning from one antifeminist that "Russia has had equal rights for women and it has failed" was seconded by another woman's avowal: "I do not want to be 'liberated' to work in factory, field, or battle—as do women in socialist countries the world over." Another passionate speaker declared that "the current trend is propelling us into irrevocable socialism," while still another affirmed just as passionately, "if you want a life like they have in the Soviet [Union], then *go there!*"[39] For each of these people, the ERA and its guarantee of equal rights for women presented a threat to America's survival.

Particularly during the early years of the amendment debate, a significant number of Oklahomans migrated to it from existing anticommunist organizations, such as the John Birch Society.[40] A September 1978 example shows that state anti-ERA advocates still held fears of communist subversion. A newsletter distributed by the Oklahoma STOP ERA PEC urged its readers to write to Louisiana U.S. congressman Gillis W. Long, as the chair of the Subcommittee on the Rules and Organization of the House, asking Long to fight "to restore the House Internal Security Committee." According to the newsletter, "beginning in early 1973, *all* of America's formal defenses against internal Communist subversion were stripped away." The newsletter then listed four committees and boards of the Justice Department, the Attorney General's Office, and the House that had been "abolished without so much as a vote," adding that subsequently "the F.B.I. and the C.I.A. have been under attack and can no longer function as they once did." The STOP ERA newsletter said that this same House resolution regarding the status of the Internal Security Committee had previously "been tied up in committee for a long, long time," but a "constant barrage of letters over the past several months" had caused its chair to refer the resolution to Long's subcommittee. "[A] sizeable flood of letters to Mr. Long might produce some results," the newsletter added. STOP ERA asked readers to "remember to pray [as] God gives us the formula for the healing of our nation, and we must not ignore it."[41] Thus Christian references were combined with fear that the nation was open to communist treason. Clearly for STOP ERA activists, the threat of communist and feminist subversion of the American way of life as they knew it was both real and personal. Anti-ratification activists believed that they must undertake the rescue of their nation with God's help.

Anti-ERA organizations in Oklahoma worked together in an apparently seamless and harmonious manner. As an umbrella organization, the state STOP ERA included WRL, Eagle Forum, Women Who Want to Be Women (WWWW)—renamed Pro Family Forum in the mid-1970s—and other anti-amendment organizations, the membership of which often overlapped, as well as Farm Bureau women. Ideology and common goals bonded anti-ratification women and antifeminist networks seemingly worked well in connecting them. A letter in the October 1981 STOP ERA PEC newsletter, for instance, testifies to the ERA opponents' camaraderie. Signed by four Oklahoma anti-ERA leaders who represented WRL and the largely Christian fundamentalist WWWW, the letter went out under the name STOP ERA.[42] In addition, another newsletter from STOP ERA referred to its being sent "[t]o Eagle Forum Members around the state," illustrating the inclusion of that organization into the fold.[43]

Perhaps due to the cooperative nature and overlapping membership of these organizations and the fact that they worked through one overarching group, STOP ERA, organized anti-ratification lobbying proved to be eminently viable and persuasive in the state. Representing one example from many of its type in extant anti-ERA sources from the decade is a detailed, well-organized, informative packet titled "Letter Writing" in the ERA Collection of the Oklahoma Historical Society. This packet shows that the anti-ERA movement was neither slapdash nor improvisational and it testifies to efficient cooperation among antifeminists.[44] Distributing a comprehensive, generic how-to letter on the best ways of getting a message across, and including customizing information for a specific area within the state, illustrates the efficiency and viability of the movement. The great number of largely similar, sometimes identical, anti-ERA letters and other messages received by politicians during the decade testify to the dynamism and systematic organization of the anti-ratification movement.[45]

By the mid to latter years of the drive, state ERA opponents began using their network, built to combat ratification, as an efficient electioneering machine. As early as 1976, a state chapter of one of the conservative women's groups formed specifically in opposition to the amendment participated actively in a reelection campaign for a like-minded candidate. A newspaper article in August that year states that the "Del City Association of W's (Women Who Want to be Women)" had endorsed incumbent state representative Ray Trent, conveying that the conservative women backed Trent above all for his stand against ratification of the ERA.[46]

By 1980 conservative women in Oklahoma were deeply involved in campaigning for and against political aspirants, often basing their efforts on a candidate's position on the amendment and other traditionalist issues. Moreover, the anti-ERA campaign inspired the rank and file to become politically active, including fundamentalist Christians. In October 1980 a Southern Baptist from Tulsa related that she was working "very hard" for Republican Dick Freeman and had campaigned "for Don Nickles, too."[47] In 1980, and again in 1982, Freeman ran and lost against Democratic congressman James Jones.[48] Two other anti-ratification traditionalists, Claudia Thomas from "north of Ochelata" in Washington County, and East Tulsa resident Martha Simms, also campaigned for Freeman during the 1980 elections. Thomas did so in her capacity as Freeman's "district chairman."[49] Regarding politics, Simms told Brown, "Christian people have a responsibility to vote." Through Simms's involvement in door-to-door campaigning for Freeman, her sister-in-law and the twenty-one-year-old daughter of her sister-in-law had both become active in the candidate's 1980 campaign. Their political participation was a pleasant surprise for Simms as her sister-in-law had "never been involved in anything like that before."[50]

In lobbying against the amendment, anti-ratification women seldom issued public statements against individual politicians. Rather, state anti-ERA activists typically sent individual and private communications to those officials. By using this tactic, ERA opponents illustrated their understanding of the importance to politicians of grassroots communications and they stayed within the bounds of their prescribed beliefs. In 1979 it was reported that, according to state legislators, "ERA generates more mail and telephone calls to lawmakers than any other issue."[51] As an example, a Chandler, Oklahoma, woman avowed to a state legislator in 1975 that the United States "was founded on Bible principles" and "strong homes," while the "ERA may be just one more tool to aid in the destruction of the home." She went on: "I know you have branded this kind of thinking emotionalism, . . . [b]ut . . . I'm convinced it's time to become emotional." In 1977 another ERA opponent, from Bristow, told the same state legislator, "[I]f you really want to help women & do what is best, let women be women [and] don't try to change the laws that God [h]as set up."[52] The intense lobbying associated with the amendment, delivered by ratification proponents and opponents alike, must have frayed the nerves of even seasoned politicians. Anti-ratification voters' greater use of personalized, private lobbying, however, had an aura of exceptional legitimacy and gave the image of a genuinely grassroots movement.

During the ERA decade, Oklahoma legislators submitted resolutions for ratification sixteen times, with the majority of those sixteen resolutions going on to become "buried in committee."[53] The legislature actually voted on the amendment five times—in the senate in 1972 and 1982, and in the house in 1972, 1973, and 1975.[54] The state's conservative women and their efficient, vibrant anti-amendment campaign deserve much of the credit for the defeat of the Equal Rights Amendment in the state. Using long-established women's networks, such as those found within churches, Oklahoma's conservative women built a viable, energetic movement that represented and spread the values traditionalists held dear. This movement, in the end, brought about the defeat of the ERA in the state.

Most importantly, the anti-ratification fight politicized many Oklahoma women who took up the cause, particularly large numbers of the state's fundamentalist Christian women. Over the course of the decade, amendment opponents carried their newfound skills into the political arena, becoming involved in campaigns for conservative candidates. The success of social conservatives during the decade of the ERA struggle has had long-term, widespread political consequences, statewide and nationally. By the end of the decade, a groundswell of traditionalists placed Oklahoma firmly within a heightened political conservatism, a movement initiated and led by women conservatives, including fundamentalist Christian women. Their success in waging the anti-ERA campaign spread their message and their influence across the state, ultimately leading to an Oklahoma political realignment from Democratic to Republican majorities.

Notes

1. Although Indians, blacks, whites, and other ethnic groups inhabited Indian Territory and the entire region after statehood, the turn-of-the-century rush of primarily white settlers "at the rate of a hundred thousand a year" established hegemony from statehood forward. For the history of migration into the two territories and the state, see James Ralph Scales and Danney Goble, *Oklahoma Politics: A History* (Norman: University of Oklahoma Press, 1982), 1–19.

2. State Legislative Council, Legal Services Division, *State Legislative Council— Memorandum of Law* (Oklahoma Legislature, September 15, 1972), David Boren, RG 8 T 5 1, box 10, folder 6, Oklahoma Department of Libraries, Allen Wright Memorial Library, Oklahoma City.

3. "Hiring by the Quota System," *Tulsa World*, December 31, 1975.

4. For Oklahoma's history of segregation and integration, see, for example, Scales and Goble, *Oklahoma Politics*, especially 36, 46–47, and Douglas Hale, "The People of Oklahoma: Economics and Social Change," in *Oklahoma: New Views of the Forty-sixth State*, edited by Ann Hodges Morgan (Norman: University of Oklahoma Press, 1982), 86. For the state's

Southern Democrat leanings, see, for example, Cindy Simon Rosenthal, *When Women Lead: Integrative Leadership in State Legislatures* (New York: Oxford University Press, 1998), 100.

5. For the state's voting patterns and state voters' late-twentieth-century penchant to vote for Republican presidential candidates, see, for example, Danney Goble, "'The More Things Change . . .': Oklahoma since 1945," in *Politics in the Postwar American West*, edited by Richard Lowitt (Norman: University of Oklahoma Press, 1995), 186–87.

6. For Oklahoma's 1971 religious makeup and confirmation that the 1971 figure of 33 percent includes state Mormons, see Samuel A. Kirkpatrick, David R. Morgan, and Thomas G. Kielhorn, *The Oklahoma Voter: Politics, Elections and Parties in the Sooner State* (Norman: University of Oklahoma Press, 1977), 29–30.

7. For descriptions of anti-ERA movement participants' religious affiliations, see, for example, Donald T Critchlow, *Phyllis Schlafly and Grassroots Conservatism: A Woman's Crusade* (Princeton: Princeton University Press, 2005), 221, and Donald G. Mathews and Jane Sherron De Hart, *Sex, Gender, and the Politics of ERA: A State and the Nation* (New York: Oxford University Press, 1990), 153, 175–80.

8. For 1980 Oklahoma population and religious adherence percentages, see *Churches and Church Membership in the United States, 1980* (Glenmary Research Center), available at the website of Association of Religion Data Archives (ARDA), www.thearda.com/mapsReports/reports/state/40_1980.asp (accessed January 11, 2013). I calculated a number of the percentages used in this study from 1980 Oklahoma figures provided by ARDA.

9. Neil J. Young, "'The ERA Is a Moral Issue': The Mormon Church, LDS Women, and the Defeat of the Equal Rights Amendment," *American Quarterly* 59, no. 3 (2007): 623–44.

10. Ruth Murray Brown, *For a "Christian America": A History of the Religious Right* (Amherst, N.Y.: Prometheus Books, 2002), 69, 76.

11. Legislative Reference Division, "Legislation for Ratification of U.S. Constitution—Equal Rights Amendment," n.d., 1, vertical file, Equal Rights Amendment, Jan Eric Cartwright Memorial Library, Oklahoma Department of Libraries.

12. Ray Parr, "State Senate Approves Women's Rights Amendment," *Daily Oklahoman*, March 24, 1972.

13. Legislative Reference Division, "Legislation for Ratification of U.S. Constitution—Equal Rights Amendment," 1.

14. For Oklahoma as the first state to defeat ratification of the ERA, see, for example, "Rights Amendment Ratification Predicted," *Daily Oklahoman*, April 20, 1972.

15. Ann Patterson, "Unpublished personal interview," interview by Ruth Murray Brown, transcript of recording, November 18, 1978, Brown family private collection, Norman, Oklahoma, and Ann Patterson, "Unpublished telephone interview," interview by Ruth Murray Brown, transcript, March 23, 1982, Brown family private collection. For "de facto head" reference, see Brown, *For a Christian America*, 30. Brown states that the house member Patterson phoned was a Republican (*For a Christian America*, 29). However, Brown's

transcripts of those original interviews at least twice provide the name of the house member, and in 1972 that representative was a member of the Democratic Party.

16. Ann Patterson, "Unpublished telephone interview," interview by Ruth Murray Brown, transcript, May 8, 1982, Brown family private collection.

17. Ibid.

18. Kim E. Nielsen, *Un-American Womanhood: Antiradicalism, Antifeminism, and the First Red Scare* (Columbus: Ohio State University Press, 2001), 52.

19. Catherine E. Rymph, *Republican Women: Feminism and Conservatism from Suffrage through the Rise of the New Right* (Chapel Hill: University of North Carolina Press, 2006), 126. According to Rymph, the quote is from historian D'Ann Campbell, *Women at War with America: Private Lives in a Patriotic Era* (Cambridge, Mass.: Harvard University Press, 1984), 216–17.

20. Rebecca E. Klatch, *Women of the New Right* (Philadelphia: Temple University Press, 1987), 4–5.

21. For Kimball as president of the LDS, see "Religion: Mormonism Enters a New Era," *Time*, August 7, 1978.

22. Ruth Murray Brown, "Ruth Murray Brown Transcript—LDS Church," unpublished manuscript, September 16, 1978, Brown family private collection.

23. Midway through the ERA debate decade, anti-ratification activists renamed their campaign "the pro-family movement." For evidence of this renaming, see, for example, Ed Montgomery, "Women Claim New Political Unit Forms," *Daily Oklahoman*, July 14, 1977.

24. Sally Rowan Bell to Candidate, October 20, 1974, ERA Collection, box 35, folder 3, Oklahoma Historical Society Research Center, Oklahoma City, emphasis in original.

25. Oklahoma STOP ERA PEC to Friends, September 8, 1978, ERA Collection, box 35, folder 13, Oklahoma Historical Society Research Center.

26. George M. Marsden, *Fundamentalism and American Culture*, 2nd ed. (New York: Oxford University Press, 2006), 5, 244–45.

27. Dee Potts, chairman, Committee for a Clean Oklahoma City, and Bart Hawkins, co-chairman, to Rep. Atkins, June 21, 1980, ERA Collection, box 35, folder 9, Oklahoma Historical Society Research Center, emphasis in original.

28. When fundamentalists stated that the U.S. Supreme Court recognized secular humanism as a religion, they most likely referred to footnote 11 in *Torcaso v. Watkins* (1961), which stated: "Among religions in this country which do not teach what would generally be considered a belief in the existence of God are Buddhism, Taoism, Ethical Culture, Secular Humanism and others."

29. Patricia Kelley (pseud.), "Unpublished personal interview," interview by Ruth Murray Brown, transcript, March 18, 1981, Brown family private collection.

30. For an explanation of fundamentalism as a "movement that mostly steered clear of direct political involvement," see Marsden, *Fundamentalism and American Culture*, 229–57, especially p. 232.

31. STOP ERA, Political Education Committee, Oklahoma City, "The E.R.A.: Equal Rights Amendment (For Men and Women)—Myths vs. Facts," undated, John Dunning Political Collection, box 56, folder 3, Oklahoma Historical Society Research Center.

32. "Eagle Forum—Leading the Pro-Family Movement since 1972—Join Eagle Forum," undated, John Dunning Political Collection, box 56, folder 3, Oklahoma Historical Society Research Center.

33. Deborah Farnum (pseud.), "Unpublished personal interview," interview by Ruth Murray Brown, transcript, November 10, 1981, Brown family private collection.

34. "Why Are Homosexuals Supporting The Equal Rights Amendment (ERA)?," Washington County Eagle Forum, undated, ERA Collection, box 35, folder 13, Oklahoma Historical Society Research Center.

35. Edith Phillips (pseud.), "Unpublished personal interview," interview by Ruth Murray Brown, transcript, October 9, 1980, Brown family private collection.

36. Velma Logan (pseud.), "Unpublished personal interview," interview by Ruth Murray Brown, transcript, July 18, 1980, Brown family private collection.

37. Wanda Dawson (pseud.), "Unpublished personal interview," interview by Ruth Murray Brown, transcript, 1980, Brown family private collection.

38. Brown, *For a Christian America*, 72.

39. State Legislative Council, "1972 Interim Hearings on the Proposed Equal Rights Amendment to the United States Constitution," January 10, 1973, 15, 60, 81, 127, Jan Eric Cartwright Memorial Library, Oklahoma Department of Libraries, emphases in original.

40. For the connection between the early Oklahoma anti-ERA movement and the John Birch Society as well as other anticommunist groups, see Brown, *For a Christian America*, 44, 81–101.

41. Oklahoma STOP ERA PEC to Friends, September 8, 1978.

42. Oklahoma STOP ERA PEC to Friends, October 28, 1981, ERA Collection, box 35, folder 9, Oklahoma Historical Society Research Center.

43. Oklahoma STOP ERA PEC to Friends, September 8, 1978."

44. "Letter Writing," 1975, ERA Collection, box 35, folder 8, Oklahoma Historical Society Research Center.

45. For extant examples of identical or largely similar letters, see, for example, Juanita Walton to Tom Steed, November 7, 1977, Tom Steed Collection, Legislative Series, box 87, folder 16, Carl Albert Center, University of Oklahoma; Mrs. W. R. Mackey to Tom Steed, November 8, 1977, Tom Steed Collection, Legislative Series, box 87, folder 16, Carl Albert Center; Polly Nye to Mickey Edwards, November 8, 1977, Mickey Edwards Collection, box 114, Carl Albert Center; and June Bryen to Mickey Edwards, n.d., Mickey Edwards Collection, Box 114, Carl Albert Center.

46. "Trent Backed by ERA Foes," *Sunday Oklahoman*, August 22, 1976.

47. Teresa Billings (pseud.), "Unpublished personal interview," interview by Ruth Murray Brown, transcript, October 10, 1980, Brown family private collection.

48. Walter Jenny, Jr., "Jones' State Legacy Longlasting" *Edmond Sun*, August 12, 2006, http://www.edmondsun.com/opinion/x519214493/Jones-state-legacy-longlasting (accessed January 10, 2013).

49. Claudia Thomas (pseud.), "Unpublished personal interview," interview by Ruth Murray Brown, transcript, October 24, 1980, Brown family private collection.

50. Martha Simms (pseud.), "Unpublished personal interview," interview by Ruth Murray Brown, transcript, 1980, Brown family private collection.

51. John Greiner, "Legislative Leaders Pondering ERA Strategy," *Sunday Oklahoman*, February 4, 1979.

52. Ruth Murray Brown, "Ruth Murray Brown transcript—Legislators' mail," unpublished manuscript, 1975, Brown family private collection.

53. For "buried in committee" reference, see Jim Young, "ERA Deadline Caps 10-year Hassle in Sooner Legislature," *Oklahoma City Times*, June 29, 1982.

54. For the sixteen resolutions as well as the dates of the legislative votes, see Legislative Reference Division, "Legislation for Ratification of U.S. Constitution—Equal Rights Amendment," 1, 6–9.

CHAPTER 12

On the Illinois

THE MAKING OF MODERN MUSIC AND CULTURE IN THE OKLAHOMA OZARK FOOTHILLS

J. Justin Castro

T he songs people play, listen to, and write contain important insights into human experience. Among other things, they help unveil elements of history, geography, conflict, and cooperation. This chapter uses song as a tool of investigation for understanding and documenting the historic cultural composition of the Ozarks of eastern Oklahoma. Other scholars have studied folk songs in the Ozarks, but this study covers a much smaller physical area, often considered distinct from the rest of the region.[1] The culture of the Oklahoma Ozarks, often associated with the Illinois River, has been unique in some ways, but in many other ways it has been similar to those in neighboring Arkansas and Missouri. The differences derive from the historical circumstances of separate but interacting cultural "groups," as well as geographical and political boundaries.[2]

Unlike the eastern part of the range, the Oklahoma Ozarks are a transition zone—physically and culturally—between the Great Plains and the eastern woodlands. This area has also been home to many of the Cherokee people since their coerced removal, beginning in the 1820s, by U.S. soldiers and settlers, from a region including parts of Georgia, North Carolina, Tennessee, and Alabama. The Trail of Tears, the path the Cherokees were forced to march over, ended in the Ozark foothills of the newly created Indian Territory. According to some geographers, this created a "cultural fault line" in the hills.[3]

The geological comparison is intriguing but is perhaps overly rigid. The area would be better described as an ethnic and cultural zone of interaction or a frontier. During the twentieth century, intermarriage—and interaction in general—broke down many cultural barriers. However, the large Cherokee presence and a unique geography still provide certain distinctive qualities.

Unlike past studies of music of the Ozarks, this one does not limit itself to folk songs. Performers in eastern Oklahoma have created multiple forms of music, including classical, religious, popular, and folk, since the arrival of the first Cherokees (and black slaves, Anglo ministers, and intermarried European Americans) in the 1820s. These forms of music, like the people that play them, often intermix and reveal distinctive characteristics. The growth of electronic media, beginning with radio, additionally instigated significant change—in both urban and rural areas—altering musical performance and what people listened to. That said, many communities, including those in the Oklahoma Ozarks, have held on to elements of oral traditions and distinctly regional attributes while including influences from the world outside and its popular culture. While most entertainers in the region today rarely include traditional songs—for example, old English and Scottish ballads—in their regular repertoires, the interplay of many forces, peoples, and technologies has created a strong and vibrant musical culture in the Oklahoma Ozarks.

The Landscape

The physical Oklahoma Ozarks region includes a high plateau and hills covered with rocky soil and thick forests. Small, scattered creeks wind their way through the shady "hollers," as they are known there, many draining into the Illinois River. At the western and northern boundaries, the densely wooded highlands yield to the flatter tallgrass and mixed-grass prairies—the wind-struck plains famous to Oklahoma—that stretch into the horizon. Physically, much of the Oklahoma Ozarks region is similar to land in adjacent counties in Arkansas and Missouri (if slightly lower in elevation) and different from much of the rest of Oklahoma. Unlike other areas of the state, the region is heavily made up of Mississippian limestone and chert, which with the water has created abundant sinkholes and caverns. The area receives more days of rainfall on average and is usually slightly cooler throughout the summer.[4]

The Oklahoma Ozarks are different from other parts of Oklahoma in other ways as well. Except for small gas deposits in southern Sequoyah County, the Oklahoma Ozarks have few of the oil and gas resources that are available to the western part of the state. Hence they lack the boomtowns and direct influence of those industries.[5] A dearth of good farming soil and grazing land also separates the Ozarks from the western prairies, and, though farming and ranching are present, it is commonly on a smaller scale.[6] Since the prairies of the central plains make up the region's western border, this area is what biologists call an ecotone—a transition area between two adjacent and different plant communities—which creates a complex and rich assortment of animal and plant life.

Culturally and ethnically the picture is similarly complicated and mixed. Situated between the Mississippi River and the Great Plains, the region has been an area of important cross-cultural interaction since prehistoric times.[7] The Cherokees, who have lived in the area longer than any other ethnic group present today, brought cultural attributes unique to them. But in addition to rituals exclusive to them, they shared numerous cultural traditions with non-Indian residents of Oklahoma and with their Arkansas and Missouri neighbors. One reason for this cultural incorporation is that beginning in the early eighteenth century, Anglo Americans, especially of Scottish and Scotch-Irish descent, married into Cherokee families. Many Anglo families similar or related to those who intermarried with Cherokees also migrated from the east into the central and eastern Ozarks. Although much less common, some Cherokees also married their black slaves.[8]

This intermarriage made life in the nineteenth-century Cherokee Nation a mixture of indigenous customs, southern white society, African American traditions, and a twist of New England religiosity. By the time the majority of the Cherokees arrived over the Trail of Tears and established towns like Vian, Park Hill, and Tahlequah, a substantial portion of them had borrowed many customs of the intermarried European Americans and their relatives to the east. They built wooden homes, institutions of higher education based on those in New England, roads, trading posts, barns with cattle, chickens, and hogs, and had Appalachian-style string bands.[9]

The Cherokees west of the Mississippi quickly rebuilt their lives. Some of the elite families owned plantations and slaves, but most lived in the valleys, on small farms.[10] Corn was the most common crop, though cotton, wheat, tobacco, and vegetables were grown.[11] Other foods and most medical remedies came from the wide variety of native plant life.[12] Multiple scholars have argued that a limited tax base had historically caused a lack of community services, but the Tahlequah and Park Hill areas were progressive in some respects.[13] A marker in front of the Cherokee Supreme Court Building still proudly claims that the community of Tahlequah was the first to receive a phone call west of the Mississippi River. Further, many Park Hill residents built large and beautiful houses with modern niceties. Cherokees constructed the first institution of higher learning in Indian Territory. Even if most of the Oklahoma Ozarks did not mirror that kind of rapid development, the Cherokee capital and the surrounding area included many impressive structures, institutions, and services by the mid nineteenth century.[14]

Over the twentieth century, demographics changed significantly. Hispanics, especially from Mexico, now make up a larger portion of the population than before. The percentage of blacks compared to other ethnicities has dropped, even if actual numbers have risen. Eastern Asian immigrants now work for or own their own businesses and attend Northeastern State University in Tahlequah. More and more whites have moved into the area (they now make up a slight majority), and Northeastern State continues to bring in a wide assortment of people from Oklahoma and around the world.[15] Yet Hispanic and Asian influences have not made significant inroads into the musical culture outside of their own specific communities.

Music Traditions

Despite the intermixing of cultures, many Cherokee preferred traditional indigenous dances and rituals (and some still do today) as a favored form of entertainment and spiritual practice.[16] Stomp dances—exhibitions of music and dance—are traditional to the Cherokees, and members have partaken in the ritual for centuries.[17] Many of these dances have been open for outsiders to observe, though certain families in the past were stricter on enforcing qualifications for entry and restricting knowledge of ceremonies considered sacred.[18] For many Cherokees, stomp grounds are spiritual and social places, which are often under the direction of a certain community or clan.[19] There are accounts of non-Indian residents participating in these dances, but overall the tradition is reserved for certain Native American groups.[20] Powwows are another venue for Cherokee music and dance. Often intertribal, involving people from multiple Native nations, these have become common since the rise of pan-Indianism after World War II. Educational institutions like the multi-tribal Sequoyah High School in Park Hill, Oklahoma, have additionally led to more twentieth and twenty-first century Cherokee powwow participants.[21]

With the inclusion of other cultures came new ideas and musical practices. Before U.S. soldiers forced the Cherokees westward, many Cherokees had taken up fiddle playing. Some carried the instrument across the Trail of Tears, and Cherokee musicians have commonly played the instrument in the Oklahoma Ozarks ever since. Picked up from Anglo-Saxon traders, the instrument became popular at social events by the early nineteenth century in the Southeast.[22] "English Dances," square dances, barn dances, house-raising dances, and jigs all became common forms of entertainment among all ethnic groups in the Southeast and in the Oklahoma Ozarks after the Cherokee removal.[23] The Cherokees have produced many talented fiddle players, and jubilees and Native stomp dances were (and are) attended by some of the same residents.

Though their fiddle-playing tradition is not as well documented as that of other ethnicities, African Americans also produced talented fiddlers who played in Civil War camps and for family and community events.[24] The blacks that came with eastern Indian groups also introduced to the region banjo playing, shouts, West African–rooted dancing, and the playing of bones.[25] In the 1930s Dennis Vann related how he had played the fiddle to fellow black refugees and Union soldiers in Franklin County, Kansas, before returning to Tahlequah in 1866.[26] Freedman John Thompson stated during the same era that his father had fiddled for Cherokee dances around Fort Gibson and Tahlequah.[27]

Other traditions dating from the nineteenth century and shared by ethnicities in the Oklahoma and greater Ozarks include hymns, gospel songs, temperance songs, and play-party tunes.[28] The latter two genres have nearly ceased to exist among present-day performers. Christian music, especially hymns, became increasingly influential as missionaries established themselves and worked with settled families. Church groups, especially Congregationalists, Baptists, and Methodists, had converted a large number of the Cherokees by the end of the nineteenth century. This trend continued into the 1900s, and most Cherokees now adhere, at least nominally, to some form of Christian faith. The music from small rural churches spread to picnics, family reunions, and performances for other celebrations. Today in the Cherokee hills it is common to hear musicians mix gospel songs with traditional and popular secular songs.[29] This phenomenon is not new—it stems from a long history of artistic mixing.[30]

Stomp dances, string band performances, and hymn singing in the Oklahoma Ozarks were established art forms that came with settlers from southern Appalachia and missionaries from New England. However, after the Civil War, new south–north migration patterns developed on the western border of the Ozark Plateau. These migrants brought their own songs and traditions, leading to an infusion of new ballads beginning in the 1840s. In the twentieth century, the genres of honky-tonk, jazz, and western swing followed similar paths from Texas and Louisiana to Oklahoma and locations further north.

The Shawnee Trail was the principle cattle road before cattlemen established the Chisholm Trail. The former passed along the edge of the Oklahoma Ozarks, bringing the culture of cowpunchers, wranglers, buckaroos, and the singing cowboy.[31] These herders stopped at Fort Gibson before moving on to the east or west fork of the trail. The post was just as much a social center for the area as a military compound.[32] In the late nineteenth century, Cherokees held traditional dances there, a church band played for balls, and Temperance Society meetings were common.[33] Beginning in that era, cowboy ballads worked their way into the repertoire of Oklahoma Ozarks musicians, including songs like "The Buffalo Skinners," and "Chisholm Trail." Here is a verse from "The Buffalo Skinners":

> Our meat it was buffalo hump and
> Iron wedge bread,
> And all we had to sleep on was a
> Buffalo robe for a bed:
> The fleas and greybacks worked on
> us, O boys, it was not slow,
> I'll tell you there is no worse hell on
> earth than the range of the buffalo.[34]

The songs these cowboys carried were but the first of a longtime movement of music between Texas and Oklahoma, including the Ozarks.

The Impact of Modern Media, Popular Music, and New Settlers

The twentieth century ushered in new music in the United States—and new technology—that significantly altered the music of the Ozark foothills. Many changes came from the influence of urban centers and the rise of "modernity."[35] One example is the development of jazz in the 1920s, in cities including New York and New Orleans, but also Oklahoma City, Tulsa, and Muskogee. Many renowned players, such as the various members of the Oklahoma City Blue Devils—William "Count" Basie, Billy King, Buddy Anderson, and Jimmy Rushing—called Oklahoma City their home. Tulsa and Muskogee also had thriving jazz scenes, and they were popular stops along the road to cities such as Kansas City, St. Louis, and Chicago. Muskogee, which lies just west of the Oklahoma Ozarks, produced numerous talented, if less renowned jazz musicians. Clarence Love, Jay McShann, Samuel Aaron Bell, Barney Kessey, Terrence Holder, and Claude Williams were all outstanding performers with Muskogee roots.[36] Williams uniquely blended jazz and fiddle playing. Talented on multiple instruments, he left his home of Muskogee in 1928 to join the thriving jazz scene of Kansas City, Missouri. There he played with Andy Kirk,

Mary Lou Williams, and Count Basie. Jazz possessed a distinct urban sound, reflective of the fast pace of life, the hustle and bustle of Ford Model Ts, electric streetcars, and new movie houses.

Although it is somewhat unclear why Muskogee produced so many great jazz musicians, most of them were black. The African American communities that came with the "civilized tribes" to Indian Territory had a rich heritage of spiritual music and work songs, and these traditions influenced the popular performers who followed. The majority of jazz musicians in the area came from families well versed in music performance.[37] Eastern Oklahoma possessed a tradition of spiritual music. "Swing Low, Sweet Chariot," one of a handful of renowned spirituals written by "Uncle Wallis" and "Aunt Minerva" Willis, Choctaw slaves, became one of the best-known religious songs in the United States.[38]

Perhaps it was a combination of musical heritage with new styles out of Oklahoma City and Tulsa that provided the right atmosphere for Muskogee musicians to flourish. New technologies also changed how music was dispersed. Since jazz developed in an era of powerful U.S. economic expansion and increasingly faster communications, this new and vibrant music rapidly influenced cultures around the globe, including the Oklahoma Ozarks. However, it would not be until the latter half of the twentieth century that jazz gained a substantial following in the Oklahoma Ozarks, and even then it was limited to larger towns like Tahlequah.

Early on, jazz had its greatest impact in urban areas, especially in black communities. Although few Oklahoma Ozarks musicians played jazz in the 1920s, it greatly influenced the music of Bob Wills, a white Texas-born musician who later established himself in Tulsa. A childhood fan of African American work songs, blues, and dance music, Wills borrowed extensively from his experiences with blacks while on the road to becoming the "patriarch of western-swing."[39] While it is questionable what African Americans thought of his attempts at emulation, Wills performed in black-face in the 1920s for a touring minstrel show.[40] He spent 1934 through 1942, his most-admired years, in Tulsa, and the close proximity of his sound to the Oklahoma Ozarks—broadcast by radio stations—made a strong and lasting impact on the area.[41]

The first experimental radio broadcast station in Oklahoma began in Oklahoma City in 1921. The spring of the following year, businesses officially commenced with stations in Oklahoma City (WKY) and Tulsa (WEH). Oil executives started the latter station, as well as KFRU in Bristow (founded in 1925). KFRU specialized in showcasing local musical talent. Otto Gray and his

Singing Cowboys became the first successful radio stars in Oklahoma, performing string band songs. The call letters changed to KVOO in 1926 and the station moved to Tulsa in 1927. It was on KVOO in 1934 that Bob Wills and his Texas Playboys entertained Oklahoma via the airwaves, on one of the longest-running radio programs in the state of Oklahoma.[42] Wills's brand of music, western swing—more or less a combination of cowboy music, string band music, the big band sound, and jazz—quickly grew in popularity throughout much of the state.

Wills and western swing influenced musicians in the Oklahoma Ozarks almost instantly. Wills had countrified the jazz horns enough to please the palates of rural Oklahomans. Guitarists and fiddlers learned his tunes and played them at barn parties and other celebrations. The new homespun bands almost always lacked the brass section and basically incorporated Wills's sound into local styles of string band music, though steel guitar became increasingly popular. Eastern Oklahoma residents, such as Sam O'Field and Curley Lewis, spent portions of their lives touring with western swing acts like Johnny Lee Wills and Leon McAuliffe and the Cimarron Boys.[43] The influence of western swing continues to be heard in the music of Oklahoma Ozark performers today, including Randy Crouch, Joe Mack, and Thomas Trapp.

"Red Dirt" music, arguably beginning in the 1970s, has also influenced Oklahoma Ozark musicians—and they have influenced it. The term has grown in popularity in the United States for describing music from Oklahoma (and sometimes Texas). Red Dirt has been a conundrum for music critics and historians, because it is hard to define. One recent author, Thomas Connor, considers the genre "a delayed reaction to [Woody] Guthrie's life and legacy, a loose musical movement with the potential to focus and synthesize the entire of Oklahoma and its music."[44] But this definition remains problematic. Musicians played Woody Guthrie songs well before the 1970s. There was no delay. The Red Dirt label has also spread beyond the boundaries of Oklahoma. The term itself has proven to be like Oklahoma weather—hard to define, and constantly changing. But Oklahoma still always seems to be a part of it.

The label relates to the color of the clay soil so common to central Oklahoma. The performers associated with Red Dirt have often come from this area. They have been influenced by traditional ballads, Texas honky-tonk, and country, as well as by the Tulsa sound connected to J. J. Cale and Leon Russell. But Red Dirt includes many types of music and is as hard to pin down as its origins. Some authors attribute the label to Jesse Ed Davis's 1972 song "Red Dirt Boogie, Brother."[45] (Davis was an Oklahoma-born Native American guitarist.) The beginning of Red Dirt has also been attributed to the record label Red Dirt Records, which Stillwater resident and singer Steve Ripley created for his band, Moses, the same year.[46] A less recognized Norman-based band called Red Dirt existed even earlier, in 1971, which previous authors have failed to mention.[47] Most living Oklahoma musicians familiar with red dirt music associate the movement to the performers and groupies who revolved in and out of "The Farm," which Conner calls "a gathering place, a makeshift commune, where mostly musicians congregated to talk, drink, and play songs" on the outskirts of Stillwater.[48] Jimmy LaFave's song "Red Dirt Roads at Night" furthered the use of the term as a genre of music from central Oklahoma. A small sample of musicians and bands that have become emblematic of the style includes Bob Childers, the Red Dirt Rangers, Stoney LaRue, Medicine Show, Tom Skinner, the Farm Couple, Jason Boland & the Stragglers, and Cross Canadian Ragweed.[49] As with western swing broadcasts in the 1930s and later, radio shows have contributed to the influence and spread of Red Dirt, swing, and folk music in Oklahoma. Present programs include KVOO's *Red Dirt Radio Hour*, KWGS's *Folk Salad, Oklahoma Rock Show*, with Steve Ripley, and *Swing on This*, with John Wooley, and a number of shows on KOSU.[50]

The Illinois River Scene

How the music of the Oklahoma Ozarks is connected to Red Dirt is another complexity. Today's Oklahoma musicians admit that there are unique qualities to the music from the hills of northeastern Oklahoma, but many people still include this music with Red Dirt. Others see music from central Oklahoma and eastern Oklahoma as interwoven but distinct: according to Oklahoma songwriter Joe Baxter, "concentric circles, where somebody belonging to one group of musician friends knows somebody who belongs to another group, and eventually the groups meet, interchange, and share."[51] This statement is likely closest to being the most accurate, although it ignores the Red Dirt label (maybe *because* it ignores it). Some artists from around Tahlequah consider their music to have more influence from the Ozarks than players from central Oklahoma, while others call themselves Red Dirt performers.[52]

Music takes on many forms in the Oklahoma Ozarks. Many musicians have formed a community out of their shared passion for music and song, including people usually known for playing in genres ranging from "traditional" to heavy metal. Oklahoma City songwriter Joe Baxter explained in 2010:

Understand that we are now experiencing the SECOND generation of "Red Dirt" music. The term has been very loosely applied and bandied about to the extent that the genre has been very watered down and expanded to include music out of Texas, Kansas, Arkansas, etc. Although the music crowd in and around Tahlequah and surrounding areas are for the most part avid Red Dirt fans, I've always noticed openness to ALL kinds of live music. This is the main difference. There are folks who actually LISTEN to my songs, understand them and seem to enjoy them. This isn't the case here in OKC.[53]

Although Red Dirt music, whatever it is, is embraced by many Oklahoman musicians and audiences, regional variations within the state continue to exist. Not only are there are differences between the western Ozark foothills and central Oklahoma, it's worth pointing out that the soil in the Oklahoma Ozarks is generally not red but brown. As far as music goes, performers seem to have stronger ties to the music scenes in Tulsa, but also to Fayetteville and Eureka Springs, Arkansas.

It is common for songs by performers along the Illinois River to include lyrics specific to the vicinity. Instead of songs about red dirt roads, clear water and forest-covered hills have been more common themes. Popular artist Randy Crouch's "On the Illinois" is clearly distinctive to the area. He wrote the song in the 1980s during the much-contested and ongoing battle between Arkansas and Oklahoma over the dumping of wastewater and chicken farm runoff into the Illinois River watershed.[54] During the first years of the twenty-first century, this ongoing conflict led other area songwriters to lend their songs about the river and the environment to an awareness campaign that resulted in a compilation album. It included Crouch's song, Eddie Glenn's "Alternative Fuel," Donnie Duree's "Lovely Illinois River Night," Dan Garber's "Highway 10," and Kelly Anquoe's "Round Dance." Local artist Murv Jacob painted an artwork for the CD cover, a Cherokee story–inspired scene titled *Rabbit and Bear Canoeing*. Regional songwriters continue to make land and water a subject. Indeed, the river has long been a theme of performers at local venues: Diamondhead Resort, Kooter Brown's, Brewdog's, the Iguana Café, the Branch, and the legendary (at least in that part of the world) Roxies Roost. Local culture and the physical environment are prominent in the work of many Oklahoma Ozark artists. Anquoe uses elements of Cherokee music, new technologies, and rock n' roll. Besides protesting against degradation of the region's main waterway, many others sing of the local natural beauty, whether born and raised in the area or latter settlers. For example, members of the Trapp family have a long lineage of talented musicians, and resident and songwriter Bill Ericson has been a longtime favorite in Cherokee County.

Figure 12.1. Fiddler Randy Crouch, Red Dirt Harvest Festival, 2007, at Okemah's Grape Ranch Winery. Photograph courtesy of Peter Henshaw.

Crouch, who moved from West Texas to the Tahlequah area in 1970, learned fiddle tips from local legend Jimmy Giles and helped initiate a resurgence in fiddle playing at Northeastern State University and in Tahlequah hangouts.[55]

Although there are unique qualities about the music from the Illinois, many Oklahomans consider Oklahoma Ozarks musicians Red Dirt artists. Tahlequah performers the Pumpkin Hollow Boys referred to themselves as playing "good old country red-dirt music" inspired by entertainers including Jason Boland and the Stragglers and Cross Canadian Ragweed.[56] Additionally, some musicians living in the foothills are originally from areas like North Texas and north-central Oklahoma. Musicians from central and northeastern Oklahoma tend to play together in shows around the state and abroad. Crouch played for many parties and in many creative endeavors at The Farm, and he has played all over Oklahoma. Further, Crouch has been the off-again, on-again fiddler for the Red Dirt Rangers. Many Red Dirt fans consider him one of the patriarchs of the genre.

Joe Mack, who lives on the other side of a hill from Crouch in Moody, Oklahoma, is a Stillwater native. Although he has written songs influenced by northeastern Oklahoma, he has also written about being an Oklahoman in general, as in his song "Oklahoma Brokedown Blues." Some of his songs, for example, "Like Mike / Gloss Mountain Breakdown," are in honor of Mack's influences from the western part of the state, in this instance Mike Hedges. Mack is good friends and often shares the stage with musicians from central Oklahoma, including Travis Linville and Carter Sampson. David Castro, another Tahlequah-area performer and songwriter who plays elsewhere in Oklahoma as well as outside the state, writes in a song titled "2010": "From Tahlequah to Oklahoma City / the grass is green, the roads are shitty / heading back we take the turnpike and pay our fees."[57]

Many musicians in the Oklahoma Ozarks do not associate with Red Dirt music at all. There are garage bands as in towns across the United States, and most are more influenced by popular mainstream music than Oklahoma roots music. Hard rock bands like Tahlequah's Soberality and Fuhgawz never regarded themselves as Red Dirt. They associate more with nationally renowned acts like Clutch and Nirvana. Many artists from the most recent generation are most influenced by the latest pop artists. A huge range of popular and not-so-popular groups has influenced Matt Gurley, a talented songwriter originally from Tahlequah, who notes shoegazer as a subgenre that has influenced his music. He describes shoegazer as "primarily started in Britain and pretty much at its peak in the late 80's and early 90's, though it still thrives today (I hope I'm living proof) . . . it usually involves dreamy, swirling textures of guitars and synths, often pairing light, breathy vocals with noisy, yet pleasant progressions and melodies."[58]

My-Tea Kind, whose members had ties to Red Dirt performers, is rarely considered a Red Dirt band. Three of the four members played as Randy Crouch's backup band, and all have played with numerous Red Dirt artists. But while roots music is apparent in the band's harmonies, not to mention the use of instruments like the musical saw and washboard, My-Tea Kind is much more experimental and eclectic. Like many performers, they play electric instruments, but they also use bullhorns, whistles, and various percussion instruments rare in Red Dirt. They did not write songs that included the name of the state, although they did play Richard Rodgers and Oscar Hammerstein's "Oklahoma!" at one of the state's centennial celebrations in 2007. Their songs tended to have a spiritual quality, which is at least partially derived from the streams, forests, and hills of northeastern Oklahoma. In comparison to Red Dirt, Joe Mack stated that "the Illinois River music pulls from the same roots, but the lyrics can contain more mystical qualities."[59] Mack and three of My-Tea Kind's members—My-Tea Kind more or less broke up when in 2007 vocalist and percussionist Bonnie Paine left to play with Elephant Revival, a popular folk band currently based out of Nederland, Colorado—joined together under various My-Tea Kinda names from 2007–2009, and in 2009 they took on the name Meandering Orange.

This infusion of the mystic has largely stemmed from the influence of hippie and psychedelic drug culture, which has influenced the Oklahoma music scene since at least the 1970s. Northeastern State University students also continue to contribute many bands little associated with Red Dirt (if any) and the institution possesses a fine program in classical music, with roots in the original school, the Cherokee Female Seminary. The traditional music of the region has not died out, although, as mentioned, performance of play-party pieces and temperance songs are growing extremely rare. It is fair to say that most Tahlequah-area musicians who have recently earned at least a partial living playing music have largely interacted with other artists in Oklahoma, commonly with self-proclaimed Red Dirt musicians, and nearly all are influenced by popular music via radio, popular recordings, and the Internet.

The abundance of cultural blending in the Oklahoma Ozarks exemplifies a history of cultural preservation, adaptation, and interaction. Multiple musical styles flourish, both in traditional and progressive variations. Some are "purer" in fashion, more influenced by past generations, though most mix influences from popular musical. The historic east–west movement of the Five Tribes, and the influx of southeasterners in general, mixing with the south–north cultures that stemmed from cowboys, western swing, honky-tonk, and jazz, have largely been responsible for Oklahoma's musical sound (whether called Red Dirt or not). Later influences have been the classic rock of the 1960s and 1970s, bluegrass, and more recently indie bands popular on college campuses. The vibrancy of the music around the Illinois River and other parts of Oklahoma derives from this long history of intermixing musical traditions and innovations. However, the musical culture of the Oklahoma Ozarks also possesses distinctive qualities deriving from its Cherokee roots, perhaps its ecological activism, and especially its connection to the river, forests, and the surrounding hills. It is this shared geographical and cultural space—and the music that it inspires—that has created a common bond among musicians on the Illinois. A part of Oklahoma and the Ozarks, the musical culture has been similar to the surrounding eco-tone; a zone of interaction where variation and ingenuity thrive at a crossroads of multiple traditions.

Notes

1. Vance Randolph, ed., *Ozark Folksongs*, vol. 1–4 (Columbia: State Historical Society of Missouri, 1946); E. Joan Wilson Miller, "The Ozark Culture Region as Revealed by Traditional Materials," *Annals of the Association of American Geographers* 58, no. 1 (March 1968): 51.The term "folk," like "tradition," has been problematic as a term for historians, although it is still useful. One problem is that often cultural traits are not as old as people make them out to be. There is a huge literature on this, but good examples are Eric Hobsbawm and Terrance Ranger, *The Invention of Tradition* (Cambridge: Cambridge University Press, 1992); Benjamin Filene, *Romancing the Folk: Public Memory and American Roots Music* (Chapel Hill: University of North Carolina Press, 2000); John Hutchinson and Anthony D. Smith, eds., *Nationalism* (Oxford: Oxford University Press, 1994).

2. I use the term "groups" in a malleable fashion. It is useful and somewhat accurate to call, for example, the Cherokee and their Anglo-American neighbors different groups, each with certain attributes more common to itself than to the other. But "groups" historically blend, borrow, fissure, or fuse into new "groups." Rigid, impermeable categories rarely, if ever, exist.

3. The term "cultural fault line" is from geographer Leslie Hewes, who wrote insightful works on "Cherokee Ozarks." See Leslie Hewes, "Cultural Fault in the Cherokee Country," *Economic Geography* 19, no. 2 (April 1943): 137–38; Leslie Hewes, "Indian Land in the Cherokee Country of Oklahoma," *Economic Geography* 18, no. 4 (October 1942): 405–12. Wilson Miller, "The Ozark Culture Region as Revealed by Traditional Materials," *Annals of the Association of American Geographers* 58, no. 1 (March 1968): 52–77, uses Hewes's term as well. Although there is significant validity to this term (this is especially true of the nineteenth century), I think Hewes overstates the case. The Cherokees intermixed frequently

with other people in the Ozarks, as well as with people on the western plains. In addition, the intermarriage of Anglo Americans into the Cherokee Nation made the ethnic differences less dramatic as previous geographers have ascribed. Because of this intermingling there are many shared cultural traits.

4. A good introductory source to the geography of Oklahoma is Charles Robert Goins and Danny Goble, eds., *Historical Atlas of Oklahoma*, 4th ed. (Norman: University of Oklahoma Press, 2006). Specifically used here from Goins and Goble are Howard L. Johnson, "Precipitation," 18–19, and Kenneth S. Johnson, "Geologic Formations," 8–9.

5. Dan Boyd, "Oil and Gas Production," in *Historical Atlas of Oklahoma*, 4th ed., edited by Charles Robert Goins and Danny Goble (Norman: University of Oklahoma Press, 2006), 28–29; Johnson, "Geologic Formations," 8–9.

6. Leslie Hewes, *Occupying the Cherokee Country of Oklahoma* (Lincoln: University of Nebraska Press, 1978), 403–408.

7. Marvin E. Tong, Jr., "Cox, an Archaic Site in the Ozarks," *American Antiquity* 20, no. 2 (October 1954): 124–29.

8. See Tiya Miles, *Ties That Bind: The Story of an Afro-Cherokee Family in Slavery and Freedom* (Berkeley: University of California Press, 2006).

9. Thomas Nuttal, *Journal of Travels into the Arkansas Territory* (Philadelphia: T. H. Palmer, 1821), 137; Cephas Washburn, *Reminiscences of the Indians* (Richmond: Presbyterian Committee of Publication, 1869), 24; William Boyd, interviewed by Wylie Thornton, July 2, 1937, Indian Pioneer History Collection, Oklahoma Historical Society Research Center (hereafter IPHC), vol. 36, pp. 311–14.

10. Devon A. Mihesuah, *Cultivating the Rosebuds: The Education of Women at the Cherokee Female Seminary, 1851–1909* (Urbana: University of Illinois Press, 1993), 21, 30, 35, 43; Hewes, "Cultural Fault in the Cherokee Country:" 138; Albert L. Wahrhaftig, "Tribal Cherokee Population of Eastern Oklahoma," *Current Anthropology* 9, no. 5, pt. 2 (December 1968): 517.

11. Hewes, "Cultural Fault in the Cherokee Country:" 136; Leslie Hewes, "The Oklahoma Ozarks as the Land of the Cherokees," *Geographical Review* 32, no. 2 (April 1942): 275.

12. E. T. Pendley, interview by Amelia F. Harris, Oklahoma City, Oklahoma, February 25, 1938, IPHC, vol. 93, p. 218.

13. Hewes, "Indian Land in the Cherokee Country of Oklahoma," 405–12; Brad Agnew, "Sustaining the Cherokees' Lamp of Enlightenment: The Establishment of Northeastern State Normal School," *Chronicles of Oklahoma* 87, no. 4 (Winter 2008–2009), 401.

14. Hewes, "Indian Land in the Cherokee Country of Oklahoma," 405–12.

15. The figure from a 2009 estimate is 6.9 percent of the population of Cherokee County. This is up significantly since the 1800s, when there is almost no mention of Mexicans or Mexican Americans in historical documents. "Cherokee County, Oklahoma," U.S. Census Bureau, http://quickfacts.census.gov/qfd/states/40/40021.html (accessed June 28, 2010).

16. Mary Townsend Crow, interview by Dayna Lee, Bartlesville, Oklahoma, June 22, 1994, Oklahoma State Arts Council Collection, Oklahoma Historical Society Research Center

(hereafter OSACC), box 3, "Crow, Mary Townsend" folder; Edward Thompson, interview by Joe L. Todd, Bartlesville, Oklahoma, February 12, 1984, Oral History Collection, Oklahoma Historical Society Research Center (hereafter OHC), t84.018 a–b; W. W. Newcomb, Jr., "A Note on Cherokee-Delaware Pan-Indianism," *American Anthropologist*, New Series, 57, no. 5 (October 1955): 1041–45; Ruth Parks, interview by L. J. Wilson, June 24, 1937, IPHC, vol. 8, pp. 66–75.

17. Other Indian peoples originally from eastern North America—for example, the Chickasaws and Choctaws—also have stomp dances.

18. Kelly Anquoe, Tahlequah, Oklahoma, e-mail correspondence to author, April 14, 2007; Tommy Wildcat, interview with Rodger Harris, March 11, 1998, east of Keys, Oklahoma, OHC, v98.017; Bill Swim, interview by L. W. Wilson, April 13, 1937, IPHC, vol. 10, pp. 240–53; Mrs. Sam Sanders, interview by C. C. Davidson, January 25, 1937, IPHC, vol. 9, pp. 154–58; Mary Riley Roberts, "Nowata Settlers," IPHC, vol. 8, pp. 426–33; Lenora Alpha Henry (Ross), interview by M. J. Stockton, June 24, 1937, IPHC, vol. 10, pp. 425–28; Minnie Hodge, interview by W. T. Holland, Tulsa, Oklahoma, August 18, 1937, IPHC, vol. 29, pp. 242–45; George W. Mayes, interview by Amelia F. Harris, Oklahoma City, Oklahoma, August 10, 1937, IPHC, vol. 71, pp. 40–48; Ida Mae Hughes, interview by Robert B. Thomas, Muskogee, Oklahoma, November 15, 1937, IPHC, vol. 30, pp. 160–62; William Boyd, interview by Wylie Thornton, July 2, 1937, IPHC, vol. 36, pp. 311–14; Lynch Sixkiller, interview by W. A. Bigby, April 19, 1937, IPHC, vol. 9, pp. 421–22; Docia Rich, interview by Ruby Wolfenbarger, August 17, 1937, Sentinel, Oklahoma, IPHC, vol. 58, pp. 42–45.

19. Anquoe, correspondence; Wildcat, interview.

20. Colonel Elsworth Walters, interview by Charles H. Holt, Skeedee, Oklahoma, March 10, 1938, IPHC, vol. 95, pp. 315–17; Loretta C. Morgan, interview by Lula Austin, Durant, Oklahoma, May 28, 1937, IPHC, vol. 37, p. 215; Night Hawk Society, photograph, Archives and Manuscript Collection, Oklahoma Historical Society Research Center, 18474.4; Lenora Alpha Henry (Ross), interview by M. J. Stockton, June 24, 1937, IPHC, vol. 28, pp. 425–28; Pendley, interview: 218; Stella Feeback Rothhammer, interview by Mary D. Doward, Tulsa, Oklahoma, January 18, 1938, IPHC, vol. 43, p. 120.

21. Wildcat, interview.

22. J. Justin Castro, "From the Tennessee River to Tahlequah: A Brief History of Cherokee Fiddling," *Chronicles of Oklahoma* 87, no. 4 (Winter 2009–2010), 388–407; John Norton, *The Journal of John Norton, 1809–16*, ed. Carl F. Klink and James J. Talman (Toronto: Champlain Society, 1970), 36–52.

23. Norton, *The Journal of John Norton*, 52; James R. Carselowey, "Thomas M. Buffington," IPHC, vol. 79, pp. 116–18; Marion Thede, *The Fiddle Book* (New York: Oak Publications, 1967), 141, 159; Andrew L. Rogers, interview by Elle Robinson in Fort Gibson, Oklahoma, July 15, 1937, IPHC, vol. 98, pp. 84–85.

24. Chaney McNair, interview by James Carsalowey, Vinita, Oklahoma, May 11, 1937, IPHC, vol. 10, pp. 442–47; Dennis Vann, interview by Reuben Partridge, March 23, 1937,

IPHC, vol. 11, pp. 65–69; Garret Garrison, interview by Nannie Burns, April 15, 1938, IPHC, vol. 84, p. 63.

25. Mabel Alexander, *Via Oklahoma: And Still the Music Flows* (Oklahoma City: Oklahoma Heritage Association, 2004), 65.

26. Dennis Vann, interview, 65–69.

27. John Thompson, interview by Ethel Wolfe Garrison, Fort Gibson, Oklahoma, 1937, in *The WPA Oklahoma Slave Narratives*, edited by T. Lindsey Baker and Julie P. Baker (Norman: University of Oklahoma Press, 1996), 421. Fiddling by slaves and freedmen in eastern Oklahoma is also included in Castro, "From the Tennessee River to Tahlequah: A Brief History of Cherokee Fiddling," 397–400.

28. Henry R. Wilson, letter to Rev. J. W. Moore, Springfield, Ohio, February 2, 1861, in Cephas Washburn, *Reminiscences of the Indians* (Richmond: Presbyterian Committee of Publication, 1869): 42–49; Charlie Hepner and Clara Clifford, interview by Arlene D. McDowell, IPHC, vol. 28, p. 435; Allen Morris, interviewed by Jas. S. Buchanan, Muskogee, Oklahoma, August 18–19, 1937, IPHC, vol. 37, p. 261; "Country Singers Planning a Big Time at Convention at High School on Sunday," *New York Times*, January 1, 1933; Althea Bass, *Cherokee Messenger* (Norman: University of Oklahoma Press, 1936), 228–31.

29. The term "Cherokee hills" is used interchangeably with "Oklahoma Ozarks."

30. J. Justin Castro, "Amazing Grace: The Influence of Christianity in Nineteenth-Century Oklahoma Ozarks Music and Society," *Chronicles of Oklahoma* 86, no. 4 (Winter 2008–2009), 446–68.

31. John R. Lovett, "Major Cattle Trails, 1866–1889," *Historical Atlas of Oklahoma*, 4th ed., edited by Charles Robert Goins and Danny Goble (Norman: University of Oklahoma Press, 2006), 116–17; Guy Logsdon, ed., *"The Whorehouse Bells Were Ringing" and Other Songs Cowboys Sing* (Urbana: University of Illinois Press, 1889), xi–xiv.

32. For more on Fort Gibson, see Brad Agnew, *Fort Gibson: Terminal of the Trail of Tears* (Norman: University of Oklahoma Press, 1989).

33. Carolyn Thomas Foreman, "Gustavus Loomis: Commandant Fort Gibson and Fort Townson," *Chronicles of Oklahoma* 18, no. 3 (September 1940): 221–23; Wildcat, interview.

34. Alan Lomax, compiler, *Hard Hitting Songs for Hard-Hit People* (New York: Oak Publications, 1967), 100–101. This song is still widely known among many "traditional" performers in Oklahoma.

35. I use the most basic definition of "modernity" here: the quality of being modern.

36. Clarence Love, interview by Joe Todd, Tulsa, Oklahoma, September 1, 1983, OHC ; John Wooley, *From the Blue Devils to Red Dirt: The Colors of Oklahoma Music* (Tulsa: Hawk Publishing, 2006), 8–12.

37. George O. Carney, "General Profile of Oklahoma Jazz Artists: A Biographical Dictionary," *Oklahoma Folklife Council Newsletter* 4, no. 1 & 2 (Fall & Winter 1992–1993): 3–4.

38. William Savage, Jr., *Singing Cowboys and All That Jazz* (Norman: University of Oklahoma Press, 1988), 5. •

39. Ibid., 13–14.

40. Wooley, *From the Blue Devils to Red Dirt*, 18.

41. Savage, Jr., *Singing Cowboys and All That Jazz*, 13.

42. Bill More, "Radio," in *Encyclopedia of Oklahoma History and Culture*, Oklahoma Historical Society, http://digital.library.okstate.edu/encyclopedia/entries/R/RA002.html (accessed June 28, 2010).

43. Curley Lewis, interview by Cynthia Taylor, Stigler, Oklahoma, April 2, 1995, OSACC, box 7, "Lewis, Curley" file; Sam O'Field, interview by the author, December 4, 2006, Claremore, Oklahoma.

44. Thomas Conner, "Woody Guthrie and Oklahoma's Red Dirt Musicians," in *Alternative Oklahoma: Contrarian Views of the Sooner State*, edited by Davis D. Joyce (Norman: University of Oklahoma Press, 2007), 91.

45. Ibid.

46. Ibid., 93.

47. 1971 show flyer, scanned copy sent to the author from longtime Oklahoma musician Terry "Buffalo" Ware, JJC.

48. Conner, "Woody Guthrie and Oklahoma's Red Dirt Musicians," 98.

49. Another work on Red Dirt music is Hugh W. Foley, Jr. and George O. Carney, *Oklahoma Music Guide* (Stillwater, Okla.: New Forums Press, 2003).

50. KWGS is the Tulsa public broadcasting station. Joe Mack e-mail correspondence to author, June 30, 2010.

51. Joe Baxter, e-mail correspondence to author, July 1, 2010. Baxter is a fourth-generation Oklahoma with ties to western and central Oklahoma. He has performed with bands and written songs for the past thirty years, mostly in central Oklahoma but also along the Illinois River.

52. David Castro Band, phone interview with author, June 30, 2010.

53. Baxter, e-mail correspondence.

54. Eddie Glenn, "Songs for the Illinois," *Tahlequah Daily Press*, July 30, 2007, www.illinoisriver.org/LetsTalk/Discussion/232020.aspx (accessed February 5, 2013).

55. Randy Crouch, phone interview with author, November 2, 2006; Randy Crouch, interview, Payne County Line, August 29, 2004, http://www.paynecountyline.com/interviews/randy_crouch_2004.htm (accessed August 22, 2006); Eddie Glenn, "Fiddlin' Folk," *Tahlequah Daily Press*, June 26, 2007, http://tahlequahdailypress.com/homepage/x519333999/Fiddlin-folk?start:int=15 (accessed June 30, 2010).

56. Pumpkin Hollow Boys, MySpace, www.myspace.com/pumpkinhollowboys08 (accessed June 30, 2010).

57. "2010," David Castro Band, EP, private copy of the author.

58. Mutt Gurely, "'Shoegazer as Subgenre': An Explanation for the Unfamiliar (pt.1.)," blog, MySpace, www.myspace.com/matthewgurley/blog/505956959 (accessed July 5, 2010).

59. Joe Mack, e-mail correspondence to author, June 30, 2010.

Contributors

Malia K. Bennett received her master of arts degree in liberal studies at the University of Oklahoma in 2008. She is director of communications for the Oklahoma state senate and has published in the *State Legislature Magazine.*

Dan T. Boyd is a certified petroleum geologist, working for Qatar Petroleum in Doha, Qatar. He was previously employed for eleven years by the Oklahoma Geological Survey in Norman, where his contribution to this book was written. He spent the first twenty-two years of his career as an exploration and development geologist in the petroleum industry, including 1978–91 work in Houston, Dallas, and Oklahoma City. He has also held a number of geological positions overseas, including extended postings in Karachi, Pakistan, and Jakarta, Indonesia. Dan received his master of science degree in geology from the University of Arizona.

J. Justin Castro graduated from Tahlequah High School in 1999. He received his PhD in history from the University of Oklahoma in May 2013. In addition to Oklahoma history, his research interests include the history of technology and Latin America. He has two publications on music and culture in the *Chronicles of Oklahoma* and an article on early radio communications in Mexico in *Mexican Studies/Estudios Mexicanos.*

Jana Vogt Catignani successfully defended her doctoral dissertation, "Oklahoma and the ERA: Rousing a Red State, 1972–1982," at the University of Oklahoma in 2010. She has taught part-time at several Oklahoma universities. She now resides in Connecticut.

Bradley R. Clampitt is assistant professor of history at East Central University. He has published numerous articles on the Civil War, and his *Confederate Heartland* (Louisiana State University Press, 2011) examines popular will and military morale in the war's western theater.

Jennifer J. Collins received a master of arts in history from the University of Oklahoma in 2001. She currently teaches history and government at Bishop

McGuinness Catholic High School in Oklahoma City, where she also serves as chair of the social studies department. She is the author of "The Lingering Shadow: The *Grapes of Wrath* and Oklahoma Leaders in the Post-Depression Era," published in the *Chronicles of Oklahoma* in 2003.

Sterling D. Evans holds the Louise Welsh Chair in Oklahoma history at the University of Oklahoma. His teaching and research interests are agricultural and environmental history and the history of the transnational Great Plains. His book *Bound in Twine: The History and Ecology of the Henequen-Wheat Complex for Mexico and the American Canadian Plains* won the 2008 Theodore Saloutos Book Award of the Immigration and Ethnic History Society.

James Hochtritt earned a PhD from the University of Oklahoma in 2000 and teaches in the Social Sciences Department at Rose State College. His dissertation was titled "Rural Cherokees, Chickasaws, Choctaws, Creeks, and Seminoles in Oklahoma during the Great Depression."

Patricia Loughlin is Professor of History at the University of Central Oklahoma and the author of *Hidden Treasures of the American West: Muriel H. Wright, Angie Debo, and Alice Marriott*, named the Outstanding Book on Oklahoma History by the Oklahoma Historical Society. Currently, she is working on an Angie Debo children's book.

Christienne M. McPherson is a doctoral candidate at Southern Methodist University, where she received the William P. Clements Fellowship, 2005–2010. Her dissertation is entitled "Private Violations in the Public Imagination: Sexual Violence against Women in Texas, 1880–1920."

Houston Mount is assistant professor of history at East Central University. He studied oil and gas law at the University of Texas where he received a juris doctorate. His PhD work at Southern Methodist University focused on Oklahoma geologist and businessman Everette Lee DeGolyer.

Linda Williams Reese, a native of Norman, Oklahoma, retired in 2010 as Associate Professor of History at East Central University, Ada, where she also served as Department Chair and Director of the Oklahoma Studies Program. Reese earned a master's degree in history at the University of Kansas in 1971 and taught for eight years at New Mexico Military Institute in Roswell. In 1991 she earned her Ph.D. in history at the University of Oklahoma. She is the author of *Women of Oklahoma, 1890–1920* (University of Oklahoma Press, 1997); *Trail Sisters: Freedwomen in Indian Territory, 1850–1890* (Texas Tech University Press, 2013); and numerous articles for scholarly journals, as well as encyclopedia and website entries and book reviews. Her current research project was honored in 2003 with the Catherine Prelinger Award of the Coordinating Council for Women in History.

Nigel A. Sellars is associate professor at Christopher Newport University, Virginia, where he specializes in American social and labor history. In 1998 he published *Oil, Wheat & Wobblies: The Industrial Workers of the World in Oklahoma, 1905–1930.*

Alvin O. Turner is emeritus dean of the School of Humanities and Social Sciences and professor of history at East Central University. He is a multi-talented scholar who has authored, coauthored, or edited six books, including *Letters from the Dust Bowl,* an edited collection of letters by Caroline Henderson (University of Oklahoma Press, 2001). He is also a poet and an authority on Oklahoma art and artists.

Index

References to illustrations are in italic type.

Abandoned Mine Land (AML) Trust Fund, 62

Acee Blue Eagle (Alex McIntosh), 6, 161–62, 165, 167

Adair, Wellington ("Wellie"). *See* Adair murder case (1920s)

Adair murder case (1920s), 6, *137*, *143*; arrest of Hardy Smith, 141; and confession by Ridge after implication by Smith, 141; donations collected for appeal, 143–44; Hardy Smith's conviction reversed, 148; and Jim Crow laws, 6, 43, 135, 149; and lynching, 135–37, *137*, 139, 142; and media attention, 147, 153n56; murder victim, Wellie Adair, 134, 141; and NAACP, 142–43, 144, 152n41; Oklahoma Appellate Court ruling for Ridge, 145–46, 153n52; and race riots nationwide, 136–38; racial climate and mob atmosphere, 144–45, 149; retrial, 146–47; Ridge's case for appeal, 144–45; Ridge sentenced to death, 142; Ridge "spirited away" to avoid vigilante mob, 141–42; Ridge tried as adult, 142, 152n39; and second appeal, 147–48. *See also* Tulsa Race Riot of 1921

Adkins, Eugene, B. (collection), 169

AFL (American Federation of Labor), 114, 117, 120, 121, 125, 126

African Americans: and demographics, twentieth century, 242; high crime rate in Tulsa blamed on, 138; and jazz musicians, 245; and Jim Crow laws, 6, 43, 135, 149; and music traditions in Ozarks, 243; as part of lynch mob, 136; prospects for in Oklahoma, 134–35, 149; and race riots, 136–38; as strikebreakers, 126, 149; and unfair treatment by justice system, 148–49. *See also* Tulsa Race Riot of 1921

Agricultural history, 57–60

Albert, Carl, 202, 205–207, *206*

Allen, Robert, 127–28

Almeda Pool, 100

"Alternative Fuel" (song; Glenn), 248

Altschuler, Samuel B., 116, 119

Amalgamated Meat Cutters: and African American strikebreakers, 126; and company unions, 119–20; concessions won by, 116; and failure of strike nationally, 128–29; and national strike of 1921, 6, 110–11; and wage cuts, 122–23. *See also* Butchers against businessmen

American Baptist Convention (1880), 161

American Federation of Labor. *See* AFL (American Federation of Labor)

American Folklife Center, Library of Congress, 32–33

American Indian Exposition (1935), 160

Amerson, Lola Maud Johnson, 185

AML (Abandoned Mine Land Trust Fund), 62

Anadarko Fair, 160

Anadarko geologic basin, 76, 85, 87

Anadarko Indian School, 157, 160, 165

Anderson, Buddy, 244

Anquoe, Kelly, 248

Ardmore-Marietta geologic basin, 76

Arkansas River Navigation System, 65–66

Arkoma geologic basin, 76, 85, 87

Asah, Spencer, 157, 159. *See also* Kiowa Five

As Long as the Waters Flow (sculpture; Houser), 42–43

Atkins, Hannah, 224, 225

Atoka Grape Project, 210–11, 219n60

Atoka mock wedding, 37

Auchiah, James, 158, 160. *See also* Kiowa Five

Avant Pool, 99

Bacone College: and Acee Blue Eagle, 6, 161–62; artists educated at, 165; and Crumbo, 162–63, *163*; declining influence of, 168; founding of, 161; and Jones, 168; and Saul, 168; and West, 164

Bacone Indian, 161

Bacone or Oklahoma style of painting, 6, 154, 167, 173n35. *See also* Bacone College

Baggett, Bryce, 224

Baird, W. David, 31, 46

Baker, Nannie Loren, 187

Barcus, Nannie, 186

Barnsdall Pool, 100

Barnum, P. T., 34

Bartlesville-Dewey Field, 62, 78, 99

Basie, William "Count," 244, 245

Bates, James C., 21

Battle of Bull Run, 16

Battle of Chustenahlah, 20

Battle of Chustotalasah, 20

Battle of Pea Ridge, 21

Battle of Round Mountain, 20

Baxter, Joe, 247–48, 256n51

Bean, Adam, 187

Bear Heart, 185

Beaver, Fred, 162, 165

Beaver River, 66–67

Beecher, Charles, 101

"Being Native to This Place" (Pierotti and Wildcat), 54

Bell, Jennie, 187

Bell, Sally Rowan, 226–27

Bell, Samuel Aaron, 244

Bellmon, Henry, 42

Bennett, Malia K., 4–5

Bennett, Mrs. Leo, 29–31, 34, 44n4

BIA (Bureau of Indian Affairs), 12, 168, 175, 176

Big Bow, Woodrow Wilson ("Woody"), 162

Binyon, H. L., 122, 123

Bison, 67, 69

Bituminous coal, 60–61

Black Kettle National Grassland, 69

Black Mountain Wilderness Area, 69

Blue Eagle. *See* Acee Blue Eagle (Alex McIntosh)

Bob Wills and His Texas Playboys, 245–46

Boland, Jason, 247, 250

Boren, David L., 62

Bosin, Blackbear, 165

Boston Pool, 99

Botanical diversity of Oklahoma, 51–52, 72n16

Bourke, John Gregory, 156

Boyd, Dan T., 5

Braddock, Anna, 122

Brewster, A. C., 141

Brock, Sidney, 113

Brooks, Jake, 127

Brown v. Spilman, 93–94

Buffalo jumps, 54

"Buffalo Skinners, The" (song), 244, 255n34

Bull Run, Battle of, 16

Burbank oil fields, 92, 100, 103, 104, 106

Burbank Pool, 104

Bureau of Indian Affairs (BIA), 12, 168, 175, 176

Butchers against businessmen, *115*, *118*, 120; African American strikebreakers, 126; Altschuler agreement made, 116; Amalgamated Meat Cutters union, 114, 116, 119, 130n13; anti-union sentiment, 112; bond bill defeated by union action, 121; boycotting and picketing of nonunion merchants, 112–13; Edward Morris Company's conditions for building plant, 113; expiration of Altschuler agreement, 119; labor movement in Oklahoma City, 110–11; lessons of strike, 128–29; lynching, 119, 128; martial law urged, 127–28; national strike (Dec. 5, 1921), 122–23, 132n35; Oklahoma City meat cutters' strike of 1921, 110–11; Oklahoma City as meatpacking center, 113, 130n10; open shop movement (1920–21), 111–13; open shop system adopted by packers, 120; packinghouse wage cuts, 119; Packingtown slums, 114; "patriotic" wartime lockouts by employers, 112; police union challenged, 117; postwar depression of 1919–21, 116–17; press in support of open shop, 124; print-shop workers' strike of 1921, 117, 119; public opinion regarding strikers, 128, 132–33n47; racism in AFL, 126; strike agreed to by union members and OSFL, 120; violence during strike, 124, 125, 126–27, 128; wages slashed by Big Five packers, 122. *See also* Amalgamated Meat Cutters
Butcher Workmen of North America, 111
Buten, J. A., 158
Butler, Nathan, 127–28

Cale, J. J., 246
Calendars, tribal, 155
Camp Napoleon Compact, 23

Camp Napoleon conference (May 1865), 22–23, 27n29
Canary, J. H., 122
CAP (Community Action Program), 203–204
Carter, Jimmy, 62
Castro, David, 250
Castro, J. Justin, 8
Catignani, Jana Vogt, 7–8
Cattle industry, 55–57, 73n30
CFL (Chicago Federation of Labor), 114
Charon Wilderness Area, 67
Cherokees: and coal, 60; and Confederacy, alliance with, 11, 18; conversion to Christian faith, 243; desertion of Drew's regiment, 20; and Five Tribes, 10; intermarriage with Anglos, 241; music traditions of, 242–43; neutrality of, 15; neutrality of reconsidered by Ross, 16–17; Opothleyahola's influence on, 19; as self-sustaining during Depression, 187–88, 190; as slaveholders, 11; and Trail of Tears, 239–40. *See also* Ross, John
Cherokee Supreme Court Building, 241
Cherokee Weavers' Association, Cherokee County, 180
Chicago Federation of Labor (CFL), 114
Chickasaw National Recreation Area, 68
Chickasaws: allied with Confederacy, 12, 13, 20; and Curtis Act (1898), 60; and Five Tribes, 7, 10, 175; and Fort Washita, 13; as slaveholders, 11. *See also* Five Tribes; New Deal programs and Five Nations people
Chickasaw Weaving Association, 180
Childers, Bob, 247
Chinese bush clover, 51
Choctaws: and Confederacy, 11, 12; and Five Tribes, 10; relocation of, 57; as

slaveholders, 11. *See also* Five Tribes;
New Deal programs and the Five
Nations people
Choctaw Spinners' Cooperative, 180, 181
Choctaw Weavers' Association, 181
Church of Jesus Christ of Latter Day Saints
(LDS), 223, 226
Chustenahlah, Battle of, 20
Chustotalasah, Battle of, 20
Cibola National Forest, 69
Civilian Conservation Corps (CCC), 70,
177
Civil War and Indian Territory, *14, 19;*
Camp Napoleon conference (May 1865),
22–23, 27n29; Confederate-Indian alli-
ance, 13, 15–16, 20–21; federal evacua-
tion of territory, 13; Fort Sumter (April
1861), 12–13; Indian alliances, 10–13;
Indian Expedition of 1862, 21; Indians
as slaveholders, 11; Indians vs. Indians,
18–19; legislation enacted to secure
Indian alliance, 12; Opothleyahola's fol-
lowers' trek north, 20; and paradox of
Indian participation in war, 24; Pea
Ridge, battle of, 21; public fascination
with, 9; and Reconstruction treaties,
23–24; significance to statehood, 4, 9;
and surrender of all Confederate Indian
forces, 23; value of Indian Territory to
both sides, 10; war's end and Indian
Territory, 22, 28n31; and war within a
war, 9–10
Civil Works Administration (CWA), 176
Clampitt, Bradley, 4
Classen, Anton, 113
Clayton Anti-Trust Act, 121
Climate of Oklahoma, 48–51
Clutch and Nirvana, 250
Coal, bituminous, 60–61
Coal-bed methane production, *77,* 88

Collier, John, 176, 182
Collins, Jennifer J., 7
Colonial Art Gallery (Oklahoma City),
160–61
Common law tradition, private ownership
of mineral rights, 93
Community Action Program (CAP),
203–204
Community Services Act (1974), 212
Connally, Claude, 122, 126
Connor, Belle Gray, 185
Conservation, New Deal measures, 59
Conservative Oklahoma Women United.
See ERA anti-ratification campaign in
Oklahoma
Coolidge, Calvin, 68, 100
Cooper, Douglas, 19, 20
Cooper, Georgia, 186
Cotton production, 57–58
Creeks (Muscogees): and Confederacy, 11,
15; and Five Tribes, 10; and Glenn pool,
96–97; mixed-blood factions among,
17; and OIWA credit program, 182; pro-
Union faction led by Opothleyahola, 18,
19, 20; as slaveholders, 11. *See also* Five
Tribes; New Deal programs and the
Five Nations people; Opothleyahola
Cross Canadian Ragweed, 247, 250
Cross Timbers, 51, 58
Crouch, Randy, 246, 248, *249,* 250
Crumbo, Woodrow Wilson ("Woody"),
162–64, *163,* 165
Curtis Act (1898), 60–61

Dancy, Ben, 125
Davis, Jefferson, 21
Davis, Jesse Ed, 246
Dawes Act (1887), 5, 92–93, 95, 96, 98, 106
Dawes Commission, 68
Debo, Angie, 8

Depression. *See* Great Depression
Doherty, Henry L., 100–101
Dome Pool, 100
Drake, Edwin L., 78
Drew, John, 18, 20
Drummond, Earl, 68
Dunbar-Ortiz, Roxanne, 47
Dunlap, John, 156
Dunn, Dorothy, 165, 167, 168
Dunn, I. L., 103
Duree, Donnie, 248
Dust Bowl (1930s), 58–59, 59, 69, 70

Eagle Forum, 232
Eastern red cedar, 51–52
Economic Opportunity Act (1964), 203, 205
Ecoregions of Oklahoma, 48–49, 49
EFMS (Emergency Food and Medical
    Service), 208, 210
Elephant Revival (folk band), 251
Elk (Rocky Mountain), 67
Emergency Food and Medical Service
    (EFMS), 208, 210
Environmental Protection Agency (EPA),
    64, 65
Environment and twentieth-century
    Oklahoma history, 46–47, 49, 61, 63,
    66; agriculture, 57–60; botanical diver-
    sity, 51–52, 72n16; cattle ranching, 55–57,
    73n30; climate, 48–50; conservation,
    67–70; ecosystems in state, 48; Native
    peoples and land, 53–55; New Deal con-
    servation measures, 59, 70; red dirt,
    47–48; stock reduction program, 56;
    wildlife species, 52–53. *See also* Natural
    resources and environmental impact
EPA (Environmental Protection Agency),
    64, 65
Equal Rights Amendment (ERA). *See* ERA
    anti-ratification campaign in Oklahoma

ERA anti-ratification campaign in
    Oklahoma, 7–8, 222, 227, 233–34; anti-
    amendment organizations, 232; anti-
    ERA letters and messages received by
    politicians, 232; and antifeminists, 232;
    arrival of proposed amendment in
    Oklahoma, 221; belief ERA was against
    God's law, 227–28, 229; and belief in
    female moral supremacy, 225–26, 227,
    236n23; and conservative influences in
    state, 223, 228; and conservative women
    as politically active, 232–33; defeat of
    ERA in state, 221, 234; ERA as threat to
    America's survival, 230–31; and ERA
    defeated in state house of representa-
    tives, 224; and fear of humanism and
    secularism, 228, 236n28; and flourishing
    of cultural beliefs in state, 221, 234n1;
    and fundamentalist doctrine, 223,
    224–25, 227, 228–29; fundamentalists
    joined by WRL as force behind, 224–25,
    232; and gender-specific laws, 221–22;
    homosexuality linked to ERA, 229–30;
    lobbying techniques, 233; long-term
    political implications of, 234; Mormons
    as disproportionate percentage of anti-
    ratification activists, 223, 224, 226; per-
    ceived threat to family, 229; state's
    affinity for GOP in national elections,
    223, 235n5; state senate approval of
    ERA, 224; STOP ERA movement, 224–
    25; STOP ERA PEC newsletter, 228,
    229, 231, 232, 236, 237; women excluded
    through gender-based, discriminatory
    laws in 1970s, 222
ERA Collection of the Oklahoma
    Historical Society, 232
Ericson, Bill, 248
Evans, Mack, 122
Evans, Sterling, 4

Extinction of species in Oklahoma, 52–53

Family Planning Program, 205, 212, 217n23, 217n27
Farm, The (musicians' commune), 247, 250
Farm Couple, The (band), 247
Farmer-Labor Reconstruction League, 120, 121, 129
Federal Art Project, 177
Federal Work Study program, 205
Fenton, Edgar, 121
Fenton, Sissy, 186–87
Fisher, A. H., 141
Five Tribes: composition of, 10, 11–12, 24n2; and cotton production, 57; federal evacuation of, 13; and Fort Smith meeting (1865), 23; relocation of, 57. See also New Deal programs and the Five Nations people; specific names of tribes
Flood Control Act (1936) (federal), 66–67
Folklore of Ireland Society, 32
Folk Salad (KWGS), 247
Ford, Gerald, 212
Fort Cobb (now in Caddo County), 13, 25n6
Fort Marion "assimilation" experience (Native art), 155–57
Fort Smith meeting, 23
Fort Washita, 13
Foster, Edwin B., 98
Foster, William Z., 112
Frazier, Bernard, 164, 166
Fred Jones Jr. Museum of Art, 169
Fred Olds statue (Guthrie), 29, 31, 32
Freeman, Dick, 233

Gadugi (defined), 188–89
Garber, Dan, 248
Gas, natural. See Natural gas in Oklahoma
Gaylord, Edward King, 113, 127
Gilcrease, Thomas, 164

Giles, Jimmy, 250
Glenn, Eddie, 248
Glenn Pool, 96–97
Goble, Danney, 31, 46
Golden, Brenda, 39
Governor's Advisory Commission on the Status of Women, 222
Grapes of Wrath, The (Steinbeck), 211
Grasses, native, 55–56
Gray, Otto, 245–46
Great Depression: and decline in coal industry, 61; and devastating effects on art markets, 6–7, 159–60; and industry in state, 116–17; and public works programs created during, 70; and renewed union organizing, 129; and tenant cotton farmers, 59. See also under New Deal programs and the Five Nations people
Greenwood (African American district, Tulsa), 138
Guardian, The (sculpture; Haney), 43, 169
Gurley, Matt, 250
Guthrie, Woody, 47–48, 58, 246

Hair, Sam, 186
Hall, David, 209
Haney, Enoch Kelly, 42, 43, 169
Harding, Warren G., 125
Harjochee, Jimmie, 185
Harlow, Victor, 121
Harmon, Charles N., 146
Harrington, M. R., 157
Harris, Fred, 209
Harrison, Walter, 127
Hayes, Mrs. I. L., 125
Head Start programs, 204–205, 212, 213, 214
Hedges, Mike, 250
Heller, Walter, 203
Higgins, Thomas, 140
"Highway 10" (song; Garber), 248

Hill, Joan, 165

History of Okmulgee County, Oklahoma,
37–38

Hochtritt, James, 7

Hodge, Minnie Wimberley, 185

Hogner, Joe, 185

Hokeah, Jack, 157, 160. *See also* Kiowa Five

Holdenville, Ind. Terr., 3

Holder, Terrence, 244

Hominy Pool, 100

Homosexuality, linked to ERA, 229–30

HOTDOG (Housewives Organized to
Defend Our Girls), 226–27

Household Service Demonstration Project
centers, 177

Houser, Alan (Apache artist), 42–43, 165,
172n29

Howe, Oscar, 165, 166

Howling Wolf (Cheyenne), 156

Hughes, Forrest, 125, 127

Hugoton Field, 64

IAIA (Institute of American Indian Arts),
168

IECW (Indian Emergency Conservation
Work), 176

Independent Producers League, 96

Indian Annual (National Exhibition of
American Indian Painting), 164–66, 167,
168–69, 174n43

Indian Arts and Crafts Board, 178–79, 181,
182

Indian Emergency Conservation Work
(IECW), 176

Indian Nations Community Action
Agency, 208

Indian Relief and Rehabilitation (IRR) program, 178–79

Indians of the Americas (National
Geographic Society), 165

Indian Territory Illuminating Oil
Company, 98–99

Industrial Workers of the World (IWW),
124–25, 127

Inhofe, James ("Jim"), 224

Institute of American Indian Arts (IAIA),
168

International Education Association
(Prague, 1928), 158

IRR (Indian Relief and Rehabilitation) program, 178–79

Irving, Washington, 51, 69

IWW (Industrial Workers of the World),
124–25, 127

Jackson, Andrew, 40, 41, 43

Jacob, Murv, 248

Jacobson, Oscar, *159*; and Acee Blue Eagle,
161–62; and Kiowa Five, 6, 158, 167;
museum established by, 168

Jake, Albin, 165

Jason Boland & the Stragglers, 247, 250

Jazz in Oklahoma, 8, 243, 244–46, 252

Jim Crow laws, 6, 43, 135, 149

Jobs Corps program, 204, 205, 213

Johnson, Lyndon B., 7, 202–203, 214

Jones, James, 233

Jones, Ruthe Blalock, 168

Jumper, John, 15

Kabotie, Fred, 165

Kemp, Fred, 122–23

Kennard, Motey, 15

Kennedy, John F., 203

Kenton cave dwellers, 154

Kerr, Robert S., 66

Kerr-McGee nuclear plant, 64–65

Kessey, Barney, 244

KI BOIS Community Action Foundation,
208

Kidwell, Clara Sue, 39

Kimball, Spencer, 226

Kimball, Yeffe, 166, 173n34

King, Billy, 244

Kinsey, Ottis, 213

Kiowa Five, *159*, 168; authenticity of work
    questioned, 167; Depression's effect on
    art markets, 159–60; discovery of, 157–
    58; international fame in 1928, 158; and
    Jacobson, 6, 158, 167; and Oklahoma or
    Bacone School, 6, 159; special classes
    arranged for, 158; and not valued by fel-
    low Kiowas, 160. *See also* Asah, Spencer;
    Auchiah, James; Hokeah, Jack; Mopope,
    Stephen; Tsatoke, Monroe

Kirk, Andy, 244

Ku Klux Klan (KKK), 143, *143*

LaFave, Jimmy, 247

Lake of the Arbuckles, 68

Land and Native peoples, 53–55

LaRue, Stoney, 247

LDS (Church of Jesus Christ of Latter Day
    Saints), 223, 226

Lead and zinc mining, 65

Leasing system for oil, 94

Ledger drawings, 156

Leon McAuliffe and the Cimarron Boys,
    246

Leopold, Aldo, 59

Lewis, Curley, 246

Lewis, James, 103

Lewis, John L., 112

Lewis, Sinclair, 3

"Like Mike / Gloss Mountain Breakdown"
    (song; Mack), 250

Lincoln, Abraham, 11

Little Dixie, 7

Little Dixie (Third Congressional District).
    See War on Poverty in Little Dixie
    (1965–74)

Livestock industry, 56–57

Livestock reduction program, New Deal,
    56–57

Long, Gillis W., 231

Longhorn cattle, 68

Love, Clarence, 244

"Lovely Illinois River Night" (song; Duree),
    248

Lynchings: and African Americans, 135,
    149; as demonstration of white superi-
    ority, 136; number of, 135–37, *137*, 150n10;
    and packinghouse strike, 6, 126–28

Lynn-Sherow, Bonnie, 47, 60, 70

Lysaght, Patricia, 32

Mack, Joe, 246, 250, 251

Mahler, Edith, 158

Main Street (Lewis), 3

Main Street, twenty-first century, 3–4

Man-ka-ih, 50

Marriott, Alice, 181

Marteney, T. L., 141

Martinez, Crestencio, 157

Matthews, W. D., 143–44

McAlester, Okla., 58, 201, 202, 213

McAuliffe, Leon, 246

McClendon, Mary Stone (Princess Ataloa),
    161

McCombs, Solomon, 165

McCullough, Willard M., 139

McDonald, Bonnie, 48

McIntosh, Alex. *See* Acee Blue Eagle (Alex
    McIntosh)

McIntosh, Chilly, 15

McIntosh, Daniel, 15

McIntosh, Dave, 186

McKinley, William, 67

McMahon, J. F., 122–23

McNeil, Vernon, 162

McNiece, Callie, 187

McPherson, Christienne M., 6

McShann, Jay, 244

Medicine Show (band), 247

Meriam Report (1928), 175

Miller, J. H., 111

Miss Indian Territory: in Atoka ceremony, 37; costume in 1907 ceremony, 29–31; costume in 1938 ceremony, 31; in script for 2007 ceremony in Guthrie, 36; on Statehood Day in Guthrie (1907), 4, 29–31; and Tom Thumb weddings, 34

Miss Oklahoma Pioneer, 40

Mitchell, Anna Belle Sixkiller, 185, 189

Mock wedding ceremonies, 30, 35, 40; in Atoka, 36; costumes in 1907, 31; criticisms of renewing vows in, 39–41; in Duncan (2007), 32, 39; elements of, 38–39; as folk drama, 32–33; in Guthrie (2007), 34–36; Irish folklore as possible source of, 32; and Jim Crow laws denounced in legislature (2008), 43; newspaper accounts of, 33–34; and 1989 Land Run centennial, 42–43; in Oklahoma City (1938), 31; in Okmulgee, 37–38; and "Reverse Wedding" protest in Guthrie, 39–41; script from 1907 ceremony, 36; on Statehood Day in Guthrie (1907), 4, 29–31, 32; and tensions among Oklahomans today, 42; and Tom Thumb weddings, 34; traditional celebration as part of Oklahoma history, 43

Momaday, Al, 165

Momaday, N. Scott, 48, 55

Montoya, Alfredo, 157

Mooney, James, 156

Mopope, Stephen, 157, 159–60. See also Kiowa Five

Morrison, Frank, 116

Morrow, Mabel, 181

Mount, Houston, 5

Mr. Indian Territory, 40, 41

Mr. Oklahoma Territory, 4, 29, 31, 34, 35, 37

Muscogees. See Creeks (Muscogees)

Music, Oklahoma Ozarks, 8, 239–40; 240–42, 247, 249; and Baxter, 247–48, 256n51; and beginning of radio (1920), 245–46; and Bob Wills, 245–46; and "The Buffalo Skinners" (song), 244, 255n34; and changing demographics, 242, 253n15; Cherokee indigenous dances, 242–43, 254n17; Christian and secular music mixed in Cherokee hills, 243, 255n29; cowboy ballads, 243–44; and Crouch, 246, 248, 249, 250; cultural blending in Oklahoma Ozarks, 239, 251–52, 252nn1–3; fiddle-playing tradition, 243; Illinois river scene, 247–52; impact of modern media, popular music, and new settlers, 244–47; intermarriage between Anglos and Cherokees, 241; and Mack, 246, 250, 251; multiple forms, 240; and music traditions, 242–44; Muskogee jazz, 244–46; Oklahoma City Blue Devils, 244; "On the Illinois" (Crouch), 248; and radio in Oklahoma, 245–47; and Red Dirt music, 246–48; and rise of "modernity" in twentieth century, 244, 255n35; and Trail of Tears of Cherokees, 239–40; and twentieth-century music genres, 243. See also names of specific artists and their works

Myers Dome Pool, 100

My-Tea Kind (band), 251

NAACP (National Association for the Advancement of Colored People), 142–43, 147

National Exhibition of American Indian Painting (the Indian Annual). See

Indian Annual (National Exhibition of American Indian Painting)

National Folklore Collection of Ireland, 32

National Forest Service, 67, 69

National Geographic, 165

National Park Service, 67, 68

Native American art in Oklahoma, *159, 162*; adaptation and blending of artistic forms, 155; annual awards, 165; and assimilationist programs, 156, 157; authenticity of works, 167; beginnings in prehistory, 6, 154; Blue Eagle, Acee, 6, 161–62, 165, 167; decline in Oklahoma School, 166–67, 173n35; educational background of artists, 168, 173n40; expositions, 160–61; Fort Marion artists, 155–57; future of, 169–70; and the Indian Annual, 164–66, 167, 168, 169, 174n43; Indian art defined, 167, 173n37; influences shaping emergence of, 157; ledger book drawings, 155–56; markets devastated by Depression, 159–60; and "New Directions in Indian Art" (1959), 167–68; and "non-traditional paintings" category, 166–67; Plains tribes, 155. *See also* Bacone College; Jacobson, Oscar; Kiowa Five

Native Americans and the land, 53–55

Natural gas in Oklahoma: coal beds as resource for, 88; cumulative production in state, 88–89; discovery through oil exploration, 86; and the economy, 85, 89; as environmentally friendly, 89; and geology, *77*, 85–86; and industrial growth in mid-twentieth century, *81*, 86–87; and oil, 85, 86; price fluctuation, 87, 89; recent activity in discovery of, 87; and shale gas, 88; and shift in 1963 from oil to gas, 86, 87. *See also* Oil and natural gas industry

Natural resources and environmental impact: lead and zinc, 65; nuclear power, 64–65; oil and natural gas, 62–64; strip mining, 61–62; water, 65–67

Nature Conservancy, The, 67, 69

Neighborhood Youth Corps (NYC), 205, 212

Nelagoney Pool, 100

Nellie Johnstone No. 1, 78, 144

New Deal programs and Five Nations people, *178, 180, 189*; communal nature of settlements, 184–85; cooperative labor groups (*gadugi*), 188–89; fraudulent activities to cover lack of success, 177–78; gendered division of labor among Cherokees, 187; goals of Office of Indian Affairs, 176; and harmony ethic, 187; and Indian Arts and Crafts Board, 179; Indian craftsmen, pressures on, 182; Indian participation in, 177; IRR program, 178–79; leases negotiated by Five Tribe members, 186; little money required by rural Indians, 186–87; living strategies, 188; Meriam Report on Indians' demoralized condition (1928), 175; mixed results in aiding Indians of Five Tribes, 176, 190n1; and part-time paid work, 186; poor results of home economics training, 178; and problems with women workers, 181–82; rural Indians' lack of cooperation with OIWA, 182–83; and self-reliance of Indians during Depression, 176, 183–84, 187–88, 190, 194n22; and U.S. Indian policy, 182; and welfare received by few Indians, 184; and women's programs, 179–80

Nickles, Don, 233

Nigh, George, 62

North Burbank agreement, 92

North Dakota History Journal of the Northern Plains (Taft), 32–33, 34, 38
Northeastern State University, Tahlequah, 242
Nuclear power industry, 64–65

OEO (Office of Economic Opportunity), 204, 209
Office of Surface Mining, 62
O'Field, Sam, 246
Ogallala Aquifer, 59–60
Ohtetoint, 156–57
Oil and Gas Journal, 92
Oil and natural gas industry, *79, 81, 83*; as central state's economy, 76, 78; cumulative production in state, 78, 90n; and the environment, 62–64; formation of, 76; future of, 89–90; and hydrocarbons produced throughout state, *76–77*; overview, 5. *See also* Natural gas in Oklahoma; Oil in Oklahoma
Oil field development on Osage Reservation, 5, *99*, 103, *105*, 106; and advantages of tribal property, 92–93; basic concept of Dunn and Lewis's plan, 103–104; and common law tradition of private ownership, 93; confusion in development of Oklahoma oil industry, 95; conservation and tribal ownership, 103, 106; consolidation of leaseholds, 103; Foster "blanket" lease, 98, 100; and Glenn pool, 96–97; largest conservation project of kind (1949), 92; mineral rights reserved by Osages as tribe, 95; multiplication of leaseholds on Osage land, 100; new pools discovered, 100; and North Burbank Field, 106; oil and gas leases, 94; Osage "headright," 98; overdevelopment and waste of oil reserves, 100; "rule of capture,"

93–94, 95; "rush to pump" problems, 94–95; secondary recovery methods, 101; South Burbank, 104; subleases executed by Indian Territory Illuminating Oil Company, 99; "underground reservation," 97–100; unitizing plan of Dunn and Lewis, 104; and waterflood recovery, 104, 106. *See also* Unitization
Oil in Oklahoma: companies founded in state, 80; discovery of, 62, 78–80; and drilling booms, 82–84; driving force behind statehood in 1907, 78; pre–World War II fields, 80; production decline, 84; resurgence of production in future, 90; trend drilling, 80–82. *See also* Oil and natural gas industry
OIWA (Oklahoma Indian Welfare Act), 182
Okesa Pool, 99
"Oklahoma" (Rodgers and Hammerstein), 5, 46, 48, 53, 251
Oklahoma: A History (Baird and Goble), 46
Oklahoma: A Land of Contrasts (McDonald), 48
"Oklahoma Brokedown Blues" (Mack), 250–51
Oklahoma City Blue Devils, 244
Oklahoma City Chamber of Commerce, 111–12, 120
Oklahoma City National Memorial, 67
Oklahoma Community Action Directors' Association, 209
Oklahoma Conservation Commission, 62
Oklahoma Cotton Exchange, 58
Oklahoma Human Rights Commission, 221–22, 222
Oklahoma Indian Welfare Act (OIWA), 182
Oklahoma National Stockyards Company, 113
Oklahoma Natural Gas Company, 86
Oklahoma or Bacone School. *See* Native American Art in Oklahoma

Oklahoma or Bacone style of painting, 6,
  154, 167, 173n35. *See also* Bacone College
Oklahoma Rock Show, 247
Oklahoma State Federation of Labor
  (OSFL), 116, 120
Oklahoma Statehood Day: in Atoka, 37; in
  Guthrie, 4, 29–31; in Haskell County, 37;
  in Holdenville, 3; in Okmulgee, 37–38;
  as tradition, 43
Oklahoma Territorial Museum, 31, 34
Olds statue (Guthrie), 29, 31, 32
"On the Illinois" (song; Crouch), 248
Open Cut Land Reclamation Act (1968), 62
Open shop movement. *See under* Butchers
  against businessmen
Opothleyahola: and Cooper's inten-
  tion to drive him from Ind. Terr., 19;
  Creek pro-Union leader, 15; and Indian
  Campaign, 21; and meeting of pro-
  Union followers, 18–19; leads pro-Union
  faction toward Kansas, 20; and Ross, 18.
  See also Creeks (Muscogees)
Optima Dam, 66–67
Osage City Pool, 99
Osage Mining and Coal Company, 60
Osage Reservation. *See* Oil field develop-
  ment on Osage Reservation
OSFL (Oklahoma State Federation of
  Labor), 116, 120
Ott, Lizzie, 186
Otto Gray and his Singing Cowboys,
  245–46
Ouachita National Forest, 68
Our Oklahoma (Wright), 46, 71n1

Packinghouse strike. *See* Butchers against
  businessmen
Page, Sarah, 138–41
Paine, Bonnie, 251
Parks, state, 70

Patterson, Ann, 224
Pawhuska oil field, 100
Paw-ne-no-pashe, Joseph (chief), 97
Pea Ridge, Battle of, 21
Pearsonia oil field, 100
Perry, Flora, 184–85, 185
Pershing Pool, 100
Peters, Susie, 157, 162
Pettee, W. J., 127
Pettit oil field, 100
Philbrook Museum of Art: establishment
  of, 164, 172n26; growing reputation of,
  165; and the Indian Annual, 164–65,
  168–69; and "non-traditional paintings"
  category, 166, 167
Phillips, Genevieve, 164
Phillips, Waite, 164
Picher, Okla., 65–66, 70
Pierotti, Raymond (Comanche), 54
Pig farms, 56–57
Pike, Albert: appointee of Confederacy to
  secure Indian alliances, 13, 15; retreat
  of Indian soldiers under, 21; trea-
  ties secured by, 15, 17, 18; and Wichita
  Agency meeting, 15–16, 26n13
Pitchlynn, Peter P., 22
Pittsburg County Community Action
  Agency, 201
Pleistocene overkill, 54
Pork industry controversy, 57
Potato Hills Field, 87
Powwows, 242
"Prairie Fire" (Bosin), 165, 166
Pratt, Richard Henry, 155–56, 157
Princess Ataloa (Mary Stone McClendon),
  161
Pro Family Forum (formerly WWWW),
  232
Public Works Administration (PWA), 176
Public Works of Art Project, 159

Public works programs, New Deal, 70
Pumpkin Hollow Boys, 250
Purdy, Victor, 122, 126

Rabbit and Bear Canoeing (CD cover by Jacob), 248
Race riots, 126, 135–36, 149. *See also* Tulsa Race Riot of 1921
Range Ecology and Management Program (Oklahoma State University), 52, 56
"Red Dirt Boogie, Brother" (song; Davis), 246
Red Dirt: Growing Up Okie (Dunbar-Ortiz), 47
Red Dirt music, 47, 246–47
Red Dirt Radio Hour, 247
Red Dirt Rangers, 247, 250
"Red Dirt Roads at Night" (song; LaFave), 247
Red Earth Festival in Oklahoma City, 169
Red Earth: Race and Agriculture in Oklahoma Territory (Lynn-Sherow), 47, 70
Reed, Agnes, 186
Reverse Wedding protest (Guthrie, 2007), 39–41
Ridge, Elias, 6, 141–42, 152n39
Ripley, Steve, 247
River and Harbor Act (1946), 65–66
Roberts, Oral, 58
Robertson, James B., 110, 125, 127, 128, 146
Roosevelt, Franklin D., 59, 70. *See also* New Deal programs and the Five Nations people
Roosevelt, Theodore, 67
Rose Cottage, *19*
Ross, John: "capture" of, 21; and Cherokee neutrality, 15, 16–17; and Opothleyahola, 18; unenthusiastic support for Confederacy, 21–22. *See also* Cherokees

"Round Dance" (song; Anquoe), 248
Rowland, Dick, 138–41
Rule of capture (oil), 93–94, 95, 96, 101, 106
Rushin, Jimmy, 244
Russell, Leon, 246

Salt cedar, 51
Sam Noble Oklahoma Museum of Natural History (Norman), 52
Sampson, Carter, 250
Santa Fe Indian School, 168
Santa Fe National Historic Trail, 67
Saul, Chief Terry, 165, 168
Savage, William W., Jr., 39
Schilling, H. C., 114
Scott, Johnson, 182
Scripps, Edward Willis, 121
Sellars, Nigel A., 6
SEOO (State Economic Opportunity Office), 209, 211
Sequoyah Orphan Training School, 180
Severe Storms Laboratory (University of Oklahoma), 48
Seward, William H., 11
Shale gas production, 88
Shartel, John, 113
Sheridan, William, 67
Shirk, John H., 111, 112, 125, 126, 127
Shoegazer (music subgenre), 250–51
Short, George F., 128
Shriver, Sargent, 204
Silkwood (film), 65
Silkwood, Karen, 64–65, 70
Silverhorn, 157
Simms, Martha, 233
Skinner, Tom, 247
Smith, Hardy, 141, 145
Smoky, Lois, 157–58, 158
Snodgrass, Jeanne, 166
Soberality and Fuhgawz (Tahlequah), 250

Soil Conservation Service, 69
Southwestern Open Shop Association, 111
Southwest Indian Art Project, 168
Sparger, Rex, 210
Spiro mounds culture (ad 500–1300), 154
Spybuck, Ernest, 157
Squint Eyes (Cheyenne), 156
Standing Bear, 157
State Economic Opportunity Office
     (SEOO), 209, 211
State parks, 67, 70
Steinbeck, John, 211
Stick, Mateo, 184–85
Stone, Willard, 162, 165
STOP ERA PEC (Political Education
     Committee), 228, 229, 231, 232, 236, 237
Story of Oklahoma, The (Baird and Goble),
     31
Strip mining, 61–62
Sunbelt Alliance, 65
Surface Mining Control and Reclamation
     Act (1977), 62
Swearingen, Jess, 213, 220n70
Sweezy, Carl, 156, 157
"Swing Low, Sweet Chariot," 245
Swing on This, 247

Taft, Michael, 32–33, 34, 38
Talimena Scenic Drive, 68–69
Tallgrass Prairie Preserve, 67, 69
Tar Creek mines, 65
Taylor, Sister Olivia, 157
Terry Don West rodeo school, 55
Third Congressional District (Little Dixie).
     See War on Poverty in Little Dixie
     (1965–74)
Thomas, Claudia, 233
Thompson, John, 243
Thompson, Mrs. Annie, 122
Tieyah, Gerald D., 40

Timber industry, 60
Tom Thumb weddings, 34–35
Tornado Alley, 50
Trail of Tears National Historic Trail, 67,
     240
Trapp, Martin, 127
Trapp, Thomas, 246
Tsatoke, Monroe, 157, 160. See also Kiowa
     Five
Tucker, Fred, 209
Tulsa Arts Association, 164
Tulsa Indian Art Festival, 169
Tulsa Open Shop Square Deal Association,
     111
Tulsa Race Riot (1921): death toll, 140–
     41; elevator incident with Rowland
     and Page, 138; Greenwood district,
     139; Higgins's account of carnage, 140;
     invasion of Greenwood, 140, 152n30;
     and martial law declared, 140; and
     media accounts, 138, 139; and release of
     Rowland, 141; and Rowland's arrest, 138;
     and white outrage at "Negro uprising,"
     140. See also Adair murder case (1920s)
Turner, Alvin O., 6–7
Twine, W. H., Jr., 143–44
"2010" (song; Castro), 250

Unitization, 101–104, 106. See also Oil field
     development on Osage Reservation
Upper Kiamichi Wilderness, 69
Upward Bound program, 205
U.S. Department of Interior Indian Arts
     and Crafts Board, 181
U.S. Geological Survey, 64

Vann, Dennis, 243

Waid, William Ash, 104
Walker, Jerald C., 42

Walton, John C., 116–17, *118*, 120, 124, 125, 129

War on Poverty in Little Dixie (1965–74), 7, 202, *206*, *214*, 215n4; and Atoka Grape Project, 210–11, 219n60; and CAP's implementation, 204; college- and university-sponsored programs, 205; and community action boards, 212–13, 219n64; and Community Services Act (1974), 212; and cooperative pharmacy plan, 210, 211, 218n51; and decline in poverty (1960–1970), 212, 219n62; and decline in population in postwar period, 202–203, 215n11; and EFMS, 208, 210; and Family Planning Program, 205, 212, 217n27; and garden program, 208, 218n37; and Head Start programs, 204–205, 212, 213, 214; high poverty rate in Little Dixie, 115nn5–6, 202, 215n10; and legislation signed by Johnson in March 1964, 7, 203, 216n17; local-initiative programs, 211–12; and Neighborhood Youth Corps, 212; and Oklahoma Plan (1970), 209–10; and poverty in McAlester, Okla., 201–202; and poverty of rural Americans overlooked, 202, 207, 215n3; and rent-a-cow initiative, 208; and rural areas, success in, 213; and Shriver as head of OEO, 204

Warren, Lavinia, 34

Water as natural resource, 65

Watie, Stand, 15, 17, 22

Way to Rainy Mountain, The (Momaday), 48, 55

Weather of Oklahoma, 48–51

Webb, Anawak Chuculate, 188

Weeks, B. D., 161

West, Louis, 181

West, Walter Richard ("Dick"), 164, 165, 167, 168, 172n25

Wheat production, 58

Wheeler, Nettie, 160, 167, 173n36

Wheelock Academy, 180

Whitby, Baxter A., 142–43

Whitman, Richard Ray, 39

Wichita Agency meeting (summer 1861), 15–16, 26n13

Wichita Mountains National Wildlife Refuge, 67

Wildcat, Daniel (Yuchi), 54

Wilderness Act (1964), 67

Wildlife refuges in state, 68

Wildlife speciation in Oklahoma, 53

Williams, Claude, 244

Williams, David, 165

Williams, Mary Lou, 245

Wills, Bob, 245–46

Wills, Johnny Lee, 246

Wilson, Charles Banks, *163*

Wilson, R. H., 121

Wilson, Thomas E., 113

Wind farms, 50–51, 64

Winding Stair National Recreation Area, 68

Wiser Pool, 99

Wobblies (IWW), 124, 127

Wolf Robe Hunt's Arrowood Trading Post (Muskogee), 160

Women for Responsible Legislation (WRL), 224–25, 232

Women Who Want to Be Women (WWWW), 232

Woodford shale, 88

Wooley, John, 247

Works Progress Administration (WPA), 70, 177

World War I, 6

Wright, Muriel H., 46, 53, 71n1

WRL (Women for Responsible Legislation), 224–25, 232

WWWW (Women Who Want to Be   Y686 oil field, 100
   Women), 232
Wynona Pool, 100   Zotom, 156

X686 oil field, 100